ETHAN FROME
Analysis in Context

Also by Eric B. Olsen

Non-Fiction

The Intellectual American: Essays

The Films of Jon Garcia: 2009-2013

The Death of Education

Fiction

The Seattle Changes

Death in the Dentist's Chair

Dark Imaginings

Proximal to Murder

Death's Head

If I Should Wake Before I Die

ETHAN FROME
Analysis in Context

A Contextual Close Reading of
Edith Wharton's Classic Novel

Eric B. Olsen

To order additional copies of this book, contact:
Xlibris
1-888-795-4274
www.Xlibris.com
Orders@Xlibris.com
788683

For my students

Contents

Books are the best of things, well used; abused, among the worst of things. What is the right use? What is the one end, which all means go to effect?   They are for nothing but to inspire.

—Ralph Waldo Emerson
"The American Scholar"

I don't believe there is any greater blessing than that of being pierced through and through by the splendor or sweetness of words, and no one who is not transfixed by [them] has known half the joy of living. I wouldn't take a kingdom for it—

—Edith Wharton
The Letters of Edith Wharton

Preface

My purpose in undertaking the Analysis in Context series of books on classic literature is primarily educational. One of the things I longed for most when I began my career as a high school English teacher was a series of books that could give me an in-depth, detailed analysis of the literature I was going to be teaching. But no such series of books existed. There are study guides like Cliff's Notes and Monarch Notes, but they were uniformly unhelpful due to their brevity. There are also a great many works of literature available in the impressive series of Norton Critical Editions, and while the mix of contemporary reviews and later criticism gathered at the end of those books offers some guidance it is in a very inconsistent way. Even books of literary analysis about a single title have their problems, primarily that they tend to break down the novel into specific components so that every chapter is about a separate literary device. As a result, these works eventually wind up going through a truncated version of the entire story in every chapter in order to deal with symbolism, theme, imagery, literary theory and the like in isolation, which gives the entire work a disjointed feel. The only other kind of book available to the educator combines the complete text with ancillary short works—essays, poems and stories—that purport to help explain the novel, but none of them contain analysis of any kind, thus making the unfounded assumption that the teacher will be able to understand and explain those connections to students in the way they were intended.

What I was looking for instead was a thorough close reading of the works I was assigned to teach so that I could come to the classroom with something like mastery of the subject. Twenty years later, there are still no books like that. In attempting to remedy this situation my goal has been to create a single work of scholarship that follows the entire story from beginning to end, providing an analysis that incorporates historical and biographical background as well as the explication of every relevant literary device in the context of the work as a whole. Thus all of the meaningful literary devices in the novel are dealt with as they appear in the text, in a holistic way that mirrors not only a chronologic reading of the work but the way in which that work is usually taught in a classroom setting. To assist in this endeavor I also wanted to preface the primary work by analyzing other short works that help provide a greater understanding of the main text. In this way I could identify ahead of time similar themes and literary devices as well as historical and other connections to the larger work. Examining similar elements in different works can help readers to understand each element in an abstract way that can then be applied more readily to any number of works, rather than identifying one highly specific example of an element that may be difficult to pinpoint later in a different context.

Despite this additional material, the book does not need to be read through from beginning to end in order to be utilized fully by educators. If teachers simply want to begin with the analysis of the novel and read nothing else, they will still find this work tremendously beneficial. But for those teachers who wish to give their students a more thorough look at the time period or examine the themes and ideas present in attendant shorter works as a way of scaffolding information about the novel for students, then that information is provided for them as well. The rather lengthy introduction to this book was something I felt necessary in order for educators and general readers alike to understand the rationale behind the series. My ultimate goal is to present the educator with something like the definitive analysis of these works. After nearly two decades of teaching literature, and in being as thorough and complete and in-depth as I can possibly be, I stand by the arguments I make in these pages. Those who take exception with what I've written are certainly welcome to do so, but for those who are looking for a way of teaching great works of literature and have no idea where to begin, a book like this will hopefully prove invaluable. Whatever this work may lack in analytical execution there is one aspect of it that is undeniable, and that is its chronological comprehensiveness. Regardless of what one thinks of the specific analytical arguments I've made, the book does analyze the complete novel in chronologic order and in doing so provides a blueprint for teaching it.

In addition to those things I felt I wanted to accomplish in this series, there are also several things I wanted to avoid. The first is an overemphasis on superfluous analysis. By superfluous I mean analytical ideas that don't serve a function within the overall story. The symbolism contained in many books of literary analysis, for example, is often identified merely for sake of doing so. The problem with this approach lies in that fact that despite how clever the author is at identifying certain symbols, if they have no connection to the rest of the analysis it doesn't really serve a larger purpose. They may be interesting ideas on their own, and many authors build fascinating chapters around them, but they don't advance a unified picture of the novel as a whole. Sometimes these interpretations can even contradict each other—and it can often happen within the pages of a single author's book. As will become clear in my introduction, it's my firm belief that the idea of an infinite number of possible interpretations of a piece of literature is a fallacy, and the most egregious examples of inaccurate analysis typically stem from the practice of interpreting passages out of context or purposefully ignoring parts of the novel that contradict a particular interpretation. My task as I saw it, then, became choosing specific literary devices and themes that, when taken together, made sense throughout the whole of the work. While that necessarily leaves some modes of investigation unexplored, especially in the realm of literary theory, another thing I wanted to avoid was the temptation to be exhaustive in my analysis. In trying to do that I felt I would only dilute the power of my argument by creating such a massive analytical infrastructure—for lack of a better word—that the original text would be in danger of getting lost.

While my vision for this series has always been as a teaching tool, I also didn't want it to be just another set of teacher handbooks full of crossword puzzles, worksheets, and quizzes of the kind that would greatly benefit public education were they to be eliminated permanently from the classroom. The best assessments will arise naturally from the material contained in the analysis and will emphasize the thinking skills of students rather than the mere fact-finding busy work of typical teacher guides. The true benefit of a series like this is to provide the raw material for the teacher, a way of seeing all of the elements that go into interpreting a work of literature as that work is being read. What the teacher or professor—or simply the curious reader—does with it at that point is up to the individual. While it's possible I may go back and provide the secondary teacher with a companion volume that demonstrates how to put this analysis to use in a classroom setting, that is not the purpose here.

Another thing I didn't want these books to be were annotated versions of the novel. While I understand the intent behind those kinds of works, not to disturb the narrative flow and allow readers to skip the annotations if they wish, it can be frustrating for the literary scholar. Being provided with dozens of pages of footnotes at the end of the book and forced to flip back and forth endlessly can be an exasperating experience for a studious reader. Finally, these books were never meant to be histories or biographies. While those elements are certainly present in my analysis, their use is very specific to the particular points being made in the text. Social and historical milieu, while important in the way they shape the narrative and the characters, are not the foundation on which any analysis should be made. Likewise, biographical information about the author, which can be crucial to understanding the intent behind much of the work, is only one aspect of understanding the text as a whole. What this book tries to do instead is to make sense of the novel in a way that integrates the author's use of language, symbolism, thematic structure, and characterization, within the larger context of the author's life and historical background, all with the singular purpose of attempting to aid the reader in truly grasping what makes a great work of literature great.

Despite the fact that I see this series of books as an educational tool, they are also written in such a way as to be accessible to every reader. They are, for the most part, free of academic jargon and arcane references that make most scholarly texts written in the past thirty years all but undecipherable to the general reading public. The ultimate goal in writing this series of books is to lead curious readers of every kind—whether that reader is an educator in the classroom or an individual at home—to a greater appreciation of classic texts, and in doing so bring the reader's thoughts back to the reason why we continue to read masterworks of literature in the first place: in the words of Ralph Waldo Emerson, for their ability to inspire.

Eric B. Olsen
May 25, 2018

A Note on the Text

One of the questions facing me as I completed the writing of this book was how best to present the variant renderings of the title of Edith Wharton's short novel *Ethan Frome*. Standard formatting today requires the titles of longer works to be printed in italics and shorter works like stories and poems to have quotation marks around the titles. But this was not always so. In the days before publishers used italics in a consistent way, titles of longer works were often put in quotations or simply capitalized. The same goes for scholarly books and journals. Even Edith Wharton herself was inconsistent, putting quotes around the title in her autobiography, but only capitalizing it in her 1922 introduction. My natural inclination was to simply let the titles stand as they appeared in the various original sources, and for many novels this would have been a workable solution. In this case, however, the title of the novel is also the same as that of the main character, and as a result I felt this could cause some confusion, as Ethan Frome the character is very different from *Ethan Frome* the novel. Ultimately, I decided for the sake of clarity to render the title in italics in all cases, even it if was not written that way in the original source.

The other decision I had to make was how best to cite sources in the text. My method has always been to cite the source and page number the first time a source is quoted in a paragraph. If the same source is used again immediately following the first quote then no source is cited at all, or if the page number is different only the new page number is indicated. In this way any unattributed quote simply corresponds to the previously cited source within a paragraph. The only minor exception to this is with Kate Chopin's "The Story of an Hour," which appeared on a single page in *Vogue* magazine and therefore is only indicated by the year of publication rather than the page number. Where there are two authors with the same last name or multiple works by a single author, the year of publication is used to distinguish between them. And where a modern edition of a book has been published I have used the original publication date in the citation, if necessary, rather than the newer date of the reprint. Finally, I wanted to devise a more streamlined solution to referencing the many newspaper articles written by a single author that appear in the section on *Ethan Frome* on film. In those cases, after the author's name I have indicated the month and two-digit year of the article, connected by a hyphen, and then followed that with the page number.

Introduction

Literary Theory in Education

The idea for a series of books analyzing classic literature came out of a number of experiences I had as a classroom teacher. Over the past two decades it has become increasing clear that teachers of literature in secondary schools tend to believe that any interpretation of a piece of literature is a valid one, when nothing could be further from the truth. The rationale behind this way of thinking seems to have come from their own experiences in college literature courses, a situation that has been written about in several essays I had my honors students read in preparation for taking those very same classes themselves. The truth about the kind of teaching that goes on in literature courses at the university level today is that it's nearly the opposite of what one would expect. Colleges and universities used to be places that challenged students to defend their beliefs by presenting them with a host of alternative ways of thinking, and one of the ways professors were able to accomplish that was by having their students read a wide variety of high-quality literature.

The goal of this kind of education was to help students begin the process of thinking for themselves by revealing to them the limited nature of their thinking thus far in their lives, to demonstrate to them the narrow pathways they had travelled intellectually as a result of appropriating thoughts and ideas from their parents, their pastors, and their peers. Allan Bloom—who himself can be a challenge to read—put the idea of what it means to go to college more pointedly than anyone has before or since in *The Closing of the American Mind* back in 1987.

True liberal education requires that the student's whole life be radically changed by it, that what he learns may affect his action, his tastes, his choices, that no previous attachment be immune to examination and hence re-evaluation. Liberal education puts everything at risk and requires students who are able to risk everything. Otherwise it can only touch what is uncommitted in the already essentially committed. (A. Bloom 1987, 370)

But for decades now professors and instructors of literature have stepped back from their responsibility as purveyors of knowledge and wisdom by allowing students to become the arbiters of truth in their classrooms. In his essay "On the Uses of a Liberal Education: As Lite Entertainment for Bored College Students," now twenty years old, professor Mark Edmundson lays out a detailed explanation for this phenomenon that centers on the economics of modern higher education in which not only schools as a whole but individual departments are forced to compete for student tuition money. The new fact of life for literature teachers is, if they make things too challenging for students, their students will simply go elsewhere.

The consumer pressures that beset me on evaluation day are only a part of an overall trend . . . Along with softening the grades, many humanities departments have relaxed major requirements. There are some good reasons for introducing more choice into curricula and requiring fewer standard courses. But the move, like many others in the university now, jibes with a tendency to serve—and not challenge—the students . . . A sure result of the university's widening elective leeway is to give students more power over their teachers. Those who don't like you can simply avoid you. If the clientele dislikes you *en masse*, you can be left without students, period. (Edmundson 1997, 44)

By removing many of the course requirements that guaranteed professors enrollment in their classes because students had to pass them in order to graduate, university faculties around the country suddenly found themselves at the mercy of their students. So naturally changes in the curriculum were made by professors to ensure that students who didn't have to would still sign up for their courses.

What this has led to is a faculty that is no longer able to challenge students, to help them see their own deficiencies, and to guide them in learning ways to correct those deficiencies. For that to be possible it would first necessitate that students see themselves as not yet fully formed, to understand that their

2

adult life has not really begun yet, and that high school not only wasn't the end of their education but perhaps was no education at all. Instead of pushing back against these student misconceptions modern college professors have retreated into modes of teaching that offer them job security rather than the ideological challenges students really need. Edmundson has plenty to say about that as well.

> Kids don't come to school hot to learn, unable to bear their own ignorance. For some measure of self-dislike, or self-discontent . . . seems to me to be a prerequisite for getting an education that matters. My students, alas, usually lack the confidence to acknowledge what would be their most precious asset for learning: their ignorance . . . A classroom now is frequently an "environment," a place highly conducive to the exchange of existing ideas, the students' ideas. Listening to one another, students sometimes change their opinions. But what they generally can't do is acquire a new vocabulary, a new perspective, that will cast issues in a fresh light. (Edmundson 1997, 47)

An unfortunate consequence of this new reality in higher education is students are taught to believe that what they think actually matters, and therefore anyone who disagrees with them is infringing on their imagined right—to quote President John F. Kennedy—to "the comfort of opinion without the discomfort of thought" (Kennedy 165). For Edmundson this includes the elimination of important tools like the Socratic method, "the animated, sometimes impolite give-and-take between student and teacher [that] seems too jagged for current sensibilities" (Edmundson 1997, 45). The reason it seems too jagged for today's students has much to do with "parents who sheltered these students, kept them away from the hard knocks of everyday life, making them cautious and overfragile, who demanded that their teachers, from grade school on, flatter them endlessly so that the kids are shocked if their college profs don't reflexively suck up to them" (42-43). One consequence of this way of growing up is that students come out of secondary school unable even to see their deficiencies, so that when they are finally shocked by the reality of their unexamined lives their immediate response is to blame the teacher. "A controversial teacher can send students hurrying to the deans and the counselors, claiming to have been offended. ("Offensive" is the preferred term of repugnance today)" (45).

The negative effects of this kind of behavior on teaching in colleges over the past twenty years are numerous, but one of the most pernicious is the continued denigration of a crucial pathway to self-examination: the literature itself. In a recent article on political correctness called "Not a Very P.C. Thing to Say: How the Language Police are Perverting Liberalism," author Jonathan Chait makes this observation about one of the many limitations put on university professors today. "At a growing number of campuses, professors now attach 'trigger warnings' to texts that may upset students" (Chait). And this continuing trend of accommodating student over-fragility extends even further: "there is a campaign to eradicate 'microaggressions,' or small social slights that might cause searing trauma. These newly fashionable terms merely repackage a central tenet of the first p.c. movement: that people should be expected to treat even faintly unpleasant ideas or behaviors as full-scale offenses." But again, immature overreactions like these come from students who have been taught not make distinctions of any kind and therefore colleges have inadvertently created an entire generation of people who are going to be offended simply because they can't think for themselves. As Tom Nichols puts it in his book, *The Death of Expertise*, an ever-increasing number of people in this country are unable understand what constitutes a valid argument and what doesn't. "Americans no longer distinguish the phrase 'you're wrong' from the phrase 'you're stupid.' To disagree is to disrespect. To correct another is to insult. And to refuse to acknowledge all views as worthy of consideration, no matter how fantastic or inane they are, is to be closed-minded" (Nichols 25).

This kind of automatic resistance to introspection exhibited by today's students is exactly what Allan Bloom means when he writes that liberal education is only able to touch "what is uncommitted in the already essentially committed." In his day, however, there were still parts of his students that were actually uncommitted. Not so today, as English professor Suanna H. Davis relates about the students she and her colleagues frequently encounter when it comes to religious indoctrination.

> Some of our students have been taught to leave a room when ungodly or demonic talk begins. If, say, a beginning-of-class conversation about a science story in the news drifts into mention of evolution or the Big Bang, a student will quietly pack up his or her books and leave, because he or she has been trained to get out of a room when Satan starts talking. It has happened to me and most of my colleagues. (Davis 2014)

The natural response to knee-jerk reactions like these is that changes begin to happen inside classrooms and lecture halls in order to circumvent this behavior—and it's important to understand that race, gender, and class distinctions provoke the same kinds of anti-intellectual reactions from students as religion does.

So in order to protect against damaging the college child's completely undeveloped sense of self, the literature has been debased to the point of meaninglessness, first by what Edmundson calls "debunking theories."

> Skeptical approaches [to literature] have potential value . . . Surely it matters that women are denigrated in Milton and in Pope, that some novelistic voices assume an overbearing godlike authority, that the poor are, in this or that writer, inevitably cast as clowns. You can't buy all of literature wholesale if it's going to help draw your patterns of belief. But demystifying theories are now overused, applied mechanically . . . Full-out debunking is what plays with this clientele. Some have been doing it nearly as long as, if more crudely than, their deconstructionist teachers. In the context of the contemporary university, and cool consumer culture, a useful intellectual skepticism has become exaggerated into a fundamentalist caricature of itself. The teachers have buckled to their students' views. (Edmundson 1997, 47)

This type of pandering to student expectations is no doubt proffered in the belief that skepticism is an important part of the maturation process, and it is, but it is only one small element of what the humanities have to offer. Another former college professor, Michael S. Roth, puts it this way in his book *Beyond the University*: "a spirit of critique is only one aspect of a well-rounded education, and its overemphasis can lead to sterility rather than creativity" (Roth 5).

By using literature as a whipping boy to reinforce inflated feelings of self-importance in students through simplistic negative interpretations, it robs it of the power to change lives. Even worse, the denigration of literature gives students a false sense of their own intelligence, something university professor and literary critic Lionel Trilling recognized in his students' reading of classic literature back in the early nineteen sixties.

> To some of us who teach and who think of our students as the creators of the intellectual life of the future, there comes a land of despair. It does not come because our students fail to respond to ideas, rather because they respond to ideas with a happy vagueness, a delighted glibness, a joyous sense of power in the use of perceived or receivable generalizations, a grateful wonder at how easy it is to formulate and judge, at how little resistance language offers to their intentions. (Trilling 1965, 4)

In an essay from that same time period on the meaning of art, "Against Interpretation," Susan Sontag makes the powerful assertion that "real art has the capacity to make us nervous. By reducing the work of art to its content and then interpreting that, one tames the work of art. Interpretation makes art manageable, comfortable" (Sontag 8). College, however, as a place of learning about one's self, should be anything but intellectually comfortable. This is another thing Edmundson makes clear, when he says that literature, as art, should be much more than just communication, it should be "intellectual work . . . a confrontation between two people, student and author, where the stakes matter.

> Is it a surprise, then, that this generation of students—steeped in consumer culture before going off to school, treated as potent customers by the university well before their date of arrival, then pandered to from day one until the morning of the final kiss-off . . . are inclined to see the books they read as a string of entertainments to be placidly enjoyed or languidly cast down? (Edmundson 1997, 46-47)

Trilling, as well, had a very clear idea about the reading of literature and the expectation readers should have if they are to get anything significant out of the confrontation. "Our typical experience of a work which will eventually have authority with us is to begin our relation to it at a conscious disadvantage, and to wrestle with it until it consents to bless us" (Trilling 1965, 62). Another former university professor, Joseph Epstein, came to the same realization during his undergraduate days at the University of Chicago, an understanding about literature that is not only absent in today's students but, in the current university climate, seems to have little hope of replicating itself. "What I do remember is the feeling of intellectual excitement while reading Plato and Thucydides and an almost palpable physical pleasure turning the pages of Max Weber's *The Protestant Ethic and the Spirit of Capitalism* as he made one dazzling intellectual connection after another" (Epstein 2012). Unlike the "delighted glibness" Trilling's students indulged in as a way of demonstrating their mastery of literary analysis, what Epstein instinctively understood is that, "mastery wasn't in the picture."

> At least, I never felt that I had mastered any subject, or even book, in any of my courses there. What the school did give me was the confidence that I could read serious books, and with it the assurance that I needed to return to them, in some cases over and over, to claim anything like a genuine understanding of them. (Epstein 2012)

Things could not be more different today, as college professors allow their students' already atrophied intellects to coast along without being challenged, leaving them comfortable in the thought that the analysis of literature is no more strenuous than tossing out whatever uninformed opinion pops into their heads. The denigration of the written word through unchallenged interpretation, then, continues to reinforce in our young people the debilitating notion that not only is beauty in the eye of the beholder, but meaning is as well. To see this kind of mindset in action one only has to go back to 1997—the same year as Edmundson's essay—in a student editorial written by college senior Erin Kirsten Stein for the *Arizona Daily Wildcat.* In an impassioned but misguided attempt to explain why poetry wasn't more popular with students at the University of Arizona she inadvertently exposes the kind of literary relativism that continues to infect high school and college literature classes to this day.

> Teachers always teach the "correct" interpretation of a poem, and it is understood to be absolute. In reality, ANY interpretation is valid. What is taught is merely the most accepted theory as to what the poem meant when he/she wrote it. But to enjoy and appreciate a poem you do not have to know exactly what was going on in the poet's mind. However the poem touches you, the feelings you get from it, even if you hate it, they are all correct interpretations. If you read it again you will find new ideas and explore symbolism, but those further interpretations are not any more valid. Poems can be read at many different levels, all of which are correct. (Stein)

The idea that any meaning a student comes up with in interpreting literature is a correct one is just the starting point. Professors are quick to guide students from there into any number of self-serving theories that, hand in hand with debunking, merely serve to reinforce their false but firmly ingrained belief that they have no responsibility at all for their own intellectual lives. This type of literary interpretation in colleges today can go by a variety of names, deconstructionism, feminism, queer theory, and the identity politics of multiculturalism, all of them different ways of achieving the same thing: taking the thinking out of education. But at its core—and as the above example amply demonstrates—it's the very idea of interpretation that is so damaging to the intellect, which is why Sontag argues so passionately against it in her essay. The interpretation of literature has been around as long as literature itself, but what is different today is the intent that motivates it. According to Sontag, "The old style of interpretation was insistent, but respectful; it erected another meaning on top of the literal one. The modern style of interpretation excavates, and as it excavates, destroys; it digs 'behind' the text, to find a sub-text which is the true one" (Sontag 6).

Sontag goes on to explain the destructive nature of this kind of teaching by using the two most influential examples of interpretive tyranny in her day, Freudian and Marxist. "According to Marx and Freud . . . events only *seem* to be intelligible. Actually, they have no meaning without interpretation" (Sontag 7). This, then, becomes the justification for ideas like deconstructionism, where the meaning in works of art must be constructed by the audience, that the work itself actually has no meaning without the audience. But this is merely an abstract dialectic argument along the lines of the tree falling in the forest without anyone there to hear it. Of course true communication depends upon two parties, the sender and the receiver, and without the receiver communication cannot be said to exist. That, however, is distinctly different from determining meaning in a work of art. The fact is, the tree that falls in a forest outside of human perception most certainly does make a noise, just as a work of art without an audience contains meaning: the meaning its creator endowed it with. This is where deconstructionist interpretation goes awry. If the only meaning of art is what the audience decides it is, then art has no intrinsic meaning, no intrinsic philosophical value, and thus art itself is devoid of meaning until the audience creates that meaning. But art does have intellectual value, and instead it is the very act of interpretation that is debasing it and making it worthless. "Like the fumes of the automobile and of heavy industry which befoul the urban atmosphere," says Sontag, "the effusion of interpretations of art today poisons our sensibilities" (7).

Joseph Epstein's explanation for the decline in the value of the liberal arts is that our modern society is one in which practical skills, that is, those skills that can be readily transferred to the workplace, are valued significantly more than the benefits of purely intellectual work. This transition has led to the intentional dismantling of the traditional way of teaching humanities courses. In an anecdote from his essay "Who Killed the Liberal Arts, And Why We Should Care" he demonstrates the lengths to which professors have gone in attempting to destroy the idea that any meaning in art is inherent in the work itself:

A bright young female graduate student one day came to ask me if I thought David Copperfield a sexual criminal. "Why would I think that?" I asked. "Professor X thinks it," she said. "He claims that because of the death in childbirth of David Copperfield's wife, he, Copperfield, through making her pregnant, committed a crime." All I could think to reply was, "I guess criticism never sleeps." (Epstein 2012)

This is no less than the wholesale destruction of intellectual thought, inculcated into generations of young people, and tantamount to making them unable to actually read. For if the literal meaning has no place in comprehending a work of art, then nothing does. Sontag also makes explicit the emphasis that this kind of interpretation has on the actual written word. "This philistinism of interpretation is more rife in literature than in any other art. For decades now, literary critics have understood it to be their task to translate the elements of the poem or play or novel or story into something else" (Sontag 8).

The true goal of interpreting literature should be to understand what the text is actually saying, not to turn it "into something else." Instead, what I used to call a valid interpretation rests on the integrity of the interpreted meaning, one that makes sense in all aspects of the literal meaning of the words on the page. But I don't even use the word "interpretation" anymore, valid or otherwise, and now I choose to use "analysis" because of the connotation of validity inherent in the word. In my method of analysis the purpose of looking at a work of art stems from a desire to know what it means. And that's really the key, what *it* means, not what *I think* it means. This is a profound distinction. For I believe that there are intrinsic meanings in works of art, especially literature. And while that ultimate meaning of a work may not be exactly what the author intended, I am quite certain that it's not simply anything I want it to be. The true meaning of a work of art is visible in the work itself, and it's not my job to overlay some allegorical interpretation on top of it or, worse yet, to "dig behind the text," as Sontag says, and thereby destroy the work in the process. The true meaning of the work is there, in the words, for all to see, and the job of formal analysis is to identify that meaning as accurately as possible, one that is valid both textually and contextually, as a way of better understanding the literal work itself.

To this end I developed a mode of analysis that I always used to think of as contextual analysis. The problem with that phrase, however, is that it's also used in colleges today as part of the deconstructionist principals that have undermined the teaching of literature. Author Michael Kowalewski explains the problem with these approaches about as well as anyone in looking at "the more recent and general trend in literary studies to turn away from an attention to language as such in favor of placing literature within the larger contexts of history, politics, class and gender concerns, and cultural conditions of production" (Kowalewski 19). Again, this is just another way of taking the thinking out of literary analysis.

What current contextual approaches too often do is conceive of literary works as merely the puppets of processes outside of themselves. They render novels and stories subsidiary to the social or cultural conditions that supposedly "account" for them . . . and they take those conditions to be more deserving of our interrogative energy than the language they are seen to originate and control . . . The problem with such arguments is that they frequently depend upon and confirm our assumptions, first, that we can indeed pinpoint such processes, and second, that they at least are clearly understood, that they are somehow less controversial, less marked with or by theoretical difficulties, than the texts they are brought in to resolve. (19-20)

The reality of this type of interpretation is that it simplifies the confrontation with the text by making the emphasis of the reading on something that is external to the text. But the assumption that there is a direct connection to be found between those external forces and the text is guesswork at best, and Kowalewski's suggestion that even the theories themselves are not understood in any meaningful way is borne out by what is actually happening in the classroom.

In his less than flattering review of *The Cambridge History of the American Novel*, Joseph Epstein also makes a scathing indictment of this kind of literary interpretation as it is used in American universities, an environment that is responsible for what he sees as the preponderance of the context-centered interpretation of literature over the text-centered interpretations of the past. Rather than those contextual theories enriching student understanding of the actual words on the page, in practice it robs literature of any meaning whatsoever.

As a former English major, I cannot help wondering what it must be like to be taught by the vast majority of the people who have contributed to "The Cambridge History of the American Novel." Two or three times a week one would sit in a room and be told that nothing that one has read is as it appears but is instead informed by authors hiding their true motives even from themselves or, in the best "context-centered" manner, that the books under study are the product of a country built on fundamental dishonesty about the sacred subjects of race, gender and class. (Epstein 2011)

The issue I have with the word "context" used in this way is that the end result is no different than "interpretation," because by this way of thinking even the context becomes whatever the reader wants it to be. The reader simply decides ahead of time that the context is—to use Epstein's words in looking at America from this perspective—"a country founded on violence and expropriation, stoked through its history by every kind of prejudice and class domination, and populated chiefly by one or another kind of victim," and from there it's just a short step to Professor X and David Copperfield as sexual criminal.

What true contextual analysis means is looking at the historical circumstances surrounding the writing for the sole purpose of better comprehending the author's words, the actual text. But this does not mean old-school interpretation in which every nuance of a writer's life was examined because it was believed to be the only way to understand the author's writing. Or stranger yet, that the only real purpose for literature is as a guide to understanding the time period in which it was written. In the introduction to his book *Close Reading: The Reader*, co-editor Andrew DuBois makes a humorous observation about this kind of history-centered interpretation by quoting the noted nineteenth century work *History of English Literature* by Hippolyte Taine, in which Taine posits the idea that context isn't to be used to understand the literature, but literature used to understand the context. In reading modern poets, Taine said, the reader would come to understand that, "they graduated from a college and travelled, wearing a dress-coat and gloves, favored by ladies, bowing fifty times and uttering a dozen witticisms in an evening, reading daily newspapers, [and] generally occupying an apartment on the second story" (Taine 2). DuBois's response to this type of interpretative theory is wonderfully acute. "Taine's vigorous, amusing writing cannot obscure the absence of a certain kind of reading . . . and we might well ask: How do you ascertain from reading *The Waste Land* what floor of his apartment building Eliot occupied, if he occupied an apartment at all, and what does it have to do with the poem?" (DuBois 5).

But that is exactly Taine's point. For Taine, the purpose of the literature isn't about the literature at all. In his hands it becomes something completely different: "The discovery has been made that a literary work is not a mere play of the imagination, the isolated caprice of an excited brain, but a transcript of contemporary manners and customs . . ." (Taine 1).

> Let us strive as much as possible to supply the place of the actual, personal, sensible observation that is no longer practicable, this being the only way in which we can really know the man; let us make the past present . . . [T]here is no other way of obtaining knowledge approximatively of bygone times than by *seeing* approximatively the men of former times. Such is the first step in history. (4)

Thus Taine's use of contextual literary analysis is for the sole purpose of understanding history. This sentiment is one that was echoed by playwright Arthur Miller in the narrative passages of *The Crucible*, his play about the Salem witch trials in Puritan New England, and there's a certain truth to it. Speaking of the Puritans in Colonial America, Miller said, "No one can really know what their lives were like. They had no novelists . . ." (Miller 4). What Miller understood from his research is that, far more than diaries or histories, or even letters, all of which carry with them the self-consciousness of the author presenting a particular image to posterity, the novelist is under no such obligation and therefore can reveal the truthful thoughts and feelings of a particular age in a way that has no equal. French novelist Émile Zola called this idea naturalism, comparing critics to zoologists who were able to construct models of dinosaurs from just a few fossil fragments. "'Today,' Zola wrote in 1866 'in literary and artistic criticism we must imitate the naturalists: we have the duty of finding the men behind their works, to reconstruct the societies in their real life, with the aid of a book or a picture'" (Wellek 15). The irony is, in today's college classrooms this outmoded way of looking at literature is the centerpiece for context-centered interpretation, and yet the "history" that they purport to have discovered is anything but. The real purpose of reading in this way is solely to reinforce a pre-conceived victim mentality for any number of perceived minority groups.

Even worse, however, Taine and Zola's naturalism has been turned on its head and repackaged as another deconstructionist exercise called New Historicism, in which the veracity of history itself is called into question, and thus no literary work can be trusted to give any kind of accurate insight into the past because no one can ever really know what the past was actually like. Unfortunately, this has led to an equally disturbing type of literary interpretation. In jettisoning context completely by calling into question the contextual reality of literature, these readings can then be used as a kind of reactionary backlash against the identity politics that informs modern context-centered interpretation. What this strictly literal interpretation seeks to do is not only look at the text and nothing but the text, but actually go out of its way to ignore contextual information that might give readers a more complete understanding of what they are reading. An extreme example of this method of interpretation comes in an essay by Lawrence Berkove about Kate Chopin's "The Story of an Hour." Chopin's brief, one-page story, which was first published in 1894, is about a woman whose husband dies and her realization that she will no longer have to submit to the oppression that many women in this country lived under at that time. "There would be no one to live for during those coming years; she would live for herself. There would be no powerful will bending hers in that blind persistence with which men and women believe they have a right to impose a private will upon a fellow-creature" (Chopin 1894).

Yet Berkove has the audacity to declare that, "in the text of this very short story there is no hard evidence whatsoever of patriarchal blindness or suppression, constant or selfless sacrifice . . . these positions are all read into the story from non-textual assumptions" (Berkove 153). The reality for anyone who actually reads the story, however, is not that they are *non-textual* assumptions but that they are *textual* assumptions. The text is very clear in saying the protagonist has been living for someone else, and while it doesn't say specifically that that person is her husband, it's incredibly disingenuous for Berkove to suggest otherwise. Likewise the "powerful will bending hers in that blind persistence" is also, obviously, her husband. But there's no mystery to the purpose behind Berkove's hyper-literal reading, as he makes his motivation clear from the start when he quotes feminist readings first in order to rebut them by claiming that the story "does not regard Louise Mallard as a heroine but as an immature egotist and a victim of her own extreme self-assertion" (Berkove 152). A nineteenth century critic couldn't have said it any better, as the prevailing patriarchal view of women's suffering at that time was that it was their own fault for not happily submitting to the maternal and domestic roles that society had relegated them to. A woman's right to vote, which came a mere twenty years after Chopin's story was published, is just one contextual fact that demonstrates the speciousness of Berkove's argument. But the disingenuousness of Berkove's reactionary interpretation is even more troubling when he goes on to say that, "while the text enables us to make certain inferences about Louise, it does not supply us with any information about the truth of her life except her perception" (Berkove 153). Even if that's literally true, what's the difference? Again, Berkove would have us ignore the narrator's clear implications as well as the character's perceptions which are, to her, the truth of her life whether he wants them to be or not. Ignoring the character's perceptions in this way is tantamount to ignoring the text itself.

Unlike colleges and universities, the most common literary theory espoused today in secondary schools is a throwback to the nineteenth century author-centered analyses that attempt to use the author's biography to explain why certain scenes or characters or thematic elements appear in their works. In one sense the exercise seems entirely pointless, as Michael Kowalewsky demonstrates in discussing the description of a character called Friend in a story by Joyce Carol Oates, and considering that character's possible biographical genesis.

There may in fact have been for Oates an actual man and car upon which she modeled those in her story. Yet even if there were, they form no part of a reader's experience of this scene . . . A reader might, of course, have recourse to a biography of Oates or to her remarks in an interview about an actual person upon whom Friend is based. Such glosses, however, would not necessarily feed into the imaginative substance of the character we encounter within the confines of the story. (Kowalewski 29, 260)

And yet, because this method of interpretation seems a much more practical approach to the use of biography, teachers are far more willing to employ it. But the problem remains that it is still entirely too limiting in attempting to explain the internal workings of the actual literature, and much too facile to give those kinds of interpretations any real merit. Author Imogen Sara Smith makes this point quite eloquently in her book on one of silent film's greatest stars, *Buster Keaton: The Persistence of Comedy*. "I am habitually skeptical of simple-minded attempts to prove that an artist must have had a certain experience because it appears in his work, or that his work must be interpreted a certain way because of events in his life. Such efforts underestimate the independence of creativity and deny artworks the right to stand alone" (Smith 11). At the same time, however, Smith is also highly conscious of the necessity for biography in coming to a complete understanding of the artist and his work, which she addresses in looking at the specific subject of her book. "But even if untangling Keaton's private and public personae is more than unusually difficult, I don't believe either can be fully understood without knowing something about the other."

Edmundson has observed a similar problem in the way that computers are used in humanities classes, taking students out of the actual text and submerging the work in an ocean of research, as though mere information can replace thoughtful reflection on the writings of the past. In his book of essays *Why Read?* he states,

Now that computers are everywhere, each area of enquiry in the humanities is more and more defined by the computer's resources . . . Instead of spending class time wondering what the poem means, and what application it has to present-day experience, students compile information about it. They set the poem in its historical and critical context, showing first how the poem is the product and the property of the past—and, implicitly, how it really has nothing to do with the present except as an artful curiosity—and second how, given the number of ideas about it readily available, adding more thoughts would be superfluous . . . The result is to suspend reflection about the differences between wisdom, knowledge, and information. Everything that can be accessed online can seem equal to everything else, no datum more important or more profound than any other. Thus the possibility presents itself that there really is no more wisdom; there is no more knowledge; there is only information. (Edmundson 2004, 14-15)

It doesn't take much effort to see how far this way of thinking has gone wrong in the teaching of literature across the educational spectrum. Context is certainly important in literary analysis, but it must be subservient to the text, not the reason for analysis. In his essay "Keats' Sylvan Historian: History Without Footnotes," Cleanth Brooks makes a beautifully truthful statement about the Grecian urn that Keats called, in Transcendental turn of phrase, a "sylvan historian."

The names, dates, and special circumstances, the wealth of data—these the sylvan historian quietly ignores. But we shall never get all the facts anyway—there is no end to the accumulation of facts. Moreover, mere accumulations of facts—a point our own generation is only beginning to realize—are meaningless. The sylvan historian does better than that: it takes a few details and so orders them that we have not only beauty but insight into essential truth. (Brooks 164)

If this idea is applied to the work of understanding and writing about literature, a "sylvan analysis" one could say, then it makes the obvious point that the analyst is under no obligation to history at all when trying to ascertain the meaning of literature. The only context that truly matters is the context of that piece of literature itself. This is not simply another version of hyper-literal reading, however, but instead a way of making sure that whatever arguments the analyst makes are valid throughout the whole of the work, a concept that Brooks addresses in his essay as well.

If we can see that the assertions made in a poem are to be taken as part of an organic context, if we can resist the temptation to deal with them in isolation, then we may be willing to go on to deal with the world-view, or "philosophy," or "truth" of *the poem as a whole* in terms of its dramatic wholeness: that is, we shall not neglect the maturity of attitude, the dramatic tension, the emotional *and* intellectual coherence in favor of some statement of theme abstracted from it by paraphrase. (Brooks 165-166)

In this way true literary analysis is content to examine the world inside the literature as a way of understanding the literature itself—Brooks' organic context—rather taking isolated parts of the work out of context or paraphrasing them as a way to support an interpretation that is not borne out by the rest of the text or as a way of trying to say something meaningful about the historical context. At the same time, this organic kind of analysis will naturally reflect the historical era in which the work was written, and that is what finally allows the reader to "go on to deal with" those external ideas of the world-view or philosophy of the writing. Nevertheless, it's important to always keep in mind that what this kind of analysis reveals about that history is a beneficial byproduct rather than the primary purpose for reading.

A genuine contextual analysis, then, which seeks knowledge and understanding and ultimately wisdom from literature, must find a middle ground in its use of context. Clearly, any meaningful analysis must begin and end with the text. At the same time, it is foolish to limit oneself to a strict formalism when studying literature. In what time period a work was written, what was happening in the writers' life and in the society when they wrote it, as well as the writers' place in that society are all important in understanding the meaning of the text, but they are still secondary to the text itself. And rather than attempting to understand the writer as a person, it is much more important to focus on the characters and their place within the universe of the writing when trying to make determinations about the content. Information about the writer's personal life is only germane, again, in looking at the specific influence it has on the actual text. One of the most articulate explanations for using this kind of context in analyzing literature comes from author Helen Lefkowitz Horowitz in her book *Wild Unrest*, about Charlotte Perkins Gilman and her writing of "The Yellow Wall-Paper."

> Language can be deceptive. Words in the past may seem transparent, their meanings fixed by a dictionary, but they carry connotations that can be specific to time, place, and social position. Although the nouns and verbs Charlotte used are current today, they were penned in a different cultural world and can relate to ideas and phenomena no longer known today. Exploring what she read makes it possible to discover the meaning of key words to her at the time she uttered them. (Horowitz 5)

While this seems to be an obvious and intelligent way of using context in analyzing literature, the fact remains that in many cases this means the reader will actually find discrimination and oppression and victims in the text, as they certainly do in "The Yellow Wall-Paper." The distinction between theoretical contextual interpretation and actual literary analysis is probably best understood by looking at the words of Professor Ann Douglas and the way in which they expose the dangers of deconstructionism. Even though her comment is about historical rather than literary interpretation, it can still be quite useful to consider in this context. "The last decades of the twentieth century have witnessed, amid vociferous protest from some quarters, the deconstruction in the academy of the racial, gendered, and economic assumptions implicit in most Western modes of 'objective' research and an increasing emphasis on subjective points of view" (Douglas xi). Douglas obviously questions the actual objectivity of Western writings by putting the word in quotes, but then to promote seeing all literary analysis as "subjective" in its point of view hardly seems to be the answer, especially in attempting to discern meaning in something as inherently subjective as fiction, because it then becomes a license to see in the text whatever the reader wants. The way her comment can be applied to this study, however, is that by using contextual information readers can discern truly objective examples of coded protest against patriarchal societal assumptions in the writings of women authors— so many, in fact, that they don't need to be invented in a subjective way by manufacturing examples that aren't really there.

This is why interpretations of literature based on identity politics, whether context-centered or hyper-literal, fail, because they have at their very conception the need to manipulate the meaning of the text in order to show how it adheres to an existing, subjective, ideological belief held by the reader. Anything so conceived, however, has to be considered invalid because it makes the text subservient to ideology rather than looking at the text objectively. What I used to call historical contextual analysis, on the other hand, takes into consideration the historical reality surrounding the creation of the story as well as that historical reality within the universe of the text in order to render the most accurate analysis of the writing possible. This is the type of analysis I have always employed in the classroom, and that I will employ throughout this book. In this way of looking at literature everything counts. Nothing that is inconvenient to a pre-existing ideological interpretation will be ignored because there is no ideological axe to grind in the first place. The words speak for themselves, and allowing them to do so makes for a much more persuasive analysis than one that tries to manipulate the author's words into saying something they don't actually mean.

Eric B. Olsen

Toward a Non-Theory of Literature

This work is not a feminist reading of *Ethan Frome*, for the simple fact that going into it I had no preconceived notion of how the novel should be read, except to look closely at the text and try to understand it in the context of the time it was written. But before I address the obvious perils associated with attempting to analyzing literature through theoretical frameworks there are other, more subtle, assumptions that can also impede an accurate analysis of Edith Wharton's novel that have to do with the very existence of the book itself. It's important to understand that not every work written by a female author at the turn of the twentieth century is going to accurately represent the experience of all women at that time. This is a concept made clear by British author Robert Roberts, who wrote about his childhood growing up in the slums of Salfort. In the introduction to his book he begins by stating the purpose for writing his story, which he felt would more accurately reflect the life he had experienced than a history written by someone else. "Many writers of modern social history have described with sympathy, and with passion even, the plight of the undermass in pre-1914 industrial Britain, when the rich seemed never so wealthy nor the poor so poor. But such description has naturally lacked the factuality that first-hand experience might have given it; few historians are the sons of labourers" (Roberts 9). In the same way, the voice of a single female writer cannot be assumed to speak for all, as not all women at the turn of the twentieth century chafed at their lot in life, but understood the trade-off inherent in their partnerships with men and felt satisfied in the bargain, especially considering the alternatives.

> Some women at least began to question—and a few to challenge overtly—their constricted place in society . . . A far greater number began, though more covertly, to see family limitation as a necessity if they would preserve health, status, economic security, and individual autonomy. Only a handful of nineteenth-century American women made a commitment to overt feminism and to the insecurity and hostility such a commitment implied. (Smith-Rosenberg 1999, 112, 115)

The danger in attempting to turn all writings by women from this era into feminist manifestos is that they are certainly not that. At the same time, to ignore the history itself—that women of that period were, in fact, restricted—is also patently false. The two extremes of the female experience at the turn of the twentieth century were summarized impressively by Edgar Lee Masters in his *Spoon River Anthology* from 1915, a look back at turn of the twentieth century life from beyond the grave. The first is told from the viewpoint of "Serepta Mason," who represents the regret of a life unlived and the bitterness associated with that recognition.

> My life's blossom might have bloomed on all sides
> Save for a bitter wind which stunted my petals
> On the side of me which you in the village could see.
> From the dust I lift a voice of protest:
> My flowering side you never saw!
> Ye living ones, ye are fools indeed
> Who do not know the ways of the wind
> And the unseen forces
> That govern the processes of life. (Masters 18)

What's so interesting is that the unconscious forces of society governing the lives of so many people at the time, both male and female, are as real to Masters as they were to the women of his day. Significantly, he is able to capture the genuine sense of helplessness in the face of oppression, one that is felt more than consciously understood, by comparing it to a force of nature in the form of wind, which man has always been powerless to control. He then goes on to symbolize the plight of his female narrator by having her compare herself to a flower that has been stunted by that force, and her bitterness in thinking about what her life might have been had it been lived in a different age that she could not yet imagine. The narrator of "Lucinda Matlock," on the other hand, lived in a very literal world in which life is to be taken as it comes, and not complained about after the fact.

> We were married and lived together for seventy years,
> Enjoying, working, raising the twelve children,
> Eight of whom we lost
> Ere I had reached the age of sixty.
> I spun, I wove, I kept the house, I nursed the sick,
> I made the garden, and for holiday
> Rambled over the fields where sang the larks,
> And by Spoon River gathering many a shell,
> And many a flower and medicinal weed—
> Shouting to the wooded hills, singing to the green valleys.
> At ninety-six I had lived enough, that is all,

And passed to a sweet repose.
What is this I hear of sorrow and weariness,
Anger, discontent and drooping hopes?
Degenerate sons and daughters,
Life is too strong for you—
It takes life to love Life. (Masters 224)

The reason why so many writings by the women of this period reflect the experience of Serepta Mason from the first poem rather than Lucinda Matlock is because the vast majority of those women writers were in a position to recognize their societal limitations intellectually, and they also had the education and the means to put their thoughts to paper in a way that allowed those thoughts to be published. But even then, the fact that many women writers were addressing this reality didn't mean that other women were necessarily reading and agreeing with their works. One of the misconceptions in studying any kind of art historically is the assumption that the best examples of that art in retrospect are the ones that the majority of people were consuming at the time. Author Elijah Wald makes this point in his book about popular music in America.

Music criticism demands studious, analytic listening, and the people who listen that way tend to value music that rewards careful attention and analysis over styles that are just fun, relaxing, or danceable—which, again, is perfectly reasonable but automatically separates them from most of the people buying and dancing to popular music. And in the same way, [music] historians tend to focus on unique, original musicians rather than typical, generic ones, even when they are supposedly studying trends and movements rather than exceptional achievements. (Wald 10)

Once can see a similar effect in the study of literature, where critically acclaimed works that stand the test of time may not be the best indicator of what the general public is reading at a given moment in history—or that they accurately reflect the ideology those readers hold—something author Janice A. Radway discovered in looking at the popularity of romance novels among female readers in the late twentieth century.

Traditional English departments . . . assumed that the most reliable and complex record of the American past could be found in the country's "greatest" works of art. In opposition to such claims, however, [is the] critique of the assumption that works selected on the basis of their aesthetic achievement would necessarily be representative of the large sections of the population that had never read such books. (Radway 3)

Ultimately, narratives like Kate Chopin's "The Story of an Hour" and Charlotte Perkins Gilman's "The Yellow Wall-Paper" emerged from the personal experiences of their authors, and those experiences happened within the context of a patriarchal society that restricted the opportunities and autonomy of women in this country. As a result, their writings are going to reflect that fact. This is a point made very clear by Marilyn Butler in her work *Romantics, Rebels and Reactionaries.* "Literature, like all art, like language, is a collective activity, powerfully conditioned by social forces . . . Authors are not the solitaries of the Romantic myth, but citizens" (Butler 4). Even with that understanding, however, the end product of analysis doesn't have to be either an indictment of this country or an apology for it simply because the reader recognizes those themes in the writing. Edith Wharton's novel *Ethan Frome* takes a different tack when dealing with the subject of patriarchy in American society and thus it is all the more impressive for it, but the same criteria applies. Looking at the historic circumstances of the time is the only thing that can put the reader anywhere close to the mindset of those authors when they wrote their works. This is just common sense, for every work of art is inspired by something, and the greatest works of art become so because they have taken on a life of their own beyond what their creators intended and achieved.

In attempting to render the most accurate analysis of a work of literature, however, it doesn't really matter what the writer's intent is, the fact of their existence and the cultural and personal experiences they have witnessed are going to become a part of the literature they create. For women, regardless of their political or personal beliefs, their experience of being a woman is bound up in everything they write. This is a point made most eloquently by Ellen Moers in her book on great women writers.

Being women, women writers have women's bodies, which affect their senses and their imagery. They are raised as girls and thus have a special perception of the cultural imprinting of childhood. They are assigned roles in the family and in courtship, they are given or denied access to education and employment, they are regulated by laws of property and political representation which, absolutely in the past, partially today, differentiate women from men. If they denied their bodies, denied whatever was special about being a woman in their time and class and place, they would be only narrowly human and would hardly be much good as writers. The great writers have always chosen brilliantly, individually, imaginatively among the varying feminine facets of the human condition; and transformed this material, along with all the other materials a writer uses, into literature [revealing] the deep creative strategies of the literary mind at work upon the fact of being female. (Moers xi)

The true goal of literary analysis, then, is to determine objectively what the work itself is saying for itself, not merely what the author intended, and certainly not what the reader would like it to say. As a result, I've taken as my models those critics who are not bound by strict adherence to what Andrew DuBois calls the "intrinsic context" of the work. By the same token, however, any analysis worthy of the name that begins from a theory outside the work has to be called into question because of the ulterior motives that must be assumed in doing so. "The *literary* critic must necessarily first establish the intrinsic context of the literary object; otherwise, all extrinsic moves (which are also 'contextual' work) are themselves suspicious" (DuBois 8). Thus context, which includes the external history of both the writer and the time period, while necessary for a complete understanding of the work, should not be the starting and ending point for analysis. One critic who epitomizes this way of thinking is Kenneth Burke in his essay on John Keats' "Ode on a Grecian Urn." Burke's ideas are equally applicable to the analysis of literature in general.

Our primary concern is to follow the transformations of the poem itself. But to understand its full nature as a symbolic act, we should use whatever knowledge is available. In the case of Keats, not only do we know the place of this poem in his work and its time, but also we have material to guide our speculations as regards correlations between poem and poet. I grant that such speculations interfere with the symmetry of criticism as a game . . . But linguistic analysis has opened up new possibilities in the correlating of producer and product—and these concerns have such important bearing upon matters of culture and conduct in general that no sheer conventions of ideals of criticism should be allowed to interfere with their development. (Burke 451)

Burke's most telling statements here are "criticism as a game," and how the "ideals of criticism" actually interfere with a true understanding of the literature. In making his argument Burke brings up another area of literary analysis that is equally as troubling as interpretation, and that is criticism.

The purpose inherent in criticism is the use of literary analysis as a way of making a value judgment about a particular work. Where pure analysis seeks to understand the work itself, as a work, criticism attempts to determine the worth of the writing as if the critic were a Roman emperor, signaling thumb up or thumb down. The essential difference between these two modes of analytical thought can be crudely understood by looking at the difference between the philosophies of Plato and Aristotle as explained by author Arthur Herman in his book *The Cave and the Light.*

> Plato used [The Myth of the Cave] to represent his most fundamental idea: that man is destined by his creator to find a path from the dark cave of material existence to the light of a higher, purer, and more spiritual truth. It's when we rise above the merely human, Plato insisted, and enter the realm of "the everlasting and immortal and changeless" that we achieve wisdom . . . Aristotle believed the philosopher's job was to explain how the world works, and how as human beings we can find our proper place in it. There is no cave; only a world made of things and facts. "The *fact* is our starting point," he once said, and that insight permeated his thinking on everything, from science to politics to drama. (Herman x).

Plato believed that truth could not be found in works of art because they were too far removed from an ideal that existed only in the mind. Looked at from this perspective, the literary critic's job is usually to measure the work in question against a perfection it can never hope to achieve in order to determine just how far it falls short. The more perfect the work, the more benefit to the reader. Aristotle, on the other hand, believed that the production of art was woven into the very fabric of humanity because man naturally sought to imitate the life he saw all around him. Looked at in this way, all art has something to teach man regardless of its relationship to perfection. Thus the relative perfection of the work of art is immaterial; the point is to discover the isolated perfections that lie within that work.

Both of these approaches to literature have their merits if the people using them understand the difference, but in practice the two wind up becoming so muddled together that neither approach is really able to function as it is supposed to. And the culprit for this is literary theory. Literary theory usually begins with a professed desire to understand the literature, but in using theories of criticism as a frameworks for beginning analysis it creates immediate problems because looking at a work with a specific expectation in mind is inevitably going to lead to value judgment. Ironically, this critical defect stems from a desire to see critical analysis as somehow scientific in nature—admittedly an Aristotelian endeavor—despite the obvious resistance to that type of analysis posed by the very nature of fiction as a creative art form. The goal is a noble one, to attempt to analyze literature in a way that aspires to reach the kind of objective conclusions achieved in scientific experimentation. Northrop Frye, in his 1951 essay "Archetypes of Literature," makes the case for this kind of comparison.

> While no one expects literature itself to behave like a science, there is surely no reason why criticism, as a systematic and organized study, should not be, at least partly, a science. Not a "pure" or "exact" science, perhaps . . . Criticism deals with the arts and may well be something of an art itself, but it does not follow that it must be unsystematic. (Frye 1951, 122)

This is a way of looking at literary criticism that Frye firmly believed in, and he was still asking in "Science and the Public Critic" six years later, "What if criticism is a science as well as an art?" (Frye 1957, 7). But by then he seems to have come down firmly on the side of science, stating emphatically that, "literature must be examined in terms of a conceptual framework derivable from an inductive survey of the literary field."

The problem with attempts like these to impose a "system" or a "conceptual framework" on a work of literature even before the book has been cracked open is that the reader comes to the process with expectations that must be fulfilled. But a scientific hypothesis is a very different thing than a critical framework. In fact, they could almost be seen as opposites. While a scientist first poses a question and then experiments to see if the facts support his supposition, literary theory begins with an already established framework that the literature is then judged by. Science is, as Frye says, "exact," and within the exacting nature of that discipline comes the search for the truth of whatever is being studied, with the understanding that there is an empirical truth that can be known and therefore discovered. Science is the discipline of finding answers, again, within the context of knowing that there is only one right answer to be found. While this isn't necessarily an inappropriate goal for criticism—as I do believe there is something like a definitive analysis of a piece of writing—applying an arbitrary external framework to a work of literature is a very different matter, and is necessarily going to lead to all sorts of problems depending on what that framework is.

Scientific inquiry works best when it deals with objective, observable phenomenon isolated from complex systems. Once science attempts to deal with something as unpredictable as human nature—the very stuff of literature—it tends to lose its way. In his *Introduction to Critical Theory*, author David Held addresses the "the illusionary nature of modern science's claim to neutrality" (Held 167). The goal of science, he states, is ultimately not one of understanding, but control, as "the concern with exactness, calculability and foresight predisposes science to seek knowledge of a particular type and form, namely knowledge suitable for prediction and, technical control." To see how inadequate this type of thinking is in accounting for human behavior, Held goes on to discuss its application to the study of history.

> Social facts are given the status of natural facts. Historical laws are given the same status as natural laws. But these concepts of social life are inadequate to their objects. Men and women are of nature but make history; nature is not, in any parallel sense, made by them . . . The laws of history cannot simply be equated with the laws of nature . . . One can speak of laws in history (for example the law of increasing concentration of capital), laws which seem natural, to which the individual is subjected. But these laws are tied to specific modes of human organization. They cannot be abstracted from the context and peculiarity of particular epochs. (168)

In the same way, a particular literary theory cannot simply be overlaid onto any piece of literature and hope to provide an accurate analysis. As with history, literature is equally tied to "the context and peculiarity of particular epochs."

More recently philosopher Irad Kimhi, in his book *Thinking and Being*, asserts that it is impossible for science to predict—and therefore control—that most basic of human functions: thinking. In his review of the book author James Ryerson says that, for Kimhi, "Thinking emerges as a unique and peculiar activity, something that is part of the natural world, but which cannot be understood in the manner of other events in the natural world" (Ryerson 21). Scientific inquiry has proven the exactitude of its predictive powers in certain areas, the reactions of atoms and molecules to each other, for instance, or the effect of forces like electro-magnetism and gravity on physical objects. But when those phenomena get more complex, like weather patterns or the growth of ecosystems, the predictive power of science diminishes rapidly. Once man is thrown into the picture, all bets are off. The unique nature of the human confluence of emotions and thoughts, as well as the highly individualized nature of past experience on future decisions, renders the claims of psychologists and social scientists to predict with any specificity what an individual will do at any given moment dubious at best. The whole point of scientific prediction and control is to be able to manipulate the natural world for the benefit of humans. The manipulation of humans themselves, on the other hand, as history has shown, is not nearly as certain.

This is what I see as the fundamental flaw in literary theory. Because it attempts to align itself with scientific inquiry it can't help but have the same objective, the attempt to achieve some kind of predictive power, or control, over the work of literature. To do that, however, it must proceed hand in hand with interpretation and deconstructionism and as a result it is always going to come out on the other end as evaluation, for that is the only possible "control" that can be claimed over a piece of literature. Echoing Frye's imperative, Evelyn Gajowski, the editor of Bloomsbury's series of books examining Shakespeare through a series of theoretical lenses, even goes so far as to say that there can be no critical analysis without theory. "There is no critical practice that is somehow devoid of theory. There is no critical practice that is not implicated in a theory. A common-sense, transparent encounter with any text is thereby impossible" (Gajowski vi). And before long we've come full circle to the kind of reader-centered deconstructionist interpretations that are taught in colleges, and with them the insidious belief that literature is devoid of meaning until the reader creates it, an idea articulated to perfection by author Fredric V. Bogel: "Rather than inhering in literary works, poetic or literary meaning emerges from the meeting of readers who employ particular interpretive assumptions or frameworks and texts realized in accordance with those assumptions and frameworks" (Bogel 7). Reading literature in this way it's fairly easy to see how the true meaning of the text itself can become lost amid of all these frameworks and assumptions.

Interestingly, there is one aspect of scientific inquiry that does seem to provide a model for true contextual literary analysis, and that is pure observation, of which Aristotle would no doubt approve. The British television film *Life Story*—eventually renamed *Race for the Double Helix* for American audiences—is about the discovery of the structure of D.N.A. Scientist Rosalind Franklin, played by Juliet Stevenson, in talking about her work as a scientist, gets to the very heart of what it should mean to analyze literature as well.

Do you know what I like about our kind of work? You can be happy, or unhappy, it makes no difference. It doesn't matter whether you like what you find or hate it. You look at it and say, "So, that's how it is." Sometimes I feel like an archeologist breaking into a sealed tomb. I don't want to touch anything; I just want to look . . . When you see how things really are, all the hurt and the waste falls away. What's left is the beauty. (Nicholson)

This gets closer to Susan Sontag's idea that the purpose of studying art is to discover "how it is what it is" rather than to assign some sort of contrived meaning to it or make a value judgment about it. (Sontag 14). Scientific inquiry begins with a hypothesis, and the purpose of testing is to confirm or deny the hypothesis—failure providing just as much information, if not more, than the success of the experiment. But literary theory begins with a framework already in place, and forces the literature to conform to that framework. Thus the search for the truth about the work quickly veers off into a search for the "truth" about the society in which it was created, usually a negative one in modern contextual criticism, or at its most simplistic—and the reason for the critic's existence—the passing of judgment on the work, and as a result there are bound to be serious flaws with those kinds of analyses no matter how well intended.

In the end, theories of literary criticism hold no interest for me. Because of the nature of the work in question, attempting to analyze it using a specific theory or attempting to determine what value it has are not tasks I believe I need to undertake. *Ethan Frome* is considered a classic work of American literature. It has stood the test of time and has, therefore, already proven its worth. This is the same criteria that the ancient Greek literary critic Longinus used when looking at what makes a work of literature sublime. "For that is really great which bears a repeated examination, and which it is difficult or rather impossible to withstand, and the memory of which is strong and hard to efface" (Longinus 57). Edith Wharton's novel is all of these things, and so the question of its greatness would seem to be a moot point. Recent trends in criticism, however, have found a way around this obvious truth by calling into question the very nature of greatness itself, for the simple fact that it necessarily robs critics of their *raison d'être*. It is a situation that can be read about with dismay, once again, in Mark Edmundson's essay:

> On the issue of genius, as on multiculturalism and political correctness, we professors of the humanities have, I think, also failed to press back against our students' consumer tastes . . . we're inclined to a programmatic debunking criticism. We call the concept of genius into question . . . Ask a professor what she thinks of the work of Stephen Greenblatt, a leading critic of Shakespeare, and you'll hear it for an hour. Ask her what her views are on Shakespeare's genius and she's likely to begin questioning the term along with the whole "discourse of evaluation." (Edmundson 1997, 48)

If even Shakespeare can be stripped of his genius by literary criticism, then who is safe? On the other hand, the motivation behind this way of thinking is fairly obvious. Literary critic Karl Shapiro once respond to the question of the purpose of literary criticism by saying, "The answer is that a good work of criticism is a work of art about another work of art. Anything short of that is failure" (Shapiro 31). Thus the work of art becomes simply the vehicle to create another work of art. Genius isn't really genius at all if a critic can tear it down and demonstrate that what the reader thought was great is actually flawed in some way. But that doesn't seem like a very artistic endeavor to me, in addition to the way the entire approach is completely backwards. According to Susan Sontag the purpose of literary analysis should be to illuminate what the work of art really is, and by doing so to show how it is a work of art. What Shapiro seems to be talking about is the job of critically analyzing ordinary works of literature in order to assess their general worth, not revisiting works of genius. The job of literary analysis in terms of great works should be to engender a greater appreciation for a work of art by helping the reader understand how it has become a work of genius rather than something else. The thought that the criticism itself should be exalted to the status of art when its very existence is utterly dependent on the work of someone else is incredibly presumptuous. But it strains all credulity to believe that it is only through achieving the status of art that the literary critic can avoid abject failure.

Instead, what I have strived to achieve in this work—in the very words of Evelyn Gajowski—is to create "a common-sense, transparent encounter" with the text. Again, the text needs to be central to any analysis, and therefore the more transparent the better. Any interpretive assumption that is brought to the work is only going to get in the way of an accurate analysis because it is necessarily going to alter the meaning of the words themselves in order to make them conform to the espoused theory. Even Northrup Frye goes into some detail in articulating this crucial distinction between criticism and scholarship.

> I realized early in my critical life that evaluation was a minor subordinate function of the critical process, at best an accidental byproduct, which should never be allowed to take priority over scholarship . . . Scholarship [may support one's judgment of a work of literature, but] scholarship will never be founded on the value judgment. (Custred 69)

There is plenty of pushback against this idea, however, because it robs literary critics of their ability to pass judgment. Of course they put it in different terms and call it evaluation, but the result is still the same. Finally, Harold Bloom, though he does state later that evaluation is part of it, nevertheless had this to say about the process. "The function of literary criticism, as I conceive it in my gathering old age, is primarily appreciation" (Bloom 2005, xiv). If the purpose for analysis of great works of literature is not appreciation, then what is it for? Apparently, it's the self-aggrandizement of the critics themselves, which is decidedly not my aim.

The other thing I consciously tried to avoid in writing this book is the adoption of a professorial tone, which serves almost the same purpose for the authors of those books as it does the literary critic, using the text merely as a way to demonstrate how intelligent the analyst is. This is yet another unfortunate aspect of the changing academic landscape over the past few decades, beyond simply the deconstructionism happening in the lecture hall. It's something that was made clear to British author and literary critic David Lodge during the thirty years of teaching he did after writing his first book of criticism, *Language of Fiction.*

> In the 1960s it was still possible to write a book of literary criticism that would simultaneously satisfy qualified scholars and interest the general reader, because there was a discourse common to both; but there was not a plethora of such books on the market, and when one appeared it was received with interest. In the succeeding decades the academic profession expanded enormously, and since advancement in it depends upon publication there has been a chronic overproduction of titles, many of which are doomed to have a tiny circulation and to be noticed only in specialized journals. (Lodge x-xi)

The reason for the obscurity of so many of these books is, ironically, the writing itself. Lodge continues: "Over the same period the language of academic criticism became more arcane and jargon-ridden, alienating the general reading public and the media that serve it" (xi). Tom Nichols puts it even more bluntly saying, "many experts, and particularly those in the academy, have abandoned their duty to engage with the pubic. They have retreated into jargon and irrelevance, preferring to interact with each other only" (Nichols 5). Finally, Joseph Epstein makes the same point in an essay exposing the cowardice of universities to hold professors on the tenure track accountable for their actions. He provides an example of just this kind of writing, which comes directly from a book written by one of his colleagues, and quotes his fellow professor thusly: "Though some writers manage to make use of modernist defamiliarization as a powerful tool in the critique of reification, most accede to the thoroughgoing fetishization of social relations that characterizes what Lukas called the 'problem commodities' in the early 20th century" (Epstein 2014, 300). Not exactly what one would call reader-friendly criticism.

In attempting to come up with a name for what I see as the only honest way of analyzing literature, I've decided to call it contextual close reading. To begin with, "close reading" as the verb, is what this type of analysis is actually doing. The term close reading has been associated primarily with the New Criticism that emerged in the middle of the twentieth century, and is usually thought of as an offshoot of, or used as a synonym for, Formalism. But since both New Criticism and Formalism come with a lot of ideological baggage, the term close reading seems much more appropriate and descriptive. DuBois gives as good a definition as any when he says, "As a term, close reading hardly seems to leave the realm of so-called common sense, where it would appear to mean something understandable and vague like 'reading with special attention'" (DuBois 2). The idea of taking a common sense approach to analyzing literature is an appealing one. Nevertheless, close reading as it is typically promoted focuses on the text to the exclusion of everything else. The idea initially makes sense, to refuse to allow anything else to interfere with the reading of the words themselves, but as was demonstrated above with Berkove's disingenuous reading of "The Story of an Hour," the very fact of ignoring contextual information that can illuminate the text is, at best, an impediment to understanding and, at worst, just another way of manipulating the text to mean only what the analyst wants it to mean. Adding the modifier "contextual" to the term allows for meaningful non-textual information to be taken into consideration, with the sole purpose of better understanding and appreciating everything the text has to say.

Karl Shapiro, whose definition of criticism as necessarily a work of art I disagree with—as well as many of his other views on criticism—was nevertheless able to articulate exactly the kind of analysis I'm talking about: "The honest critic has no system and stands in no dread of contradicting himself. And because he abhors systems he is in a better position to view a work of art in its wholeness and in its relations to other things" (Shapiro 9). This is exactly the approach I have taken in looking at *Ethan Frome*.

Analyzing *Ethan Frome*

Edith Wharton's *Ethan Frome* is one of the great works of American literature, and yet even in its day it wasn't fully recognized as such. Well known literary critic Edmund Wilson asked the following rhetorical question of the author as early as 1923: "Has Mrs. Wharton ever been given her rightful place as the foremost of living American novelists and one of the foremost living novelists of the world? I have seen very little intelligent criticism of her by American and none by English critics" (Wilson 1923, 872). And about her most famous novel he asked another question: "Has Thomas Hardy ever done anything better than *Ethan Frome*?" The novel is taught in public schools throughout the United States, but in reading criticism going back to its publication it seems clear that much of what is great about the novel has been missed by generations of readers. The purpose of this book is to rectify that situation and expose readers and teachers alike to a way of finding deeper meaning in a work that has obviously resonated with audiences over the last hundred years. Author Parley Ann Boswell's summation of Wharton's continued ability to enthrall readers is also—with a minor exception—a fairly astute summation of *Ethan Frome*. "Wharton's fiction . . . continues to attract readers for many reasons: her acute understanding of the limited opportunities of American women and artists; her sardonic portrayal of an age of excess; her ability to discriminate between illusion and delusion; her juxtaposition of graceful, lucid prose with ruthless cruelty and emotional atrophy" (Boswell 111).

Though *Ethan Frome* doesn't deal directly with the "age of excess," it can be assumed that the vast majority of its readers are much better off than the characters in her novel, and without even trying Wharton is able make the reader's problems seem fairly insignificant by comparison. There is also no doubt that the limitations placed on those characters by society were very real, something Edmund Wilson was again able to discern before most of his colleagues. "Mrs. Wharton was perhaps the first American to write with indignant passion against American values as they had come to present themselves by the end of the last century" (Wilson 1926, 204). The result of these oppressive values, which could more appropriately be labeled a rigid code of behavior, is that they led to necessary illusions that might become dangerous when they turned into delusions. And yet again, it was Wilson who was able to articulate the unconscious mode of those behaviors early on. "One of the most depressing features of the American world of this period was that it hardly knew what was the matter with it. It was only at a later date that people like Edith Wharton . . . began to diagnose and describe" (Wilson 1924, 98-99). All of these elements come together in Wharton's writing, and especially in *Ethan Frome*, where she is most clearly able to contrast the elegant style of her prose with the grim story she was telling.

Yet there's another aspect to Wharton's writing in *Ethan Frome* that accounts in great part for the real power of her narrative, and this comes in the form of the symbolism she infused into the story, a level of meaning that can easily be overlooked in concentrating too closely on the literal text. This is where the true nature of the story appears, as well as in the masterful way the author was able to use the symbolism of the story to convey a far more important idea—and a subversive one in her day—than a strictly literal reading of the story ever could. The significance of this way of writing as an art form, especially for readers, is expressed in this paraphrase of the philosophy of Theodor Adorno by David Held:

> In his own writings Adorno always insisted that art loses its significance if it tries to create specific political or didactic effects; art should compel rather than demand a change in attitude, [and by doing so demonstrate] the capacity of art to restructure conventional patterns of meaning . . . The truth-value of art resides in its capacity to create awareness of, and thematize, social contradictions and antinomies. (Held 83, 84)

Rather than arguing, then, a true work of art couches its philosophy in such a way that it makes the underlying meaning obvious, though not necessarily on a conscious level.

At the same time, it's important to note that the ubiquitous nature of the symbolism in this work does not abnegate the responsibility of the literary analyst to begin with the literal meaning of the text. In fact, a great majority of the meaning in Wharton's novel has to do with looking quite literally at what the characters say and do. This was a point made by author R.B. Hovey in his own analysis of *Ethan Frome* in which he criticizes the same kind of interpretation decried by Susan Sontag in light of the recent book-length works of biography about Edith Wharton by Elizabeth Ammons and Cynthia Griffin Wolff.

> I am discomfited by the "creativity" some of our contemporary commentators avail themselves of: a freedom to erect with ingenuity such elaborate and intricate critical scaffoldings as nearly to overshadow the literary work in question. My premise is not purism. My trouble is that Wolff and Ammons reshape Wharton's art almost beyond recognition. (Hovey 4)

In the introduction to David Mulroy's book *The War on Grammar*, his editor and colleague Charles I. Schuster related an even more elemental philosophy shared by one of his own professors when he was in college. "How can you engage in interpretation, she'd admonish, unless you understand literally what the words on the page mean?" (Mulroy viii). While Mulroy himself understands the complex relationship between the two ways of looking at a text, he rightly emphasizes the primacy of the literal meaning in any kind of literary analysis.

> Literal meanings should be of special concern to literary scholars . . . In creating the aesthetic effects for which they are valued, the literal meanings and broader meanings of a text are inextricably intertwined—i.e., the text with its literal meaning properly understood becomes an occasion for reflection. If we do not understand the literal meaning of a literary text, then we cannot really claim to be responding to it *as literature* when we reflect upon it, because literal meaning is the distinctive characteristic of literature in the realm of art. (Mulroy 26)

To understand the symbolic foundation of much of the literature produced by American women at the turn of the twentieth century, it is instructive to look at other examples of this style of writing. The first example presented in this book is by Kate Chopin, the author of *The Awakening*, which was published in 1899. Her frequently anthologized work "The Story of an Hour" appeared five years earlier, and can be viewed as a template for the longer work to come in that the only way the protagonists in both stories can continue to maintain the freedom they have achieved is to die at the end. Likewise, "The Yellow Wall-Paper" by Charlotte Perkins Gilman is a glimpse into the life of a woman who is unable to escape her oppression physically and therefore escapes inwardly by retreating into her mind. In Edith Wharton's *Ethan Frome* the lack of freedom is also a central concern of all three principal characters and therefore the author uses similar symbolic devices as these other female writers to demonstrate the true impact of societal restrain on her characters' lives. In fact, author R. Baird Shuman goes so far as to say, "There is probably no more pervasive single element in *Ethan Frome* than the symbolism" (Shuman 90).

Because of this emphasis on symbolism, what is also necessary in order to achieve complete comprehension in reading of all of these works is not only to understand the historical context in which they were written, but also the societal context that explains the *way* in which they were written. In the BBC documentary *A Personal Journey with Martin Scorsese through American Movies*, the director discusses similar restraints faced by Hollywood directors working within the studio system of the 1940s.

We've talked about the rules, the narrative codes, about the technical tools, and we've seen how Hollywood filmmakers adjusted to these limitations. They even played with them. Now's the time to look at the cracks in the system, and what slipped through these cracks has always fascinated me . . . The forties directors found that they could exercise more control on a small budget movie than on a prestigious A-picture. Also, they'd have [fewer] executives looking over their shoulder and they could introduce unusual touches, weave in unexpected motifs, and even transform routine material into a much more personal expression. So in a sense, they became smugglers. They cheated, and somehow got away with it. (Scorsese)

Scorsese calls these directors smugglers for their ability to get into their films themes and ideas that the studio heads or the production code would ordinarily have prevented, and the same holds true for women writing at the turn of the twentieth century. Certain themes and ideas that would have been unacceptable for a woman to write about overtly in print needed to be expressed symbolically, which is what makes the fiction written by women during this period so incredibly rich in symbolic content.

It was during the mid-nineteenth century that publishing in the United States first became a big business, and it was then that publishers began to consider the financial benefits of publishing writing by women authors. They envisioned an expansion of the reading audience by women who would naturally gravitate toward writers of their same sex, especially fiction that was highly sentimental in nature, romances, gothic novels and the like, and they were rewarded for their prescience. Unfortunately, their vision did not extend beyond the societal limitations of their day and many women authors found themselves relegated to a critical cul-de-sac in which their writings could easily be dismissed or patronizingly categorized by critics. In the introduction to her anthology of short fiction, *Great Short Stories by American Women*, editor Candice Ward makes this observation about the position female authors found themselves in at the time:

Sentimental literature gave women writers a voice even as it perpetuated stereotypes and locked them (and their characters and readers) into the passive postures associated with the feminine. Thus, while Rebecca Harding Davis's "Life in the Iron-Mills" helped establish American realism, some critics dismissed it as yet another piece of sentimental melodrama; Louisa May Alcott wrote autobiographical fiction that addressed issues such as abolition and women's suffrage yet was heralded as America's foremost children's author . . . The local color movement of the late nineteenth and early twentieth centuries played a paradoxical role in the reception of works by other women writers, including Sarah Orne Jewett, Kate Chopin, Mary E. Wilkins Freeman, Willa Cather, Susan Glaspell and Alice Dunbar-Nelson. While an ability to realistically depict scenes from various regional settings earned them critical praise, it also contributed to a limited perception of their work. (Ward v)

Part of this limitation has to do with the kind of fiction many of their predecessors were encouraged to write, as Chopin scholar Emily Toth attests: "In 1850s popular fiction, young girls immerse themselves in housewifely service arts. They learn to pour tea and serve small refreshments; to sew; to care for the sick; to pray; and, if they are wealthy and somewhat worldly, to dance and sing and play the piano as womanly accomplishments" (Toth 1999, 17). That began to change, prior to the work of the authors listed above, but only in very prescribed ways. Until the emergence of the kind of subversive symbolism that female authors used for smuggling their message to a receptive audience, positive resolutions for female characters could only occur within the already established societal norms for women, as author Elizabeth Ammons makes clear. "Authors showed women escaping in droves from bad matches into happy ones (the acceptable way to do this was to have the tyrannical first husband die) and thus they affirmed at one and the same time woman's right to be happy and self-determined, and society's insistence that the highest estate for her was the married one" (Ammons 12). Historian Larzer Ziff, in his book on American society in the 1890s, points out another factor that limited women writers in the very subjects they could address. "To be a serious female author in the nineties was to be a writer of stories about women and their demands. The woman novelist was trapped by her affiliations to her sex in precisely the same manner as was the twentieth-century Negro writer in the 1950s trapped by affiliation to his race. The condition of women inescapably had to be the material of her art" (Ziff 283).

As a result, the way many of these writers were forced to work in the late eighteen- and early nineteen-hundreds parallels the constraints movie directors were forced to adhere to by the production code in effect some forty or fifty years later in Hollywood. Another way to look at it, however, is that this constraint was not so much an imposition on women writers as much as it forced them to be more creative—and as a result more persuasive—in the process. This is the stance that Virginia Woolf took in 1929 in *A Room of One's Own.*

It is fatal for a woman to lay the least stress on any grievance; to plead even with justice any cause; in any way to speak consciously as a woman. And fatal is no figure of speech; for anything written with that conscious bias is doomed to death. It ceases to be fertilized. Brilliant and effective, powerful and masterly, as it may appear for a day or two, it must wither at nightfall; it cannot grow in the minds of others. (Woolf 104)

Woolf's observations were more than theoretical for Edith Wharton, as the author had actually experienced something similar in her career. Her early stories and novels not only emphasized the cruel suffering and sacrifice of women, but caricaturized men as evil villains who used women and destroyed their lives. "Choice and execution of theme create problems in almost all of Wharton's early fiction," says Elizabeth Ammons, as they "have for their premise male exploitation and conceive of it in crude, melodramatic terms . . . In her hands they remain incredible, lurid examples of male depravity. As a result, theme, rather than being provocative in these early books, is merely angry and superficial" (Ammons 23). This is a facet of her work that Wharton herself was painfully aware of, as she eventually related to one of her editors. "They were all written at the top of my voice," she confessed, in "one long shriek. I may not write any better, but at least I hope I write in a lower key" (7).

Rather than metaphorical shouting in print, then, it is finally the ability of their arguments to "grow in the minds of others" that makes the symbolism of women writers in this period so powerful. By adhering to accepted modes of behavior in terms of plot, or forcing on their protagonists expected moral outcomes as far as punishment, female authors had to use all of their skills as writers to get across themes and ideas that challenged the status quo. Kate Chopin's protagonist in *The Awakening* shocked readers with her decision to leave her husband and children, live on her own and take a lover, and as a result the novel was almost universally excoriated in the press. But her protagonist couldn't be seen as "getting away with it" and so Chopin was forced to have her die as punishment. It's doubtful the novel would have been published otherwise. In conforming to the morality of the period, her protagonist even commits suicide so that she can be seen as tacitly admitting her transgressions in the process. What readers at the time didn't understand, and many still don't today, is that killing herself was the character's symbolic way of remaining free, a covert refusal to go back to the life that everyone in the novel demanded she return to and may have even forced her into at the end.

Charlotte Perkins Gilman's story "The Yellow Wall-Paper" achieves much the same effect. Outwardly her protagonist goes mad at the end of the story, and for contemporary readers it was a fitting end for a woman who never stopped complaining in the face of all the love and care and attention that anyone could expect in this world. But her mind had other ideas, and mentally she was able to free herself by retreating inward, thus separating her inner self from the outward oppression that she sensed but couldn't intellectualize. The words of Shakespeare, while literally addressing suicide as in the case of *The Awakening*, are also appropriate to a mind that refuses to be imprisoned.

> Nor stony tower, nor walls of beaten brass,
> Nor airless dungeon, nor strong links of iron,
> Can be retentive to the strength of spirit;
> But life, being weary of these worldly bars,
> Never lacks power to dismiss itself.
> If I know this, know all the world besides,
> That part of tyranny that I do bear
> I can shake off at pleasure. (Shakespeare 1599, 31)

Likewise, Edith Wharton's novel *Ethan Frome* deals primarily with societal imprisonment, but in an entirely unique way. Elizabeth Ammons probably comes closer than any other Wharton scholar in her ability to articulate the true motivation behind the author's fiction, which is reflected in the title of her book, *Edith Wharton's Argument with America*. "Her governing themes rise from the recurrent situation of a heroine perceiving an enormous and cruel lack of fit between her personal expectations of life and the social reality. Where there is rebellion it almost always meets with failure" (Ammons 5). But simply demonstrating the oppression that women in her day faced was to point out the obvious, and in doing so those fictional women were typically forced into predictable ends. For Edith Wharton, however, this was not nearly enough. Ammons goes on to explain why.

> On the issue of most concern to her—the issue of woman's life and liberty—she obviously believed that any "solution" would have to consist of revolutionary changes in men's, not women's, attitudes: in a patriarchy only the opinion of men matters. It is that simple. And not one of her books . . . which bring to a close the Progressive Era phase of her argument with America, suggests that men in any way want, or have ever wanted, minor let alone revolutionary change. (Ammons 156)

What this necessitated was a new approach to the same old problem for women's literature, one that would have the power to address the problem at its source in an entirely new way. And in *Ethan Frome* Edith Wharton found that way. She was able to hold up for examination the utterly senseless way that women were limited by society in her day by symbolically representing that female experience in the character of her male protagonist. Her feat was so effective that even forty-five years later no less a critic than Lionel Trilling remained completely dumbfounded. Trilling, who felt his mission was to explore the morality inherent in literature, was initially unimpressed with what Wharton had done. In his analysis of Wharton's novel entitled "The Morality of Inertia" he begins by damning the book because of his perception of the author's gratuitous cruelty.

> We can never speak of Edith Wharton without some degree of respect . . . But she was a woman in whom we cannot fail to see a limitation of heart, and this limitation makes itself manifest as a literary and moral deficiency of her work, and of *Ethan Frome* especially. It appears in the deadness of her prose, and more flagrantly in the suffering of her characters . . . Whenever the characters of a story suffer, they do so at the behest of their author—the author is responsible for their suffering and must justify his cruelty by the seriousness of his moral intention. The author of *Ethan Frome*, it seemed to me . . . could not lay claim to any such justification. (Trilling 1956, 35-36)

Trilling goes on to describe this suffering as "an image of life-in-death, of hell-on-earth, which is not easily forgotten . . . It is terrible to contemplate, it is unforgettable, but the mind can do nothing with it, can only endure it" (36). He concludes by saying that, in terms of moral lessons that can be taken away from reading the novel, "there is nothing to say about *Ethan Frome*. It presents no moral issue at all."

For many women of the time, however, their lives actually were a living hell, a living death, as those lives were completely subsumed by the domestic roles they had been relegated to. Husbands left for work during the day and participated in social functions through their work or fraternal orders in the evenings, while women were left at home with the cooking, the cleaning, and the children. But then this was seen as the natural order of things at a time when women, by virtue of their position in nature as procreators of the species, were assumed to be naturally suited to the role of mother and wife. As a biological imperative, it was commonly assumed, there was nothing to argue with. In their article "The Female Animal: Medical and Biological Views of Women and Her Role in Nineteenth-Century America," authors Carroll Smith-Rosenberg and Charles E. Rosenberg articulate the prevailing view of physicians at the time, one that justified a woman's limited role in society by virtue of her physiology.

> Physicians saw woman as the product and prisoner of her reproductive system. It was the ineluctable basis of her social role and behavioral characteristics, the cause of her most common ailments; woman's uterus and ovaries controlled her body and behavior from puberty through menopause . . . It was, another physician explained in 1870, "as if the Almighty, in creating the female sex, had taken the uterus and built up a woman around it." A wise deity had designed woman as keeper of the hearth, as breeder and rearer of children. (Smith-Rosenberg 1999, 112-113)

What's so telling—and as a result so effective—about Wharton's manipulation of these circumstances in *Ethan Frome* is that when the same indefensible obligations are foisted on a man, it becomes incomprehensible to men. But this is one of the dangers women writers faced in having to cloak their most salient arguments under layers of metaphorical disguise in order not to be dismissed out of hand. Marilyn French makes this point about Wharton's work specifically, though she still tends to be dubious about the exact nature of male ignorance. "Wharton is subtle, delicate, and precise. The seeming innocence of male critics about the difference between a woman's life and a man's, about the profound effects of learning to adapt the self to a small anteroom life, has led to an impercipience about Wharton's work" (French vi). French then alludes to Wharton's own metaphor in identifying the paradox for the author and other women writers like her, who were forced to express their ideas in an oblique way. "She does not shout: therefore she is not heard. Had she shouted, she would not have been published." Elizabeth Ammons goes on to state that this was not an accident on the part of Wharton. "Early in the first decade of the twentieth century she seems to have made a decision, now that she had some experience and confidence, to try novels that penetrated rather than tried to manufacture contemporary social questions" (Ammons 23). In that respect *Ethan Frome* was her greatest triumph in presenting the inequity of societal expectations in a way that was immediately apparent to the unconscious mind. But perhaps she was a little too successful, as demonstrated by the struggle of Trilling and so many other readers to make conscious sense of a truth they could only feel.

To his credit, Trilling eventually manages to come up with a justification for the book's existence—and that is just about how one would describe the faint praise he is able to muster. But to see how far he misses the mark one only has to look at the comparative literary works that sprang to his mind but then immediately were dismissed as far more exalted than Wharton's work.

> Her aim is not that of Wordsworth in any of his stories of the suffering poor, to require of us that we open our minds to a realization of the kinds of people whom suffering touches. It is not that of Flaubert in *Madame Bovary*, to wring from solid circumstances all the pity and terror of an ancient tragic fable. Nor is it that of Dickens or Zola, to shake us with the perception of social injustice, to instruct us in the true nature of social life and to dispose us to indignant opinion and action. (Trilling 1956, 40)

The tremendous irony here is that *Ethan Frome* does all of these things, and Trilling's reference to *Madame Bovary* is more accurate than he realizes. While Flaubert's novel is similar in spirit to Chopin's *The Awakening*, the similarity ends there. Thematically, it is much closer to *Ethan Frome*. What's so telling about Trilling's description of Flaubert's novel is that he calls it a "fable," as though the character of Emma Bovary is not even human, more like a simplistic personification out of Aesop than a real, flesh and blood woman. But this was to be the fate of so many female characters in turn of the century literature about women. If, like Chopin's characters, they rebelled against the status quo they were seen as evil and deserving of punishment for threatening a way of life that had evolved into strictly distinct spheres for men and women. The fact that men were the recipients of a far more beneficial and rewarding sphere was not to be questioned, and at the same time jealously guarded. Had Wharton's protagonist been female the novel would no doubt have been mentioned in the same breath as *Madame Bovary*, for teaching the same moral lesson: that to strive above one's lot in life and—especially if one is female— to be unhappy with a loving husband and a family is to be ungrateful for the good things that have been given and deserving of moral retribution.

The opening chapters of Flaubert's novel are instructive in understanding the kind of fable Trilling was talking about, as well as how Wharton effectively manipulated that device in her story to achieve the same results. The essential characteristics of Emma Rouault, a young woman who attempts to win the affections of, and eventually marry, the young doctor Charles Bovary yet still craves more, are eerily similar to those that Wharton attributes to Ethan Frome. First, there is the dissatisfaction with the life in which they have found themselves after the death or illness of their parents.

> BOVARY: Mademoiselle Rouaut did not at all like the country, especially now that she had to look after the farm almost alone. (Flaubert 13)

FROME: When they married it was agreed that, as soon as he could straighten out the difficulties resulting from Mrs. Frome's long illness, they would sell the farm and saw-mill and try their luck in town. Ethan's love of nature did not take the form of a taste for agriculture. (Wharton 1911, 76)

Then comes the skill of perception that allows them to be seen as unique in the eyes of their intended partners.

BOVARY: [Dr. Bovary] began rummaging on the bed [for his whip], behind the doors, under the stairs. It had fallen to the floor, between the sacks and the wall. Mademoiselle Emma saw it and bent over the sacks of flour. (13)

FROME: They had sat for a few minutes on the fallen log by the pond, and she had missed her gold locket, and set the young men searching for it; and it was Ethan who had spied it in the moss. (167)

Finally, there is the philosophical disdain for a life of obligation and responsibility, and a yearning for a fantasy life that they can never obtain.

BOVARY: Accustomed to calm aspects of life, she turned, on the contrary, to those of excitement . . . And the shade of the argand lamp fastened to the wall above Emma's head lighted up all these pictures of the world, that passed before her one by one in the silence of the dormitory. (28, 30)

FROME: He let the vision possess him as they climbed the hill to the house. He was never so happy with her as when he abandoned himself to these dreams . . . The wave of warmth that went through him was like the prolongation of his vision. (55-56)

In making her protagonist a man, and putting him in exactly the same position as women all over the country, it left male critics like Trilling with no way to make sense of it other than to assume that Wharton was punishing him needlessly. "All that Edith Wharton has in mind is to achieve that grim tableau of which I have spoken, of pain and imprisonment, of life-in-death. About the events that lead up to this tableau, there is nothing she finds to say, nothing whatsoever" (Trilling 1956, 40). Which was exactly Edith Wharton's point. By showing the frustration and onerous demands of domestic responsibility that the majority of women faced daily, but in the life of a man, it seemed to make absolutely no sense to men—reinforcing Wharton's position that it makes no more sense to force the same thing on women. Using Trilling's own words against him Edith Wharton was able to, with a simple change of gender in her main character, "require of us that we open our minds to a realization of the kinds of people whom suffering touches" (40). Emma Bovary was a woman who was not satisfied with her life. In attempting to have something more, something better, something else, she ruined herself. That is an idea a male audience could understand because it reinforced their belief that a woman belonged in her place, and when God or nature was displeased with her overreaching she was punished for it. But in making the same thing happen to Ethan Frome, Edith Wharton was very deftly able "to shake us with the perception of social injustice, to instruct us in the true nature of social life and to dispose us to indignant opinion and action" (40). The only problem is, critics like Trilling missed it completely.

The point here is not to disparage Lionel Trilling but to show just how persistent male patriarchal views were that they could last well into the middle of the twentieth century and beyond. It would have been interesting to see Trilling review the work shortly before his death in 1975, at the height of the women's movement. Though even that doesn't necessarily guarantee he would have been any more enlightened, as more recent scholarship following his example goes to show. Harold Bloom's view of *Ethan Frome* from the mid-nineteen-eighties sees him heading down the same path as Trilling and coming out at the other end at exactly the same place. "The book's aesthetic fascination, for me, centers in Wharton's audacity in touching the limits of a reader's capacity at absorbing really extreme suffering, when that suffering is bleak, intolerable, and in a clear sense unnecessary" (Bloom 1986, 4). As with Trilling, the irony is thick. The suffering of Ethan, as a man, is seen not only as "bleak" and "intolerable" by Bloom but, more tellingly, clearly "unnecessary." Truer words were never spoken. It was not the reader's capacity for "absorbing really extreme suffering" in a work of fiction that was in question in Wharton's day, but a woman's capacity to do the same thing in her real life. That is what is demonstrated by Ethan's plight. And in Ethan's role as an unconscious symbol for the oppression of women, it's quite easy to see how placing women in that very same position is just as intolerable and unnecessary.

The real moral lesson to be learned from *Ethan Frome* is that for human beings to be trapped in life by others in any way is immoral on its face. One only has to begin with the most obvious example, slavery, which had ended officially in the U.S. less than fifty years before Wharton's novel was published. There were many slaveholders who insisted to the end that it was

God's desire that blacks should be enslaved. But the abolitionist movement and the Civil War put a definitive punctuation on the end of the practice in a way that clearly demonstrated its immorality. Likewise, even the apparently blameless oppression of poverty is something that Trilling recognizes as immoral when he cites Wordsworth and Dickens as requiring the reader to understand the inherent unfairness in society that manages to create a class of suffering poor. How immoral is it then, for an entire gender to oppress fully half of the population by claiming their innate superiority and an obligation to protection women from the vagaries of the outside world that, for all intents and purposes, is no different than keeping them imprisoned in domestic servitude? It is Wharton's genius that in making her protagonist a man his suffering can't be summarily dismissed by men, which only goes to prove how immoral it was to intentionally inflict that same suffering on women. Trilling blames Wharton, not God, for Ethan's suffering, as she is the architect of his suffering. How telling, then, that Trilling cannot see men as complicit in inflicting the very same suffering on women.

What Trilling finally manages to dredge up as a way of explaining the purpose of the book is something he calls the morality of inertia, that is "the *not* making of moral decisions [that] constitutes a large part of the morality of humanity" (Trilling 1956, 41). His point is that Ethan's sense of morality lies in the mindless devotion to duty he has allowed to envelope his life, and further implies that Ethan actually has a moral imperative to break out of his obligatory torpor in order to make everyone's life better. How ironic that this is the very same thing Kate Chopin allowed her protagonist to do in *The Awakening* and she was castigated for it. Trilling believes that in choosing to take his own life at the end of the story, Ethan is purposely not making a choice between Mattie and Zeena. In a life made up solely of duty and obligation, Trilling says, "choice is incompatible with his idea of existence; he can only elect to die" (42). What is so fascinating about this kind of desperate attempt to wring some meaning out of a story that is incomprehensible to him is that he conveniently forgets Ethan doesn't have a choice to make. He is married to Zeena and they have no money. He can't run away with Mattie, not because he believes it is morally wrong to leave his wife, but because he is penniless. All of this plays out over the course of an entire chapter in which Ethan goes to great lengths to think through all the possible choices he might be able to make, which is in direct contradiction to Trilling's assertion that, "It is quite impossible for him to deal with the dilemma in the high way that literature and moral philosophy prescribe, by reason and choice" (41). In the end, his choice is the same as that of Edna Pontellier in *The Awakening.* Rather than go back to a life he hates, after having found the love of his life, he decides "that part of tyranny that I do bear / I can shake off at pleasure."

But the really astounding part of Trilling's analysis comes in his conclusion. "The morality of inertia, of the dull, unthinking round of duties, may, and often does, yield the immorality of inertia" (Trilling 1956, 43). Again, people who put their heads down and do their duty because they feel a moral obligation to someone or something else, are really behaving immorally because they fail to see and stop the evil that their inaction has allowed to flourish. This conveniently ignores the women's movement in the nineteenth-century that was routinely attacked for advocating legal and cultural changes its detractors claimed went against God and society, even though they were simply attempting to combat the "immorality of inertia" in their day. Instead, Trilling comes up with a very different analogy. "The example that will most readily occur to us is that of the good simple people, so true to their family responsibilities, who gave no thought to the concentration camp in whose shadow they lived" (43-44). Of course this is the analogy that would immediately come to mind for a Jewish man writing in the post-World War Two era. But what of women writing at the turn of the twentieth century? Wouldn't they likely see the immorality of inertia as the good and simple husbands, so true to their family responsibilities, who gave no thought to the women who were imprisoned in the very houses where they lived?

Like so many men of the late-nineteenth and early-twentieth century, Lionel Trilling was a product of the societal prejudice and blindness in which he lived. By the time he wrote "The Morality of Inertia" in 1955, women had been writing serious novels about the female experience in America for decades, especially since the passage of women's suffrage in 1920. Looking backward, then, to analyze works from a different era—in this case a time before the right of women to have equality before the law and equal participation in society—it is incumbent upon the literary critic not only to be able to see the world in a different way from his own, but from an entirely different perspective. What seemed in Wharton's day like the nearly universal ignorance of men to the suffering of women required a way of storytelling that would allow men to see the results of that suffering in a way they could understand. This is an aspect of *Ethan Frome* that author Helge Normann Nilsen points out in addressing contemporary negative criticism of the novel.

> Her narrative is said to be deficient because it does not make the disastrous fates of its characters meaningful in some larger, perhaps metaphysical sense. But Wharton's point is precisely that no meaningful context is to be found, though this does not mean that her tale lacks such a dimension.

> It emerges in its awareness of the inequalities and injustices of socio-economic circumstances . . . It is as if Wharton is saying that even if a man is a helpless victim, one must yet protest and take a stand against the injustice and indifference of society and the universe. (Nilsen 89).

But it's clear that Nilsen is still viewing the novel from the context of her own time at the end of the twentieth century, because that is not what Wharton is saying at all. *Ethan Frome* does point out "inequalities and injustices," but not of "socio-economic circumstances." Critics in Wharton's day—and much later—had no problem whatsoever understanding and protesting the treatment of Ethan, and taking a stand against the author because her "helpless victim" was a man. In fact, that was the whole point of criticism like Trilling's. What Edith Wharton was really saying to the men of her time was that the same "injustice and indifference of society" those critics were decrying when the victim was a man, is just as wrong "even if" that helpless victim is a woman.

Kate Chopin's
"The Story of an Hour"

"The Story of an Hour," though written when the author was forty-three years old, emerged directly out of events Kate Chopin experienced during childhood. Her father, Thomas O'Flaherty, had come from Ireland to New York in 1823 and a few years later moved west to settle in St. Louis. He began a business there selling boats and groceries, which also allowed him to participate in the lucrative trade equipping expeditions for travel further west, and he became a rich man in a short period of time. In 1840 his first wife bore him a son, George, but she and a second child died in childbirth four years later. At the same time, Eliza Feris, barely sixteen years old, had been dealing with the aftermath of her mother's failed marriage. Her father had left her mother broke and with seven children. Eliza's two older sisters had already married, and to avoid destitution a marriage was arranged between her and the widower Tomas O'Flaherty, who was thirty-five years her senior. What little information that exists paints O'Flaherty as a hard and unsympathetic man, but there had to have been some measure of generosity in him considering that after their marriage he took in Eliza's three younger sisters and her younger brother, as well as her mother, to live with them in his red-brick mansion on Eighth Street in the heart of town. Eventually the two would produce three more children, Tom, Kate, and Jane, and the family was further expanded by the presence of four slaves and two slave children, also possibly fathered by O'Flaherty. By the time of Kate O'Flaherty's fifth birthday, in 1855, she was part of a large, stable upper-class family. But on November 1st of that year, young Kate's life changed forever—though not necessarily for the worse.

Thomas O'Flaherty, in his role as a well-known and respected businessman in St. Louis, participated in the ceremonial opening of the Pacific Railroad's new track that had been built out to Jefferson City. O'Flaherty was one of the railroad's founding investors and was part of a contingent making the inaugural journey between the two cities when, just outside the town of Gasconade, the bridge that spanned the river of the same name collapsed even before the train had reached the water. All but one of the cars tumbled off the tracks, killing thirty people and injuring seventy more. One of those who had died was Thomas O'Flaherty. Kate was attending the Sacred Heart boarding school at the time, so she was not present to witness her mother's immediate reaction to the news, but she no doubt talked about it with her in the years that followed. Besides the shock of losing her husband, young Eliza O'Flaherty also inadvertently came into possession of her own life. In *Unveiling Kate Chopin*, author Emily Toth relates the unique position Eliza found herself in and how different it was from her life before, circumstances her daughter would never forget.

> At twenty-seven, [Eliza] suddenly found herself a wealthy widow in charge of a very large estate . . . Widows controlled their property, as wives did not; widows also had legal control of their own children, as wives did not. And so Eliza's first act as a young widow was to bring her daughter Katie home. From then on, Eliza would be the one making decisions about her daughter—and for the rest of her life, Kate would brood about her father's sudden death, and what it meant for her mother. (Toth 1999, 9-10)

Though it would happen slightly later in her life than it did for her mother, Kate O'Flaherty would go through a similar experience. After her father's death Kate's youngest sister died, and so her maternal great-grandmother, Victoria Charleville, moved into the house and made it her mission to instruct her only great-granddaughter. "Madame Charleville understood that marriage was a practical arrangement, undertaken for social standing and security. Romantic love might come later . . . But the greatest lesson, one her great-granddaughter repeated so tellingly in her later stories, was that a woman had to be independent" (Toth 1999, 14-15). After the end of the Civil War—during which she lost both her great-grandmother and her half-brother George—Kate entered St. Louis society. By this time she had become a thoughtful and intelligent young woman. But even though she had received a solid, independent-minded education at the Sacred Heart School, as well as from Madame Charleville, and had grown up in a house run by women, the reality from here on out would be very different: "Men . . . would be making the rules" (44). In 1870 she married Oscar Chopin, from Louisiana, who had attended college in France during the war and was not only a romantic but appreciated intelligence in women. In him Kate believed she had made a good choice of husband, and she had. "Oscar was a rare man who preferred an original woman, one who was neither quiet nor stay-at-home" (67). One of those independent acts that drew the scorn of friends and neighbors was Kate Chopin's preference for taking long solitary walks during their marriage, a desire that would also inform *The Awakening*. "I always feel so sorry for women who don't like to walk; they miss so much—so many rare little glimpses of life; and we women learn so little of life on the whole" (Chopin 1899, 176).

But in other respects, Chopin's life was wholly conventional. The couple moved to Louisiana after their marriage, and in the eight years from 1871 to 1879 Kate Chopin gave birth to six children, five boys and the youngest a girl. Unlike many of her characters, Chopin apparently understood the limitations that child rearing placed on women but did not seem to chafe against them herself. As her writings show, however, she was also very conscious of the way in which marriage and motherhood could work on a woman's psyche in painful and destructive ways. It was only three years after the birth of their daughter, in 1882, that Kate Chopin's husband Oscar died. At thirty-two years of age she found herself, like her mother before her, the head of a large family. Unlike her mother, however, Kate's husband had not been rich and so she had to find a way to continue making a living for that family. "Most women of Kate Chopin's class would have turned their financial affairs over to the most capable or eager male relative. But the widow Chopin . . . chose instead to run Oscar's business herself" (Toth 1999, 93-94). Kate also fell into an affair with a married man the following year, which made things untenable in Louisiana, and so in 1884 she moved her family back to St. Louis to be with her mother. But if she had sought comfort and safety in the role of a daughter after the tumultuous aftermath of her husband's death, Kate Chopin was once again forced to resume the mantle of responsibility when her mother died in 1885. The result of all this turmoil is that Chopin became intimately familiar with the difference between the kind of independence she and her mother had experience, and the suffering that so many wives endured in the late nineteenth century.

"The Story of an Hour" was written after her move back to St. Louis, when Chopin had the freedom and independence to imagine a life for herself as a writer. It's important to note that the original title of the story was, "The Dream of an Hour." The implication of that word as Chopin intended, however, is one of a vision for the future rather than the fantasy world of a sleeping dream. The title wasn't changed until the late 1960s, when Chopin scholar Per Seyersted noticed that the author had crossed out the word "Dream" and written "Story" on a copy of it she had kept from the magazine in which it first appeared. The story bore the new title in Seyersted's compilation of the complete works of Kate Chopin and has done so in print from that day forward. It may not seem like much, but that change allows the reader to take a much more literal approach to the story. In fact, it nearly invites it. The danger of using the word "dream" in the title is that it gives the reader permission to dismiss the protagonist's desires as mere fantasy, which only serves to undercut Chopin's intent. Even worse, it can lead to fallacious interpretations on the order of arguing that the entire story itself is metaphorical. Chopin's instinct then, after thinking about it further, was to change the word to "story" and thereby root the narrative more firmly in the reality of the moment. The result is that any subsequent temptation toward interpretation, such as looking at that hour as the only real life the protagonist ever had, at least manages to get closer to the truth.

In making this subtle change to the story that the author never realized in her lifetime, Seyersted was able to collaborate with Chopin in the kind of symbolic coding that was so essential to works by women in this period, as author Janet Beer attests.

> Chopin's fictions, and particularly her short stories, are subversive documents. There are a number of levels on which the stories work . . . The narrative organization is often the main subversive instrument, with the surface meaning apparently conventional, apparently moving toward closure and a restoration of previously accepted social order but actually . . . being undermined by the processes of revelation that have occurred throughout the tale. (Beer 1997, 28)

This technique was no accident. "She was expert in her manipulation of both form and language so as to position herself to write about issues which she found compelling—issues which were often controversial" (Beer 2008, 1). The first sentence of the story bears this out—a sentence that is also its own paragraph, which therefore demands even closer reading. "Knowing that Mrs. Mallard was afflicted with a heart trouble, great care was taken to break to her as gently as possible the news of her husband's death" (Chopin 1894). If the story is just a story, then the circular nature of the plot—which ends with doctors saying her husband's return was too much for her weak heart—fits neatly with a literal reading in which it was merely the unexpected nature of his return that killed her. It certainly makes for an ironic twist to the tale, on the order of O. Henry or Guy de Maupassant, but little more. If the reader takes the time to examine the text more closely, however, other possibilities emerge.

To begin with, the protagonist is referred to as "Mrs. Mallard." This lets the reader know that at this time in American history she is not a separate person, as she is completely defined by her relationship to Mr. Mallard. Chopin biographer Emily Toth writes something similar about the author's recognition of that fact in her own life on her wedding day. "She would now be, forever, defined as a wife, and take her assigned, and much more narrowly defined, place in a patriarchal world. She was now, as she wrote, 'Mrs. Chopin and not Miss Katy'" (Toth 1999, 56). More importantly, however, Chopin uses the indefinite article "a" to modify "heart trouble." If the sentence doesn't contain the article then it clearly suggests a medical condition: she died of heart trouble. With the article the phrase means something very different, not heart trouble but a troubled heart. Thus, the character's heart trouble actually has more to do with her emotional state than her physiology. Olivia Weisser addresses this idea in her book *Ill Composed: Sickness, Gender, and Belief in Early Modern England*, in which she writes about a young woman named Alice Thornton who became violently ill on her wedding day.

> She was particularly anxious about marriage, a fear encapsulated in her description of "sickness at my heart." Marriage signified full female adulthood in this period and marked a crucial turning point at which women relinquished legal and civic identity to their husbands. What is more, Thornton professed not to love her husband. She had only agreed to marry him out of duty to her family, as he would be able to restore the family's perilous financial status. (Weisser 1-2)

Here is an actual young woman who uses almost the identical phrase that describes Mrs. Mallard in Chopin's work. For Mrs. Mallard, the love relationship that she has with her husband is clearly troubled. This is the foundation that explains what happens in the rest of the story, and as a result it provides an even better circular closure than a literal reading does. It is also the same kind of "heart trouble" that informs *Ethan Frome*, in which both Ethan and his wife find themselves trapped in a loveless marriage.

The second paragraph of the story is mere reporting. Her husband's friend Richards was at the train station and heard news of a train crash. He stayed at the station to verify by telegram that Brently Mallard's name was on the list of those who had died, and rushed to their house to make sure that his friend's wife didn't hear the news accidentally. It was Mrs. Mallard's sister who tried to break it to her as gently as she could. The third paragraph is an important one in establishing the protagonist's character.

She did not hear the story as many women have heard the same, with a paralyzed inability to accept its significance. She wept at once, with sudden, wild abandonment, in her sister's arms. When the storm of grief had spent itself she went away to her room alone. She would have no one follow her. (Chopin 1894)

The first sentence says a lot. It makes it clear that Mrs. Mallard is different from other women, especially in her ability to fully accept that her husband is dead. Importantly, this is not mere resignation that he is gone but an actual acceptance that implies it is something she subconsciously desires. Her metaphorical "storm of grief" is therefore a short one, suggesting that once her weeping is over so too is her grief. In this way she already has begun the transformation from wife to widow and all that will mean for her in the future, though she doesn't consciously realize it yet. In addition, the fact that she doesn't want anyone to go with her to her room bespeaks the desire of a woman who unconsciously longs for separation from the society that is responsible for her unenviable position in the first place.

Women at the turn of the twentieth century still had very few rights, and even fewer if they were married. This is reflected in the text by the fact that, throughout the story, the protagonist's first name is never referred to by the narrator. In the first line she is Mrs. Mallard, and in the last she is Brently Mallard's wife. Though certain legal rights to property they brought into marriage were granted in a few states and localities at this time, the laws that primarily governed women in America were the same ones that had made their way over to the English colonies in the early seventeenth century, as professor Sara J. Evans states in her book *Born for Liberty: A History of Women in America*.

Under English common law a married woman was "covered" by her husband. The name given to her status was *feme covert* and as such she had no independent legal standing. She could neither own property nor sign contracts; she did not even own the wages she might earn. Her legal existence merged into that of her husband. Only single women over the age of twenty-one, and widows with a status known as *feme sole*, had legal rights to make contracts and hold property in their own names. Widows in particular exercised considerable legal rights as the agents of their deceased husbands. (Evans 1989, 22)

Thus Mrs. Mallard's flight from both Richards and her sister represents her desire for independence from society as a whole as it is symbolized in those two characters, the man who is the embodiment of the dominance of patriarchy in American culture, and the woman who represents the submission to that patriarchy.

The next paragraph is comprised of only two sentences. "There stood, facing the open window, a comfortable, roomy armchair. Into this she sank, pressed down by a physical exhaustion that haunted her body and seemed to reach into her soul" (Chopin 1894). Both doors and windows are literary symbols of freedom and opportunity, especially an open window with its view to the outside world. In this way the house functions as a metaphorical prison, the symbolic confinement in which a woman lives her married life, while the window provides an escape to something new, something different, something apart from what she has thus far experienced in her marriage. Chopin biographer Emily Toth explains how this imagery was spurred by a trip her father took her on as a child to see where he worked during the day— and reinforced by the long walks she would take as an adult.

> The trip also inspired Kate with a lifelong interest in the world that respectable young ladies did not see—and she connected being outdoors with freedom from social restraints. Twenty years later, as a young wife in New Orleans, she described riverfront scenes in her diary, including a cotton "pickery"; more than forty years later, she wrote *The Awakening* about a woman who swims out, "where no woman had swum before." (Toth 1990, 25)

This image of freedom through the open window is also coupled with the protagonist sitting in the armchair as exhaustion presses down upon her. The narrator says that it haunted her body, which tells the reader that this exhaustion isn't simply about the death of her husband but something much greater that has been going on ever since she married. Haunting is typically thought of as resulting from a soul that is not at rest, a person from the past, long dead, who has unfinished business in this world. Mrs. Mallard's physical exhaustion can be seen in the same light. The unfinished business, however, is that of women everywhere who had yet to gain legal rights and freedoms because of an unfair system that stretched back centuries. The invisibility associated with haunting also continues to reinforce the idea that she is still unconscious as to the exact nature of the oppression she has suffered.

It seems clear from the text that there are no servants about, which doesn't mean they don't have any. Nevertheless, even if she isn't doing them herself, it is still Mrs. Mallard who has been responsible for overseeing the cooking and cleaning as well as every other chore that goes on in the household. In the early colonial era and throughout the expansion into the West, both men and women worked at home, on the farm, and though each had their sphere of responsibility all of their labor was seen as necessary for the survival of the family. But once urban men began going off to work in jobs separate from the household, all of that changed. In their book *A History of Women in America*, authors Carol Hymowitz and Michaele Weissman explain the division of labor in the home that began in the eighteenth century and essentially robbed women of their economic value in marriage ever after.

> Among the new middle class, home and family came to be seen as separate from the world of work and money. Women were affected by this change in very significant ways. In their homes, middle-class women continued to perform their traditional work—to cook and clean, make clothing and other household goods, and care for children. What they did, however, was no longer considered "real work," because, unlike men, they earned no money thereby. (Hymowitz 64)

The fact that this oppression has reached down into her soul is another strong suggestion of Mrs. Mallard's subconscious unhappiness with her lot in life. Because of this, the next paragraph, describing what she sees and hears through the open window, is heavily freighted with symbolic meaning for her.

"She could see in the open square before her house the tops of trees that were all aquiver with the new spring life" (Chopin 1894). The season of spring traditionally symbolizes the beginning of new life after the death of winter, a foreshadowing of the new future she will soon imagine for herself. "The delicious breath of rain was in the air." Similarly, rain symbolizes cleansing, the washing away of her old life in preparation for a new one. "In the street below a peddler was crying his wares." This is a wonderfully subtle symbol, but it reflects the new economic freedom Mrs. Mallard will have as a widow instead of the financial dependence she has experienced as a married woman. In Joyce W. Warren's book *Women, Money and the Law*, in which she makes the case for greater economic participation by women in society than previously thought, she nevertheless articulates the societal expectations of the time in regard to a woman's economic worth.

> Nineteenth-century culture defined upper- and middle-class white women as inherently domestic and assumed their exclusion from the market economy, while working-class families and the free black bourgeoisie expected their women to remain in the home if they could afford to do so. The concept of woman's economic dependence was an established "truth"

of the dominant discourse in American society, and any counterdiscourse was effectively silenced, excluded or marginalized. (Warren 1)

Finally, "The notes of a distant song which some one was singing reached her faintly, and countless sparrows were twittering in the eaves" (Chopin 1894). Here is both the song of a person singing as well as that of birds. The singing of the person is a clear symbol for happiness because that is when most people sing. The addition of the birds expands the symbolic element of freedom in the scene because of their ability to fly. But even more can be added to this idea as the reference to birds also brings to mind the 1875 poem "To the Mockingbird" by Albert Pike in the way in which it makes birds a symbol of freedom beyond the mere fact that they can fly.

> I would, sweet bird, that I might live with thee,
> Amid the eloquent grandeur of these shades,
> Alone with Nature!—but it may not be:
> I have to struggle with the stormy sea
> Of human life until existence fades
> Into death's darkness. Thou wilt sing and soar
> Through the thick woods and shadow-chequered glades,
> While pain and sorrow cast no dimness o'er
> The brilliance of thy heart; but I must wear,
> As now, my garments of regret and care,
> As penitents of old their galling sackcloth wore. (Pike 111-112)

Thus the bird is a symbol of freedom not just because it can "sing and soar," but also because it does not "struggle with the stormy sea of human life." Without the human intellectual concerns of "regret" for the past and "care" about the future, the bird is able to live in the moment, free from the "pain and sorrow" of human existence.

Once again Chopin makes the next sentence its own paragraph, emphasizing its importance. "There were patches of blue sky showing here and there through the clouds that had met and piled one above the other in the west facing her window" (Chopin 1894). The blue sky indicates peace and tranquility, especially after the storm of grief that has passed. Significantly, the clouds in the sky are in the west, the direction of the setting sun and because of that the traditional symbol of death or the end of something. With Mrs. Mallard's marriage at an end, the clouds and all their associated discontent have moved on to the west and she will now be free to live her life for herself. But it is more than just her individual conflict that the receding clouds represent. The societal expectations for widows were much less severe than those for single women. A widow could choose not to remarry and still maintain a high social standing in a way that an unmarried woman—an old maid, whose life in every other respect was identical—could never do. Then comes yet another paragraph composed of only one sentence.

"She sat with her head thrown back upon the cushion of the chair, quite motionless, except when a sob came up into her throat and shook her, as a child who has cried itself to sleep continues to sob in its dreams" (Chopin 1894). This is an interesting simile, because it says far more about the protagonist's position as a married woman at the time than the merely descriptive purpose it serves in a literal reading. In comparing Mrs. Mallard to a child, the simile draws attention to her place as a dependent in her husband's household. And the reference to a child crying itself to sleep and continuing to sob in its dreams reinforces the idea of her marriage as a nightmare. The idea of childlike innocence, especially in looking at her own lack of cognizance about the position she is in, also tells the reader that her acceptance of society's expectations for women has been an unconscious one rather than choice on her part, for the simple reason that there were no other options available for her to consider.

In the next paragraph Chopin finally gives the reader a sentence of description about her protagonist, and manages to say something about her character at the same time. This she couples with another reference to the blue sky.

> She was young, with a fair, calm face, whose lines bespoke repression and even a certain strength. But now there was a dull stare in her eyes, whose gaze was fixed away off yonder on one of those patches of blue sky. It was not a glance of reflection, but rather indicated a suspension of intelligent thought. (Chopin 1894)

The effect of these two seemingly disparate sentences is intriguing. Mrs. Mallard is a young woman, which again reinforces the innocence and acceptance suggested by the child simile in the previous paragraph. She is also attractive, her face fair and calm. But the lines in her face tell of the repression she has suffered. This is an important distinction because rather than oppression, in which the oppressed understands consciously that they are being held back in some way, the repression here is unconscious. In living out societal expectations that were chosen for her rather than selected by her, she has had to suppresses or dismiss her desires at an early age in order to fit in and conform to the way life is lived all around her.

Significantly, this is followed by the dull stare at the patch of blue sky. The phrase "suspension of intelligent thought" is important to understand because it has so often been misinterpreted. Louise Mallard has not been hoping for her husband's death, or even wishing that she could be free and on her own. Her life has been lived according to the expectations of the time and she has conformed to them as best she could. The repression in her face tells the reader that beneath her conscious thoughts lies something else, but it is not something that she could have articulated if asked. It is simply a part of her life as a woman at the turn of the twentieth century. When the narrator says this is not a look of reflection, it means she is not thinking about the past, about her husband, or what might have been. But because she has always conformed to societal norms and knows nothing else, she actually must suspend her intellect in order to allow herself to be open to something new, something that she had never considered before. And it's also significant that this new idea is coming from the blue sky rather than the clouds. In this respect the clouds that have prevented her understanding have now moved away, which means there is knowledge coming to her from the blue sky. "There was something coming to her and she was waiting for it, fearfully. What was it? She did not know; it was too subtle and elusive to name. But she felt it, creeping out of the sky, reaching toward her through the sounds, the scents, the color that filled the air" (Chopin 1894).

An important aspect of freedom for any oppressed person comes in the first line of this paragraph when it mentions the fear that Mrs. Mallard feels. The simplistic expectation about someone who has just been released from bondage is that they will celebrate and revel in their newfound freedom. But this is an outsider's view, which forgets that things that are new and unfamiliar can also be frightening. It's a sentiment expressed by Maya Angelou in her poem "I Know Why the Caged Bird Sings" in addressing black oppression. "The caged bird sings with a fearful trill, of things unknown but longed for still" (Angelou 183). Mrs. Mallard may be entering a phase in her life of emotional and economic freedom—one she may even unconsciously long for—but the fact that she has never experienced those things, has never had to shoulder the responsibility for them, makes them initially fearful. This will be a new experience for her, and put in that same position a lot of people would be unwilling to take the chance and as a consequence they would retreat to the safety and familiarity of their former oppression. Wonderfully, this nameless idea that is coming to her from the blue sky makes its way to her "through the sounds, the scents, the color that filled the air," demonstrating that what is coming to her is not only associated with the peace and tranquility of the blue sky, but with all of those symbols of freedom that she could see and hear through the open window.

Nevertheless, the fear of the unknown is still present when Chopin writes, "Now her bosom rose and fell tumultuously. She was beginning to recognize this thing that was approaching to possess her, and she was striving to beat it back with her will—as powerless as her two white slender hands would have been" (Chopin 1894). It's clear from this description that the freedom coming for her is not simply going to be one more element in her new life going forward. The narrator says that this thing is "approaching to possess her," which means it is going to mean everything to her; it will become the driving force in her life, her reason for living. It is absolutely vital to understand this idea in order to make complete sense of the ending of the story. This dramatic change in her character can be seen in the very next paragraph.

> When she abandoned herself a little whispered word escaped her slightly parted lips. She said it over and over under her breath: "free, free, free!" The vacant stare and the look of terror that had followed it went from her eyes. They stayed keen and bright. Her pulses beat fast, and the coursing blood warmed and relaxed every inch of her body.

This is the turning point in the story, when Mrs. Mallard finally abandons herself to the thought of being "free" for the very first time in her life—even the word has to "escape" from her lips. The "vacant stare and the look of terror" are also suddenly gone. Not only has the unconscious aspect of her life that has followed society's dictates been exposed, but the fear of the unknown has also left her. Her eyes, now "keen and bright," are suddenly conscious of the way she has had to live her life before, and the mere thought of this new freedom is then equated with blood, the life giving fluid that flows through her body and which she cannot live without. Again, this is an extremely important association in the way that it foreshadows the ending.

Now comes the complete consciousness of the protagonist, Louise Mallard, in which she can see things for what they really are for the first time in her life. "She did not stop to ask if it were or were not a monstrous joy that held her. A clear and exalted perception enabled her to dismiss the suggestion as trivial" (Chopin 1894). First, she understands that the joy overtaking her could be interpreted by some as "monstrous" because it has only been realized through the death of her husband. But the fact remains that this is not something she brought about herself or even conceived of before, so of course the suggestion is "trivial." One of the most important points of the story comes next. "She knew that she would weep again when she saw the kind, tender hands folded in death; the face that had never looked save with love upon her, fixed and gray and dead. But she saw beyond that bitter moment a long procession of years to come that would belong to her absolutely. And she opened and spread her arms out to them in welcome." It's vital to the power of this story that the husband not be a tyrant or abusive to her, because that's not the issue. It's the same concept as the benevolent slaveholder in the American South. A slaveholder can be the nicest person in the world and want only the best for his slaves, but that still doesn't justify possessing another human being. In the same way, it doesn't matter how nice Louise's husband was to her, the societal expectations and legal limitations on her life are just as onerous and oppressive. This is a crucial point Chopin is making, because it's not Louise's husband as an individual that she is escaping from but rather a way of life in general that has been imposed upon women by men.

Now that she fully understands what her own unconscious participation in society has been, she can finally see her relationship with her husband for what it really was.

> There would be no one to live for during those coming years; she would live for herself. There would be no powerful will bending hers in that blind persistence with which men and women believe they have a right to impose a private will upon a fellow-creature. A kind intention or a cruel intention made the act seem no less a crime as she looked upon it in that brief moment of illumination. (Chopin 1894)

The first sentence of this paragraph was actually changed the second time the story was published. In the first appearance of the story, in *Vogue* magazine in 1894, the sentence was printed as it is here. The second appearance, a year later in *St. Louis Life*, added the word "her" to the sentence, making it read, "There would be no one to live for [her] during those coming years; she would live for herself." (Koloski 2005) While the addition of the pronoun changes the meaning of the sentence slightly, it does not change the overall intent of the paragraph. The meaning of the sentence without the pronoun is that Louise has been living *for* someone else all these years, namely her husband. With the pronoun added it simply means that her husband had been living her life *for her* while she stayed isolated at home. In both variations the sentence that follows the semicolon makes the same point. Either she is going to live for *herself*, in the first instance, or *she* lives for herself in the second.

Chopin begins the paragraph by stating that women's role in society has always been as a support mechanism for their husbands, either living *for* them and their aspirations or *through* them. But with the death of Louise's husband all of that is now over. Further, the imposition of the "private will upon a fellow-creature" is something she equates with a crime. It's also interesting to note that she sees women as participants in this behavior as well as men, due to the fact that other women, mothers and sisters and the like, could be every bit as coercive in attempting to maintain the status quo as their male counterparts. And just as before, Chopin goes out of her way to make the point that it isn't any specific instance of oppression that a woman experiences that is repugnant, it's the very idea itself. Whether or not her husband is a brute or a benevolent is immaterial to the reality of what his wife has to endure on a psychological level every day. In John Stuart Mill's contemporary essay, "The Subjection of Women," he states their situation this way:

> I am far from pretending that wives are in general no better treated than slaves; but no slave is a slave to the same lengths, and in so full a sense of the word, as a wife is. Hardly any slave, except one immediately attached to the master's person, is a slave at all hours and all minutes; in general he has, like a soldier, his fixed task, and when it is done, or when he is off duty, he disposes, within certain limits, of his own time, and has a family life into which the master rarely intrudes. "Uncle Tom" under his first master had his own life in his "cabin," almost as much as any man whose work takes him away from home, is able to have in his own family. But it cannot be so with the wife. (Mill 155)

Thus the idea that the oppression of women is a crime isn't mere hyperbole. While the slavery of blacks had been criminalized at the end of the Civil War, the more subtle enslavement of women was still ongoing. This is powerfully demonstrated by the next two sentences. "And yet she had loved him— sometimes. Often she had not" (Chopin 1894). There's a strong sense here that Louise's initial declaration of love for her husband is really just her past, unconscious conformity to society's expectations coming out to express what she thinks she's supposed to feel, and she immediately attenuates that by saying it was only sometimes that she had loved him. Then Chopin allows her to take a breath and begin a new sentence that reflects her character's newfound consciousness, confirming the fact that she had never really loved him at all. And her response to that realization is equally powerful.

"What did it matter! What could love, the unsolved mystery, count for in the face of this possession of self-assertion which she suddenly recognized as the strongest impulse of her being!" (Chopin 1894). It's typical of the male, patriarchal view that this sentence has been misinterpreted as an example of Louise Mallard simply being selfish. Conservative intellectual Harold Bloom, in describing the protagonist from Chopin's *The Awakening*, could just as easily be describing Louise Mallard here when he says that the dynamic change of the character is simply "a narcissistic self-investment that constitutes a new ego for the heroine. Unfortunately, she fails to see that her passion is for herself, and this error perhaps destroys her" (H. Bloom 1987, 1). It's obvious that Louise's passion is going to center on herself, because up until now she has had to live her entire life for someone else. And in that context, what could the idea of romantic love really have to offer her? Even were she to find herself falling in love with a man in the future, once she had married him she would wind up in exactly the same position she had been in before. In fact, Chopin used this very situation in *The Awakening*, and had her protagonist turn down the offer of marriage from the young man who was in love with her. It's very easy for men to label this as narcissistic behavior and see it as an error on her part because the nineteenth-century man never had to make that choice. The irony is, his life had always been a narcissistic one and supported as such by the rest of society. In saying that her new self-possession is now the "strongest impulse of her being," Chopin is allowing Louise Mallard to behave in exactly the same manner that men had always behaved, but the fact that she has never experienced it before will make it that much more important to her. "'Free! Body and soul free!' she kept whispering" (Chopin 1894).

It seems that with each successive sentence Chopin exposes yet another layer of the oppression women had to suffer in the nineteenth century. In this case Louise's declaration that not only has her soul been liberated but her body as well is so subtle that the significance can easily be missed. In the days when women had no rights within the bonds of marriage, that also included the right to their own bodies. This is a legal concept addressed by Rose Weitz in her book, *The Politics of Women's Bodies: Sexuality, Appearance and Behavior.*

> Upon marriage a woman experienced "civil death," losing any rights as a citizen, including the right to own or bestow property, make contracts or sue for legal redress, holding custody over minor children, or keep any wages she earned. Moreover, as her "protector," a husband had a legal right to beat her if he believed it necessary, as well as a right to her sexual services. These principles would form the basis of marital law in the United States from its founding. (Weitz 3)

Part of a man's marital rights included unfettered access to his wife as a sexual object, and in the context of a marriage in which the woman had no feelings of love for her husband it's not a big step to equate the act with rape. Again, it is John Stuart Mill who, with unvarnished frankness, explains the wife's true position in a loveless marriage. "However brutal a tyrant she may unfortunately be chained to—though she may know that he hates her, though it may be his daily pleasure to torture her, and though she may feel it impossible not to loathe him—he can claim from her and enforce the lowest degradation of a human being, that of being made the instrument of an animal function contrary to her inclinations" (Mill 155-156).

It's only at this point in the story that Chopin allows her protagonist to interact with the rest of society, as symbolized by her sister and her husband's friend. But Louise is a changed person now, a dynamic character who is a very different woman from the one who went up to her room alone an hour earlier. Chopin begins with the sister, who symbolically bears the diminutive of a male name. "Josephine was kneeling before the closed door with her lips to the keyhole, imploring for admission. 'Louise, open the door! I beg; open the door—you will make yourself ill. What are you doing, Louise? For heaven's sake open the door'" (Chopin 1894). Josephine, who is still unconsciously conforming to society, is shown in a position of submission, on her knees. But this isn't enough for Chopin and she also has the character's "lips to the keyhole, imploring for admission." If the door is symbolic for change and opportunity, then the keyhole is the way in. This initially might seem as if Josephine wants to have what her sister has achieved, especially when this is the only place in the story that the protagonist's first name is even mentioned, but in reality the comparison between the two sisters is simply a way to reinforce the consciousness that Louise has achieved. Josephine's lack of understanding is demonstrated by what she actually says to her sister. First she begs her sister to open the door by claiming Louise is making herself sick. The implication here is that the freedom Louise has gained, and more specifically her embracing of it, is unhealthy. From the view of society her desire for freedom is an illness, something that she needs to be cured of. Second, when that doesn't work Josephine invokes religion, "for heaven's sake," to further imply this deviance goes against God's injunction for married couples.

"Wives, submit yourselves unto your own husbands, as unto the Lord. For the husband is the head of the wife, even as Christ is the head of the church: and he is the savior of the body. Therefore as the church is subject unto Christ, so let the wives be to their own husbands in everything" (Ephesians 5:22-24). Biblical directives such as these have been used for centuries to justify the subjugation of women to their husbands. In her book *Women and Christianity, Volume III: From the Reformation to the 21st Century*, author Mary T. Malone makes clear the kind of unfair burden these ideas have placed on women since the birth of Christianity and, as with law and medicine, have taken much too long to rectify because of their general, unconscious acceptance by both perpetrators and victims alike.

> Traditional [Christian] ethics has been fundamentally authoritarian, that is, it has used power to bolster its authority, from the power of God's sanctions to the use of sometimes extreme violence. There has never been a place for the voice of the weak. Traditional ethics has also been sexist and has reinforced sexism in the implementation of its decisions. The main emphasis has always been put on the passive virtues of submission, patience, resignation, acceptance of one's own lot, and obedience . . . With this fixation, the traditional ethical perspective prevented creativity, risk and real self-actualization. This lack of personal growth was partly a result of the emphasis on law rather than on the development of a mature conscience, again, with more direct consequences for women, for whom obedience was seen as a 'natural' state. (Malone 287-88)

The belief that women are naturally weaker or naturally less intelligent than men is one of the most insidious in Western culture and one that continues to undermine attempts to achieve equal status for women well into the twenty-first century. But here Chopin's character Louise Mallard expresses in no uncertain terms her unwillingness to conform to the ideas that her sister represents by saying, "'Go away. I am not making myself ill.' No; she was drinking in a very elixir of life through that open window" (Chopin 1894). By this time there is no doubt what the open window symbolizes, as everything outside represents something that has been denied to Louise, something that she can now have for herself only because of the death of her husband. Far from making her ill, the world that is represented by life outside the house is one that has suddenly become a life-giving force for her. And this can't be emphasized enough, because if that "elixir of life" is ever taken away from her it can only mean that life itself will be taken along with it.

Next comes the evidence of Louise Mallard's complete transformation of character. "Her fancy was running riot along those days ahead of her. Spring days, and summer days, and all sorts of days that would be her own. She breathed a quick prayer that life might be long. It was only yesterday she had thought with a shudder that life might be long" (Chopin 1894). Again, the emphasis on life and death is easy to miss here because of the character's understanding that she is now living for herself and no one else. This is the actual joy that will be referred to in the final line of the story, and her prayer for long life must also be considered part of that as well. Whatever kind of unconsciousness there has been before in Louise's life about her own lack of opportunity, or in Mary Malone's words the lack of "creativity, risk and real self-actualization," there is clearly a conscious sense now that what she has been relegated to in her past life isn't something she is willing to accept anymore. Her shudder at the thought of a long life just the day before is evidence enough of that.

At this point in the story Louise Mallard has fully achieved her dynamism as a character and has completely changed. But despite the optimism of the next paragraph, it also contains some serious symbolic foreshadowing that should be alarming to the careful reader. "She arose at length and opened the door to her sister's importunities. There was a feverish triumph in her eyes, and she carried herself unwittingly like a goddess of Victory. She clasped her sister's waist, and together they descended the stairs. Richards stood waiting for them at the bottom" (Chopin 1894). In the first place, she is giving in to her sister's pleas, however much she has changed. Significantly, after opening the door the sister doesn't come in but instead Louise goes out. The triumph in her eyes is feverish, but she nevertheless carries herself "unwittingly like a goddess of Victory." The capital letter Chopin uses for Victory, rather than the proper name Nike, is a nice touch. The practice of capitalizing certain, or nearly all, nouns was briefly in vogue prior to the standardization of the English language in the nineteenth century. Used here it suggests that this isn't any ordinary victory, and like a similar use of the phrase "the Surrender" in the American South to denote the end of the Civil War, Louise's victory over the oppression of societal expectations and her ability to now be free of them is worthy of a proper noun. Nevertheless, she does clasp her sister's waist, bringing the two of them together, and descends the stairs, which has the effect of lowering herself from her formerly exalted status, to the waiting Richards—the symbol of male dominance—who is standing there below.

Finally, the climax of the story fulfills all of the foreshadowing of the previous paragraph and provides the true rationale for the twist ending.

> Some one was opening the front door with a latchkey. It was Brently Mallard who entered, a little travel-stained, composedly carrying his grip-sack and umbrella. He had been far from the scene of the accident, and did not even know there had been one. He stood amazed at Josephine's piercing cry; at Richards' quick motion to screen him from the view of his wife. (Chopin 1894)

There is a tremendous significance to Brently Mallard's ignorance of the whole affair that goes along with the male ignorance of patriarchal dominance in marriage Chopin has already illuminated. But Louise's assertion earlier in the story that he "had never looked save with love upon her" is not enough to absolve him of his responsibility for unconsciously going along with societal dictates that severely limited a woman's ability to live her life in something other than a prescribed manner that centered on the home and family. In this context Brently Mallard is also clearly an example of Lionel Trilling's "immorality of inertia." Another important element of the paragraph is that it is not Louise who screams. This is left to Josephine, who represents traditional expectations for females and the unconscious acceptance of the status quo. For Richards, his role is that of protector, a convenient rationalization for the subjugation of women in nearly every aspect of American life. All of which leads to the concluding line of the story. "When the doctors came they said she had died of heart disease—of the joy that kills."

It's important to remember that this line comes from the doctors' point of view. In those days doctors were nearly all male, and their findings were that Louise died of "heart disease," not "a heart trouble" as stated in the first line of the story. So while it is clear they are thinking only of a physiological weakness of her heart, Chopin has taken great care in the opening line to let the reader know this isn't the real reason for her death. The joy the doctors are referring to is their belief that she was so happy to see her husband alive her weak heart could not stand the shock. In fact, the very opposite is true. Louise Mallard had transformed completely as a character, and that change could not be undone. For her, there was no going back. It was impossible. The joy that killed her was the joy of freedom she had briefly experienced. And because she had been fully possessed by that joy, staying alive and going back to the way things had been before, especially in light of her newfound consciousness, was a literal impossibility. Author Mary E. Papke puts it this way: "only Louise and the reader perceived the earlier 'death' of the true woman 'Mrs. Mallard;' and that what murdered her was, indeed, a monstrous joy, the birth of individual self, and the erasure of that joy when her husband and, necessarily, her old self returned" (Papke 54). But her old self couldn't return, as her old self had already died, and as a result she was actually "murdered" by the return of her husband. Just as with Chopin's protagonist in *The Awakening*, the only way for Louise Mallard to maintain her freedom and not be reeled back in by a society that would never be able to accept her status as an independent woman, was to die.

In retrospect, it doesn't seem surprising that much of the subtlety of Chopin's story was lost on the readers of her day, especially considering the deceptive nature of the final sentence, which was no doubt read by many at the time as a reinforcement of conventional attitudes. But Chopin biographer Emily Toth explains why this was done.

To make her story publishable, Kate Chopin had to disguise reality. She had to have her heroine die. A story in which an unhappy wife is suddenly widowed, becomes rich, and lives happily ever after . . . would have been much too radical, far too threatening in the 1890s. There were limits to what editors would publish, and what audiences would accept." (Toth 1999, 10)

As if to emphasize this disconnect, the 1895 version of the story as it was published in *St. Louis Life* was immediately followed on the same page by this attempt at humor:

Man of the House (in a loud and angry voice)—Confound it! Shut that door, you, out there! Shut that door this minute!

Servant (appearing with dignity)—Do ye know who yez hollerin' at?

Man of the House (collapsed)—Oh! excuse me, Bridget. I thought it was my wife. (Moore 5)

In fact, even *Vogue* refused to publish the story when Chopin first submitted it, as did three other magazines she offered it to subsequently. It wasn't until after the critical success of her first book of short stories, *Bayou Folk*, that she resubmitted the story and it was accepted.

The story also marked the beginning of an artistic awakening for the author as well, as her stories more frequently began to address inequities for women in society.

Three of the most striking were about wives. One is attracted to her husband's best friend; another is wildly happy to hear that her husband is dead; and a third one leaves, after her own death, hints of adultery that drive her living husband to despair ("A Respectable Woman"; "The Story of an Hour"; "Her Letters"). Only the third actually commits adultery—but the first clearly has it in mind. (Toth 1999, 158)

According to Toth, "By the end of 1894, Kate Chopin was already coming into conflict with traditional views of what should be written, particularly about independent women. But she did not seem inclined to stop . . ." (Toth 1990, 253). The absolutely fascinating aspect of the criticism of her work at this time was not the implication that she was somehow lying about a woman's place in American society, as this seemed to be a fact beyond dispute. In discussing

The Awakening, author Bernard Koloski claims, "It was not the truth of her book that came under attack in 1899 but the fact that Chopin had put that truth on paper and published it" (Koloski 2012, 3). H.L. Mencken addressed this very issue as late as 1925 in an otherwise insulting article on women writers in America.

> Women, and especially American women, write very few good novels, and almost none of the first rank. Why is this? I believe it is mainly because the display of their talent is still greatly hampered by convention—because it would still cause a frightful scandal if they began to tell the truth—that is, if they began to describe human existence as they actually see it . . . She knows that if she told the whole truth [men] would be shocked to death and flee her as the pestilence. So she compromises . . . (Mencken 7)

What sets "The Story of an Hour" apart from Chopin's other works like *The Awakening* and "The Storm," which deal more nakedly with infidelity, is her conscious use of symbolism and her ability to "smuggle" into the story ideas and criticisms that—while missed by many readers who were unable to see beyond the literal story that seemed to reinforce societal expectations of the day—were there to be found for anyone who understood the inherent inequality of the status quo, especially as "Chopin, characteristically, does not tell her readers what to think" (Toth 1999, 176). "The Story of an Hour" remains a powerful indictment of marriage at the time, as well as an example of the style of writing that the times imposed on women writers.

More importantly, the story also provides insight into the way to read *Ethan Frome*. Many of the themes of female oppression are also easy to miss in Wharton's novel because of the way they are made manifest in her male protagonist, and stories like Chopin's are crucial in providing a method for understanding those themes. One of the unanswered questions in Chopin's story is why Louise would have married her husband in the first place if she never loved him. But this assumes that Louise had anything like a choice, or that she was willing to risk never getting another proposal had she turned Brently Mallard down, a situation that a close reading of *Ethan Frome* makes clear was also facing Zeena when Ethan proposed to her. The themes of financial dependence, physical and emotional oppression, the loss of the self in marriage, the true meaning of freedom, the fear of independence, the onus of morality, matters of life and death, and visions of happiness in "The Story of an Hour" are all present in *Ethan Frome* as well. And it is only through a clear understanding of the way in which these works were written that they can be appreciated fully in light of what their authors were actually able to achieve.

Charlotte Perkins Gilman's
"The Yellow Wall-Paper"

Just as it had been with Kate Chopin, the influence of Charlotte Perkins Gilman's father on her life and career was vitally important, but in a completely different way. Where the death of Chopin's father allowed her mother to live a life unknown to most women of her day, with money and freedom, and provided an example for the young Kate, Charlotte's father influenced her life through reading. She was born into a distinguished New England family in 1860. Her father, Frederick Beecher Perkins, was related to the Beecher family that included preacher Henry Ward Beecher and novelist Harriet Beecher Stowe, while her mother, Mary Westcott, was from a prominent Rhode Island family of merchants. Like Chopin, Charlotte Perkins grew up without a father, though it was because he had left her mother when she was young; unlike Chopin she grew up destitute, as her father's financial support was infrequent and insufficient. What he did pass on to her, though, was a love of books.

> A published author of short stories, Frederick Perkins became a librarian in Boston and later San Francisco. As the compiler of the reference book *The Best Reading*, he helped shape the literary choices of the nation and his daughter. As Charlotte matured, she found a way to reach her father by asking him to suggest books for her reading. (Horowitz 9)

Whereas Kate Chopin had a flesh and blood example of a truly independent woman in her mother, something unique in her day, Gilman's ideas of the inherent inequality between men and women in society initially came from her reading. But she also had her own personal experiences that reinforced these ideas, especially after she turned twenty-one and began to be courted by men.

Once she and her mother settled in Rhode Island she started seeing a young man who had graduated from Brown College, "but she did not like the way he browbeat her as they conversed about ideas and religion. At some point . . . she made a decision that she would distance herself from him, and . . . [eventually] he had ceased to call" (Horowitz 13). As a result of this disillusionment with men, Charlotte became infatuated with a girlfriend of hers she had known since childhood, Martha Luther, and she allowed the infatuation to become an all-consuming passion, a relationship that she believed would enable her to focus on her reading and writing and the development of her mind.

> Charlotte wrote to Martha that she was "really getting glad not to marry," for she reasoned that "the mother side" of herself was so strong that, if she married, she would experience "an interminable war between plain duties and irrepressible instincts." Even now, she felt "rage" at domestic confinement. Were she married, she would dissipate her energy and get nowhere. (14)

Charlotte was naturally devastated when Martha announced that she was getting married. Though it's to her credit she never felt betrayed by Martha's choice, that didn't make the pain any less acute. Charlotte's desire to spend her life with Martha had nothing to do with homosexuality, but was instead a reaction to the realities of married life for women in her day. In her imagined relationship with Martha she thought to escape all of that, living a life of the mind rather than of the body, and sharing her life in equality with another woman rather than becoming the virtual possession of a man. Nevertheless, she was able to move on herself after Martha's announcement, marrying Charles Walter Stetson in 1884 and giving birth to their daughter a year later.

The importance of Gilman's story "The Yellow Wall-Paper" in understanding *Ethan Frome* is that it deals specifically with the one area of women's oppression at the turn of the twentieth century that Chopin's "The Story of an Hour" doesn't, and that is women's health, both mental and physical. In her biographical account of the story, *Wild Unrest: Charlotte Perkins Gilman and the Making of "The Yellow Wallpaper,"* Helen Leflowitz Horowitz has put Gilman's most famous work into its proper historical context. Along with Charlotte's voracious appetite for all kinds of books as a young woman, from fiction to philosophy to science, also came a tendency toward despondency in her emotional life that today would have been diagnosed as clinical depression. Back then, however, physicians had no conception of this psychological condition. At the same time, the two sides of her personal identity—one that wanted desperately to experience the love and devotion of motherhood and marriage, along with the conscious understanding that such an act was a death sentence to her intellect—continued to war within her. This is something she recognized even before her marriage, and which she tried to convey to Stetson. "I have lost *power.* I do not feel myself so strong a person as I was before. I seem to have taken a lower seat, to have become less in some way, to have shrunk . . . Since I have been with you I have lost in great measure that strong self-confidence which was my greatest happiness" (Horowitz 60). Stetson's response to her vacillation about marriage was typical: "There must be something very morbid in her brain . . . sensitive nerves and ready brain play as strange freaks—and I think hers are running riot with her" (59).

Like Louise Mallard's realization that love counted for very little in the face of her newfound freedom, Charlotte wrote something similar to her fiancé when she declared on the threshold of their marriage, "the delight in your love is lost entirely in the horrified shrinking at confinement, restricting possession" (Horowitz 61). Echoing Harold Bloom's denunciation of the protagonist in Kate Chopin's *The Awakening,* Charlotte's future husband, "labeled her desire for work and self-sufficiency as selfishness" (40). His ideas about women had been thoroughly absorbed from the society in which he lived, especially when it came to Charlotte's reading as an explanation for her behavior. "She thinks much of her irregularity comes from her father. It may be: but more comes from ill-digested reading of philosophical works mixed with her imagination" (60). As a result, Charles thought of her as "a mere child. She has ideas of life founded on slight hints from books" (62). Charlotte nevertheless went on to marry Charles Stetson, but the post-partum depression she suffered after the birth of her daughter was anything but imaginary, and forms the basis for "The Yellow Wall-Paper." Gilman described her descent into melancholy and enervation at the time in her diary, especially severe after a doctor was called for against her wishes. "I had had one of my bad times when he was first sent for. The next day was bad too; highly excited, hysterical, seeming to myself wellnigh insane" (95-96). Charlotte was eventually persuaded to undergo a rest cure for hysteria under the direction of the renowned doctor S. Weir Mitchell in Philadelphia, which only seemed to make matters worse. Finally, she separated from her husband and moved to Pasadena, California in 1888 to live on her own for a while with her daughter, and it was there, after processing everything she had gone through, that she was able to write about her experience in "The Yellow Wall-Paper."

The title signals to the reader that the wallpaper is at the center of the story, and that the primary themes and ideas Gilman is attempting to covey will be found there. The opening sentence, like Chopin's, is its own paragraph, and it makes a couple of subtle but important points in the process. "It is very seldom that mere ordinary people like John and myself secure ancestral halls for the summer" (Gilman 1892, 1). The fact that the narrator and her husband are ordinary reflects the same type of philosophical argument that is made in "The Story of an Hour," where it is not specific instances of oppression by men that are the point, but the very idea of societal oppression in general. Thus, these two characters represent a normal view of male dominance in married relationships rather than extreme cases resulting in physical or mental abuse. The second point has to do with the author's reference to "ancestral halls," which shows that this way of thinking is something that did not begin in this era or with this couple but, as the previous chapter has shown, goes back to biblical times and further. In this way Gilman establishes that her story is not something out of the ordinary but a common occurrence in the lives of the people of her day. The next sentence builds on that idea, but extends it to foreshadow what is to come.

"A colonial mansion, a hereditary estate, I would say a haunted house, and reach the height of romantic felicity—but that would be asking too much of fate!" (Gilman 1892, 1). The colonial mansion fixes the setting as America, while the hereditary nature of the estate reflects not only the legal inferiority of women who came over to North America from England, but also the historical fact that women in England couldn't inherit estates at all, that the property of the landed gentry went to the next living male heir, bypassing any closer female relatives completely. Then the narrator calls it a "haunted house," which suggests the same idea of haunting that informed "The Story of an Hour." The literal conception in this case, however, is very different. Here the narrator is speaking of haunting in the tradition of eighteenth- and nineteenth-century gothic romances, in which the excitement of the mysterious unexplained is ultimately followed by a more benign and rational resolution that completely discredits the previous supernatural experience. What she seems to be hoping for is that this romantic idea of a haunting will parallel her illness, and that the ultimate cause for it will turn out to be nothing after all. But then immediately afterward she says this is too much to expect of fate, and suddenly the haunting becomes closer in meaning to its use in Chopin's story. The unfinished business of a society that has yet to recognize a woman's right to individuality and autonomy will ultimately haunt her in the form of the wallpaper.

"Still," she says, "I will proudly declare that there is something queer about it . . . John laughs at me, of course, but one expects that in marriage" (Gilman 1892, 1). In these next lines, just like the textual implications made by the third-person narrator in Chopin's story, the first-person narrator here states quite explicitly that her beliefs and feelings are routinely ridiculed in the context of her married life. Furthermore, it's clear that she, like Louise Mallard, has no expectation otherwise in the absence of any alternative in American society at the time. Yet beneath it all she knows what she knows, and it will be that unconscious knowledge in the face of the resistance of an entire society that will be her ultimate undoing. Unlike the single change to one of the sentences in Chopin's story that resulted in a distinction without a difference, Gilman's story was subjected to far more frequent and insidious alterations in the years since its initial publication in 1892, all of which are meticulously analyzed by Julie Bates Dock in her book, *"The Yellow Wallpaper" and the History of Its Publication and Reception*. This sentence is one that was changed significantly in subsequent reprints of the story.

> The first important variant, and the one most noticeably resonant with meaning, appears in the fifth paragraph of the story . . . Texts that follow *The Golden Book Magazine* (and Lane's more recent *Gilman Reader*) print the following: "John laughs at me, of course, but one expects that." Omitting "in marriage" radically transforms the line. Why on earth would one "expect that?" . . . Clearly other readers do not know either, for several have attempted to clarify this ambiguity . . . These readings either personalize the statement specifically to John or universalize it to include all men [but in either case] it distorts Gilman's focus: here she is bashing marriage in particular, not men in general. (Dock 7)

Because these stories are so heavily dependent on the literal word choices their authors make in getting across symbolic meaning, great care must be taken to ensure that the author's intent is respected by analyzing the most accurate version possible. In order to accomplish this, the page numbers cited here refer to the 1899 monograph published by Small, Maynard & Co., but corrected to conform to the definitive version published by Dock.

It's tempting for some readers to credit the underlying thematic elements of great fiction to inspiration or providence, but that ignores the diligence and the artistic gifts that great writers possess. As was seen in Chopin's work the main thrust of the story, despite it's symbolic coding, came directly from the author's experiences. Charlotte Perkins Gilman was even more forthcoming about the genesis of her work, and made numerous references to it in letters and her other writings. And while some of the figurative meaning in her work may have been unconscious, it was by no means accidental. Not only does "The Yellow Wall-Paper" have a clear overt meaning, but it also sends a very deliberate symbolic message. And Gilman wouldn't have had it any other way. In fact, she saw this story in particular as one that transcended the

Eric B. Olsen

limitations of fiction and over time began to view it as a manifesto of sorts. "A few years ago Mr. [William Dean] Howells asked leave to include this story in a collection he was arranging—*Masterpieces of American Fiction*. I was more than willing, but assured him that it was no more 'literature' than my other stuff, being definitely written 'with a purpose.' In my judgment it is a pretty poor thing to write, to talk, without a purpose" (Gilman 1935, 121).

Next comes a straightforward recounting of the prevailing ideology of the day concerning the differences between men and women. "John is practical in the extreme. He has no patience with faith, an intense horror of superstition, and he scoffs openly at any talk of things not to be felt and seen and put down in figures" (Gilman 1892, 1-2). Again, much of this way of thinking was rationalized by an interpretation of the biological differences between men and women that reinforced those social distinctions.

> Women's physiology and anatomy, physicians habitually argued, oriented her toward an "inner" view of herself and her worldly sphere. Logically enough, nineteenth-century views of heredity often assumed that the father was responsible for the child's external musculature and skeletal development, the mother for the internal viscera, the father for analytical abilities, the mother for emotions and piety . . . The Victorian woman was more spiritual than man, yet less intellectual, closer to the divine, yet prisoner of her most animal characteristics, more moral than man, yet less in control of her very morality. (Smith-Rosenberg 1999, 113-114)

As a result of nothing but her sex, the narrator's feelings, premonitions, and beliefs are now things that may be scoffed at openly by the more superior and rational intellect of man.

To make matters worse her husband isn't just any man, but to her credit she also realizes that just because he is in control it doesn't mean he truly understands what is going on with her. "John is a physician, and *perhaps*—(I would not say it to a living soul, of course, but this is dead paper and a great relief to my mind)—*perhaps* that is one reason I do not get well faster. You see he does not believe I am sick!" (Gilman 1892, 2). This sentence is actually the key to understanding the entire story, for two reasons. First, the narrator realizes that something is wrong in her life, something doesn't make sense, and she will spend the rest of the story desperately trying to figure out what that is. Yet unlike Louise Mallard in "The Story of an Hour," who comes to recognize the inequity of the role she has assumed in her married life, the narrator of "The Yellow Wall-Paper" never does. That is what finally drives her mad. The second important point in this sentence is her recognition that writing makes her feel better. The exercise of her intellect is actually her pathway to recovery, but because her husband is a physician and blinded by the medical beliefs of his day he will do everything in his power to stop her from doing the very thing that will help her get better.

Another important aspect of the narrator's character is revealed when she responds to all of this with the phrase, "And what can one do?" (Gilman 1892, 2). This reinforces the idea that she is so deep in the conformity of the era that it will be impossible for her to imagine a way out. It's the very reason Chopin's protagonist had to undergo a "suspension of intelligent thought" first, before she could imagine a different life for herself, something Gilman's narrator is unable to do. She goes on to say that her husband is a physician of high standing and that he believes there is nothing wrong with her except for "temporary nervous depression—a slight hysterical tendency," and again she finishes the paragraph with "what is one to do?" (2). The mention of the word hysteria brings with it a host of historical associations, almost none of them good. One of the more recent works on the subject is *Hysteria: The Disturbing Story* by Andrew Scull. Early in the book he mentions Philadelphia neurologist Silas Weir Mitchell, the very doctor that Charlotte Perkins Gilman went to for her depression, and on whose prescription for her cure the story was based. "Like most of his medical colleagues," Scull recounts,

> he pronounced himself baffled by much of what he saw: the trances, the fits, the paralyses, the choking, the tearing of hair, the remarkable emotional instability, all with no obvious organic substrate. Hysteria was, "the nosological limbo of all un-named female maladies," a condition that so challenged his powers of understanding and his therapeutic skills that he often referred to it in tones of exasperation as "mysteria." (Scull 7)

The historical shame of the frequent reliance on a diagnosis of hysteria by doctors was based on the medical mythology and misinformation that underlies its use. "One very common view of the disorder [is] that it was rooted in the female reproductive organs, more specifically, the womb—as its very name, deriving from the Greek word for that organ, *hystera*, would imply" (Scull 23). And just to reinforce further the idea that the narrator is at a disadvantage in understanding the true nature of her condition, she says, "My brother is also a physician, and also of high standing, and he says the same thing" (Gilman 1892, 2-3). It's no wonder, then, that she feels helpless in her situation.

And yet even with all of this working against her, very early in the story she demonstrates that she has the means within her to achieve the same kind of understanding that Louise Mallard did.

> So I take phosphates or phosphites—whichever it is—and tonics, and journeys, and air, and exercise, and am absolutely forbidden to "work" until I am well again. Personally, I disagree with their idea. Personally, I believe that congenial work, with excitement and change, would do me good. But what is one to do? (Gilman 1892, 3)

This is an incredibly frustrating passage to read because of how close the narrator comes to realizing what her trouble is, and yet she is not even allowed to express her feelings openly because they lack any kind of scientific justification—and also because she is a woman. It's significant that the word "work" is in quotes, and more so because she is "forbidden" to engage in this work. This experience will be the basis for the central conflict in the narrative and is repeated throughout the story, as the narrator's thoughts and feelings lead her right up to the precipice of discovery, only to see her become discouraged and then back off because she has been conditioned by society that she can't go against what the doctors say. It's even worse in her case because the doctors are her family members. And yet again, her acceptance of the status quo is reflected in the phrase, "what is one to do?"

The next sentence reveals what her "work" actually is. "I did write for a while in spite of them; but it *does* exhaust me a good deal—" (Gilman 1892, 3). The sentence construction here is marvelous. The first half seems to imply that perhaps writing is not good for her because of how tired it makes her feel. But the second half of the sentence then comes in to show what the real cause of her exhaustion is: "having to be so sly about it, or else meet with heavy opposition." The idea of opposition to her thoughts and feelings, as well as her writing, is another theme that is repeated throughout the story. As a result, the next sentence is freighted with subtextual meaning. "I sometimes fancy that in my condition if I had less opposition and more society and stimulus—but John says the very worst thing I can do is to think about my condition, and I confess it always makes me feel bad" (3-4). The narrator again frustrates the reader because of her seeming complicity in the circumstances of her condition, and Gilman's sentence structure reflects this. She doesn't even finish the first half of the sentence—the implication of which is that "society and stimulus" would help her get better—before it is interrupted by her husband. A further idea that Gilman explores in the course of the story is that it was not only men who were conditioned by society's expectations, but women as well. In many ways they were just as unable to comprehend the artificiality of their assigned gender role as men. When the narrator uses the word "fancy" to describe her own thoughts the meaning is the nineteenth-century definition of the word as a synonym for imagination. As such, she can't even admit to herself that her thoughts are legitimate. This is reinforced by what her husband says, that she should not even be thinking in the first place. And directly following that comes her sense of guilt for the way she feels.

This is yet another important point that the author makes in the story. Charlotte Perkins Gilman did quite a bit of reading in the relatively recent scientific field of psychology in her day. In analyzing her story it seems she understood intuitively what she might not have understood consciously, that at some deep, unconscious level many women felt there was something wrong with their lives. The problem for those women was that they lacked the background and education that would have enabled them to explain their feelings rationally. In some cases, when the subconscious mind goes to work to solve a problem for the individual it often takes the outward form of insanity. For these women, working in the house all day cooking, cleaning, taking care of children must have been exhausting, and if somewhere in the back of their minds the fact that they were expected to carry out all of these tasks and be grateful in the bargain didn't make sense, their mind could sometimes solve the problem for them by making them so ill that they couldn't work. This is the most likely cause of what was labeled hysteria at the time, "an unspoken idiom of protest, a symbolic voice for the silenced sex, who were forbidden to verbalize their discontents, and so created a language of the body" (Scull 7).

The fact that this malady was unconscious, however, created further problems for these women when they were seen—not only by others but by themselves—to be shirking their responsibilities. "It does weigh on me so not to do my duty in any way!" says Gilman's narrator. "I meant to be such a help to John, such a real rest and comfort, and here I am a comparative burden already!" (Gilman 1892, 10). Diane Price Herndl, in her impressive study of feminine illness in late nineteenth and early twentieth century American fiction, *Invalid Women*, puts it this way: "Americans, the celebrants of robust heartiness and self-sufficiency, are suspicious of illness as a manifestation of laziness or willful attention seeking" (Herndl xiii). The guilt that naturally followed only compounded the negative aspects of the situation for these women, especially when doctors were unable to discover any physiological cause for their symptoms. Thus it was that the severe limitations imposed on women were not just physical ones but emotional as well, and the frustration with their seeming lack of options can be found in Gilman's poem, "In Duty Bound," which was published in January 1884, four months before her marriage to Charles Stetson.

> In duty bound, a life hemmed in
>> Whichever way the spirit turns to look—
> No chance of breaking out, except by sin—
>> Not even room to shirk—
>> Simply to live, and work. (Gilman 1884, 30)

Significantly, it is a woman's spirit that is "hemmed in" in this stanza and, with no other options that could possibly meet with society's approval, other ways of living their lives that did not involve indentured servitude were looked on as somehow sinful. This included even the most basic of rights given to salaried workers: the right to strike. Because women were not hired workers their lives more closely approximated that of the slave, "simply to live, and work," something John Stuart Mill acknowledged when he asserted that, "no slave is a slave to the same lengths, and in so full a sense of the word, as a wife is" (Mill 155).

Gilman continues to demonstrate her genius as a writer when she has her narrator try to stop thinking about her problem. "So I will let it alone and talk about the house" (Gilman 1892, 4). As much as any woman in America at the time, Gilman understood that the home was a woman's metaphorical prison. This was hinted at by Kate Chopin in "The Story of an Hour" when Louise Mallard looks out of the window to a world beyond the home, but in Gilman's story it is the symbolic foundation on which the rest of the subtextual meaning is built. Another stanza in Gilman's "In Duty Bound" deals specifically with the married woman's relationship to her home.

> A narrow house with roof so darkly low
>> The heavy rafters shut the sunlight out;
> One cannot stand erect without a blow;
>> Until the soul inside
>> Shrieks for a grave—more wide. (Gilman 1884, 30)

Tragically, this was simply one part of an overall theory of women on the part of men that justified female subjugation, as Carroll Smith-Rosenberg makes clear in citing an 1869 medical paper she says is "strikingly reminiscent of some midtwentieth-century writings."

> Mentally, socially, spiritually, she is more interior than man. She herself is an interior part of man, and her love and life are always something interior and incomprehensible to him . . . Woman is to deal with domestic affections and uses, not with philosophies and sciences . . . She is priest,

not king. The house, the chamber, the closet, are the centers of her social life. (Smith-Rosenberg 1999, 114)

The physical and intellectual imprisonment of women in the home, however allegorical it might have seemed in reality, was nevertheless made real by societal expectations. In Gilman's poem the description of the physically oppressive nature of the house itself is followed by the woman's attempt to stand erect, which only results in her being beaten down. This represents the desire on the part of women to be their own person and the consequences that typically followed, until the final two lines imply that the grave provides more freedom for women than the home—the very concept that both "The Story of an Hour" and *The Awakening* are based on.

Gilman's narrator, on the other hand, is completely unconscious of the way her description of the house reinforces the prison-like conditions she has acquiesced to in her married life.

> The most beautiful place! It is quite alone, standing well back from the road, quite three miles from the village. It makes me think of English places that you read about, for there are hedges and walls and gates that lock, and lots of separate little houses for the gardeners and people. There is a *delicious* garden! I never saw such a garden—large and shady, full of box-bordered paths, and lined with long grape-covered arbors with seats under them. There were greenhouses, too, but they are all broken now. (Gilman 1892, 4-5)

First of all the house is separated from other people, three miles from the village, the opposite of the "more society and stimulus" the narrator consciously knows she needs. Second, the references to England again bring with them associations with the legal restrictions on women that came over to this country, including primogeniture, the inability to inherit her husband's property on large estates that lingered on in Great Britain well into the twentieth century. Finally, there is the more explicit nature of the "hedges and walls and gates that lock" that directly state the way the property itself is going to affect her. And while she gushes about the beautiful gardens with their stately shade trees and grape vines—plants that were planted long ago and have existed for generations, thus symbolizing the status quo—it's significant that, "There were greenhouses, too, but they are all broken now." The greenhouses, which signify new life and a change in the status quo, are broken. Nevertheless, her unconscious seems to understand all of this at once: "There is something strange about the house—I can feel it" (5).

Eric B. Olsen

Throughout the story there are actions taken by the narrator that the rest of the characters respond to negatively. Her writing has already been shown to be one of those. Later, she expresses her uncomfortable feelings about the house to her husband one night, "but he said what I felt was a *draught*, and shut the window" (Gilman 1892, 5). The implication couldn't be clearer. Windows and doors represent freedom and opportunity but her husband, as the symbol of her oppression, is the one who closes the window. She continues by saying, "I don't like our room a bit. I wanted one downstairs that opened on the piazza and had roses all over the window, and such pretty old-fashioned chintz hangings! But John would not hear of it" (6). This extends the symbolism even further. The narrator wanted the room on the ground floor that had a door opening up to the outside. The flowers symbolize the flowering of her life—similar to the idea expressed in the *Spoon River Anthology*—and the chintz decorations are also typically festooned with floral patterns. But once again, the patriarchal directives of her husband must be obeyed and she is denied the room of her choice. The episode was one that had a parallel in Gilman's personal life. In writing *Wild Unrest* Helen Lefkowitz Horowitz was able to draw extensively from the diaries and letters of Gilman and her first husband. Shortly after getting pregnant, during a heat wave in August, "Charlotte wanted to sleep on the roof. 'I humbly ask if I can sleep there tonight, and am told "No, you cannot!" Serves me right for asking'" (Horowitz 93).

Far more subtle, however, is the context in which the narrator's discussion with her husband takes place. "I even said so to John one moonlit evening" (Gilman 1892, 5). While the meaning for light and dark symbolism is typically assumed to represent variations of good vs. evil, or innocence vs. impurity, in the vast majority of cases the symbolic use of light is equated with knowledge and understanding. In simple terms this can be seen in the root of the word enlightenment, or when a person says, "I see," to mean that they now understand something. Crude visual imagery also reinforces this idea when animated characters are shown with a light bulb over their heads to indicate they have just realized something they didn't know before. By the same token, darkness indicates ignorance or the lack of understanding. Again, the phrase "in the dark," which coveys a person's a lack of knowledge about something, reinforces this idea. But because of the specific context of Gilman's story, this symbolism is used in a slightly different way, which will become more apparent later on. Essentially, the moonlight is the light that illuminates the narrator's mind and makes things easier for her to understand. Daylight, on the other hand, represents the façade that is shown to the rest of the world and reinforces expected behaviors. This is associated with a symbolic blinding of the narrator, and is thus more difficult for her to resist.

But it's more than just the physical space of the room downstairs that is denied to her; it is her very feelings themselves. "I get unreasonably angry with John sometimes. I'm sure I never used to be so sensitive. I think it is due to this nervous condition" (Gilman 1892, 5). It is only the narrator's inability to understand the problem on a conscious level that leads her to believe her anger is unreasonable. The fact that she is more sensitive now speaks to a growing awareness—however unconscious—that something in her life is not right. Yet her ability to express her feelings and potentially uncover the source of her disquiet is denied to her by her husband. "But John says if I feel so [angry], I shall neglect proper self-control; so I take pains to control myself—before him, at least, and that makes me very tired" (5-6). The result is that she goes to great lengths to control herself "before him," acting in a way that is not natural because it is not the way she truly feels. And just as when she tries to hide her writing from him, she becomes exhausted by the deception. Whenever this occurs, as will be seen, she retreats back into feelings of guilt over being sick in the first place and then tries to rationalize her husband's behavior. "He is very careful and loving, and hardly lets me stir without special direction. I have a schedule prescription for each hour in the day; he takes all care from me, and so I feel basely ungrateful not to value it more" (6). Even her guilt is a clue to the problem, because it arises specifically from John directing her every movement during the day. But instead of understanding this oppression for what it is, which should be clear by the fact that she doesn't value it, she lapses back into rationalizing his behavior according to society's dictates.

After being forced to sleep in a different room than the one she originally wanted, her description of their actual bedroom is also telling, and alarmingly so. "So we took the nursery at the top of the house. It is a big, airy room, the whole floor nearly, with windows that look all ways, and air and sunshine galore. It was nursery first and then playground and gymnasium, I should judge; for the windows are barred for little children . . ." (Gilman 1892, 7). Rather than allowing the narrator to have the room downstairs that opens up to the outside world, her husband instead forces her upstairs into a room with bars on the windows. The insult of his action is even more egregious because she is able to see all around to the world outside and yet is forced to remain in the room like a prisoner. But the room also has another important layer of symbolic meaning in which it represents the actual mind of the narrator. In this sense the room contains all of the information she needs to understand what is wrong with her, which is reinforced by the windows that look all around to the outside world. Like the bars on the windows, however, her indoctrination and participation in the perpetuation of societal norms prevents her from grasping what her unconscious mind is trying to show her. The bedroom, then, has become the battleground of her psyche, simultaneously holding the answer to her illness as well as revealing its cause. Finally, the key to that understanding is also located within the room: the yellow wallpaper.

In Gilman's story the wallpaper symbolizes society, both its expectations and the oppression of women that result from the conformity of men and women to those expectations. In this way every single description of the paper can be read as if the narrator were literally describing the social inequities for women at the time.

> I never saw a worse paper in my life. One of those sprawling flamboyant patterns committing every artistic sin. It is dull enough to confuse the eye in following, pronounced enough to constantly irritate and provoke study, and when you follow the lame uncertain curves for a little distance they suddenly commit suicide—plunge off at outrageous angles, destroy themselves in unheard of contradictions. (Gilman 1892, 8)

Her description begins by saying the paper commits "artistic sin," in other words the things that the eye normally associates with beauty are not only completely absent, but somehow perverted. She also uses words like "confuse," "irritate," "lame," and "contradictions," all of which are readily applicable to the belief that a woman's only function is to be an appendage of her husband, and that she is somehow unworthy of being a self-actualized individual. It is a belief that is, indeed, constantly irritating and that, in attempting to thoroughly study and understand the contradictions inherent in such a belief it commits suicide in the way it reveals an utter lack of reason and sense.

"The color is repellant, almost revolting; a smouldering unclean yellow, strangely faded by the slow-turning sunlight . . . a dull yet lurid orange in some places, a sickly sulphur tint in others" (Gilman 1892, 8). Yellow has any number of negative connotations, from the mild implications of age or cowardice, to the more extreme connections with physical illness like jaundice or puss. "It is the strangest yellow, that wall-paper! It makes me think of all the yellow things I ever saw—not beautiful ones like buttercups, but old foul, bad yellow things" (39). All of this is an apt description of the nature of societal imperatives in that day for women. The reference she makes to the color suggesting something old is also a way of demonstrating the long history of these beliefs, leading the narrator to an unequivocal unconscious assessment of that entire way of life and the natural human response to such an unnatural way of living. "The paint and paper look as if a boys' school had used it. It is stripped off—the paper—in great patches all around the head of my bed, about as far as I can reach, and in a great place on the other side of the room low down . . . No wonder the children hated it! I should hate it myself if I had to live in this room long" (7-8, 9). Thus the narrator's unconscious mind understands exactly how she would feel if she consciously understood the societal impositions placed on her. But there's a further connection that can be made between this description and Edith Wharton's conceptual framework in *Ethan Frome.* Gilman's narrator makes the natural assumption that if males had been placed in a similar situation as women, "as if a boys' school had used it," that they would respond to the lack of inherent reason in that way of living by stripping off the paper from the walls, literally destroying symbolic societal dictates that make no rational sense.

The narrator's description of the room ends with her having to hide her writing—the conceit of the story is that she is writing a diary of some sort. "There comes John, and I must put this away—he hates to have me write a word" (Gilman 1892, 9). As before, the association of writing with intellect and reason makes her husband naturally antagonistic to it. But the narrator also knows and understands how important this work is to her emotional life. Like other women of her day, writing was much more than a hobby for Gilman. In discussing the early life of Margaret Fuller, the spiritual progenitor of women writers at the turn of the twentieth century, biographer Megan Marshall had this to say about her father's—and by extension, society's—expectations for her. "To her father's and her own dismay, [she] struggles through years of singing lessons, unable to shine at this one accomplishment . . . [and] Timothy [Fuller] will prod when he offers to buy her a piano. But she continues to *write every day* that she has paper and pen to hand, except in times of sickness, until she becomes a woman. And then too, when she will write of music, art, literature, politics, and travel for a nation of readers" (Marshall 6-7). For Gilman, the process quite naturally became her "work," a term that equated the life of the mind with that of sustenance and necessity. All of which made her bouts of depression that much worse when the author found herself "hopelessly despairing, at my total inability to *work*" (Horowitz 9). Again, it was Gilman's personal experience that informed this idea. Her doctor told her specifically to "have but two hours' intellectual life a day," she explained in a brief essay about writing the story, "and 'never to touch pen, brush, or pencil again' as long as I lived. I went home and obeyed those directions for some three months, and came so near the borderline of utter mental ruin that I could see over" (Gilman 1913, 271).

The male belief that intellectual exertion in women was one of the reasons for the unexplained symptoms of hysteria held sway for at least a century and, more insidiously, even convinced many women writers of its truth. This is one reason the literature by women from that period is so rich in addressing the issue, especially in the United States. Author Diane Price Herndl sees this belief by both sexes as so widespread at the time that it even caused modern feminist authors to make generalizations to that effect. "Gilbert and Gubar claim that it was the stress of making art that caused women writers' illnesses in the nineteenth century, that moving from the 'feminine' art of the body to the 'masculine' art of the pen was illness inducing" (Herndl 126-127). But Herndl sees this view as far too simplistic when trying to explain the complex variables of societal restraint that manifested in the extreme range of physical symptoms women exhibited at the time. She also notes that all three of the authors represented in this particular analysis understood that writing was psychologically beneficial rather than debilitating. "Gilman and Wharton both came to believe that writing made them feel better—Wharton had, in fact, used 'making up' stories as a kind of therapy since she had been a child. This was true of other women writers, too. Kate Chopin consciously took up writing as therapy for the depression she experienced after her husband's and mother's deaths" (127).

In the story John's sister is named Jennie, and in her association with the narrator's husband as his relative she becomes just as much a part of the oppression as Louise Mallard's sister in "The Story of an Hour." This is reinforced by the way she shares the same beliefs as John when it comes to the narrator's writing. "There comes John's sister. Such a dear girl as she is, and so careful of me! I must not let her find me writing. She is a perfect and enthusiastic housekeeper, and hopes for no better profession. I verily believe she thinks it is the writing which made me sick!" (Gilman 1892, 17-18). The narrator at first commends Jennie for her attentive nature, and consequently reinforces the guilt she has for being sick in the first place. But the description of Jennie as such an "enthusiastic housekeeper" explicitly aligns her with the status quo, especially as she "hopes for no better profession." Thus she is joined in opposition against the narrator with her brother the doctor, as she also believes that the narrator's writing is responsible for her symptoms. "I know John would think it absurd," the narrator says about her writing. "But I *must* say what I feel and think in some way—it is such a relief!" (25). This shows she understands at some level that the writing is helping her, but since she doesn't exactly know how to articulate that belief to others she has no way of arguing for what she intuitively knows to be true. The same goes for her obsession with the wallpaper, which stems from the unconscious knowledge that it holds the key to understanding her illness. "Of course I never mention it to them any more—I am too wise—but I keep watch of it all the same" (28).

The narrator's determination to speak aloud her thoughts and feelings is met with equal resistance. Of her husband she says, "I tried to have a real earnest reasonable talk with him the other day, and tell him how I wish he would let me go and make a visit to Cousin Henry and Julia. But he said I wasn't able to go, nor able to stand it after I got there; and I did not make out a very good case for myself, for I was crying before I had finished" (Gilman 1892, 25-26). Here is another aspect of male-female relationships at the time that does not get enough attention. Rather than being able to see his own behavior—both as a representative of prevailing social conventions and as an individual—as part of the reason for his wife's breakdown, John is only able to see her tears as a confirmation of his erroneous beliefs. This is reflected in his behavior toward her. "And dear John gathered me up in his arms, and just carried me upstairs and laid me on the bed, and sat by me and read to me till it tired my head" (26). In the first place his immediate reaction is to treat her like a child by carrying her upstairs and putting her to bed. But his reading to her is even more telling. The act of reading the book can be equated with the attempt to reinforce societal norms. The very physicality of the book brings with it the connotation of truth because of its concreteness, and yet just because something is in a book does not make it any more reliable that any other form of communication. In the same way, while the ubiquitous nature of society's adherence to specific behaviors argues for its truth, it is no more a guarantee of truth than a book. In fact, the extremely anti-intellectual nature of popularity itself is an indication that it cannot reflect the truth, which is demonstrated when the narrator says that her husband's reading has "tired my head."

At this point in the story the symbolic oppression becomes so overt as to be unavoidable. The narrator says, "John does not know how much I really suffer. He knows there is no *reason* to suffer, and that satisfies him" (Gilman 1892, 10). This is a pointed description of people in society who refuse to see any reason to doubt their beliefs. No less a luminary than Sir Francis Bacon recognized this tendency in human reasoning back in the seventeenth century.

> The human understanding when it has once adopted an opinion (either as being the received opinion or as being agreeable to itself) draws all things else to support and agree with it. And though there be a greater number and weight of instances to be found on the other side, yet these it either neglects and despises, or else by some distinction sets aside and rejects, in order that by this great and pernicious predetermination the authority of its former conclusions may remain inviolate. (Bacon 97)

John's inability to see beyond his own "pernicious predetermination" is once again reinforced by his behavior. At first he agrees to repaper the room, but then decides against it. "He said that I was letting it get the better of me, and that nothing was worse for a nervous patient than to give way to such fancies. He said that after the wall-paper was changed it would be the heavy bedstead, and then the barred windows, and then that gate at the head of the stairs, and so on" (11-12). In this way the oppression of women is nothing more than a "fancy," and giving in on one area would only lead to a slippery slope which would necessitate removal of the "bars" from the windows of opportunity and the "gate" that leads downstairs to the wider world. And as before, when confronted by him the narrator backs down and rationalizes away her desires. "But he is right enough about the beds and windows and things . . . I would not be so silly as to make him uncomfortable just for a whim" (12-13). Another point that Gilman addresses here is that the resistance of so many men to women's desire to change their restricted role in society was based on the belief that it was unnatural, or strange, or uncomfortable for men, none of which are rational reasons for the continuation of oppressive behavior toward half of the population.

It's not enough for the husband to simply assert power over his wife, however; he must also humiliate her in the process in order to make his argument that much more unassailable. The narrator says, "he laughs at me so about this wall-paper!" (Gilman 1892, 11). And when she urges him again that they take the bedroom downstairs he reacts in a like manner. "Then he took me in his arms and called me a blessed little goose, and said he would go down to the cellar, if I wished, and have it whitewashed into the bargain" (12). But John has no intention of doing what she wishes. His reference to her as a "blessed little goose" is a way of dehumanizing her and in doing so he is able to completely dismiss her thoughts and feelings. Worse than that is his conception of moving downstairs. Instead of the room she wanted, he suggests bypassing it all together and going down to the basement, thus replacing her tower prison with a dungeon. Whitewash, as a synonym for cover up, is particularly appropriate as well. Something similar happens one night when the narrator gets up out of bed to look at the wallpaper and her husband says, "What is it, little girl? . . . Don't go walking about like that—you'll get cold" (30). Referring to his wife as a child and ordering her about in a similar manner infantilizes her and results in the same kind of condescension as referring to her as an animal. But this is all established behavior at the time and confirmed by the narrator on the first page of the story when she says, "John laughs at me, of course, but one expects that in marriage" (1). The remark is almost chilling it its unquestioned acceptance of patriarchal dominance as it appears in marriage.

The battle between the narrator's unconscious determination to be free and her conscious desire to please her husband and conform to society's expectations is addressed when she talks about her writing again. "John has cautioned me not to give way to fancy in the least. He says that with my imaginative power and habit of story-making, a nervous weakness like mine is sure to lead to all manner of excited fancies, and that I ought to use my will and good sense to check the tendency. So I try" (Gilman 1892, 13-14). Again, there is the use of the word fancy defined as imagination, and the way in which John has tried to stop her from using her mind. This kind of warning is usually couched in such a way that it draws on the idea of the inferiority of the female mind, that the danger in letting women use their minds is they do not have the mental capacity to make sense of the things they think and therefore end up frustrated and sick as a result. In reality, the unconscious nature of this argument by men seems far more likely based on their fear that if women actually did stop to think about their lives they would of course rise up in rebellion. For Gilman's narrator the idea is connected to her work, which she addresses immediately after this. "I think sometimes that if I were only well enough to write a little it would relieve the press of ideas and rest me . . . It is so discouraging not to have any advice and companionship about my work" (14). Her own consciousness understands the importance of her work in keeping her mind active and alert, but immersed as she is within a system that doesn't make sense this awareness brings with it unintended consequences. This she makes clear in speaking about the wallpaper again.

"This paper looks to me as if it *knew* what a vicious influence it had! . . . I get positively angry with the impertinence of it and the everlastingness" (Gilman 1892, 15). In the context of a literal reading of the story, the moment when the narrator starts to personify the wallpaper can be seen as the beginning of her mental breakdown. But when the paper is instead seen as a representation of society, the "influence," "impertinence," and "everlastingness" of the patriarchal imperatives they represent are actually providing her with the opportunity to connect what she intuitively understands about the paper with the unconscious demands and expectations that society has unfairly placed on her. "The wall-paper, as I said before, is torn off in spots, and it sticketh closer than a brother—[the children] must have had perseverance as well as hatred. Then the floor is scratched and gouged and splintered, the plaster itself is dug out here and there, and this great heavy bed, which is all we found in the room, looks as if it had been through the wars" (17). That the room was once a nursery is extremely significant, as the narrator is acutely affected by the way the ideas of society are indoctrinated in succeeding generations— well before their mature conscious minds can allow them to make their own decisions. And yet the children who had been imprisoned there seem to have unconsciously understood this as well, which accounts for their attempt to strip the paper off the walls. For the narrator, however, the idea is even more personal for the fact that she has just had a child herself. "It is fortunate Mary is so good with the baby. Such a dear baby! And yet I *cannot* be with him, it makes me so nervous" (11). The reason the child makes the narrator nervous is that he is a male and as such he will eventually grow up to take his father's place in the perpetuation of female oppression, all of which continues to be represented by the wallpaper. "There's one comfort, the baby is well and happy, and does not have to occupy this nursery with the horrid wall-paper. If we had not used it, that blessed child would have! What a fortunate escape! Why, I wouldn't have a child of mine, an impressionable little thing, live in such a room for worlds" (27). The problem for the narrator is that she doesn't understand the symbolic nature of her feelings and the way they represent her actual life.

Further personification of the wallpaper begins to take on ominous tones. At first it is the shapes themselves, which suggest female oppression in stark relief. "There is a recurrent spot where the pattern lolls like a broken neck and two bulbous eyes stare at you upside down" (Gilman 1892, 15). Before long, however, the narrator begins to sense that there is something more to the pattern than these evocative shapes. "This wall-paper has a kind of sub-pattern in a different shade, a particularly irritating one, for you can only see it in certain lights, and not clearly then. But in the places where it isn't faded and where the sun is just so—I can see a strange, provoking, formless sort of figure, that seems to sulk about behind that silly and conspicuous front design" (18-19). Ironically, the beginning of her dissociation with reality in the literal story, her obsession with the wallpaper, is a way for her to consciously understand all of her problems. Her unconscious mind senses the disconnection between the everyday experience of the life she has always lived and the actual reality of that life, something she feels but can't put a name to. This is the meaning of the two patterns. The outer pattern is the one that doesn't make sense, the day-to-day existence of women as they become subsumed in the never-ending tasks that they have been saddled with—something the narrator describes as "silly and conspicuous." But underneath, in the place where reality waits to enlighten the narrator, is the skulking figure that is only visible under certain conditions. In another literary parallel, Professor Michael Krasny had this to say about the main characters in Chekov's story "The Lady and the Dog."

> It's also a story about secret lives, Gurov's realization that there is a life underneath the one that we live. Within the mundane, the quotidian, that exists on the outside, there's a hidden real life that's authentic and it's concealed. And ironically, Anna tells her husband—when they're having

the affair and they're separated from Yalta—that she has to travel to Moscow because of a female disorder. It's a wonderfully apt metaphor for what drives her secret life. (Krasny)

This "female disorder" metaphor is also similar to Chopin's "heart trouble," where the physiological illness is simply a euphemism for an emotional one. The problem for the narrator in Gilman's story is that she is unable to consciously understand this division, and will struggle throughout to make sense of what the wallpaper is trying to tell her.

One of the absolutely inspiring elements of the story—despite its traumatic subject matter—is the way that Charlotte Perkins Gilman singles out a real doctor by name for his suspect methods. "John says if I don't pick up faster he shall send me to Weir Mitchell in the fall. But I don't want to go there at all. I had a friend who was in his hands once, and she says he is just like John and my brother, only more so!" (Gilman 1892, 20). Mitchell is the Philadelphia physician who developed the idea of what amounted to sensory depravation in his "rest cure" for women suffering from hysteria, and of course the friend of the narrator is none other than the author herself. But the idea for his treatment was based on a complete misunderstanding of the malady. In the story the narrator states, "I don't feel as if it was worth while to turn my hand over for anything, and I'm getting dreadfully fretful and querulous. I cry at nothing, and cry most of the time" (20-21). To doctors this appeared to be a simple case of overstimulation, that there was too much activity in the lives of these women—and there was, just not the right kind—and as a result they felt that these women would benefit from getting away from everything in order to rest. But this diagnosis was wrong on three points. In the first place the physical symptoms that occurred were more akin to cabin fever than overstimulation. Being trapped in a world of someone else's devising, and unable to comprehend why they were miserable, simply made women more nervous. They didn't need rest; they needed escape. Which feeds into the second misconception. By eliminating their work during this rest cure, women became overwhelmed by a sense of guilt at not living up to their responsibilities as wives and mothers. Finally, with no one to talk to about what they were feeling there was no possibility that they would be able to improve, all of which accounts for why Mitchell's cure was such a dismal failure.

The enforced infantilization, the absence of all intellectual nourishment or stimulation, the utter boredom, the attempts to suppress their own individuality were a source of horror and wretchedness, vividly represented in Gilman's short story "The Yellow Wallpaper," a literary document that ensured that Weir Mitchell's name would reverberate in feminist circles in our own century as the epitome of the brusque, misogynist, paternalistic Victorian nerve doctor. (Scull 102-103)

One of Gilman's special gifts in writing this story is the way in which she was able to convey a distinct sense of the two patterns in the wallpaper that is matched by her actual narrative. The outer pattern is paralleled by the literal story in which the narrator's obsession with the wallpaper looks for all intents and purposes like mental illness. "I'm getting really fond of the room in spite of the wall-paper. Perhaps *because* of the wall-paper. It dwells in my mind so!" (Gilman 1892, 21-22). The reader's initial response to this is obviously one of concern. But what at first seems like a kind of Stockholm syndrome, with the hated wallpaper now becoming the reason behind her fondness for the room, is actually quite purposeful. As stated earlier, the wallpaper holds the answer to all of the narrator's mental problems. Specifically, the symbolism of the wallpaper is the key to the narrator's understanding. If she can figure out the message the paper is telling her on a metaphorical level, she will have the opportunity to grasp on a conscious intellectual level what she is actually feeling and why.

> I lie here on this great immovable bed—it is nailed down, I believe—and follow that pattern about by the hour. It is as good as gymnastics, I assure you. I start, we'll say, at the bottom, down in the corner over there where it has not been touched, and I determine for the thousandth time that I *will* follow that pointless pattern to some sort of a conclusion. (22)

The inner pattern then, the conclusion she is looking for, is the answer to her emotional struggle, and in that context her obsession with the paper is not so much a sign of metal illness as it is an unconscious realization of exactly what she must do in order to get well again. Almost unnoticed in all of this is the symbolism of the bed nailed to the floor. Like Chopin's protagonist uttering the phrase, "body and soul free," the bed here is a symbol of sexual obligation in marriage and the fact that it is nailed to the floor further symbolizes its resistance to change. "The women's movement objected to the concept of what were known as men's marital rights. That a husband had an unlimited right under law to sexual intercourse with his wife was a source of disquiet among women, surfacing early in the women's rights movement" (Horowitz 87).

It's also here where the symbolic play of light and dark begin to reveal their true meaning. One night the narrator makes another attempt to talk to her husband about her feelings. "It was moonlight. The moon shines in all around just as the sun does. I hate to see it sometimes, it creeps so slowly, and always comes in by one window or another. John was asleep and I hated to waken him, so I kept still and watched the moonlight on that undulating wall-paper till I felt creepy" (Gilman 1892, 29). In addition to the two separate patterns the narrator detects, there is the influence of light that also serves to highlight or conceal those aspects of the paper. First there is the sunlight that is associated with the outer pattern, something that doesn't make any sense to the narrator during the daytime. These are the expectations of society that, in the light of day, are regularly adhered to. People go about their business at work or play, in the company of others, conforming openly to the only kind of society they've ever known. When the sun goes down, however, and people are alone with their thoughts, this is when the sub-pattern becomes visible. There is just enough enlightenment, without the interference from anyone or anything else—represented by the blinding omnipresence of the sunlight—to make the connection. A similar effect is seen in "The Story of an Hour" to explain why when Louise Mallard goes up to her room she insists on being alone.

The truth that the moonlight reveals about the inner pattern is also something the narrator initially dislikes. She hates to see it, and it makes her feel creepy. Again, this is similar to the way Louise Mallard initially feared the freedom that was coming to her from the blue sky. But just as in Chopin's story, for Gilman's narrator the truth of the inner pattern of the paper must also come in through the windows of her bedroom. Because the inner pattern of the wallpaper is where the truth lies it is only in the moonlight, alone or with her husband asleep, that she can begin to understand what the paper is trying to tell her. "The faint figure behind seemed to shake the pattern, just as if she wanted to get out" (Gilman 1892, 29). The frustration for the reader comes from the fact that while the narrator is increasingly able to articulate the difference between the two patterns of the literal wallpaper, she is still maddeningly uncomprehending about the way it symbolizes her real life.

> There is one marked peculiarity about this paper, a thing nobody seems to notice but myself, and that is that it changes as the light changes . . . On a pattern like this, by daylight, there is a lack of sequence, a defiance of law, that is a constant irritant to a normal mind . . . It is like a bad dream . . . By moonlight—the moon shines in all night when there is a moon—I wouldn't know it was the same paper. At night in any kind of light, in twilight, candlelight, lamplight, and worst of all by moonlight, it becomes bars! The outside pattern, I mean, and the woman behind it is as plain as can be. (33, 34)

In this way the daily existence of people operating in concert with the assumptions of male patriarchy makes no logical sense and constitute, "a defiance of law." Once again, this is similar to Louise Mallard's belief that the blind adherence to this behavior made it "no less a crime." Gilman's narrator then likens it to a "bad dream." By moonlight, however, the reality becomes clear: there is a woman behind the pattern, and the societal expectations of the daylight can clearly be seen as the bars of her imprisonment.

There's also an unfortunate irony that reveals itself at this point in the narrative. Because the narrator has been hiding her writing and her emotions from her husband, he begins to think she is actually improving. When she tries to tell him that she wants to leave the house and go away, he says, "Of course if you were in any danger, I could and would, but you really are better, dear, whether you can see it or not. I am a doctor, dear, and I know" (Gilman 1892, 30). The condescension is thick as he essentially tells her that he knows better than she does what she really needs. And then, as if to reinforce his belief, he says, "But now let's improve the shining hours by going to sleep, and talk about it in the morning!" (31). The "shining hours," of course, means the daylight, when society is at its most powerful in making the doubts of the nighttime seem unreasonable. "Really, dear," he says, "you are better!" To which she replies, "Better in body perhaps—" At this, her husband becomes genuinely alarmed. "He sat up straight and looked at me with such a stern, reproachful look that I could not say another word" (31-32). As a physician, her husband is used to dealing with specific physical symptoms, but in matters of mental illness—which he doesn't comprehend her condition to be—his skills become irrelevant. And worse, with no "cure" for insanity the prognosis is a grim one. "There is nothing so dangerous, so fascinating," he says "to a temperament like yours. It is a false and foolish fancy. Can you not trust me as a physician when I tell you so?" (32). Of course she agrees with him for the moment, but still refuses to go to sleep. The symbolism here is important, too. Sleep signifies the unconsciousness of her husband's behaviors and beliefs, and in the context of the story it is the opposite of her highly conscious attempt to figure out what the real cause of her illness is by staying awake to examine the wallpaper.

Another dichotomy occurs when the narrator seems to fall completely under the sway of her delusions. But the devastating effect on the reader of her obsession in the literal story is counterbalanced by a sense of exquisite suspense as she approaches ever nearer to understanding what she is really seeing. "The fact is I am getting a little afraid of John" (Gilman 1892, 35). Her paranoia here is parallel to the negative feelings she has around her baby; as males they are both the active and passive agents in perpetuating male dominance in society. Therefore the closer she comes to discovering the true meaning of the paper, the more she suspects those who are directly associated with its symbolism. "I have watched John when he did not know I was looking, and come into the room suddenly on the most innocent excuses, and I've caught him several times *looking at the paper*! And Jennie too. I caught Jennie with her hand on it once" (36). Where her husband is essentially oblivious to the stultifying effects of society's dictates because he benefits from them, it's interesting to see the sister contemplating the paper. But like the sister in "The Story of an Hour" she is much further away from understanding its significance and thus she becomes identified more with the husband than the narrator.

> She didn't know I was in the room, and when I asked her in a quiet, a very quiet voice, with the most restrained manner possible, what she was doing with the paper—she turned around as if she had been caught stealing, and looked quite angry—asked me why I should frighten her so! . . . Did not that sound innocent? But I know she was studying that pattern, and I am determined that nobody shall find it out but myself! (36-37)

This mental determination, in the guise of obsession, is actually the narrator's path to recovery, and as she comes ever closer to that revelation her drive to understand it can be seen as salvation rather than dissipation. As a result, she can't allow herself to be taken away from the wallpaper yet. "I don't want to leave now until I have found it out. There is a week more, and I think that will be enough" (38).

At this point the narrator finally realizes that the key to understanding the negative feelings she has been having for so long are to be found in the wallpaper. The task now is to be able to decipher the message that it has to tell her. The first clue is the difference between daylight and dark, especially the way that the expectations of society are so much stronger during the day. "I'm feeling ever so much better! I don't sleep much at night, for it is so interesting to watch developments; but I sleep a good deal in the daytime. In the daytime it is tiresome and perplexing" (Gilman 1892, 39). Because of the way that most people behave during the day, it is almost impossible to figure out what is wrong during that time. So the narrator concentrates on what she can learn during the night. Her next discovery is that the influence of the paper is not confined to their room, but can roam about at will with a volition that would be necessary for it to be able to touch the lives of every person in society. The symbolism for this is the smell. "But there is something else about that paper— the smell! . . . It creeps all over the house. I find it hovering in the dining-room, skulking in the parlor, hiding in the hall, lying in wait for me on the stairs" (39-40). It is only her heightened sensitivity to the message imparted by the paper—in symbolic terms the repression of women by society—that allows her to sense this, whereas most people are unable to detect it at all. "It is not bad—at first—and very gentle, but quite the subtlest, most enduring odor I ever met" (40). Because patriarchy was so ingrained in society, and absorbed at such an early age, it seemed normal, almost pleasant at first. But by this time in the story the two adjectives Gilman uses to describe the smell, subtle and enduring, only make sense in symbolic terms. It is, in fact, the very subtlety of societal expectations, as well as their unquestioned good, that accounts for their ability to endure for so long.

And yet the symbolic connection of the paper to her real life continues to elude the narrator, no matter how close she gets. "I really have discovered something at last. Through watching so much at night, when it changes so, I have finally found out.

> The front pattern *does* move—and no wonder! The woman behind shakes it! Sometimes I think there are a great many women behind, and sometimes only one, and she crawls around fast, and her crawling shakes it all over. Then in the very bright spots she keeps still, and in the very shady spots she just takes hold of the bars and shakes them hard. And she is all the time trying to climb through. But nobody could climb through that pattern—it strangles so; I think that is why it has so many heads. (Gilman 1892, 42-43)

There's a tantalizing sense of the possible in this description. From the narrator's perspective she realizes that an impact can be made on the outer pattern, but it will no doubt take the effort of "a great many women" rather than just one. During the day, in the bright spots, it is more difficult because that's when society's dictates have their strongest hold on people. It is only in the shady spots that the symbolic meaning becomes perfectly clear.

Just as Louise Mallard in Kate Chopin's story came to her realization completely within her own mind, the same thing must happen for the narrator in Gilman's story, and by extension all other women. It is the intellectual understanding of what their lives are truly like that must happen first, before they can band together and make substantive changes in those lives. Maddeningly, the narrator seems to understand—on a strictly literal level— the importance of the female mind in comprehending the subtle subjugation that women have unwittingly participated in, and how that is the real cause of the physical manifestations that had been labeled as hysteria. And yet even when women do come to understand their plight, society is always at the ready to subvert their efforts. "They get through, and then the pattern strangles them off and turns them upside down, and makes their eyes white! If those heads were covered or taken off it would not be half so bad" (Gilman 1892, 43). The covering of the head, not to mention its complete removal, is symbolic of the lack of intellect necessary to allow a person to willingly submit to their own oppression. The irony, once again, is evident, as males continually argued that women made themselves miserable by thinking. Which was true, but that was only because in thinking through the reality of their position they came to realize how little sense it made for them to participate in an inherently unfair social construct. Their misery actually came from the equally powerful realization of their own inability to do anything to change it.

The next section of the story deals with the apparent paradox of the daylight. "I think that woman gets out in the daytime!" (Gilman 1892, 44). This is a crucial point that Gilman addresses. How does one mount an effective protest against imprisonment, when women aren't literally imprisoned? One of the challenges in attempting to convey the oppression felt by women is that many women had an undeniable freedom of movement while their husbands were at work. Along with that freedom, though, was the sense that they had an obligation to put on a brave face for people they interacted with during the day. In identifying the woman she sees outside, the narrator says, "I can see her out of every one of my windows!" (44). The true meaning behind this line, in which the woman she sees is apparently free, comes from the fact that the narrator's windows are barred. In this way the freedom and opportunity associated with the windows is not freedom at all, but simply the illusion of freedom. All of this is reinforced when she says, "It is the same woman, I know, for she is always creeping, and most women do not creep by daylight . . . I see her on that long road under the trees, creeping along, and when a carriage comes she hides under the blackberry vines. I don't blame her a bit. It must be very humiliating to be caught creeping by daylight!" (44). Gilman's reference to creeping here is an acknowledgement of the position of submission that women are forced into. They are certainly not going to complain about it and go against the majority opinion during the daylight hours because it would only bring immediate resistance, along with implications that something is wrong with the woman who does this. And so those feelings must be repressed, symbolized by the creeping woman hiding from the sight of others, inwardly embarrassed by the role in society she has been forced to assume.

The phenomenon of the creeping woman outside also suggests another way of looking at the narrator's specific situation. Louise Mallard, as was mentioned earlier, experienced fear at the thought of the freedom that is symbolized by the outside world. "There was something coming to her and she was waiting for it, fearfully. What was it? She did not know; it was too subtle and elusive to name. But she felt it, creeping out of the sky, reaching toward her . . ." (Chopin 1894). Gilman's narrator makes a similarly incongruous statement about the wallpaper when she says, "I'm getting really fond of the room in spite of the wallpaper. Perhaps *because* of the wallpaper. It dwells in my mind so!" (Gilman 1892, 21-22). In both of these scenes the success of societal indoctrination is evident. While women unconsciously chafed at being forced into a specific role by society, there was sometimes an even stronger conscious fear of moving into a world that they had been left utterly unprepared to operate within. Edith Wharton biographer Cynthia Griffin Wolff makes this point in looking at the psychological underpinnings of the author when it came to the position the house played in her life as an adolescent. "The implications of independence were apparently more frightening than the consequences of submission: the beast who embodied her fears stalked her only when she was outside, and her dreadful anxieties could only be relieved by reentering [the] house" (Wolff 169). So while there are forces at work compelling the narrator to understand the significance of the wallpaper as a way to free her mind, there are equally powerful societal forces working to suppress those very same ideas.

The sense of the narrator's inability to comprehend what the paper is telling her is also found in this scene. She speaks of the way that the woman in the paper who has escaped during the daylight is too fast for her to really see in full. "I often wonder if I could see her out of all the windows at once. But, turn as fast as I can, I can only see her out of one at a time. And though I always see her, she *may* be able to creep faster than I can turn! I have watched her sometimes away off in the open country, creeping as fast as a cloud shadow in a high wind" (Gilman 1892, 45). A disappointment on the part of the reader is inevitable at this point in the story. Were the narrator able to see the woman through all of the windows at once it would allow her to understand the symbolism of why she is creeping along rather than walking upright. The fact that she can only see the woman out of one window at a time means that the narrator is never going to understand the extent to which she has been oppressed and therefore will never make the connection between the symbols in the wallpaper and her own life. The fact that the woman can creep as fast as a cloud's shadow is testament to the extraordinary ability of all women to function under such oppression. But in the same way that the narrator's decision to hide her writing from her husband makes him think she's improving, the fact that women were able to function so well within the confines of societal expectations actually limited the ability of men to discern the severity of the imposition on them. Therefore it is only the nighttime, when the outer pattern of the paper fades away, that is left to the narrator to uncover the true nature of her plight. "And John is so queer now, that I don't want to irritate him. I wish he would take another room! Besides, I don't want anybody to get that woman out at night but myself" (45). Here she seems to intuitively understand everything she needs: that only in the darkness does the true nature of the paper become apparent, and that it is her responsibility to figure out how that symbolizes her actual oppression.

The narrator's unconscious understanding of how the daylight attitudes of people prevent them from seeing the consequences of their behavior is demonstrated when she says, "If only that top pattern could be gotten off from the under one! I mean to try it, little by little" (Gilman 1892, 46). And yet the problem remains that the narrator is able to see the paper only at the literal level. She has not been able to move beyond the actual pattern of the paper itself and understand the symbolic message that it is telling her. This is going to provoke a crisis in her mind that must be resolved if she is going to have any peace. Her mind can only allow this cognitive dissonance to go on for so long before it must step in and resolve the crisis for her if she does not begin moving toward a figurative understanding of the wallpaper. "There are only two more days to get this paper off, and I believe John is beginning to notice. I don't like the look in his eyes . . . He asked me all sorts of questions, too, and pretended to be very loving and kind. As if I couldn't see through him!" (46-47). At first this seems entirely in keeping with the mental illness she is suffering in a literal reading of the story, as her paranoia toward her husband increases. But when seen in conjunction with what she unconsciously understands about the wallpaper it makes perfect sense. Her husband's behaviors are not really benevolent but harmful to her, and she is beginning to understand that now. "Still, I don't wonder he acts so, sleeping under this paper for three months. It only interests me, but I feel sure John and Jennie are secretly affected by it" (47). So there it is, if she could only understand it. It is not her husband and his sister, specifically, who are the guilty parties here, but merely the way that they represent society. Ultimately, they have been as victimized by the influence of what the paper symbolizes as anyone else. It's the same point Chopin makes through the mild and loving behavior of the husband in "The Story of an Hour." Gilman reinforces this further through her use of the name John for the narrator's husband, the most generic of male names to suggest that it is not John specifically who is at fault, but the patriarchal social order.

The narrator's true cognitive break comes next, as she cannot get past the literal paper to discover its symbolic meaning and as a last resort she begins physically removing it from the wall one night. "As soon as it was moonlight and that poor thing began to crawl and shake the pattern, I got up and ran to help her. I pulled and she shook, I shook and she pulled, and before morning we had peeled off yards of that paper" (Gilman 1892, 48). But along with the daylight comes interaction with society in the form of other people, which is also reflected by the paper. "And then when the sun came and that awful pattern began to laugh at me, I declared I would finish it to-day!" (48-49). This personification speaks to how deeply rooted and permanent gender roles in society seem, so much so that the idea they can be changed would be laughed at by society. Though it seems there is even hope for Jennie when she comes into the room and sees what the narrator has done. "Jennie looked at the wall in amazement, but I told her merrily that I did it out of pure spite at the vicious thing. She laughed and said she wouldn't mind doing it herself, but I must not get tired. How she betrayed herself that time!" (49). Even the narrator's unconscious understanding is beginning to fail her now that her mind has given up attempting to decipher the symbolic message of the paper. Jennie's statement that she "wouldn't mind doing it herself," is a sign that she also unconsciously recognizes the symbolic meaning in the paper. But the narrator sees her lack of complete understanding as a betrayal, even though she has yet to fully understand it herself.

Once the furniture has been removed from the room in preparation for the family's departure, the narrator rushes Jennie out of the room and locks the door. "So now she is gone, and the servants are gone, and the things are gone, and there is nothing left but that great bedstead nailed down, with the canvas mattress we found on it." (Gilman 1892, 50). Though everything else has been removed, the bed, a permanent symbol of the oppression of marriage, remains. And as if the children instinctively understood this as well, she states, "How those children did tear about here! This bedstead is fairly gnawed!" (50). Even so, she comes excruciatingly close to figuring things out, but is only able to continue to act literally by trying to remove all of the wallpaper when she should be acting symbolically. "I forgot I could not reach far without anything to stand on! This bed will *not* move! I tried to lift and push it until I was lame, and then I got so angry I bit off a little piece at one corner" (51). Thus society's dictates prevent her from accomplishing her goal, and this inability will lead to more drastic measures. "I've got a rope up here that even Jennie did not find. If that woman does get out, and tries to get away, I can tie her!" (51). The apparent paradox of this statement actually makes sense in two ways. First, the symbolic woman behind the pattern cannot be allowed to escape because the narrator comprehends that somehow she is the key to curing her illness. As such, she can't let her get away until she fully understands what she represents. On another level, however, it simply reflects the unconscious and unwitting participation of women in their own subjugation.

The fact that the narrator will never be able to achieve complete understanding is demonstrated by her own continued inability to break free of society's conventions in her own mind. "I am getting angry enough to do something desperate. To jump out of the window would be admirable exercise, but the bars are too strong even to try" (Gilman 1892, 52). In contemplating this act she does see a way to end the oppression, as Louise Mallard did unconsciously, by killing herself. Society, however, in the form of the bars, will not allow it. More significantly, however, is that even had the bars not been there she would not have allowed herself to try. "Besides, I wouldn't do it. Of course not. I know well enough that a step like that is improper and might be misconstrued" (52). Gilman is magnificent in her ability to demonstrate the insidious nature of societal expectations in the way that they not only manifest themselves in those who benefit by them, but in those who must suffer. And she reinforces this idea in the next sentence. "I don't like to *look* out of the windows even—there are so many of those creeping women, and they creep so fast. I wonder if they all come out of that wall-paper as I did?" (52). By now her frustration with the inability to understand the symbolic content of the paper is complete. In refusing to look out of the windows she eliminates the frustrations that the windows represent: not only the opportunities that she will never have in this society, symbolized by the bars, but the grim reality for women who must continue to submit to patriarchal authority, symbolized by the creeping women. Yet at the same time the reader is equally frustrated, as the narrator has all but completely solved the problem by counting herself among those women who have been trapped by the pattern of the paper. Unfortunately, the symbolic nature of that entrapment still escapes her and she continues to focus on the literal paper rather than its underlying meaning. Thus she uses the rope to tie herself, now completely identifying with the literal figure in the wallpaper. "But I am securely fastened now by my well-hidden rope—you don't get *me* out in the road there! I suppose I shall have to get back behind the pattern when it comes night, and that is hard!" (52-53).

This idea, that women's unconscious acceptance of the status quo is as much to blame as its unconscious perpetuation by men, is reflected in the final passage of Gilman's poem "In Duty Bound," in which she equates the behavior of women with the posture of stooping—in both its literal and figurative sense.

The high ideals of the grand and pure
  Die, as of course they must
  Of long disuse and rust.

That is the worst. It takes supernal strength
  To hold the attitude that brings the pain;
And there are few indeed but stoop at length
  To something less than best,
  To find, in stooping, rest. (Gilman 1884, 30)

Gilman's poem, like her story, recognizes that women must first comprehend the possibilities that have been denied to them, the "ideals of the grand and pure," before they will be able to understand that those ideals must necessarily die in an environment in which they have been suppressed. Significantly, she says, "That is the worst." The stooping that women do, not only in the attitude of submission they take on but, with incredible insight by Gilman, also meaning behavior that is beneath their dignity, "takes supernal [supernatural] strength" to maintain, to remain in the very secondary position in society that "brings the pain." Her final declaration is how few women truly understand what they have given up in order to conform to the dictates of societal conventions, and that by stooping they are only able to achieve something that is "less than best." Finally, the foundation upon which everything in "The Yellow Wall-Paper" is built, the idea that conforming to society is the easier path than resistance and the consequences it brings, and because of that, unintentionally equating in the minds of women the supernatural effort of stooping with "rest."

Gilman's narrator does finally realize that she is the woman behind the pattern, the woman behind the bars, but she has been unable to grasp the symbolic nature of that imprisonment, and thus her mind has finally given her a way of escaping from her mental quagmire by allowing her to fully identify with the paper on a literal level. "It is so pleasant to be out in this great room and creep around as I please! I don't want to go outside. I won't, even if Jennie asks me to" (Gilman 1892, 53). When her husband returns home and finds the door locked he pleads with her to open it—similar to the scene in "The Story of an Hour." "Why there's John at the door! It is no use, young man, you can't open it!" (53). The significance here is that her husband is every bit as unable to change society as she is, especially when both of them are equally unconscious about what must be done. She tells him she has thrown the key out the window and that it is somewhere near the front door. "Then he said—very quietly indeed, 'Open the door, my darling!' 'I can't,' said I. 'The key is down by the front door under a plantain leaf!'" (54). The narrator here recognizes that she no longer has the power to unlock the symbolism that can set her free physically. So because she was unable to understand that symbolism on a conscious level, her mind allowed her to escape by going inward. Rather than continuing the passive submission to society undertaken by most women, the narrator understands that this is impossible for her. Like Louise Mallard, she can't go back. Unlike that character's physical death, however, the narrator here undergoes the death of her mind.

> "I've got out at last," said I, "in spite of you and Jane! And I've pulled off most of the paper, so you can't put me back!" Now why should that man have fainted? But he did, and right across my path by the wall, so that I had to creep over him every time! (55)

The conclusion to the story is a fascinating one, especially in the sudden appearance of the name Jane. By identifying so completely with the woman in the wallpaper, the narrator seems to be referring to herself by name in the third person, the person who represents her old identity as Jane. In doing this she not only condemns John for his adherence to societal norms, but herself as well. Of course it's highly probable that the name is simply a misprint for Jennie, as most critics over the last hundred years have suggested. But the idea that the narrator now recognizes her former self as an entirely separate entity who, along with her husband John, is equally responsible for the perpetuation of the oppressive behaviors of a patriarchal society makes for a far more satisfying ending. Not only does it allow the narrator to be free from her own repressed intellect, but it allows her to achieve in a literal sense what her intellect was unable to. That literal victory, regardless of the horrific cost, is finally symbolized in the way she repeatedly crawls over the unconscious body of her husband.

Of course Gilman was able to fight her way out of her own illness by understanding that her need to write, or work as she called it, was essential to her survival, defying the prescription of Weir Mitchell and doing instead what she intuitively knew to be right for her. "Using the remnants of intelligence that remained, and helped by a wise friend, I cast the noted specialist's advice to the winds and went to work again—work, the normal life of every human being; work, in which is joy and growth and service, without which one is a pauper and a parasite—ultimately recovering some measure of power" (Gilman 1913, 271). As such, the story became a cautionary tale for the author rather than a strict recounting of her experience: "I never had hallucinations or objections to my mural decorations." She claimed she sent a copy of the story to Mitchell but never heard back from him, and then recounted sometime later,

Eric B. Olsen

"that the great specialist had admitted to friends of his that he had altered his treatment of neurasthenia since reading 'The Yellow Wallpaper.' It was not intended to drive people crazy, but to save people from being driven crazy, and it worked." Though Mitchell's reaction to her story, if there was one, has never been documented, for Gilman the mere suggestion that he had was the final validation she had always believed was due her, a validation that was denied to the narrator in her story.

While there's a case to be made that Gilman had no idea of the larger symbolism inherent in her wallpaper, and that the prison-like existence of the symbolic woman within the paper was only meant to refer to her medical treatment, it's not a very convincing one. Her entire adult life prior to writing the story had been lived in the bitter conflict between the desire for a relationship with a man and the attendant loss of self that would necessarily entail. Even the poetry she was writing just before turning her hand to this story attests to that fact. "You are a fool—" says the man to the woman in her poem entitled "The Quarrel," "I mean an angel! Here, go back! You're a slave—I mean a queen! . . . It is absolutely impossible for you to get out from behind; and therefore I will fight till I die to keep you behind." (Horowitz 167). And in a speech she gave at a public meeting in Pasadena a year before writing the story, she said about the social limitations put on women, "In the subtlest and most civilized form we suffer under it in those delicate but rigid conventions of society which hamper and confine our daily lives and crush out all happy human intercourse between men and women . . ." (172). She may have begun the story with the sole intention of exposing the ineffectiveness of the rest cure for women suffering from depression, but it's difficult to believe that she was entirely unaware of the larger implications of her narrative.

This understanding of the symbolic meaning in Gilman's story can also be seen in some contemporary reviews. One of the many myths surrounding "The Yellow Wall-Paper" is that audiences of the day believed it was simply the story of a woman gone mad, or that the woman behind the pattern was somehow real, making the story a supernatural one in the tradition of Poe. And to be fair, many readers understood the story in exactly that way. But Julie Bates Dock argues convincingly against this and other myths surrounding the tale. "Contemporary reviews demonstrate that the story's first readers did recognize its indictments of marriage and of the treatment of women, even if they did not label them with modern terms like 'sexual politics' . . . We flatter ourselves if we think we are the first to apprehend Gilman's 'polemical intent' or her commentary on the sexual politics of marriage in the nineteenth century" (Dock 19). To be sure, the vast majority of these reviewers really were unable to grasp the underlying meaning of the story, but those who did were incredibly insightful. Most of the initial reviews came on the occasion of the story's first reprint, in book form, from the publisher Small, Maynard & Co. in 1899. Henry B. Blackwell, writing in *The Woman's Journal*, said, "This is a most striking and impressive study of morbid psychology, in the shape of a story. A woman goes insane through the effort of her husband, a well-meaning physician, to cure her of a 'temporary nervous depression' . . . by keeping her confined in a quiet house" (Dock 107). The suggestion that it is the husband's fault for the narrator's worsening condition is even more pointed in an unattributed review in the *Newport Daily News*. "Those familiar with Mrs. [Gilman's] work know that she writes nothing meaningless, and guess that the author would rejoice if her lifting the surface from one woman's subdermal process of thought should illuminate for some other blundering, well-intentioned male murderer the affect of a persistent aversion upon knotted and jangled nerves" (111-112).

Most reviewers, however, tended to see the story as an anomaly, something quite apart from Gilman's other writings. Anne Montgomerie, in *The Conservator*, is representative of this view. "It is in style quite different from what may be considered her customary and contemporary, or in a sense even her most serious, mood . . ." (Dock 104). And yet there is an undeniable irony as Montgomerie goes on to articulate the specific ways in which she sees the story as a departure from Gilman's other writings. "It is almost uncanny to come upon Mrs. [Gilman] in the act of making literature of this sort—she is so interested, heart and soul, in such other things as women's economic status, and so identified with the philosophic assertion of sex independence." The irony is that this is precisely the subject matter of "The Yellow Wall-Paper." But while Montgomerie may have missed that fact, she must be commended as the only reviewer of her day to grasp the symbolic nature of the wallpaper, even if she didn't understand its precise meaning. "It is a condition, not a wall paper, of course. Anything would have served her fancy," she says about the narrator. "If she had not referred her malady to that yellow wall paper it would have attached itself to some other phenomenon." But the most prescient comment comes, finally, from Henry Blackwell, and his observation about Gilman's story tenuously connects it to *Ethan Frome*, which wouldn't be publish for another dozen years.

> Nothing more graphic and suggestive has ever been written to show why so many women go crazy, especially farmers' wives, who live lonely, monotonous lives. A husband of the kind described in this little sketch once said that he could not account for his wife's having gone insane— "for," said he, "to my certain knowledge she has hardly left her kitchen and bedroom in 30 years." (Dock 107).

Both "The Story of an Hour" and "The Yellow Wall-Paper" are very complimentary in the way they are able to critically address specific aspects of societal expectations for woman, while at the same time symbolically condemning the entire notion of female subjugation in marriage and society in general. Each of these stories also provides a way for the text to be read literally and allow unsophisticated readers the ability to reinforce their unconscious bias. In Chopin's story the protagonist dies at the conclusion, seemingly punished for gleefully hoping to capitalize on the death of her husband and embracing her newfound freedom, but in reality her death resulted from a refusal to once again submit to the repression that had informed her entire married life. In Gilman's story the narrator goes insane, seemingly punished for not appreciating the love and care of her husband, but in reality escaping the repression in her marriage by retreating inwardly in her mind. What these two stories also do is provide a more accurate way to read Edith Wharton's *Ethan Frome*, by examining how women writers at the turn of the twentieth century were able to smuggle ideas into their work through the use of symbolism. As stated earlier, R. Baird Shuman's contention that "There is probably no more pervasive single element in *Ethan Frome* than the symbolism" means that a precise understanding of that symbolism is crucial because of the isolated nature of Wharton's narrative (Shuman 90). Her characters have only limited interaction with society, and so she is left to demonstrate the insidious nature of societal expectations in the way that those expectations have been thoroughly absorbed by her characters and thus inform their inner lives as well as their actions.

Edith Wharton's
ETHAN FROME

Wharton's work, especially when it comes in period camouflage, is not always as it first seems.

—Laura Rattray
Edith Wharton in Context

One of the frequent comments made about *Ethan Frome* is how different the lives of the characters in the novel are from the life of the author. The hardscrabble existence of her rural New England farmer and his wife at first seems miles away from the upper class urban atmosphere in which Edith Wharton spent her own life. And yet it is also evident from Wharton's fiction she was well aware that the strictures placed on women by a patriarchal society made no concession to class or privilege. While poor and working class women may have dealt with different issues—namely physical and sexual abuse, as well as economic privation—their wealthy counterparts were not immune from an oppression that was more psychological in nature. Author Dale M. Bauer states quite emphatically this fundamental truth as Wharton understood it: "that women under capitalist patriarchy form an oppressed class on their own, regardless of the class they enter upon marriage" (Bauer 1994, 100).

Richard Ruland and Malcolm Bradbury make a similar point in their history of American literature when looking at the wider context of Wharton's social criticism and her attempt to point out the devastating effect that societal expectations had on women.

The tragedy [in her works] came from her sense of social and sexual imprisonment and her fundamental awareness of the discrepancy between civilization and the harsh economic laws on which its privileges were founded. Her own society marriage was unhappy; she was disquieted not only by the direction American society was taking but by her own role as commodity and sexual victim within it. (Ruland 245)

Author Elizabeth Ammons puts the matter bluntly when she suggests that much of Wharton's early fiction "focuses in one way or another on the pain of being a woman" (Ammons 5). Most important, however, was Wharton's understanding of the way in which that pain cut across all levels of society. "Typical women in her view—no matter how privileged, nonconformist, or assertive (indeed, often in proportion to the degree in which they embodied those qualities)—were not free to control their own lives, and that conviction became the foundation of her argument with American optimism for more than twenty years" (3).

Edith Wharton began her life as Edith Newbold Jones on January 24, 1862. Her father, George Frederic Jones, was a member of the American gentry who, by the time he graduated from Columbia College, had already completed an extensive tour of Europe with his father and afterward settled into the life of the leisure class dividing his time between homes in New York City and Newport, Rhode Island. While her mother, Lucretia Rhinelander, was from a similar upper class background, the Rhinelanders had fallen on hard times after the early death of Lucretia's father, though they still managed to retain most of the outward trappings of their wealthy lifestyle. After their marriage in 1844, according to Wharton biographer Hermione Lee, the couple maintained a neatly bifurcated life that continued throughout Edith's childhood. "At the country house in Newport there were outdoor pastimes like walking, riding, and archery contests . . . there were fishing parties, boat races, and the endless, ritualistic rounds of drives and calls, in one's very best clothes from Paris," while "in New York, her parents did what everyone did: a few charities, walks in the Park, endless 'calls,' and outings to the newly fashionable Italian opera . . . [but] her parent's main social occupation was their dinner parties" (Lee 28-29). Edith had two brothers who were much older, and whom her mother seemed to prefer. As a result, she bonded more closely with her father, and the two shared "a passion for books, an enthusiasm for travel, a delight in nature (especially gardens) and an appreciation for art" (Fournier 8). But there was another side to her father Wharton observed in which can be seen a model for the character of Ethan Frome.

I imagine there was a time when his rather rudimentary love of verse might have been developed had he had any one with whom to share it. But my mother's matter-of-factness must have shriveled up any such buds of fancy . . . and I have wondered since what stifled cravings had once germinated in him, and what manner of man he was really meant to be. That he was a lonely one, haunted by something always unexpressed and unattained, I am sure. (Wharton 1934, 39)

When she was only four years old her father made the decision to take the family on an extended trip to Europe for six years, renting out their homes in New York and Rhode Island in order to ride out the lengthy recession that followed the Civil War. This experience was formative for Edith and resulted not only in numerous trips to Europe during her lifetime, but a permanent move to Paris in 1909 where she stayed throughout the whole of World War One. She began writing at a young age, publishing poetry and completing an unpublished novella at age fifteen. In 1882 she became engaged to Harry Leyden Stevens, whom she had been seeing since she was eighteen, and when she ended the engagement a short time later a society reporter suggested that it was a direct result of her literary aspirations—even quoting Shakespeare to emphasize the point. "The only reason for the breaking of the engagement hitherto existing between Harry Stevens and Miss Edith Jones is an alleged preponderance of intellectuality on the part of the intended bride. Miss Jones is an ambitious authoress, and it is said that, in the eyes of Mr. Stevens, ambition is a grievous fault" (Dawson 43). The actual reason for the breakup is that the Stevens' family was new money, and Lucretia and her family had blocked their entrance into New York's old money society years earlier. Mrs. Stevens never forgot, and because she controlled her son's finances she would not allow him to marry into the family, forcing Edith to take the blame.

There may have been some truth, however, to the effect her writing had on her personal relationships with men. After the end of her engagement and the death of her father later that same year, she became acquainted with Walter Van Rensselaer Berry, a Harvard graduate who was studying for his bar exam. The two of them shared an instant connection over the things that stirred Edith's imagination. In Berry, "she discovered a companion who satisfied her deep need for conversation about the authors and the works that absorbed her" (Fournier 12). Unfortunately, while Edith also seemed to satisfy Berry's intellectual needs, according to Wharton biographer Richard Lewis she was not the kind of wife he was looking for. "Berry maintained a careful lack of final seriousness in his relations with women. His tastes, then and later, drew him betimes to women more frivolous and fluttery than Edith, not to say more beautiful and rich . . . He wearied a little of Edith's persistent intellectuality . . . (Lewis 49). Even if that hadn't been the case, Hermione Lee argues that Berry might not have been the best match for Edith, despite their mutual interests. "It would also be rash to assume that if she *had* married Walter Berry it would have been a story of happiness and fulfillment. He was the pre-eminent example of the kind of man whom she found—and who found her—interesting and magnetic. This was not a type who would necessarily make a good husband" (Lee 65). Despite a sort of falling out at the time, the two would reconnect years later and remain friends for the rest of their lives. "About thirteen years later, Edith Wharton and Walter Berry became intimate friends by which time she had been married for over ten years and was at last starting to write professionally. Walter arrived at precisely the point when she needed literary encouragement and advice" (Lee 64). Berry was also an important part of the process for Wharton when she was writing *Ethan Frome*. "In Paris I wrote the tale as it now stands, reading my morning's work aloud each evening to Walter Berry . . . We talked the tale over page by page, so that its accuracy of 'atmosphere' is doubly assured" (Wharton 1934, 296).

Edith eventually married Edward Robbins "Teddy" Wharton, who she began to see socially shortly after Berry had exited the scene. Wharton, whose family was from Boston, had been a friend of Edith's older brother Harry Jones. Boston, as Edith soon discovered, was a different world from New York—and also explained in some measure Teddy's lack of ambition. "A joke she liked to make was that in Boston she was a failure because she was thought 'too fashionable to be intelligent,' in New York because she was 'too intelligent to be fashionable'" (Lee 73). Though the match met the approval of Lucretia, Edith may have had reasons other than love for accepting his proposal. "Still unmarried six years after her debut, she was growing concerned about her prospects for her own home and her own place in society" (Fournier 13). Teddy Wharton did not make enough of an income from his investment capital to enable them to purchase a house together, so after their wedding they stayed in a cottage on her mother's estate in Newport for much of the year, and then travelled to Europe in late winter after the holidays, returning to Newport in the spring. It wasn't until Edith received an inheritance from an elderly cousin in 1888 that the couple was finally able to move back to New York City. At first they rented a small house on Madison Avenue, but before long they moved to a house of their own, a five-story brownstone on Park Avenue. A few years later she even purchased her own summer home in Newport.

Throughout these years Edith lived a decidedly upper-class existence, but the absence of sexual intimacy in her marriage to Teddy soon began to take an emotional toll, complete with the illnesses that afflicted a large

Ethan Frome: Analysis in Context

number of married women at the time, an inner psychological stress that was reflected outward by their bodies. According to Wharton biographer Shari Benstock, "Edith's frequent illnesses and breathing problems prevented her from sharing a bedroom, even when they travelled . . . The humming eroticism of her youth turned back on itself, draining her energies and feeding self-doubt and unfulfilled longings" (Benstock 60). As a result, the two failed to have any children. "Teddy was no authority on female sexuality, and he was surely unprepared to deal with the consequences of Edith's sexual ignorance and fear. These failures, never openly acknowledged, foreshadowed other failures of psychological and intellectual intimacy." Eventually Edith and Teddy sold their house in Rhode Island and purchased a summer home in the Berkshires, in Lenox, Massachusetts in the far western part of the state, which she named the Mount. Lenox would eventually become the setting not only for *Ethan Frome* but another novel, *Summer*, written in 1917. First, however, she concentrated her energies on writing *The House of Mirth* in 1904, one of the novels she would become best known for in her day, which examined the lives of the people in the New York high society in which she had grown up.

Because Edith was less than satisfied in her marriage to Teddy, it was natural that she eventually sought out the companionship of other men. The first was Berry, who would reappear in 1896. The other was William Morton Fullerton, with whom Edith would carry on a brief love affair just prior to the writing of *Ethan Frome*. She convinced Teddy that the two of them should take an apartment in Paris at the end of 1906, in the hope that the literary atmosphere would inspire her. But that wasn't the only attraction that Europe held for her. "Wharton had another reason to settle in the City of Lights, for she was beginning an affair with Morton Fullerton, Paris correspondent for the *London Times*. The two shared a number of interests . . . An urbane companion, he offered her the passion and the sexual fulfillment which she had not experienced in more than twenty years of marriage to Teddy" (Fournier 18). 1907 was also notable as the date that Edith began writing a story about a young man and his wife who were trapped—literally and figuratively—in the harsh, New England countryside, though at the time it was never intended to be one of her published works of fiction. The story was initially an exercise to improve her conversational French, and its main characters were named Hart and Anna rather than Ethan and Zeena. The story is fascinating, less for its differences from *Ethan Frome* than for the way that she shaped and expanded on the similarities between the two, and in doing so created a much more intimate and compelling work.

Wharton's French precursor to *Ethan Frome* begins *in medias res*, with Hart and Mattie walking through the woods on a winter evening, Hart trying to hide the embarrassment he feels at having confessed his love for his wife's niece, and assuring her that she doesn't have to leave because of it. Unlike the novel, the two have declared their feelings for each other prior to the start of the tale, as Hart says as much later in the narrative. When they return to the house Anna is waiting to let them in, and the next day a cousin comes to visit and convinces Hart's wife to go to Worchester to see a new doctor. Instead of reveling in a night alone with Mattie, however, Hart becomes convinced that Anna is planning on returning in secret to catch them in a compromising position—something Hart clearly believes he will be unable to resist. To avoid this he manufactures any number of reasons to stay in the village until late at night. When Anna returns home she announces that her doctor wants her to hire a servant girl, and so she essentially dismisses Mattie. Hart, while devastated, refuses to confront his wife, and it is during his trip back from the train station to deliver Mattie's trunk that the story ends. His devastation at Mattie's departure causes Hart to despise having to live the remainder of his life without her, though when he suggests that he could go with her it is Mattie who threatens suicide. In the final line of the story Mattie's acceptance of her banishment almost suggests a similar motivation as the sacrifice of Kate Chopin's protagonist in *The Awakening*: "You're not happy together—and it makes you unhappy, I know it—but if you leave her to marry me, what humiliation for her, what infamy for me!" (MacCallan 47).

It was only in the intervening years, when Edith Wharton's personal life began to reflect the challenges faced by her characters in the story, that she would expand upon her language exercise and turn it into *Ethan Frome*. While most commentators emphasize the differences between the French story and the later novel, what is more remarkable is how similar the two are. Everything is there, from Zeena's illness and dominance over her husband, to Ethan's indecisiveness and tortured inner dialogue, the pursuit of Mattie by a younger rival, and even the desire for suicide by both characters. In the end, when Wharton began anew and turned her hand to reimagining her original idea she managed to transform it into one of her most important and long-lasting works. It's this autobiographical aspect of the novel that accounts for so much of its power, authenticity, and longevity. Author R.W.B. Lewis put it this way in his 1976 biography of Wharton: "Into no earlier work of fiction, not even *The House of Mirth*, had she poured such deep and intense private emotions. *Ethan Frome* in this regard was a major turning point, whether or not it was also the finest of her literary achievements. Edith had hitherto reserved her strongest feelings for poetry; henceforth, they would go into her novels and stories . . . From this moment forward, and with obvious exceptions,

Edith Wharton's fictional writings began to comprise the truest account of her inward life" (Lewis 308).

Another inspiration, this time for the ending of the novel, was a fatal sledding accident that happened in Lenox in 1904 in which an eighteen-year-old girl was killed and four of her friends injured, one of them permanently. The *Berkshire Evening Eagle* reported on March 12, 1904 of the accident that had occurred the evening before. Five high school students had decided to ride together on a large sled. Observers said that the sled attained a high rate of speed very quickly on the icy slope, and a minute later they heard a crash from the bottom of the hill. After rushing to see what had happened, they found all five of the students lying unconscious in the snow with various injuries. The most severely hurt was Hazel Crosby, who was steering the sled, and who died the following day. Three other girls and a boy were taken to various houses and the doctor called. It was only discovered decades later that one of the injured girls, Kate Spencer, had been well acquainted with Mrs. Wharton. Spencer's hip was dislocated as a result of the accident and her face was also badly scarred. Wharton had been a volunteer at the public library in Lenox—one of the settings in her novel *Summer*—since 1902 during her summers in the Berkshires, and a year after the accident Spencer was hired on as part of the regular staff. A letter Wharton wrote to Spencer from 1909, as well as several gift tags attesting to presents received by the young girl from the author, indicated a friendship that coincided with the beginning of Wharton's work on *Ethan Frome.*

Wharton moved permanently to France in 1909, selling her house in New York to do so, while Teddy stayed with his sister in Boston. Edith's husband came to Europe briefly at the end of the year but didn't stay long, though Teddy did confess to her before returning to the U.S. that he had lost a substantial portion of Edith's capital in bad stock market speculations. Of course he was allowed to do this because, as the man in their marriage, he legally controlled all of Edith's money. The move to Paris, where she stayed for the next thirteen years almost uninterrupted, was also a way to establish residence in a country that would allow her to more freely seek a divorce. In the meantime she demanded that Teddy return the money he had essentially stolen, and he did, but it nearly wiped out his own personal finances, the bulk of which he had inherited from his mother after her death. At the same time, Wharton's affair with Morton Fullerton was becoming increasingly difficult to sustain because of their separate lives and the need for secrecy, and she was spending most of her time attending to Teddy's welfare by seeking treatment for him both in the United States and in Europe. Wharton began working on *Ethan Frome* in the summer of 1910, but after a short illness and a trip to New York, did not return to it until the beginning of 1911. Back in France she applied herself diligently to completing the work, seemingly drawing inspiration from her current situation, as biographer Shari Benstock recounts. "By winter 1911, her hours of sexual passion had come and gone. Disillusioned with her lover, her husband in the throes of mental illness, Edith felt as tied to Teddy as Ethan Frome was to his bedridden wife, Zeena" (Benstock 247).

Wharton's most recent biographer, however, strongly resists the idea that the literary merit in her work at this time was solely a result of her personal difficulties. According to Hermione Lee, "It would be a travesty to suggest that all the stories of failed love, sexual treachery and claustrophobic marriages Wharton published during this period issued from her relationship with Morton Fullerton. These themes were already her specialty. The qualities that make Wharton a great writer . . . were the product of years of observation, reading, practice and refinement, not of a love affair" (Lee 348-349). The story was first serialized in *Scribner's Magazine* in the fall of 1911, and *Ethan Frome* came out in novel form by the publisher in September, the same month the third and final installment appeared in the October issue of the magazine. Reviews at the time were fairly mixed, though the positive reviews were far more laudatory than the negative ones critical, which generally pleased the author. As a result, Wharton assumed that sales of the book would be in the nature of the windfall she received from *The House of Mirth*, which had sold nearly one hundred and thirty thousand copies, but she was disappointed when Scribner's informed her that the slim volume had managed to sell only about sixty-seven hundred. What angered her most were reports from friends in New York that bookstores were frequently out of stock, indicating to her that Scribner's had been too conservative in its estimates for the first printing. But *Ethan Frome* was not destined to be a popular sensation and instead gained its reputation gradually over time.

Though her most critically acclaimed work was yet to come—*The Age of Innocence*, which won her a Pulitzer Prize in 1920—Wharton's novel of rural New England remains her most important work, primarily for its accessibility to modern audiences. While her novels about the decay of upper crust New York society are in many ways relics of a bygone age because of their subject matter, *Ethan Frome* is primarily about the emotional lives of its characters and, as such, transcends the limitations of time. This is an aspect of the novel that historian Carl Van Doren recognized. "In the desolate communities which witness the agonies of Ethan Frome and Charity Royall [the protagonist of *Summer*] not only is there a stubborn village decorum but there are also the bitter compulsions of a helpless poverty which binds feet and wings as the most ruthless decorum cannot bind them, and which dulls all the hues of life to an unendurable dinginess . . . Without filing down her characters into types she contrives to lift them into universal figures of aspiration or disappointment" (Van Doren 98-99). This ability on Wharton's part to make her characters resonate with readers in a way that goes beyond the specifics of the plot and setting is what has made her, to this day, one of America's great literary figures. "By creating literature that replicated the universal, the abstract principles of human relationships, Wharton had earned a place in the pantheon of important writers" (Wagner-Martin 246). Wharton's gift was the ability to make her characters—primarily Ethan—fully developed and multi-dimensional, while at the same time allowing the underlying symbolic imagery and severity of the landscape to emphasize the universal truth of the limitations that society had imposed on them, and that to a great extent were responsible for their suffering.

Looking at *Ethan Frome* critically, the first thing that becomes apparent is the nature of the work itself. Rather than the world of her most popular novel to that point, *The House of Mirth*, which examined the wealthy American life of her childhood and early adulthood, in this work Edith Wharton explores a bleak, rural landscape and characters who are as trapped by their poverty and station in life as the leafless trees lying dormant beneath the snow. And yet this was a world she was just as familiar with as that in Manhattan, by virtue of having made her home there for nearly a decade. "*Ethan Frome* was written after I had spent ten years in the hill-region where the scene is laid, during which years I had come to know well the aspect, dialect, and mental and moral attitude of the hill-people" (Wharton 1934, 296). This kind of literary intimacy is one that, Wharton knew from her reading, had a long precedent. On the opening page of her book on literature, *The Writing of Fiction*, she makes a pointed reference to what she considered the first piece of fiction to delve into the psyche of its characters rather than simply put them through a series of actions in a plot. About Madame de La Fayette's novel, *La Princesse de Clèves* she had this to say, calling it "a story of hopeless love and mute renunciation in which the stately tenor of the lives depicted is hardly ruffled by the exultations and agonies succeeding each other below the surface" (Wharton 1925, 7). With the exception of the "stately tenor" of their lives, Wharton could just as easily have been describing the characters in *Ethan Frome*. The idea that the primary action in the characters' lives is happening "below the surface," is the main one, but there is also the undeniable fact that no matter what the characters feel, whether it is the exultation of Ethan or the agony of Zeena, the grim reality of their lives is "hardly ruffled" by the emotions they experience.

Eric B. Olsen

Several scholars have commented on the implications of this type of heavily symbolic writing, where the truth of the story would have to be understood through more than just the dialogue and actions of the characters, especially given the stoicism and circumspection of those characters. "The nature of her subject imposed certain difficulties on Wharton," says author Kenneth Bernard, "particularly her characters' lack of articulation. How could she, without over-narrating, get at a deep problem involving such characters when they do not speak enough to reveal that problem? Frome's character and his marital relationship are at the heart of the novel, but they are revealed only indirectly. Wharton solved her difficulty in a masterful way by her use of imagery and symbolism. It is in her use of imagery and symbolism that the depths of the story are to be found. Without an understanding of them the reader *would* find the characters unmotivated and the tragedy contrived" (Bernard 178-179). Bernard, more than most writers, realized the importance of symbolism in this particular novel. "With the understanding of the imagery and symbolism [the reader] can look into the heart of the book and see the characters as full-bodied people in the grip of overwhelming emotional entanglements" (184). Even Wharton scholar Blake Nevius, while somewhat dismissive of the author's general talent in this area, nevertheless expressed admiration for the ability she displayed in writing *Ethan Frome*. "Edith Wharton's imagination could occasionally be roused to symbol-making activity by the conjunction of a theme and a setting both deeply cherished and understood" (Nevius 129). It is that very intersection between her comprehension of the theme of oppressive societal dictates and a beloved setting in the Berkshires that accounts for *Ethan Frome*'s continued reputation as a classic of American literature.

Elsewhere in her book on writing fiction can be seen a way of understanding the kind of gender reversal that is at the heart of *Ethan Frome*, as well as the subtle implication that Frome's love is not returned by the object of his affection. In her discussion of the way in which Marcel Proust, in *Remembrance of Things Past,* was able to shed a "prophetic ray on his characters," and in doing so simultaneously flash "a light . . . on the central theme of the book," she identifies that theme as "the hopeless incurable passion of a sensitive man for a stupid uncomprehending woman" (Wharton 1925, 116). Nevius mentions several of Wharton's stories that deal with a similar theme, *Ethan Frome* among them, but then goes on to make the following claim, that "in each case the emphasis falls on the baffling, wasteful submission of a superior to an inferior" (Nevius 108). Author Grace Kellogg goes on to explicitly connect this idea to *Ethan Frome*. "This is the case of Ethan Frome, trapped within the narrow, self-centered nature of Zeena"

(Kellogg 112). Just like Trilling, Nevius is "baffled" by the fact that a superior male is held in societal captivity by an inferior woman. But that confusion falls away when Nevius's statement is considered in its actual gender-neutral wording. How many women in Wharton's day were tied down to "stupid uncomprehending" males? As Wharton's biography clearly demonstrates, the author herself was a perfect example ot a superior woman wastefully tied to an inferior man. Thankfully, Wharton herself never actually submitted. The same, however, cannot be said of Ethan. And while this idea most clearly describes his relationship with Zeena, there is also an aspect of it to be found in Mattie's inability to comprehend Ethan's desire for her.

Much has been made of Ethan's passive nature throughout the book, and there has been almost no scholarship that makes sense of it in a way that could even remotely be called satisfying. For most authors that passivity is simply a character trait, a given from which his further action—or more precisely, inaction—derives. But that is only half the story. While much of Ethan's behavior does result from his passive nature, that passivity must have come from somewhere. And likewise, most of the attempts to discover its source are equally unsatisfactory. Author Suzanne J. Fournier, for instance, sees Ethan's submission to Zeena as a consequence of his fear of disrupting the fantasy world he creates for himself. "Ethan's passivity is a function of his desire to observe (or dream) rather than act" (Fournier xiii). But in reality that relationship is reversed. Ethan's dream world is actually the result of his passivity, and it is not an innate passivity any more than it was for the women of his day; it was one that was imposed on him by the dictates of society. In fact, it is only in looking at Ethan as a female surrogate that his passivity makes any sense at all. Like most women of his day, he has been forced into a passive role his entire adult life, first abandoning his studies to take care of his parents, then after making his ill-advised proposal to Zeena, and their subsequent marriage in which she has dominated him ever since. Therefore Ethan's passive reaction to these events can be seen as a typically feminine one because of similar social pressures exerted on him.

In 1934 psychoanalyst Karen Horney questioned whether the idea of feminine passivity was actually a feminine trait at all, but instead that it "must be considered as importantly conditioned by the culture-complex or social organization in which the particular [patient] has developed" (Horney 232-233). Horney also addressed the specific sociological reasons that this behavior was primarily associated with women, suggesting doctors and therapists ask themselves,

Under what social or cultural conditions do we find more frequently in women than men (1) the manifesting of inhibitions in the direct expression of demands and aggressions; (2) a regarding of oneself as weak, helpless, or inferior . . . (3) a becoming emotionally dependent on the other sex; (4) a showing of tendencies to be self-sacrificing, to be submissive, to feel used or to be exploited . . ." (Horney 229)

The answer, of course, is the cultural condition of the patriarchal society of late nineteenth and early twentieth century America. By putting her male protagonist, Ethan, in the position of restriction from the same societal pressures that oppressed females, Wharton was actually demonstrating society's complicity in causing so many of the negative traits that were typically associated with women and erroneously assumed to be an inherent part of their psychological makeup. Seen in this way Ethan is not, as so many critics want to portray him, a tragically flawed character—any more than the women of his day were—but instead he has been unconsciously created by a society that is ultimately indifferent to the consequences of the conditions under which he has been forced to live.

In addition to the use of symbolism that underpins the novel, a close reading of *Ethan Frome* reveals three primary thematic elements in the narrative, each of them corresponding roughly to one of the main characters. The first concerns the title character. Looking at Ethan Frome in the specific way that Wharton has rendered him, he becomes a surrogate for the women of her day. The author has been able to make all of the inherent incongruities that arise from the subjugation of women seem—if not cruel, in Lionel Trilling's view—at least preposterous when presented in the guise of a male character. The second element has to do with Zeena's illness. Ethan's wife represents that aspect of the female character absent in Ethan, demonstrating one of the significant responses of women to societal oppression: mental and emotional stress that manifests itself physically. The third element, though primarily concerning Mattie, also comes by way of Ethan. In his obsession with Mattie as an object of love and desire, Ethan has created a fantasy world that doesn't really exist. Careful study of the text reveals that Mattie does not return Ethan's love, and in this way Wharton exposes one of the final consequences of the subjugation of women. By excluding women from participating fully in society it forces them into a fantasy world that may have no connection with reality, and in doing so can cause them to behave in ways that are detrimental to their own lives as well as the lives of those around them.

The standard interpretation by contemporary readers of the way in which female oppression is rendered in the novel exclusively centers on Zeena and

Mattie. This is a view best articulated by Wharton scholar Suzanne J. Fournier. "Although the novel focuses most closely on the blighted life of Ethan Frome, it also illuminates the unsatisfactory circumstances of the two women trapped with him in a dilapidated farmhouse" (Fournier 86). But the elements of that oppression in the lives of Mattie—marriage as the only way out—and Zeena—marriage as an equally strong trap—had long been rationalized away by a patriarchal society. Much more compelling is the idea of how female oppression is demonstrated in the character of Ethan. In looking at the novel this way it's important to note that the use of male characters in literature to symbolize female challenges in life is not unique to Wharton. One of the earliest examples of this occurs in Mary Shelley's *Frankenstein* from 1818. Author Ellen Mores makes the argument that the primary theme in Shelley's novel is not one of the usually accepted ones: the hubris of usurping God's authority, the immorality of unchecked scientific experimentation, or even the imposition of modernity on a largely pastoral way of life. *Frankenstein*, she argues, is a story about the trauma of birth.

> *Frankenstein* brought a new sophistication to literary terror, and it did so without a heroine, without even an important female victim. Paradoxically, however, no other Gothic work by a woman writer, perhaps no literary work of any kind by a woman, better repays examination in the light of the sex of its author. For *Frankenstein* is a birth myth, and one that was lodged in the novelist's imagination, I am convinced, by the fact that she was herself a mother. (Moers 91-92)

While Mores calls Shelley's novel a "birth myth" the true power of *Frankenstein*, as she sees it, is to dispel the myth of childbirth as it had been erroneously represented in literature. "Fear and guilt, depression and anxiety are commonplace reactions to the birth of a baby, and well within the normal range of experience. But more deeply rooted in our cultural mythology, and certainly in our literature, are the happy maternal reactions" (93).

The result of this unconscious revelation about the truth of childbirth for women in the early nineteenth-century—Shelley herself lost three of her children before they had reached the age of three—is that her novel has become one of the most famous works in all of literature. If her story had been about a woman, however, it's doubtful that it would be more than a footnote today, with the same lack of name recognition some of her other novels like *Valperga, The Fortunes of Perkin Warbeck,* and *Lodore* have for modern readers. It was the ability to frame her story through the use of a male protagonist that allowed *Frankenstein* to circumvent the natural prejudice against that same theme had it been contained within the pages of a mere "women's novel." A similar phenomenon is also responsible for the lasting success of *Ethan Frome*. Consciously or not, Edith Wharton was able to address the mistaken notion of female inferiority by demonstrating the way in which those limitations impacted her male protagonist. In part this comes from a proclivity to take the events of her own life and reverse the gender roles when writing about them in her fiction. In discussing *Ethan Frome* specifically, biographer Richard Lewis stated,

> The great and durable vitality of the tale comes at last from the personal feelings Edith Wharton invested in it, the feelings by which she lived her narrative. *Ethan Frome* portrays her personal situation, as she had come to appraise it, carried to a far extreme, transplanted to a remote rural scene, and rendered utterly hopeless by circumstance. As she often did, Edith shifted the sexes in devising her three central characters. (Lewis 309)

And just as with Mary Shelley's creation, what accounts for the story's impressive longevity is the way that Wharton's shift in sexes was able to bypass cultural filters in order to reveal the truth in a way that resonated with readers on an unconscious level. It could also be argued that she was able to recognize this effect on readers at the time, saying about reviewers who struggled explain the book's positive qualities, "They don't know *why* it's good, but they are right: it *is*" (Lauer 84).

The issue of women's illness is far more straightforward, and made its appearance in literature by women almost from the time they began writing. Lauer and Wolff's ancillary materials for the Norton Critical Edition of *Ethan Frome* include an excerpt from an 1868 medical article in *The American Journal of Insanity* that outlines the special emotional difficulties encountered by women who move to rural areas after their marriage, a situation identical to Zeena's.

> The early married life of the wives of some of our smaller farmers seems especially calculated to predispose to [nervous prostration]. Transferred to an isolated farm-house, very frequently from a home in which she had enjoyed a requisite measure of social and intellectual recreation, she is subjected to a daily routine of very monotonous household labor . . . Remote from neighbors, as in sparsely settled districts, for weeks together, she sees only her husband and the generally uneducated man who shares his toil . . . Her daily life . . . is exhausting and depressing to a degree of

which but few are likely to form any correct conception. From this class come many applications for the admission of female patients. (Lauer 98)

It's interesting to note that this is an idea Wharton herself was familiar with, as she expressed a very similar sentiment in her French draft of *Ethan Frome*. More importantly, however, she made that point in reference to Mattie, who had been forced to shoulder the responsibilities that the wife had abdicated because of her illness. "In her features she expressed all the deep anguish of the long line of women who, for two hundred years, had worn out their lives and devoured their hearts in the narrow and gloomy existence of the American countryside" (MacCallan 47).

Zeena's illness then, as it was for many women, does not seem an unreasonable reaction to the never-ending drudgery that country life offered the wives of farmers. In a fascinating footnote to her book on gender in Victorian America, Carroll Smith-Rosenberg enumerates a number of factors that went into the unconscious choice by women to rebel through the manifestation of symptoms that would eventually be brought together under the single medical diagnosis of hysteria.

Three complex factors interacted to make hysteria a real behavioral option for American women: first, the various experiences that caused a woman to arrive at adulthood with significant ego weakness; second, certain socialization patterns and cultural values that made hysteria a readily available alternate behavior pattern for women; and third, the secondary gains conferred by the hysterical role in terms of enhanced power within the family. Individual cases presumably represented their own peculiar balance of these factors. (Smith-Rosenberg 1985, 331)

There are literary precedents for this aspect of *Ethan Frome* as well, of which Gilman's "The Yellow Wall-Paper" is the most obvious example. But even Wharton's previous novel, *The House of Mirth*, addresses the idea of a woman's illness as a reflection of the intractable nature of societal pressures. Author Diane Herndl sees these examples as part of a larger narrative in American literature.

In fictions like Charlotte Perkins Gilman's "The Yellow Wallpaper" (1892) and Edith Wharton's *The House of Mirth* (1905), we find the same passive and defeated invalid that had figured in the fictions of Southworth, Hawthorne, and Poe fifty years earlier . . . The woman in "The Yellow Wallpaper," like Poe's women, goes mad, and apparently takes her husband with her . . . driven insane by her intellectual needs. In the same way, Lily Bart in *The House of Mirth*, like Georgiana in "The Birthmark," Beatrice in "Rappaccini's Daughter," and Zenobia in *The Blithedale Romance*, dies at the end of the story. (Herndl 112-113)

But the literary character whose behavior most closely resembles Zeena Frome's form of illness was created by Harriet Beecher Stowe in Marie St. Clare from *Uncle Tom's Cabin* in 1852. In this manifestation "The invalid is a selfish, hateful, and spoiled woman whose illnesses are feigned to enable her to avoid any kind of work; she lives in luxury and thinks only of herself and her imagined ills. Her servants wait on her hand and foot; her every need, real or imagined, is answered because no one wants to listen to her continual complains" (Herndl 51). Unlike Marie St. Clare, Zeena is far from rich, but this simply goes to show that the form hysterical illness could take in the nineteenth-century had nothing to do with socio-economic factors. The real disease, as Gilman and Wharton and, by extension, Chopin, saw it, was society itself. Modern feminists are sometimes embarrassed by the seeming inability of many female protagonists of this period to rise above their subjugation and triumph. But not only was that kind of fiction unrealistic, it failed to properly address the very real consequences of societal oppression by offering happy endings that were unavailable to most women at the time. "Gilman and Wharton use their heroines as proof that women's lives needed to be changed, that it was the social structure that was really sick" (Herndl 143).

Finally, Ethan's imaginary love affair with Mattie brings to the fore one of the little explored aspects of the oppression of women in the nineteenth-century, that of the self-destructive fantasy. Ironically, this was initially thought to be an inherent weakness in women that was acerbated through the act of reading, as Honoré de Balzac's 1829 *Physiology of Marriage* makes clear.

To think of leaving a woman at liberty to read the books which her character of mind may prompt her to choose! This is to drop a spark in a powder magazine; it is worse than that, it is to teach your wife to separate herself from you; to live in an imaginary world, in a Paradise . . . Moreover, in reading plays and romances, woman, a creature much more susceptible than we are to excitement, experiences the most violent transport. She creates for herself an ideal existence beside which all reality grows pale; she at once attempts to realize this voluptuous life, to take to herself the magic which she sees in it. (Balzac 148-149)

With women confined by society to the drudgery of domestic duties and childrearing, it's little wonder they sought some measure of escape through reading. At the same time, however, there was a decided lack of comprehension by men that it was these very limitations that were the root cause of the need for women to seek out vicarious experiences through literature. One of the older relatives of Kate Chopin's childhood girlfriend, it's said, "spent most of her time shopping, which her devoted husband . . . preferred her to do. Otherwise, he said, she'd fill her head with impossible ideas from romantic novels and expect him to spend all his time loving her" (Toth 1999, 19).

The concept was one that would be understood completely only in the mid-twentieth century—too late for women suffering at the turn of the century but provides for the modern reader a way of looking back in order to truly understand their lives, both real and fictional, as well as the motives behind their behaviors. German psychoanalyst Karen Horney identified different reactions that women—and by association Ethan—had to the severe limitations imposed on them by society, which to her way of thinking were a part of a learned masochism that naturally fed into the sort of fantasy life that Ethan developed for himself. Horney's use of the masculine pronoun makes that connection even more pointed. "There are several ways in which one can find reassurance against deep fears. Renunciation is one way; inhibition another; denying the fear and becoming optimistic, a third one; and so on.

> Being loved is the particular means of reassurance used by a masochistic person. As he has a rather free floating anxiety, he needs constant signs of attention and affection, and as he never believes in these signs except momentarily, he has an excessive need for attention and affection. He is therefore, generally speaking, very emotional in his relations with people; easily attached because he expects them to give him the necessary reassurance; easily disappointed because he never gets, and never can get, what he expects. The expectation or illusion of the "great love" often plays an important role. (Horney 227)

This could almost be a psychological description specific to Ethan Frome. Tied down to a loveless wife, he naturally seeks out the affection and attention he has been denied in the form of Mattie. But this "great love" is just an illusion, and necessarily so as Wharton's text clearly shows. Because there is nothing else in his life that is worthwhile, he can't afford to risk learning the truth.

The major problem with the construction of this kind of fantasy world for women, like the ones Ethan represents, is the potential for self-destruction. The most obvious example of this in literature is Emma Bovary from Gustav

Flaubert's *Madame Bovary*. For Emma Roualt, the romantic ideal that life promised did not begin with her marriage to Charles Bovary. In fact, that is when it ended. And while she attempts to make peace with her docile and sedate surroundings, she cannot shake the feeling that she is missing out on all of the passion and excitement she has read about in the pages of the fiction she devours. Her long-term lovers therefore become merely the means to achieve a dream that she chases without success, an illusion she can never obtain. She also lives in a fantasy world of social class when she takes over her husband's finances and begins spending money they don't have, taking trips and buying gifts for her lovers, decorating her home and buying expensive clothes in the mistaken belief that she will find happiness in the excesses she witnesses in the upper class. In the end, Emma commits suicide to avoid the shame of the debts she has incurred along with the full exposure of the sexual exploits she had been able to keep hidden for so long.

While *Ethan Frome* is a very different novel, the parallels with *Madame Bovary* are informative. Ethan, too, had dreams, though they were based on the very real experiences he had while attending college. He also married for the same reason as Emma, in order to leave the farm and advance in life. "When they married it was agreed that . . . they would sell the farm and saw-mill and try their luck in a large town . . . His period of study at Worchester, increased his faith in his ability as well as his eagerness to see the world; and he felt sure that, with a 'smart' wife like Zeena, it would not be long before he had made himself a place in it." (Wharton 1911, 76). But when Zeena refused to leave, Ethan found himself just as disappointed as Emma. Though Emma and Ethan's fantasies seem very different—and they are—there is still a strong association the characters have with each other. While Emma indulges in actual adultery, her dream is really one of achieving ecstatic love that will manifest itself in what she imagines to be the perfect life. Ethan, while his affair remains imaginary, essentially has the same dream. He wants a relationship with Mattie that will transform his mundane existence into a perfection only achieved in his dreams. In the end, however, neither character can obtain the life and love they imagine for themselves.

The self-destructive nature of these dreams for each character is, nevertheless, very different. Emma Bovary never changes in her single-minded desire to achieve the perfection of her fantasies, and it is only the threat of public exposure of her ruinous behavior that drives her to take her own life. For Ethan the process is very different, as his inability to achieve his dream warps his character to the point where he allows Mattie to convince him to take his life. Author Suzanne Fournier has done a nice job in articulating the mechanism that accounts for this process of Ethan's inner decay.

An introspective figure who has endured years of silence with his ill mother and then his hypochondriac wife, he is accustomed to dreaming about the life he cannot have. Throughout the novel, he is inclined to retreat from the conditions of his life on the farm into reveries about nature or private fantasies about Mattie . . . The relation between dream and reality is a complicated one for Ethan, who delights in Mattie's presence chiefly because it sustains and enriches his vision of her . . . This other world does not exist, of course, and Wharton directs potent irony against Ethan as he retreats from life into the illusions that he has generated. (Fournier 83, 84, 85)

Ultimately, it is the actions these characters take as a result of their thwarted dreams that demonstrate the real danger in the kind of inhibited life that nineteenth-century expectations imposed on women. Despite Emma's suicide, her family still has to deal with the consequences of financial ruin and scandal after she is gone. In the same way, not only do Ethan and Mattie suffer from Ethan's actions but Zeena must suffer as well. The real tragedy, therefore, is not the fantasy itself. When women attempted to act out these fantasies in their real lives in a way that was self-destructive, it only served to reinforce patriarchal prejudices rather than reveal those fantasies as the natural outgrowth of a system that denied women the very freedom they needed in order to be happy with their lives as they were.

Edith Wharton's unique take on male-female relationships in her lifetime arose from a complex series of factors. One of the most important was that of her desire to write works of literature rather than simply the popular women's fiction of the day. What that necessitated was the ability to write convincingly from the male point of view. According to author Linda Wagner-Martin, "She believed that if she were to become a truly significant literary figure, she must not write as if she were a woman . . . Wharton was trying to avoid writing the somewhat predictable stories of women characters who managed to overcome social restrictions that coerced them into becoming less than they might be" (Wagner-Martin 243). Part of her ability to do this rested on her close association with men. Unlike the female dominated household of Kate Chopin's mother in St. Louis, or the community of women that Charlotte Perkins Gilman gravitated to in California, Edith Wharton typically chose to surround herself with male friends. Part of this desire came from the poor relationship she had with her mother, and part of it was a result of the incomplete sexual union she had with her husband. Biographer Shari Benstock claims this was especially true early in her marriage. "Rather than bringing her into the magic circle of feminine self-knowledge, marriage isolated her from women. In her Newport years, Edith appears to have had no close women friends." (Benstock 60). Wharton scholar Marilyn French, in her introduction to *The House of Mirth*, went so far as to say that Wharton "preferred the company of men to that of women and somewhat resented the wives of her male friends: she liked to be queen in a room full of men. She was stubbornly uninterested in meeting accomplished women like Virginia Woolf and Katherine Mansfield" (French xii).

Though Edith Wharton exhibited this preference throughout her life, it should in no way imply exclusivity. Author Susan Goodman actually wrote two books about the author's inner circle of friends, one primarily about men, and the other called *Edith Wharton's Women: Friends and Rivals*. Even French goes on to say, "Wharton's most faithful friends were women" (French xii). Nevertheless, while Wharton did have women friends, they tended not to be associated with her vocation of writing of literature. That position was reserved for men. "She valued the patriarchal hierarchy that had distinguished her through the years. Her reputation among the male literary elite gave her extraordinary access to the world of men and afforded her the prestige to continue to publish into the 1930s" (Boswell 32). In fact, Wharton frequently measured herself against the male literary world, and viewed her place in it as the equal of the men of letters she associated with, though never allowing that position to subsume her knowledge and experience of being a woman.

> She herself encouraged this view by describing her writing as that of a male, explaining in a November 1907 letter to Robert Grant, "I conceive my subjects like a man—that is, rather more architectonically and dramatically than most women—and then execute them like a woman; or rather, I sacrifice, for my desire for construction and breadth, the small incidental effects that women have always excelled in, the episodical characterization . . ." (Wagner-Martin 246)

The result of this acute consciousness of gender distinctions in her writing, combined with her own stylistic conventions, is that it allowed her to approach her characters from a decidedly gender-neutral frame of mind. In doing this Wharton was able to give to her characters exactly the traits she needed to fit whatever piece she was writing.

In some ways this emphasis on the male point of view makes ascertaining Wharton's feminist credentials through her fiction difficult at times because, like many of the women novelists of her day, she was operating within the very strict guidelines that were allowed her. "Marilyn French's essay . . . used the title "Muzzled Women" to reflect on the fact that many women writers never managed to draw women characters who were as adventurous, as bold, as acclaimed as those writers themselves had been or were . . . 'This disparity is so pervasive that one is inclined to believe it is caused by censorship—external and internal, the more insidious sort'" (Wagner-Martin 248). The limited amount of Wharton's non-fiction dealing with feminist issues also serves to disguise the fact that she had very strong opinions about the nature of patriarchal society and its negative effect on women. But Wagner-Martin quotes an unpublished eulogy Wharton delivered during World War One that should dispel any doubt about the author's complete understanding of the society she lived in. "The only thing that matters, in the feminist movement, is the fate of . . . those poor hard-working women who accept their long misery with an animal fatalism because they do not know they have a right to a more humane existence" (Wagner-Martin 247-248). The challenge, then, was how to get this point across to a male audience that had absolutely no stake in sharing power and therefore refused to acknowledge that there even was a problem.

Wharton's genius is that her extensive travelling in the world of men, including the primarily male occupation of writing and publishing, gave her access to thoughts and ideas, behaviors and motivations, that the ordinary woman writer was unable to draw upon. At the same time, however, male prejudice and bigotry were readily apparent to a woman who did not share in the same legal and societal freedoms as her male companions. "As comfortable as Wharton might have felt among her prestigious male colleagues and friends, her fiction reveals that she did not always share their perspectives on popular culture. Perhaps *because* she had access to and experience with the privileges of a man's world, Wharton understood better than her male colleagues the powerlessness of women" (Boswell 32). As such, Edith Wharton's ability to demonstrate the consequences of societal expectations on women in the form of her male protagonist is not a feature of her writing that is strictly limited to *Ethan Frome.* Wharton scholar Elizabeth Ammons has observed a similar concept at work in male characters from her other major novels, and sees a pattern in the way the author renders, "human beings such as Lawrence Selden, Ethan Frome, or Newland Archer, characters who may be weak but who are so at least partially because they are almost as trapped and victimized by the patriarchy as the women they love" (Ammons 15).

Introduction

In Scribner's 1922 edition of *Ethan Frome* Edith Wharton closes her introduction by saying it was a practice she had never indulged in before, "the first I have ever published of any of my books" (Wharton 1911, ix-x). As a result, this makes her introduction—something Joseph X. Brennan dubbed "brief but illuminating"—one of the most important parts of the novel (Brennan 348). And because her introduction is so important it is incumbent upon the reader who wishes to fully comprehend the story to first understand these short remarks the author makes "as to why [s]he decided to attempt the work in question, and why [s]he selected one form rather than another for its embodiment" (Wharton 1911, x). Much like the novel itself, while Wharton claims that these two things are the only ones "of any value to [her] readers" the actual information she conveys does so much more, giving the reader a veritable blueprint for understanding the entirety of the work as well as the specific elements that must go into any analysis worthy of the name. In that light it's incomprehensible why the editors of so many modern editions of the novel—especially those intended for students—make the conscious choice to omit Wharton's introduction.

One of the major criticisms Wharton endured on the publication of the novel was the specious charge that she was writing about a people and a setting that she knew very little about. Thus, Wharton begins with her own expertise in rendering the story and its characters:

I had known something of New England village life long before I made my home in the same country as my imaginary Starkfield; though, during the years spent there, certain of its aspects became much more familiar to me. Even before that final initiation, however, I had an uneasy sense that

> the New England of fiction bore little . . . resemblance to the harsh and beautiful land as I had seen it. (Wharton 1911, v)

The particular choice of setting for her novel is what struck so many readers at the time, something Wharton biographer Hermione Lee describes as "the violent switch from her usual upper-class, sophisticated, international territory to the remote hills and poor farmers' lives of nineteenth-century New England" (Lee 378). In doing so, Wharton moved away from examining the psychology of the rich to in order to explore the inner lives of characters that had a more universal relationship to the ordinary reader. This is actually one of the things that accounts for the book's continued relevance, as well as its importance in secondary education—something that was not achieved by any of her other works, and which itself is a reflection of the reputation *Ethan Frome* has attained in the last hundred years. In the words of Elizabeth Ammons, "This multileveled book belongs in the continuum of classic American romance" (Ammons 76).

The other major criticism against the book at the time was a perceived artificiality that arose from the use of a narrator as a framing device for the internal story of the title character. Wharton addressed this as well, citing literary precedent, "in following a method of which 'La Grande Bretèche' and 'The Ring and the Book' had set me the magnificent example" (Wharton 1911, ix). Both Balzac's short story from 1831 and Robert Browning's long narrative poem from 1868 used similar framing narrations, though certainly not in the way that Wharton manipulated the device for her novel. In the opening essay of her book *Edith Wharton in Context*, author and editor Laura Rattray makes a telling statement about Wharton's writing: "Wharton was a writer whose fiction often captured the very moment of social transition" (Rattray 4). But the only explanation for what induced Wharton to write an introduction to *Ethan Frome* is that the author herself was conscious that she had participated in a moment of artistic transition as well. The kind of regional realism in American literature that held sway almost from the end of the Civil War was finally giving way to a more grim realism that would come to be called naturalism, and Wharton felt compelled to offer an explanation for purposefully turning away from the more idealized American literature of the past.

Realism, as a literary theory, was itself a reaction to perceived excesses of the romanticism of the early nineteenth century, and its stated intent is probably best articulated by the poet William Wordsworth in his preface to the *Lyrical Ballads* written by both he and Samuel Taylor Coleridge.

The principal object, then . . . was to choose incidents and situations from common life, and to relate or describe them, throughout, as far as was possible in a selection of language really used by men, and, at the same time, to throw over them a certain colouring of imagination, whereby ordinary things should be presented to the mind in an unusual aspect; and, further, and above all, to make these incidents and situations interesting by tracing in them, truly though not ostentatiously, the primary laws of our nature: chiefly, as far as regards the manner in which we associate ideas in a state of excitement. Humble and rustic life was generally chosen, because, in that condition, the essential passions of the heart find a better soil in which they can attain their maturity, are less under restraint, and speak a plainer and more emphatic language. (Wordsworth vii)

In many ways, this could be just as apt a description of *Ethan Frome*. Nevertheless, it was this kind of transition, from a romanticized realism to a more modern realism that opened up the book to criticism.

In Europe the heightened emotion of adventure novels like those by Sir Walter Scott, or the supernatural gothic novels of Anne Radcliffe and Mary Shelley gradually gave way in the Victorian era to more socially realistic depictions of life by authors like Charles Dickens, Gustav Flaubert and Fyodor Dostoevsky. According to authors Richard Ruland and Malcolm Bradbury, the literary emphasis was different in the United States. "America was a land of nature; though immigrants now poured in, its cities were not dominant; though industry grew rapidly and the workplace became familiar ground, nature seemed the space to root national identity and possibility" (Ruland 142-143). But the American brand of romanticism that had been perfected by authors as diverse as Walt Whitman, Nathaniel Hawthorne and Edgar Allan Poe began to alter drastically alter after the carnage of the Civil War, and a new American realism became the norm. Unlike the social realism of Europe, this American version emphasized regional variation in the country and was exemplified by the writings of Mark Twain, William Dean Howells, and Stephen Crane. As the newly reunited country rapidly turned from a rural agrarian to an urban industrialized society, the kind of realism that authors sought to convey in their works more frequently began to reflect that fact. "The strength of [the] regional tradition . . . also gave expression to the as yet unvoiced and radical, thus introducing new aspects of American life—the immigrant experience, the black experience, the experience of women—and pointing the path toward social criticism and naturalism" (193).

Edith Wharton belonged to that group of writers from the turn of the twentieth century, many of them women, who were working in an area that combined a certain kind of regionalism that harkened back to an earlier era in American literary history, with a realism that also reflected the harsh reality of life in the United States as it really was—in her case, for women. Rather than dealing with heroic protagonists who influenced events and their environment though sheer force of will, writers like Frank Norris, Kate Chopin, Theodore Dreiser and Willa Cather were exploring the challenges faced by everyday people who were powerless to control their lives in an increasingly modernized world. In this context it seems counter-intuitive to proclaim that *Ethan Frome* is not a realistic novel. After all, the story is rich in detail and depth of description about the people and a place Wharton had observed for over a decade. In writing about the book in his biography of Wharton, R.W.B. Lewis said, "The treatment both of setting and character shows Edith Wharton in perfect command of the methods of literary realism; in its grim and unrelenting way, *Ethan Frome* is a classic of the realistic genre" (Lewis 309). But that is not what Wharton's introduction attempts to defend. In point of fact, *Ethan Frome* is a fantasy. It's not the accurate recounting by the author of what happens to a character, but instead the completely fictional story within the novel of what happened to that character in the past through the eyes and imagination of a different character. Modern critics seem to understand better than those in Wharton's day that in practical terms this makes little difference. Harold Bloom, commenting on Lewis's statement, even goes so far as to say, "literary 'realism' is intensely metaphorical, as Lewis keenly knows. *Ethan Frome* is so charged in its representation of reality as to be frequently phantasmagoric in effect" (H. Bloom 1986, 4).

The reviewer from *The Baltimore Sun*, however, decried what he saw as "the impossible construction of the story. There is no way that the engineer who tells us the story could have learned it. The author [would have] done better to tell a straight tale . . ." (Grasty, 31). Wharton's decision to use a narrator was equally vexing for the unnamed reviewer from *The Brooklyn Daily Eagle*, who gives the fullest account of this critical view.

> Mrs. Wharton seems to have committed an inexplicable error of form. The story is a story of the innermost souls of her people. Both the feelings which moved them and the few and timid expressions given to these feelings, could be known only to the characters themselves or to their creator. But Mrs. Wharton puts this story into the mouth of a visiting engineer who worked in Starkfield for the winter. In theory it is the story which this engineer picked up in the neighborhood, chiefly from the gossip of the village and in part from a drive with Ethan Frome himself. But a visitor must pick up merely the facts and the outer shell of a story

in that way. The significant things in this story are not the facts but the passion which inspired the facts . . . [things] Ethan Frome never would or never could have told . . . (Hester, 5)

Interestingly, the reviewer does seem to understand the true nature of the narrator, as a surrogate for the author herself. "Those are things which the engineer could only have got, as Mrs. Wharton got them, from his imagination . . . precisely the thing which Mrs. Wharton has made vivid and true by her narrative imagination." But that isn't nearly good enough. In this way of looking at literature not only isn't the narrator sufficiently realistic, he actually impedes the realism of the novel and simultaneously baffles the critic. "Therefore, the engineer, at the beginning and the close of the book, is a superfluity and an intruder . . . Why did she ever introduce the engineer, to serve as a screen between herself and the readers and to make a blot on what, without him, would have been one of the strongest, most direct and deepest stories she has ever told?"

But those critics at the time who objected to this new mode of writing were operating from a very different sense of what the "rules" of writing a novel should be, and it wouldn't be until decades after Wharton's death that the common sense of critics like Joseph Brennan would first begin to see the novel's structure in its proper context.

Once one recognizes [the] fact, however, that we have to deal here with an overt fiction within a fiction, it is expedient, if not indeed necessary, to accept this arrangement as the very form of the novel and to analyze it as such. Hence the need for a close examination of the "vision" within the novel in relationship to its narrator as well as on its own terms. (Brennan 348)

The choice to use this particular literary conceit was not one that Wharton made lightly, but emerged only after considering the problems associated with the particular characters she was writing about. In discussing the New England countryside and patterns of speech as they were usually rendered in the literature of her time she said, "Even the abundant enumeration of sweet-fern, asters and mountain-laurel, and the conscientious reproduction of the vernacular, left me with the feeling that the outcropping granite had in both cases been overlooked" (Wharton 1911, v). This is an important statement for two reasons. In the first case, she felt that earlier writers had ignored the literal stone that is such a prominent feature of the landscape in favor of the more verdant aspects of the setting. It is the second case that is more interesting, however, because of the metaphorical way the stone represents the people themselves.

Like an iceberg in the ocean, in which the vast majority of its bulk lies hidden beneath the water, Wharton sensed the same characteristic in the people of rural New England that she lived with in her day. And she says as much to the reader by comparing them directly to the stone hidden beneath the ground. "They were, in truth, these figures, my *granite outcroppings*, but half-emerged from the soil, and scarcely more articulate" (Wharton 1911, vi). There's a certain irony in Wordsworth's description of a kind of realism in fiction that speaks "a plainer and more emphatic language," when Wharton's characters barely speak at all. This is something Hermione Lee calls, "the great shock" of the novel. "*Ethan Frome* is a story of silence and speechlessness, numbness and dumbness" (Lee 378). How then, was Wharton going to accurately portray lives which were, in a sense, hidden from sight, and characters who had no motivation to explain their lives to anyone, much less the inclination to think about them for themselves? The answer—realistically—is that she couldn't.

> This incompatibility between subject and plan would perhaps have seemed to suggest that my "situation" was after all one to be rejected . . . But I had no such fear . . . in the case of *Ethan Frome*. It was the first subject I had ever approached with full confidence in its value, for my own purpose, and a relative faith in my power to render at least a part of what I saw in it. (Wharton 1911, vi-vii)

The specific "situation" she speaks of is more than just the reticence of her characters, but the very construction of the novel itself. "The problem before me, as I saw in the first flash, was this: I had to deal with a subject of which the dramatic climax, or rather the anti-climax, occurs a generation later than the first acts of the tragedy" (vi). While she is speaking here about the ending of the novel, the real issue is that the bulk of the story had to be set in the past. Not only would it prove challenging at best to get the story of the present-day Ethan out of her New England farmers, it would have been literally impossible to obtain from them an accurate rendering of his past. In this way the fantasy element of *Ethan Frome* actually springs from the very reality of the situation that Wharton was facing. For Wharton, the answer was a simple one: someone else would have to tell the tale.

At the same time, just because the narrator of her tale had to imagine the actual story, didn't mean that Wharton felt she could abandon the dictates of reality altogether. "It appears to me, indeed, that while an air of artificiality is lent to a tale of complex and sophisticated people which the novelist causes to be guessed at and interpreted by any mere looker-on, there need be no such drawback if the looker-on is sophisticated, and the people he interprets are simple" (Wharton 1911, viii). Simple, in this case, does not mean unintelligent, but lacking in guile. If her characters don't want to talk about themselves, they simply don't. But this wasn't enough for her contemporaries and, as she states about this necessary construction, it "met with the immediate and unqualified disapproval of the few friends to whom I tentatively outlined it." Realism in literature at this time wasn't just important to literary critics and authors; it was seen as the only thing. Later in the twentieth century Lionel Trilling castigated the writings of Theodore Dreiser because he felt that the author's emphasis on realism actually stunted the artistic value of his works. "Everyone is aware that Dreiser's prose style is full of roughness and ungainliness, and the critics who admire Dreiser tell us it does not matter . . . But it has been taken for granted that the ungainliness of Dreiser's style is the only possible objection to be made to it, and that whoever finds in it any fault at all wants a prettified genteel style, and is objecting to the ungainliness of reality itself" (Trilling 1950, 14)

Wharton's fear, and it was a legitimate one, was that in apparently foregoing "reality" altogether, her book risked being rejected by critics out of hand—and as a result of that, by readers—because of its abandonment of the real in favor of the imagined. The great irony in all of this is that fiction, by its very nature, is unreal. The fact that Wharton's narrator in *Ethan Frome* imagines what happened to the protagonist in the past is not at all different from an author who is essentially doing the same thing. Beyond that, however, is what fiction offers to the reader that reality can't. This is another point made by Trilling in the same essay when it came to critics who disapproved of Henry James and the way that he portrayed artists in his work. Much like Wharton in her introduction, in James' rebuttal he was able to articulate the importance of fiction in that respect.

> More significant, is the comment Granville Hicks makes in *The Great Tradition* when he deals with James's stories about artists and remarks that such artists as James portrays, so concerned for their art and their integrity in art, do not really exist: "After all, who has ever known such artists?" This question, as Mr. Hicks admits, had occurred to James himself, but what answer had James given to it? "If the life about us for the last thirty years refused warrant for these examples," he said in the preface to volume XII of the New York Edition, "then so much the worse for that life . . . There are decencies that in the name of the general self-respect we must take for granted, there's a rudimentary intellectual honor

to which we must, in the interest of civilization, at least pretend." And to this Mr. Hicks, shocked beyond argument, makes this reply, which would be astonishing had we not heard it before: "But this is the purest romanticism, this writing about what ought to be rather than what is!" (Trilling 1950, 13)

Whatever her intended goal in writing *Ethan Frome*, Edith Wharton was very pointedly able to turn James' idea around and address "what ought *not* to be rather than what is." By the simple feat of imbuing her male protagonist with the attitudes and repressions necessarily adopted by the women of her day, Wharton adroitly demonstrated the folly of imposing such behaviors and expectations on anyone.

Wharton never abandoned the idea of making the story itself as believable as possible, especially considering the necessity of its imaginative construction. But that believability has to be understood in the context of the overall conceit of the novel. Wharton was especially sensitive to charges that her story did not really reflect the true nature of the people living in that part of western Massachusetts in which she spent a decade of summers. Even at the end of her life she felt compelled to defend herself in her autobiography, *A Backward Glance*.

In an article by an American literary critic, I saw *Ethan Frome* cited as an interesting example of a successful New England story written by some one who knew nothing of New England! *Ethan Frome* was written after I spent ten years in the hill-region where the scene is laid, during which years I had come to know well the aspect, dialect, and mental and moral attitude of the hill-people . . . [This] might have sufficed to disprove the legend—but once such a legend is started it echoes on as long as its subject survives. (Wharton 1934, 296)

One of her harshest critics, writing a few years after the novel's release, was Elizabeth Shepley Sergeant who created a faux dialogue between herself and an imaginary friend who liked the book. "I was born with . . . the kind of people, the kind of place, yes and the kind of drama of weakened will she is so relentlessly describing," says Sergeant's character. "And I tell you that in spite of the *vraisemblance* of the surface, she has got them all wrong. She has nowhere dug down into the subsoil" (Lauer 122-123). The great irony is that Wharton really didn't need to defend herself from this charge, and Sergeant inadvertently reveals the answer why. When the friend remarks that she will never forget the heightened realism of a certain passage, Sergeant launches in with her sarcastic reply. "Of course you can't. Neither could Mrs. Wharton. You both look at Starkfield with the eyes of the sophisticated stranger . . . You notice the superficial things that would make you miserable" (124). But that is finally the point. The story isn't *told* by Ethan, and so it was never going to represent the thoughts and feeling of someone who grew up and lived there all of his life. The story is the narrator's vision—which is why the novel resonates so profoundly with its readers, the vast majority of whom are also outsiders.

Finally, it is Joseph Brennan who lays the entire argument to rest in the conclusion of his essay on the novel. He recognizes first that, "it would be much more reasonable to judge the novel in terms of the special character of the narrator's mind—his predilection for poetic, symbolic design and an abstract ideal of human nature—rather than in terms of psychological realism. For even within the formal structure and statement of the work, Ethan and Mattie and Zeena are much more imagined than real characters" (Brennan 356). It is only in following Brennan's suggestion that the reader is able to move beyond the simplistic motivations and relationships of the characters as calculating villains and helpless victims operating within a specific plot. In looking at them from the narrator's perspective readers are able to better understand the issues that those imaginary characters face in the very real society in which they operate. "One may take issue, perhaps, with the rightness of the narrator's vision, but certainly not with his right—or the right of the author—to imagine it as his peculiar sensibility dictates." In this way the inner story of *Ethan Frome* attains the same reality that any other novel does. In the grand scheme of things, no matter how realistic an author attempts to make a novel the reality of any work of fiction is that it is only an idealized version of the truth. Brennan makes this clear when, just like Trilling, he quotes Henry James. "It may be well to recall what Henry James wrote in defense of *Daisy Miller*, that his 'supposedly typical little figure was of course pure poetry, and had never been anything else.'"

As stated earlier, within the confines of her fictional world Wharton purposely made her narrator more sophisticated than the inhabitants of Starkfield. "If he is capable of seeing all around them, no violence is done to probability in allowing him to exercise this facility; it is natural enough that he should act as the sympathizing intermediary between his rudimentary characters and the more complicated minds to whom he is trying to present them" (Wharton 1911, viii). What Wharton almost dismisses as a "minor detail," however, is actually one of the most powerfully realistic aspects of the entire novel, as there was still the matter of how the narrator was going to come by the information that he uses to create his vision of the story of Ethan Frome. "I might have sat him down before a village gossip who would have poured out the whole affair to him in a breath," she writes (viii-ix). This is a perfectly legitimate way of telling a story, but it does come with certain drawbacks of which Wharton was well aware when she stated that in doing so her tale would lack a sense of "roundness" that is "produced by letting their case be seen through eyes as different as those of Harmon Gow and Mrs. Ned Hale" (ix). More importantly, however, she also understood that it would have violated the essential reality of the characters she was writing about. "In doing this I should have been false" in characterizing "the deep-rooted reticence and inarticulateness of the people I was trying to draw." Ultimately her method is successful because "each of my chroniclers contributes to the narrative *just so much as he or she is capable of understanding* of what, to them, is a complicated and mysterious case; and only the narrator of the tale has scope enough to see it all."

Cynthia Griffin Wolff has made the best case for the importance of seeing Wharton's novel in terms of its narrator as the de facto author of the tale, especially in the way that it shifts the emphasis away from the literal story. "It is the *relation* of the tale to the narrator's larger categories that must be our primary interest, the focus of the story as Wharton has defined it" (Wolff 158). As Wolff implies, Wharton's need to provide an introduction, especially as it addresses her defense of the novel's structure and the primacy in the tale of the narrator, gives the reader a way to understand that the significance of *Ethan Frome* is less about the characters than it is the narrator's response—as a surrogate for the reader—to those characters. Wharton herself would expand upon this idea in her book on the writing of fiction a few years later.

> In every form of novel it is noticeable that the central characters tend to be the least real. This seems to be partly explained by the fact that these characters, survivors of the old "hero" and "heroine," whose business it was not to be real but to be sublime, are still, though often without the author's being aware of it, the standard-bearer of his convictions or the expression of his secret inclinations. They are *his* in the sense of tending to do and say what he would do, or imagines he would do, in given circumstances, and being mere projections of his own personality they lack the substance and relief of the minor characters, who he views coolly and objectively, in all their human weakness and inconsequence. (Wharton 1925, 94-95)

What's so interesting about this observation in relation to *Ethan Frome* is the way that Wharton's narrator takes on the role of the "author" of the story. If Ethan and Mattie seem the "least real" in the story—as Elizabeth

Shepley Sergeant complained—it is because their true purpose is not as "real" people at all, but as symbolic representations of society. Thus the interior story of Ethan's past has far more to do with the narrator's "projection of his own personality" and makes of Ethan as a character the "standard-bearer of his convictions or the expression of his secret inclinations." In this way Wharton's ability to use Ethan as a symbolic representation of women is not simply presented as such by her, a female writer, but instead through the eyes of her male narrator. While Joseph Brennan's comment along this line deals with only one specific aspect of the narrator's view of the characters, it is also reflective of Wharton's larger point.

> The narrator's acute sensitivity to the beauty of nature, in fact, accounts for much that is profoundly moving and memorable in *Ethan Frome* . . . It is not surprising, therefore, that in projecting the character of Ethan, the narrator has liberally endowed him with much the same sensitivity he himself possesses. Though there is not the slightest indication from any source of evidence to which the engineer has access that either Ethan or Mattie was especially sensitive to the beauties of nature, the narrator has so thoroughly imbued the two of them with this susceptibility that it both motivates and dominates their relationship. (Brennan 349)

The tremendous irony in all of this is the way that Edith Wharton's symbolic rendering of Ethan, Mattie, and Zeena through her narrator turned out to be more realistic than much of the regional fiction published in her day. "Other writers," says Cynthia Wolff, "the venerable regionalists of New England, had already given us the surface view that Wharton scorned: a prettified spectacle of billboard art, a pastoral land seen through awestruck eyes. Wharton would look through the surface to discover what was timeless in the human mind . . ." (Wolff 159). And the word timeless is key here, as it soon becomes apparent that *Ethan Frome* is not just as story of particular people in a particular place and time, but a symbol for the emotional struggle of humanity in all times. "In the end," says Wolff, "such a method focuses our attention more clearly and precisely on the narrator than on anything else. Refracted thus, a particular event may gain significance beyond the limitations of its time and place, may finally tell us about human consciousness itself. That is the function of Art."

Prologue

Just as with the two preceding short stories in this volume, the first sentence in Wharton's novel is also a separate paragraph. And as with those other two stories, it also demands special attention. The first word in the novel is the personal pronoun "I." This makes it clear that it is the narrator who will be telling the entirety of the tale. But just as important to consider is the rest of the sentence: "I had the story, bit by bit, from various people, and, as generally happens in such cases, each time it was a different story" (Wharton 1911, 3). Thus the construction of Wharton's novel takes the form of a frame story. She begins with a prologue in which the narrator introduces the main characters and the circumstances that ultimately allow him to put into place the pieces of Ethan's life he has learned from the people in the village. The other nine chapters that comprise the interior of the novel contain the story that the narrator tells about Ethan, a story that none of the other people he has talked to completely understands.

This story-telling aspect of the novel is reinforced in a very clever way in the second paragraph by having the narrator speak in second person, directly to the reader.

> If you know Starkfield, Massachusetts, you know the post-office. If you know the post-office you must have seen Ethan Frome drive up to it, drop the reins on his hollow-backed bay and drag himself across the brick pavement to the white colonnade; and you must have asked who he was. (Wharton 1911, 3).

In this way the narrator's curiosity becomes the reader's own, and the episode that opens the novel is the impetus for the narrator's desire to know more about this singular individual. His description of Ethan is as striking as the man himself, a "ruin of a man" who nevertheless possessed a "careless powerful look." He was a commanding presence "in spite of a lameness checking each step like the jerk of a chain." Here Wharton foreshadows Ethan's life with Zeena through the symbolism of the chain, as though Ethan's feet are in legcuffs as he walks. But that won't become apparent until later, and so it's the description of his face, "bleak and unapproachable" that stands out on first reading, as well as his disabled body, "so stiffened and grizzled that I took him for an old man and was surprised to hear that he was not more than fifty-two" (3-4).

The narrator learns from Harmon Gow, the stagecoach driver, that Ethan's injuries were the result of a "smash-up" that had occurred some twenty-four years earlier "which, besides drawing the red gash across Ethan Frome's forehead, had so shortened and warped his right side that it cost him a visible effort to take the few steps from his buggy to the post-office window" (Wharton 1911, 4). One of the many masterful techniques Wharton uses in *Ethan Frome* is that of juxtaposition. In fact, recognizing her use of this device is one of the keys to understanding the entire novel. It is also one of the ways that her writing, in the words of Laura Rattray, "is not always as it first seems" (Rattray xx). After describing the visible effort that Ethan must expend to pick up his mail, "drag[ging] himself across the brick pavement," the narrator adds almost matter-of-factly that "he used to drive in from his farm every day about noon" (Wharton 1911, 4). The connotation of the verb "drive" to modern audiences brings with it images of automobile travel. But the fact is Ethan makes the trip every day in a horse-drawn buggy, which requires much more effort to prepare than merely hopping into a car. And because the narrator mentions it so casually it's easy to miss the importance of the following observation. "I noticed that, though he came so punctually, he seldom received anything but a copy of the *Bettsbridge Eagle*, which he put without a glance into his sagging pocket" (5).

The question then becomes why Ethan would go to the tremendous effort, especially given his extensive injuries, of hitching up his horse and driving all the way into town and back every day when there was rarely anything there waiting for him? The answer comes in the following sentence. "At intervals, however, the post-master would hand him an envelope addressed to Mrs. Zenobia—or Mrs. Zeena—Frome, and usually bearing . . . the address of some manufacturer of patent medicine . . ." (Wharton 1911, 5). Ethan's wife is apparently sick, as she has the need for mail-order medication. But whatever the exact nature of her illness is, it must make conditions at home severe enough that Ethan goes through the pain and effort every day of harnessing his horse and hitching up his buggy in order to achieve the brief respite that going to the post office provides. Regardless of how much the people in the village may or may not know about his personal life, they seem to have a great respect for the man. "Every one in Starkfield knew him and gave him a greeting tempered to his own grave mien; but his taciturnity was respected and it was only on rare occasions that one of the older men of the place detained him for a word."

Though many contemporary critics, as well as later biographers, attempted to tie Wharton's New England stories to the writings of Nathaniel Hawthorne, there is very little evidence on which to make that case. Though the settings are naturally similar, the differences in the writing style and intention of the two authors are quite distinct. There is, however, the matter of Wharton's choice of names for the two main characters in the novel that suggest something of an attempt on her part to place her work within the American tradition of Hawthorne, or at the least to pay homage to the author. In her original French version of the story Wharton had named her characters Hart and Anna. The most notable Ethan in American literature comes from the short story "Ethan Brand," Hawthorne's tale of a man who goes in search of the Unpardonable Sin, and after returning home decades later decides to kill himself because he realizes the search itself has made him guilty of that very sin. But that hardly describes Ethan Frome. Says author Cynthia Wolff, "Wharton was not interested in sin, but she was interested in the effect of isolation upon the workings of a man's emotional life" (Wolff 159). Zenobia too, is the main character in one of Hawthorne's works, his novel *The Blithedale Romance.* Unlike Wharton's Zeena, Hawthorne's character is a charismatic woman at the center of the creation of a utopian society, and like Ethan Brand she also commits suicide. There is one similarity she has to Wharton's character, however. According to Elizabeth Ammons, the two eligible men in her life "decide to love childlike Pricilla rather than her mature sister Zenobia" (Ammons 76). The only other connection Wharton's novel has to Hawthorne is a tenuous one, as Suzanne Fournier suggests, "The figures Wharton chose from Hawthorne's romances both take their own lives, thus completing the act which Ethan Frome and Mattie Silver unsuccessfully attempt at the climax of *Ethan Frome*" (Fournier 60).

It's only after Ethan has climbed back into his buggy and set off for his farm that the narrator questions Harmond Gow as to the severity of the smash-up that crippled him. "Wust kind . . . More'n enough to kill most men. But the Fromes are tough. Ethan'll likely touch a hundred" (Wharton 1911, 6). At this the narrator is shocked, especially given the nature of Ethan's injuries, but what he says in reply reveals something more than just his perception of Ethan's physical pain. "That man touch a hundred? He looks as if he was dead and in hell now!" From the narrator's point of view the brutal nature of the accident that has disabled Ethan is such that another fifty years on the planet seems inconceivable in terms of pain and suffering. But what is more informative in his response is that Ethan looks to him as if he is in hell already. Beyond simply the pain associated with death, the connotation of hell is one of everlasting torment. What it is that torments Ethan specifically is not known at this point in the story, though part of it must be related to the sickness of his wife if it drives him to town every day. For Gow, the real torment seems to lie in the oppression of the weather. "Guess he's been in Starkfield too many winters. Most of the smart ones get away."

Again, Wharton is not content to simply let one answer present itself before she tacks on even more information. The effect of the weather on the people of Starkfield will be addressed by the narrator shortly, but for now it's important to look at the last part of what Gow says because that is what the narrator responds to first. It would be easy to misread his statement that "Most of the smart ones get away," as an implication that Ethan is not one of the smart ones because he never escaped (Wharton 1911, 6). But in context it becomes clear that Ethan is one of the smart ones when the narrator asks, "Why didn't *he*?" (7). Wharton even italicizes the personal pronoun in order to make it more explicit: if most of the smart ones get away why hasn't Ethan, as one of their number, been able to do likewise? Gow says that it was because he had to take care of his parents. "There warn't ever anybody but Ethan. Fust his father—then his mother—then his wife." Oddly absent from this list of reasons is the one the narrator points out in accounting for what he takes as the primary cause for Ethan's inability to escape. "And then the smash-up?" Which makes Gow's response all the more curious. "Harmon chuckled sardonically. 'That's so. He *had* to stay then.'" While the narrator takes the information at face value, it's worth noting that Gow's response of laughter to the accident is not what one would expect, and Wharton's choice of adverb only heightens the effect. Something about the accident is not quite what it appears to be, and things become even more curious after Gow responds to the narrator's next question: "And since then they've had to care for him?" But in answering why the accident forced Ethan to stay in Starkfield Gow says, "Oh, as to that: I guess it's always Ethan done the caring." At this point the narrator realizes that there is much more to the story than Gow is telling him, and at the same time that he isn't going to get any more from him. "Though Harmon Gow developed the tale as far as his mental and moral reach permitted there were perceptible gaps between his facts, and I had the sense that the deeper meaning of the story was in the gaps."

It's here the narrator returns to something Gow said earlier, that one possible explanation for the haunted and tortured look in Ethan's eyes is that he had spent too many winters in Starkfield.

> Before my own time there was up I had learned to know what that meant. Yet I had come in the degenerate day of trolley, bicycle and rural delivery, when communication was easy between the scattered mountain villages, and the bigger towns in the valleys, such as Bettsbridge and Shadd's Falls, had libraries, theatres and Y.M.C.A. halls to which the youth of the hills could descend for recreation. But when winter shut down on Starkfield and the village lay under a sheet of snow perpetually renewed from the pale skies, I began to see what life there—or rather its negation—must have been in Ethan Frome's young manhood. (Wharton 1911, 7-8)

Here Wharton begins to lay the groundwork for the primary story to come by contrasting the relative ease of the present day with the way things had been a generation earlier. The key word in this description is communication, as it is the isolating effect of the snows that has the greatest impact on the people of Starkfield during the winter, so much so that the narrator refers to it as the "negation" of life. Wharton herself called the story a "tragedy of isolation," one taking place "before the coming of the motor and the telephone" (Wharton 1932, 77, 78). It's also here the reader learns that the narrator is an engineer working on a construction project at a power station in Corbury Junction. A carpenter's strike, however, has stranded him in the village for several months and given him some insight into the difference between the experience of winter for ordinary urban dwellers versus those who live in this tiny farming community.

At first the narrator is irritated to find himself stuck for the winter in Starkfied, but eventually, "under the hypnotising effect of routine, I gradually began to find a grim satisfaction in the life" (Wharton 1911, 8). Nevertheless, the beauty of the scenery as he observes it during the early portion of his stay appears to be at odds with the way the inhabitants of the village experience it. "One would have supposed that such an atmosphere must quicken the emotions as well as the blood; but it seemed to produce no change except that of retarding still more the sluggish pulse of Starkfield" (9). What he begins to realize is that the single winter he was forced to stay in the village—the first for him—is nothing compared to the accumulated effect of numerous winters on the people who have spent their entire lives there. "When I had been there a little longer . . . I began to understand why Starkfield emerged from its six months' siege like a starved garrison capitulating without quarter.

Twenty years earlier the means of resistance must have been far fewer, and the enemy in command of almost all the lines of access between the beleaguered villages . . ."

Wharton uses the metaphor of war to describe the isolating effect of the winter months on the inhabitants by calling it a "siege." The reality for farmers, even as late as the early twentieth century, is that their lives had changed very little from those who had immigrated to North America nearly two hundred years earlier. With their dependency on horses for transportation, the weather limiting travel and communication, as well as the inability to grow more food, the impact of the winter months on people was a sobering one. Families had to stock pile as much food as they could manage in order to make it though the winter, and then they spent those months watching that supply gradually dwindle, hoping they could survive until the spring. Even if neighbors had extra food to share with a household that was running low, they might be miles away and extreme weather conditions could limit their ability to get the food to those in need much less even know about that need. Two decades earlier, the narrator instinctively understands, the ability to withstand nature's onslaught would have been reduced even further. Again, Wharton's reference to that era is preparing the reader for the shift in time periods when the main story begins.

It's also important to note that the entire novel takes place during the winter, not only in the current timeline but also the inner story set in the past within the frame. As such, all of the characters, but more specifically Ethan, must deal with a force of nature over which they have no control, an unstoppable fact of life that seems to sap their spirit and energy, leaving them somehow less than they were before. Over time the cumulative effect of this assault on the people has had the consequence of diminishing them as people. In this context it's not difficult to equate the natural force of winter with the very unnatural force of societal expectations for women. One only has to remember Edgar Lee Masters and the metaphor he uses in the cautionary warning that comes from Serepta Mason:

Ye living ones, ye are fools indeed
Who do not know the ways of the wind
And the unseen forces
That govern the processes of life. (Masters 18)

Wharton also invokes the wind as part of her martial description of the winter, "when the storms of February had pitched their white tents about the devoted village and the wild cavalry of March winds had charged down to their support" (Wharton 1911, 9). In this way Wharton is able to provide a symbolic parallel to the kind of covert oppression that society imposes on women by turning it into the oppression of nature, one that more accurately represents the unconscious way that societal expectations were accepted by people in her day. As such, Ethan has no more power to control the weather than the women of Wharton's day had to control the "unseen forces" to which they were compelled to submit. Much like Lionel Trilling would do four decades later, the narrator thinks back to Gow's phrase that most of the smart ones get away and thinks to himself, "If that were the case, how could any combination of obstacles have hindered the flight of a man like Ethan Frome?" (9-10).

The association of the weather with the seemingly intractable nature of society's expectations for the women of her day is not only present in *Ethan Frome*, but informs a great deal of Edith Wharton's other works. Wharton biographer Richard Lewis sees this phenomenon as stemming from the naturalist philosophy she had absorbed in her reading and was thus reflected by the "implacable power of the environment" seen in much of her writing (Lewis 56). The word environment here is not simply a reference to weather, but any environment that serves to repress the natural instincts of her characters. "Those fictional figures of hers who struggle pathetically against their stifling surroundings are belated offsprings of the tutelage of Egerton Winthrop—a combination, as it were, of Flaubert's *Madame Bovary* and Herbert Spencer" (Lewis 56-57). The association between societal expectations and the indifference of nature is not only evident in the overt symbolism of the winter weather in the natural environment of *Ethan Frome*, but in the man-made environments found in Wharton's other stories. "Wharton's familiar setting of Old New York, for example, often serves as arena for the Darwinian struggle between a desiccated upper class and a brash, rising middle class" (Fournier 74). Even the great V.L. Parrington summed up Wharton's primary impact as an author as "an observer whose irony springs from noting the clash between men and social convention" (Parrington 382). When viewed in this way the rural New England setting of *Ethan Frome* functions in much the same way as the settings in Wharton's other novels, as it is the reaction of the characters to those restrictive environments—not necessarily the environments themselves—that she is interested in. This also applies to the specific struggle of women at the time, as author Barbara A. White attests when she says about the author, "she seems to have used New England settings . . . as symbolic means of exploring favorite subjects, such as the absence of high culture in modern life, the permeation of the present by the past, and the claustrophobia of female experience" (White 54).

The narrator's mystification about what has kept Ethan in Starkfield for so long is followed by his recounting of the circumstances of his own residency in Starkfield, as a lodger in the home of the widow Mrs. Ned Hale, née Ruth Varnum. Mrs. Hale's fortunes had diminished over the years, forcing her to rent out rooms in the family home, "the most considerable mansion in the village," where she lived alone with her mother (Wharton 1911, 10). At first his stay there seemed fortuitous. As she nightly informed her visitor about the people and events that made up the "Starkfield chronicle . . . I had great hopes of getting from her the missing facts of Ethan Frome's story, or rather such a key to his character as should co-ordinate the facts I knew" (10-11). But while the narrator finds her to be "a store-house of innocuous anecdote [on] any question about her acquaintances," to his dismay he discovers that "on the subject of Ethan Frome I found her unexpectedly reticent. . . . 'Yes, I knew them both . . . it was awful . . .' seeming to be the utmost concession that her distress could make to my curiosity" (11). It should be noted that her reference to "them both" indicates someone else was involved in the accident along with Ethan. Of course, as soon as he is able he confronts Harmon Gow with this information, hoping to get from him more of the story than he was willing to part with previously. "I put the case anew to my village oracle, Harmon Gow; but got for my pains only an uncomprehending grunt." In attempting to explain Mrs. Hale's behavior, however, Gow confirms the presence of another person in the accident that disfigured Ethan. "Come to think of it, she was the first one to see 'em after they was picked up . . . I guess she just can't bear to talk about it" (11-12).

The irony for the narrator is that the more he learns about Ethan, or rather the more bits and pieces he manages to accumulate about him, it still does nothing to explain the haunted countenance of the man that caused the narrator to exclaim that Ethan seemed as if he were already in hell. "No one gave me an explanation of the look in his face which, as I persisted in thinking, neither poverty nor physical suffering could have put there" (Wharton 1911, 12). Wharton, however, keeps him from associating the things he has learned with the episodes at the post office, in which she put the fact of Zeena's medication together with Ethan's daily trips as a way of explaining his need to escape from whatever is going on in the house. Having no regular contact with anyone else in the village to consult, there seems to be little more the narrator can do in attempting to solve this mystery. But then the unexpected happens. "I might have contented myself with the story pieced together from these hints had it not been for the provocation of Mrs. Hale's silence, and—a little later—for the accident of personal contact with the man" (12-13). The closest thing Starkfield has to a livery stable is run by Denis Eady, who also owns the grocery story, and the narrator had hired Denis take him up to the Corbury Flats every day in order to catch his train. But when Eady's horses get sick, and the illness spreads to the rest of the horses in the village, the narrator finds himself essentially stranded.

Wharton presents the reader with a wonderfully droll exchange between the narrator and Gow that captures the essence of the kind of rural New England characters she was writing about.

> Then Harmon Gow suggested that Ethan Frome's bay was still on his legs and that his owner might be glad to drive me over.
>
> I stared at the suggestion. "Ethan Frome? But I've never even spoken to him. Why on earth should he put himself out for me?"
>
> Harmon's answer surprised me still more. "I don't know as he would; but I know he wouldn't be sorry to earn a dollar." (Wharton 1911, 13)

It's here the reader learns of Ethan's poverty. "I had been told that Frome was poor, and that the saw-mill and the arid acres of his farm yielded scarcely enough to keep his household through the winter; but I had not supposed him to be in such want as Harmon's words implied." (14). According to Gow, "I don't see how he makes out now." In bringing up this new topic of conversation, however, Gow is also inspired to divulge more information about Ethan's past.

> Fust his father got a kick, out haying, and went soft in the brain, and gave away money like Bible texts afore he died. Then his mother got queer and dragged along for years as weak as a baby; and his wife Zeena, she's always been the greatest hand at doctoring in the county. Sickness and trouble: that's what Ethan's had his plate full up with, ever since the very first helping. (14-15)

What's interesting is that, along with the sickness of Ethan's father and mother, Gow also mentions that Zeena is one of the best at "doctoring in the county." This actually seems at odds with the fact that Zeena receives medicine on a regular basis, especially if her illness is such that it drives Ethan out of the house every day. But it won't be until much later in the novel that this seeming paradox is resolved.

The narrator agrees to have Gow ask Ethan, and the next day Ethan shows up in front of the Hale residence with his swayback horse and for the next week he takes the narrator the three miles to the train station and picks him up at the end of the day to bring him back. The horse is slow, and it takes an hour each way, but that's not the most remarkable aspect of the journey. "Ethan Frome drove in silence, the reins loosely held in his left hand . . . He never turned his face to mine, or answered, except in monosyllables, the questions I put, or such slight pleasantries as I ventured" (Wharton 1911, 15). While on the surface this refusal on the part of Ethan to engage in conversation with the narrator simply seems to be in character for the people as Wharton describes them in her introduction, there is a deeper meaning that emerges as the narrator concludes his observation. "He seemed a part of the mute melancholy landscape, an incarnation of its frozen woe, with all that was warm and sentient in him fast bound below the surface . . . I simply felt that he lived in a depth of moral isolation too remote for casual access" (15-16). This somber description, when taken symbolically, begins with the "melancholy landscape" of American society for women. However positive their lives might have been on the surface, there was no denying their inability to live those lives to their fullest expression. Further, the "frozen woe" attests to the inability to affect any meaningful change in that society which, for many women, resulted in a "depth of moral isolation" that could not be accessed casually.

Then, for the third time, Wharton brings up the isolating influence of winter. "I had the sense that his loneliness was not merely the result of his personal plight, tragic as I guessed that to be, but had in it, as Harmon Gow had hinted, the profound accumulated cold of many Starkfield winters" (Wharton 1911, 15-16). Like Shakespeare, Wharton is alerting the reader to something important in thrice mentioning the season in this way, which gives added credence to the idea of her use of winter in the novel as one that contains significant symbolic meaning for the character beyond just the obvious oppression of that time of year. In fact, the first half of the sentence seems to make this abundantly clear, that the isolation Ethan feels is "not merely the result of his personal plight." In the same way that the house signifies the oppressive restraints on women in "The Yellow Wall-Paper," the weather signifies the way society's expectations have trapped Ethan. Wharton's use of a more appropriate symbol for a man also reverses the idea of the outside world as one that represents freedom in "The Story of an Hour." Ethan's responsibility for earning a living is centered on the exterior world, the opposite of the woman trapped by the interior responsibilities of the home. Thus for Ethan, his ability to work outdoors and deal with business matters in the village seems no more liberating than a woman's trips to the grocery store. In either case, the psychological onus of societal expectations is in no way diminished by the character's apparent physical freedom.

On two occasions, however, the narrator is able to penetrate Ethan's silence. The first is when he mentions that he spent the previous winter working in Florida and what an extreme difference there is between the two climates. "Yes," says Ethan, "I was down there once, and for a good while afterward I could call up the sight of it in winter. But now it's all snowed under" (Wharton 1911, 16). The moment implies what the narrator had thought about Ethan all along, that he never would have stayed in Starkfield by choice, and the evidence of a brief sojourn south seems to confirm that. The second occasion is when the narrator accidentally leaves a book of popular science on the sleigh, and when Ethan returns it to him that evening he is compelled to mention the impact it had on him. "There are things in that book that I didn't know the first word about" (17). The moment provides yet another crucial insight into the character of the man. "I wondered less at his words than at the queer note of resentment in his voice. He was evidently surprised and slightly aggrieved at his own ignorance." The narrator offers to loan the book to him, and though Ethan initially hesitates he eventually agrees. The hope, on the narrator's part, is that this will lead to some kind of discourse between the two men, "but something in his past history, or in his present way of living, had apparently driven him too deeply into himself for any casual impulse to draw him back to his kind" (18). As a result, on their next meeting "he made no allusion to the book, and our intercourse seemed fated to remain as negative and one-sided as if there had been no break in his reserve" (18-19).

The event that changes all of this for the narrator, and allows him enough of a glimpse into Ethan's life that he is compelled to tell his story, is the snowstorm. He wakes up one morning to find that a heavy snow has been falling all night, and though he predicts the train will be delayed, he decides that if Ethan shows up he'll go on ahead to the Flats, as he does have work he needs to do at the power station. "I don't know why I put it in the conditional, however, for I never doubted that Frome would appear. He was not the kind of man to be turned from his business by any commotion of the elements; and at the appointed hour his sleigh glided up through the snow like a stage-apparition behind thickening veils of gauze" (Wharton 1911, 19). The interesting thing to note in this passage is another of the apparent gaps in the narrator's perception. While Ethan's daily trips to the post office suggest that he is escaping from some torment at home, and his dogged determination to transport the narrator is evidence that he is loath to miss an economic opportunity no matter how small, there is another suggestion that can account for both of these behaviors, namely, that Ethan is lonely. Further, the suggestion that Ethan refuses to be controlled by the weather actually reinforces the idea that the elements represent the limitations imposed on him by society when the snow successfully stops him later in the scene. As the stories by Chopin and Gilman demonstrate, it is only when women begin successfully challenging the status quo that society redoubles its efforts to force them back into conformity.

After climbing up into the sleigh the narrator is surprised when instead of being taken to the train station Ethan turns his horse in the opposite direction. On questioning his driver, Ethan answers plainly, "The railroad's blocked by a freight-train that got stuck in a drift below the Flats," and says he's taking the narrator "Straight to the Junction, by the shortest way" (Wharton 1911, 20). This moment is probably the closest thing the two ever get to something that could be called a relationship. Earlier, the narrator had said, "I was getting to know him too well to express either wonder or gratitude at his keeping his appointment," but that doesn't last for long (19-20). The real question becomes what difficulties Ethan had to go through to get the information about the railroad blockage in the first place and, more importantly, what his motivation was for obtaining that information. Again, there seems to be something at work here that goes beyond merely making a dollar. Ethan tells him, "You said you had some business there this afternoon. I'll see you get there" (20). To this the narrator responds by saying, "You're doing me the biggest kind of a favour." His expression of appreciation actually has the effect of opening the way for more communication with Ethan than the narrator has had with him the entire week previously.

The trip to the Junction also provides the narrator with further opportunities for exposition about the setting and Ethan himself. He is first taken past the schoolhouse and along a road the narrator had walked before, near Ethan's moribund sawmill. Interestingly, he views the mill "between hemlock boughs bent inward to their trunks by the weight of the snow" (Wharton 1911, 20-21). Hemlock serves as a foreshadow here, not of literal death but of the symbolic death Ethan has undergone, reinforced by the disfigured branches of the trees that seem to mirror Ethan's own limbs, as well as the fact they are weighed down by snow that represents the oppression of societal expectations. Later on, however, the narrator sees a small apple orchard, and his description harkens back to Wharton's introduction, with its "starved apple-trees writhing over a hillside among outcroppings of slate that nuzzled up through the snow like animals pushing out their noses to breathe" (21). Once beyond the orchard Wharton makes another of her brilliant juxtapositions as the narrator examines "one of those lonely New England farm-houses that make the landscape lonelier," which is followed by Ethan's comment, "That's my place." It's a humbling moment for the narrator who has, until now, been conscious of Ethan's poverty but has had no direct experience of it and, "in the distress and oppression of the scene I did not know what to answer" (21-22). As she does with the description of the outcroppings of stone in comparing them to animals trying to breath, Wharton also personifies the house as it sits in frigid isolation: "the thin wooden walls, under their worn coat of paint, seemed to shiver in the wind that had risen with the ceasing of the snow" (22).

Had this scene taken place at the beginning of their time together, it's doubtful Ethan would have said much of anything to his passenger. But with the greater development, however small, of their relationship, combined with the narrator's expression of appreciation toward Ethan, the latter becomes uncharacteristically expressive during this part of their journey. At first he tells the narrator a little more about his home, though he certainly doesn't seem to be apologizing for it. "The house was bigger in my father's time: I had to take down the 'L,' a while back" (Wharton 1911, 22). With this information in hand the narrator studies the dwelling more closely.

> I saw then that the unusually forlorn and stunted look of the house was partly due to the loss of what is known in New England as the "L": that long deep-roofed adjunct usually built at right angles to the main house, and connecting it, by way of storerooms and tool-house, with the wood-shed and cow-barn. (22).

Then the narrator goes on to make this seemingly incongruous statement. "It is certain that the "L" rather than the house itself seems to be the centre, the actual hearth-stone of the New England farm" (23). At first thought it would seem that the fireplace—typically built in the middle of the house rather than on one of the outer walls as it would be in the twentieth century—has the best claim as the "actual hearth-stone" of the New England home. But Wharton isn't referring to the house here; she's talking about the farm. It's the working aspect of the farm that is centered in the "L," as "it enables the dwellers in that harsh climate to get to their morning's work without facing the weather." Kenneth Bernard, in his essay on imagery and symbolism in Wharton's novel, sees in the denuded building, as well as the winter landscape, a symbol for Ethan's emotional life. "The separation of feeling from its expression, the idea of emotion being locked away, separated, or frozen, just as Starkfield is bound by ice and snow, is demonstrated also by the Frome farm . . . Frome's home is disjointed, separated from its vital functions even as he is" (Bernard 179-180).

Bernard's reference to the "vital functions" of the home and its association with Ethan is that the "L" Ethan was forced to tear down was the business end of the house. What this symbolizes is that Ethan is no longer able to work because of his physical injuries, and the narrator goes on to make that comparison directly. "Perhaps this connection of ideas, which had often occurred to me in my rambles about Starkfield, caused me to hear a wistful note in Frome's words, and to see in the diminished dwelling the image of his own shrunken body" (Wharton 1911, 23). But the "L," in the narrator's words, also protects its owners from the weather. And here is another reference to what society's expectations have done to Ethan, though the reader at this point has very little to go on by way of understanding how those expectations have manifested themselves in Ethan's life. Nevertheless, Ethan's newfound willingness to converse with this stranger provides a few more clues. "We're kinder side-tracked here now . . . but there was considerable passing before the railroad was carried through to the Flats . . . I've always set down the worst of my mother's trouble to that." Along with the weather, the remoteness of the farm is another aspect of the isolation that Ethan feels, though he presents the episode in terms of the way it affected his mother. When rheumatism confined her to her bed she would spend her days looking out at a road where people used to pass, but by then was almost entirely empty of traffic. The only thing that roused her from her illness was when the main road was flooded out and Harmon Gow and his stage used their road to transport his passengers. "She picked up so that she used to get down to the gate most days to see him. But after the trains begun running nobody ever come by here to speak of, and mother never could get it through her head what had happened, and it preyed on her right along till she died" (24).

As if to reinforce the idea of isolation, the snow begins to fall again and Ethan lapses back into silence. The wind has also picked up and turned the trip into something of a slog against the storm. Fortunately, the weather calms by the time the narrator has finished his work, and the two of them head back to Starkfield, "with a good chance of getting there for supper" (Wharton 1911, 25). But while the wind has ceased, the snow begins falling again in earnest, "a soft universal diffusion more confusing than the gusts and eddies of the morning. It seemed to be a part of the thickening darkness, to be the winter night itself descending on us layer by layer." The trip back in the dark really is harrowing, in a countryside with no electric lights, as the snow continues to fall and accumulate in ever-greater quantities. "Two or three times some ghostly landmark sprang up to warn us that we were astray, and then was sucked back into the mist; and when we finally regained our road the old horse began to show signs of exhaustion." The narrator eventually climbs down and walks beside the horse, while Ethan struggles to find the gate to his property. But once there, Ethan refuses to take the narrator any further. "I understood that he was offering me a night's shelter at the farm, and without answering I turned into the gate at his side, and followed him to the barn, where I helped him to unharness and bed down the tired horse" (26).

The narrator follows Ethan up to the door of the house as his host clears off the snow from the porch and the two enter. Once inside, at the end of the passageway is a closed door with light shining beneath it to guide them, "and behind the door I heard a woman's voice droning querulously" (Wharton 1911, 27). In the symbolism of doors and windows the closed door initially bars the narrator from a complete understanding of Ethan, but there is light underneath, which indicates that the answer is on the other side. And it is the entrance into that room that provides him with the answers he has been searching for. As Ethan opens the door and they walk into the room the querulous voice quiets. In the final sentence of the Prologue the narrator makes it clear to the reader that the rest of the story within the frame is merely conjecture, based not only on the facts as he knows them up to that point, but also from what he will learn in spending the night at the Frome's house. "It was that night that I found the clue to Ethan Frome, and began to put together this vision of his story." It's Wharton's use of the word, "vision," that indicates the inner story will be comprised of the narrator's speculation about Ethan's life. Author Candace Waid describes the moment this way: "The narrator projects his vision at the moment we are to see behind the closed door, and his fiction fills the elliptical center of the book . . ." (Waid 76).

Wonderfully, Edith Wharton goes out of her way to emphasize that fictional aspect of the narrator's vision by concluding the sentence with fully three rows of ellipses. This idea of using punctuation to suggest a major shift in the narrative is something author Jean Frantz Blackall calls "Edith Wharton's Art of Ellipsis," a technique she has identified in the author's works in which she sees "a highly calculated and contrived way to achieve certain kinds of effects" (Blackall 145). One of these uses of ellipses by Wharton, she posits, is "to entice the reader to enter into imaginative collaboration with the writer." This is an important concept, because the ellipses here do not just indicate a time shift to the past, but one in which the reader participates in imagining Ethan's past along with the narrator. Though readers intuitively understand how significant this is, it's not always clear to them why. As Cynthia Griffin Wolff so evocatively puts it, "The 'story' of Ethan Frome is nothing more than a dream vision, a brief glimpse into the most appalling recesses of the narrator's mind. The overriding question becomes then—not who is Ethan Frome, but who in the world is this ghastly guide to whom we must submit as we read the tale" (Wolff 161). The simple answer is, he is all of us. The narrator is merely holding up a mirror as a way of forcing the reader to acknowledge, in Kate Chopin's words, "that blind persistence with which men and women believe they have a right to impose a private will upon a fellow-creature" (Chopin 1894).

Chapter I

Along with Chapter One of Mark Twain's *Huckleberry Finn*, the first chapter of *Ethan Frome* is one of the greatest opening chapters in all of American Literature. In it, Edith Wharton lays down the entire symbolic foundation for the rest of the novel, giving the reader a context in which to understand the subtext of the story, as well as some backstory for all of her characters. In addition, she provides the motivation and the central conflict for Ethan. Significantly, Wharton begins with the weather, the snow, the primary symbol for societal restrictions that will play a major part in Ethan's frustration, as well as the resolution of the story. "The village lay under two feet of snow, with drifts at the windy corners. In a sky of iron the points of the Dipper hung like icicles and Orion flashed his cold fires. The moon had set, but the night was so transparent that the white house-fronts between the elms looked gray against the snow, [and] clumps of bushes made black stains on it" (Wharton 1911, 28). The symbolism of the oppression of winter is found not only in the snow itself but in the description of the sky as "iron," like the door of a dungeon cell, and stars that threaten, in the form of hanging icicles and cold fires. Wharton also ends her first paragraph with the most significant symbolism in the novel. According to Kenneth Bernard, "There is hardly a page throughout the book that does not have some reference to light and dark" (Bernard 180).

The light/dark symbolism that had been somewhat altered by Charlotte Perkins Gilman in "The Yellow Wall-Paper" is used in its purest form here, as "the basement windows of the church sent shafts of yellow light far across the endless undulations [of snow]" (Wharton 1911, 28). Thus the front of the houses—Gilman's symbol for a woman's societal confinement—are gray, indicating a lack of consciousness by their occupants, and even nature seems to conspire in this ignorance as the bushes cast black shadows on the snow. But from the basement of the church comes knowledge and understanding for the protagonist in the form of "shafts of yellow light." As a young Ethan Frome makes his way along the deserted streets of the village he notices Michael Eady's new store, the one that Dennis Eady has inherited by the time of the Prologue, and the house of Lawyer Varnum, the home of Ruth, who first comes upon Ethan and Mattie after the accident. But Wharton makes another symbolic statement when Ethan looks up at the church. "As the young man walked toward it the upper windows drew a black arcade along the side wall of the building" (28-29). This blackness not only represents the ignorance of religion when it comes to a woman's place in society, but it is the windows—the very symbol of opportunity and freedom—that are darkened. As was demonstrated earlier, religion was one of the primary means of justifying the continued subjugation of women by men, and so its solution is not to be found in the church. As a result, religion plays no part in the novel. This ignorance, however, is juxtaposed with "the lower openings, on the side where the ground sloped steeply down to the Corbury road, [and] the light shot its long bars, illuminating many fresh furrows in the track leading to the basement door" (29). Again, Wharton emphasizes that there is enlightenment to be found for the protagonist in looking at what is going on in the basement of the church.

Wonderfully, Wharton delays Ethan's interaction with the light in order to deliver some backstory. First she clears the way for his enlightenment by eliminating any possibility of interference with what he needs to learn and understand. "The night was perfectly still, and the air so dry and pure that it gave little sensation of cold. The effect produced on Frome was rather of a complete absence of atmosphere, as though nothing less tenuous than ether intervened between the white earth under his feet and the metallic dome overhead" (Wharton 1911, 29). Next, Ethan references an "exhausted receiver," the glass jar used to create a vacuum, and the narrator connects this with the protagonist's brief studies at a college in Worcester, which explains Ethan's interest in the book of popular science the narrator had left on the sleigh in the Prologue. The reason for cutting short his studies was due to "His father's death, and the misfortunes following it." But it's also here that Wharton delivers the most important information of the whole novel, a concept that explains the entirety of Ethan's character and informs every aspect of the story.

In relating Ethan's brief experiences in higher education the narrator says, "though they had not gone far enough to be of much practical use they had fed his fancy and made him aware of huge cloudy meanings behind the daily face of things" (Wharton 1911, 30). Ethan's studies are of no practical use precisely because they had "fed his fancy." Fancy, as it does in both the stories by Chopin and Gilman, refers to imagination, a fantasy more than a desire.

The way this informs Ethan's character is that his incomplete education has made him aware of "meanings behind the daily face of things," but for Ethan those meanings remain "cloudy." This is actually the defining character trait of Ethan Frome. He knows that there is truth behind the actual things said and done by people, just as Gilman's narrator understood that there was a true pattern beneath the outer pattern of the wallpaper, and like Gilman's narrator Ethan is equally unable to discern exactly what those truths are. Clouds in this case, like their association with Louise Mallard's consciousness in "The Story of an Hour," symbolize a lack of clarity, something hidden or disguised. But within that general inability to discern reality, author Suzanne Fournier also sees the central internal conflict of the novel for the protagonist. "Torn between his duty to Zeena and his passion for Mattie, Ethan spends much of the novel in solitary thought as he tries (vainly) to overcome his deepening confusion" (Fournier 82).

Back in the narrative, however, Ethan has the opportunity to dispel some of that confusion via the light emanating from the windows in the basement of the church. The light's association with windows also implies that the knowledge will set Ethan free. And he is seen as ripe for understanding when Wharton states, "As he strode along through the snow the sense of such meanings glowed in his brain" (Wharton 1911, 30). With the atmosphere around him as clear as that in a vacuum, his brain glowing with the sense that there is more to learn, Wharton is still in no hurry to get to Ethan's encounter with the light. "He stood there a moment, breathing quickly, and looking up and down the street, in which not another figure moved." So there are also no people around to distract Ethan from the enlightenment to be gained through his exposure to the light coming from the building. Much of the village is apparently in attendance in the church basement, "from which strains of dance-music flowed with the broad bands of yellow light." At last Ethan is ready for his interaction with the light, and this is what he does:

> The young man, skirting the side of the building, went down the slope toward the basement door. To keep out of range of the revealing rays from within he made a circuit through the untrodden snow and gradually approached the farther angle of the basement wall. Thence, still hugging the shadow, he edged his way cautiously forward to the nearest window, holding back his straight spare body and craning his neck till he got a glimpse of the room. (31).

While there is knowledge to be gained in the light, important knowledge for him, Ethan chooses instead to "keep out of range of the revealing rays from within," thus avoiding the revelations to be gained inside by "hugging the shadow." The truth is, Ethan doesn't want to see what's there, the reason for which will become apparent as the chapter progresses. Nevertheless, he does crane his neck in order to catch a "glimpse" of what he needs to see, though because he is not fully enlightened it will be much easier for him to suppress the significance of that vision.

In addition to the partial view Ethan has of the dance in the basement, "from the pure and frosty darkness in which he stood, it seemed to be seething in a mist of heat," which has the effect of obscuring his understanding even further (Wharton 1911, 31). What he is watching is the very end of the church dance. The musicians are putting away their instruments, the young people are heading for the door, while the older people who were watching begin to put on their coats and hats. But before they can start leaving a young male dancer runs back to the middle of the floor and claps his hands, causing the musicians to stop and pick up their instruments again, while the rest of the people return to take their former places. "The lively young man, after diving about here and there in the throng, drew forth a girl who had already wound a cherry-coloured 'fascinator' about her head, and, leading her up to the end of the floor, whirled her down its length to the bounding tune of a Virginia reel" (32). The girl in the cherry scarf is actually the object of Ethan's curiosity, and the information he gains from seeing her through the window is what he must come to understand—the very understanding he is so desperately trying to avoid.

Wharton also manages to introduce conflict into the scene, but again it is in the context of what Ethan should be learning about the girl who is dancing. "Frome's heart was beating fast. He had been straining for a glimpse of the dark head under the cherry-coloured scarf and it vexed him that another eye should have been quicker than his" (Wharton 1911, 32). This is also the first of many examples of the sense of ownership that Ethan will exhibit for the girl under the scarf, as well as the feeling that he is competing for her affection. While she is dancing, Ethan is given the first clue to her character. Her head is described as dark, an obvious reference to her hair color, but in the light/dark symbolism of the novel that darkness is read as ignorance, in this case it indicates she is unaware of Ethan's intentions toward her. Further, her head, as the seat of knowledge and understanding, in addition to its dark coloring, has also been covered with the scarf. "As she passed down the line, her light figure swinging from hand to hand in circles of increasing swiftness, the scarf flew off her head and stood out behind her shoulders, and Frome, at each turn, caught sight of her laughing panting lips, [and] the cloud of dark hair about her forehead" (33). Twice now, Wharton has combined the two symbols of the hair and the scarf, but here she adds an additional symbol in order to make her meaning perfectly clear. The girl's dark hair, which has also been covered with the scarf, is not only falling over her forehead and covering the prefrontal cortex of her brain, it is also described as a cloud, Wharton's symbol for vagueness or obscurity. The full meaning of this is to reinforce the idea that the girl has absolutely no idea how Ethan feels about her.

Nevertheless, as the dance continues Ethan's intentions become perfectly clear to the reader. He feels as if the reel is going on forever, indicating his desire for it to be over, and then discloses why. "Now and then he turned his eyes from the girl's face to that of her partner, which, in the exhilaration of the dance, had taken on a look of almost impudent ownership" (Wharton 1911, 33). The irony is thick here. Ethan characterizes the look that the young man gives the girl as "impudent ownership," and yet it's clear from the initial symbolism Wharton has constructed that the girl has no idea Ethan is interested in her. In this context the impudence of the young man, then, is actually directed toward Ethan rather than the girl, the very same impudent sense of ownership Ethan is guilty of having for her as well. The young man, it turns out, is none other than Denis Eady, the owner of the village store in the Prologue, but here, twenty-four years earlier, still working for his father. Ethan predicts that he will eventually take over the store, and from his perspective Eady is exhibiting that same sense of entitlement toward the young woman with whom he is dancing, provoking Ethan to even greater outrage. "Hitherto Ethan Frome had been content to think him a mean fellow; but now he positively invited a horse-whipping" (34). Along with that observation comes another part of the lesson that the enlightening rays of light from within should be revealing to Ethan. "It was strange that the girl did not seem aware of it: that she could lift her rapt face to her dancer's, and drop her hands into his, without appearing to feel the offence of his look and touch." What Ethan needs to realize is that she actually doesn't take offence at Denis Eady's look and touch, something he describes as "strange." But from his limited vantage point outside, craning his neck to get merely a glimpse of the scene, he is able to rationalize what he sees by telling himself that she only appears not to be offended.

At last Wharton decides to divulge the identity of the girl. Her name is Mattie Silver, and she is a distant cousin of Ethan's wife Zeena. Commentators tend to make much of Mattie's last name, Silver, in the way that it seems to be the antithesis of the sluggish Starkfield, or how the reflective nature of silver contrasts the element of light with Ethan's darkness. And there are other associations of the character's name that have been made with springtime, nature, and the singing she does. But just as with Wharton's selection of Ethan and Zeena as the names of the other two main characters, the name seems to have little true symbolic value. Much more persuasive is the idea that Mattie's last name is simply a reflection of her personality. She is a happy girl who has her whole life ahead of her, and at the moment she is making the best of her situation. If one wanted to posit a symbolic significance to her name more relevant to the novel as a whole it might be in the form of quicksilver, or mercury, a metal that is liquid at room temperature and therefore unable to be grasped by the hand in the same way as its solid counterpart, the metal silver. This reinforces the idea that her words and actions are not what they appear to be, and therefore assumptions made about her feelings and motives—not only by Ethan but by the reader—are likely to be incorrect.

Ethan regularly walks to the village to escort Mattie home from whatever amusement she has been allowed to attend. What's fascinating about this particular paragraph is the way in which it succinctly defines Ethan's relationship with his wife Zeena, as well as reveals a major misconception about her character throughout the novel. What the reader must keep in mind at all times in order to accurately analyze *Ethan Frome* is that the entire story within the narrator's first-person frame is told from Ethan's point of view. And yet this is often misunderstood, as author Van Meter Ames demonstrates in his *Aesthetics of the Novel*. "The importance of the argument is heightened by the frame into which it is put, that is, by the first-person narration of the introduction and conclusion, which is sharply set off from the omniscient narration of the body of the story" (Ames 187). In point of fact, the internal narration is not "omniscient," as there is absolutely no attempt by Wharton to delve into the thoughts and feelings of either Zeena or Mattie, which a truly omniscient narrator would be able to do. One could even argue further that the interior story is merely a continuation of the first-person narration of the frame story, but because the narrator isn't present in Ethan's past there is no need for first-person pronouns.

Ames' confusion comes from his assumption that there are other things beyond Ethan's frame of reference presented in the third-person narration. "While Ethan's point of view is kept all the time, there is skillful shifting to things outside it for the benefit of the reader" (188). But this is a misreading of the novel. Everything in the internal narration is something that Ethan knows, even if he is not observing it at the time or wouldn't put it exactly that way in his thoughts. In that respect third-person limited is a better description of the narration, as the narrator may be omniscient in terms of his access to Ethan's thoughts and history, but that omniscience is strictly limited to Ethan in a way that, ironically, even Ames eventually seems to understand. "The point of view is consistently that of Frome; his wife, Zeena, is always treated dramatically, never subjectively; and her cousin, Mattie Silver, is presented as a lovable girl, but never allowed to take the theme" (187). Because Ethan is the central third-person character, it is exclusively his thoughts and prejudices that account for the descriptions and interpretations of the other characters he interacts with, especially Zeena and Mattie. The character of Ethan Frome, then, is a classic example of an unreliable narrator. Even though he may say or think certain things about the other characters, it doesn't mean they are true.

Wharton has given the reader a forewarning of this when she said that Ethan's brief education "had fed his fancy and made him aware of huge cloudy meanings behind the daily face of things" (Wharton 1911, 30). The reality is, while Ethan understands that there are hidden meanings behind the events he experiences, most of the time he is wrong about what they mean. Further, because Ethan's interpretations are going to be fed by his "fancy," or his imagination, the reason they are going to be wrong is because they are intrinsically self-serving. Shakespeare makes the same point in *Romeo and Juliet* when he writes about dreams, which apply to Ethan's conscious desires as well as to those unconscious dreams of sleep. After Romeo accuses Mercutio's lengthy speech describing Queen Mab, the creator of dreams, of being about nothing, his friend responds by saying,

> True, I talk of dreams,
> Which are the children of an idle brain,
> Begot of nothing but vain fantasy,
> Which is as thin of substance as the air (Shakespeare 1591, 40-41)

The key to Shakespeare's description of dreams is that they are created by "vain fantasy." Thus these fantasy visions, or fancies, are vain—not in the sense of being useless, but from the root word of vanity—in that they are merely expressions of the dreamer's desires rather than anything real. They are also created by a brain that is doing little conscious work in the case of sleeping—or in the case of Ethan, sublimating his thoughts to his desires—and therefore both are as insubstantial as the air. In this context Ethan sees only what he wants to see, and he believes what he wants to believe because he is unable to see things objectively. All of which is symbolized in the first chapter by his aversion to the light.

The first thing the reader actually learns about Zeena is that she is the person responsible for Mattie attending these dances. "It was his wife who had suggested, when the girl came to live with them, that such opportunities should be put in her way" (Wharton 1911, 34). Mattie, it turns out, is something of an indentured servant, brought to Ethan's house "to act as her cousin Zeena's aid . . . without pay." And yet Ethan manages to dismiss Zeena's generosity out of hand. "But for this—as Frome sardonically reflected—it would hardly have occurred to Zeena to take any thought for the girl's amusement" (35). It must always be remembered that thoughts of these kind are strictly from Ethan's viewpoint and are often, as in this example, contradicted by the actions of the characters themselves. Joseph X. Brennan makes this clear in his 1961 essay on *Ethan Frome*, explaining that while the narrator is the one writing the story, he is really writing it *as* Ethan, and therefore that close association means they are actually one in the same. "The characterization of Mattie and Zeena, however, though ultimately derived from the narrator's sensibility also, nevertheless becomes the immediate responsibility of Ethan in the envisioned story, for it is through his sensibility and from his point of view that this vision is projected. This distinction, of course, is a logical rather than a real one, since the two sensibilities are really only one" (Brennan 351). So even though it is the narrator who is envisioning the story, the "responsibility" Brennan speaks of for the characterization of the other people inhabiting the novel, is entirely Ethan's.

This makes perfect sense, as it is very much in keeping with Wharton's description of the characters from her introduction. Her "granite outcroppings" would not be able to think and understand in the elegantly descriptive language the narrator uses. Ames explains the way this manifests itself in Ethan's mind. "If Frome were going over this matter he would hardly do it in the elaborate way in which it is presented, a man's own thoughts proceeding more by symbols and images, scraps of sentences" (Ames 189). Thus the more orderly and intellectual prose of the narrator is not to be read as separate from Ethan. Instead, it is a conceit the reader readily accepts: that this is the way Ethan would have put it had he possessed the education and intelligence of the narrator. According to Wharton scholar Geoffrey Walton in his book *Edith Wharton: A Critical Interpretation*, "The implication is, as Edith Wharton wished to suggest, of rural inarticulateness and exasperating inconsequence, which the narrator has ordered and disciplined" (Walton 85). This is very similar, in fact, to the more natural conceit the reader accepts in the complex prose of *To Kill a Mockingbird* that the adult Scout narrates for the younger version of herself who is actually experiencing the story in the novel.

The next paragraph is made up of a single sentence, and can go by so quickly that it's easy to miss its importance, especially in its relationship to the previous paragraph—as well as the fact that its full significance won't be made clear until later in the chapter.

When his wife first proposed that they should give Mattie an occasional evening out he had inwardly demurred at having to do the extra two miles to the village and back after his hard day on the farm; but not long afterward he had reached the point of wishing that Starkfield might give all its nights to revelry. (Wharton 1911, 35)

It is Zeena who first suggests that Mattie should be given the opportunity for amusement, so as "not to let her feel too sharp a contrast between the life she had left and the isolation of a Starkfield farm" (34-35). But at the same time it is Ethan who "inwardly demurred" at the imposition that walking home with Mattie had caused him. Living in isolation on their farm, with little other human interaction, it's difficult to imagine that the complete reversal of Ethan's attitude toward Mattie, from that of onerous obligation to the point where he wished that he could walk her home every night, was not noticed by Zeena. Given that, it's also not very difficult to imagine that the simultaneous change in Zeena's attitude toward the girl, at first making sure she doesn't suffer from isolation to that of complete neglect, has far more to do with Ethan's behavior than it does Mattie's—a speculation that will be confirmed by the end of the chapter.

Mattie has been living with the Fromes for a year at this point in the story. And though Ethan has occasion to see her frequently during the day, "no moments in her company were comparable to those when, her arm in his, and her light step flying to keep time with his long stride, they walked back through the night to the farm" (Wharton 1911, 35). His affection for the girl—along with his attendant jealousy of Denis Eady—is apparent at this point, but Wharton also gives another indication of the unreliability of Ethan's thoughts when he claims, "He had taken to the girl from the first day, when he had driven over to the Flats to meet her." This hardly gibes with his professed unhappiness at having to escort her home from village functions after she had first arrived. And yet again, in thinking back to their first meeting he provides another clue to her behavior that should have helped him better understand her actions later on. "He reflected, looking over her slight person: 'She don't look much on housework, but she ain't a fretter, anyhow'" (36). This aspect of Mattie's personality, an absence of worrying about circumstances she is powerless to control, is completely misunderstood by Ethan and instead becomes the foundation for the fantasy world he gradually begins to create around his relationship with her. The nature of this fantasy is revealed in his observation that, "the coming to his house of a bit of hopeful young life was like the lighting of a fire on a cold hearth." The hearth of the house, especially at this time in New England, was vitally important for providing heat and comfort for the inhabitants, and because of that the warmth of the fireplace is also symbolic of the familial love within a home. Thus Ethan's description of the house before Mattie as "a cold hearth," demonstrates a decided lack of love between husband and wife. The transformation of the hearth by Mattie's warmth, then, is indicative of the transfer of Ethan's affection from his wife to Mattie. In short, he is now in love with the girl, as opposed to honoring the cold marriage he has to Zeena.

The way that Ethan's love for Mattie manifests itself in his mind is as a possession of the girl. He begins the paragraph by saying that Mattie had "lived under his roof for a year," and at the end he closes with his observation that "She had an eye to see and an ear to hear: he could show her things and tell her things, and taste the bliss of feeling that all he imparted left long reverberations and echoes he could wake at will" (Wharton 1911, 35-36). In this way Ethan sees himself as a teacher of sorts. In his life experience and schooling, however truncated, he feels he is her superior in the way that he can teach her things she can see and hear. It's important to note, however, that this inclination to teach comes not from a desire to improve Mattie, but in the thrill he will take when she references the things he has taught her, and tastes the "bliss of feeling" from awakening those lessons "at will." Author Dale M. Bauer sees this as just one example of the way sexual expression by the characters in Wharton's novels operates more as a vehicle for understanding themselves rather than demonstrating a desire for true intimacy. "The object of sexual desire is really an inverted or distorted version of the way the subject sees herself or himself. Thus, sexuality becomes a primary way of understanding how the self *is* what it avows it is not. In this way, Wharton came to see sex expression . . . as an experience of alienation rather than intimacy" (Bauer 2003, 116).

In Bauer's view the continued sense of ownership demonstrated toward Mattie by Ethan is merely a means by which Ethan can better understand himself. Ethan is a man who is trapped by society, by his marriage, by his economics, and yet for years he has been able to conveniently deny all of that. Therefore it is his recent desire for Mattie, a desire for the happiness and the ease of life she exhibits, as well the freedom of youth she represents, that will ultimately demonstrate to him that he is, in actuality, the opposite of her. And it is only through that implied "sex expression" that Ethan can discover just how alienated he really is. Author Linda Costanzo Cahir reinforces the first half of this idea when she writes about Ethan's purposeful avoidance of reality. "Continually occupying a dream-life that is better than his real one, Frome, despite repeated opportunities, cowers before any act that would improve his circumstances. His passivity allows him to remain insular, outlying, and securely detached from the materiality of his milieu. His vision-life provides an enticing repose, a numbing inertia that Frome finds addictively comfortable" (Cahir 222-223). In this way it is only the symbolic sexual act of coasting with

Mattie at the end of the novel—"Riding horses and sledding down hills, in Wharton's fiction," claims Bauer, "displace heterosexual intercourse and lead to destruction"—that is finally able to reacquaint Ethan, rather brutally, with the true reality of his life (Bauer 2003, 136).

But the emphasis on teaching here is more to the point, as it is another way that Ethan can be associated with female characters in literature as they are perceived by women writers. Ethan's feelings for a girl who has had little education and absolutely no money stems from a desire to mold her into the woman he wants to spend his life with, and by extension to thereby exert some control over that romantic life. This is an issue that transcends sex and gender. Even in the Victorian literature that long preceded Wharton's, there was a noticeable shift in the types of relationships feminist writers imagined for women. According to author Ellen Moers, the author of *Literary Women: The Great Writers*, where men of the period wrote about "the poor girl who wants a rich man," women were already writing about "the rich girl who wants a poor man. The latter situation was seized upon by every woman writer who was a feminist in love, because it gave her a chance to do the scene of her choice: the heroine choosing and demanding her love" (Moers 157). Moers sees this as a move away from the accepted convention that women must always marry "up," the belief that their goal in attracting a husband was not only to obtain a marriage proposal but one that would secure her financial future. The problem with this cultural imperative is that in real life so many of the men of financial means made such poor lovers, while men of the lower classes had never been put in a position to have their passion socialized out of them.

A woman's choice, then, of a man who really loved her—and was genuinely able to express that love—was the true sign of feminism for women who had been taught that social and financial upward mobility were the only criteria on which to base a proposal. As to life afterward, Moers cites the author Flora Tristan as articulating the way feminists saw these unconventional matches ultimately playing out to their mutual advantage.

> In the future, when woman is conscious of her power, she will free herself from the need for social approval, and those little tricks which today aid her to deceive men, will become useless; when that time comes, woman will say:—"I choose this man for my lover, because my love will be a powerful force on his intelligence, and our happiness will be reflected on others." (Moers 157)

Her love as a "powerful force on his intelligence" implies that regardless of his lack of traditional education, the passionate lover will be in a position to benefit intellectually from his relationship with an educated partner. In looking at Ethan's relationship with Mattie in this light, his character moves away from the stereotypical male attitude of sexual domination and instead toward a more typically female attitude of seeking long term emotional compatibility and security. Instead of settling for the woman he has married, he can instead create in Mattie the woman who will fulfill his every need. Ethan's association with the feminine in terms of his love relationships is further strengthened by Zeena's equally strong association with male domination in marriage.

For Ethan, his imagined love relationship with Mattie must necessarily remain an unspoken one as he is married and, because of his desire to avoid learning the truth about her feelings, this rationalization ultimately satisfies him. In fact, it is the basis for any number of flights of fancy involving the two of them. His teacher-student relationship is certainly one area in which he believes that his feelings are reciprocated by her. "It was during their night walks back to the farm that he felt most intensely the sweetness of this communion" (Wharton 1911, 36). It's important to remember, however, that this statement is from Ethan's viewpoint. There are numerous examples of this kind of assertion throughout the novel that can cause even serious scholars to be misled. Suzanne Fournier, for example, sees in this sentence the way in which nature in the novel provides the context in which "Ethan and Mattie experience a closeness" (Fournier 101). But that way of seeing their relationship can only be achieved through a reading that ignores the central conceit of the novel, namely that Ethan is the sole viewpoint character in the internal part of the story. As such, there's simply no way around the fact that the "communion" he speaks of is being experienced strictly from his point of view. And because of that, there is absolutely no way of knowing at this point in the story if Mattie truly shares that feeling with Ethan.

Wharton even goes to far as to remind the reader of this when she expands upon the idea of Ethan's fantasy world at length in the following paragraph. As was pointed out earlier, because his life with Zeena has been unfulfilling he has shifted his affections to Mattie. It's here that Ethan's fantasy of love and possession most powerfully associates him with female characters of the turn of the twentieth century literature produced by both men and women. Wharton describes him in particularly feminine terms when looking at his emotional life, especially as it relates to nature.

He had always been more sensitive than the people about him to the appeal of natural beauty. His unfinished studies had given form to this sensibility and even in his unhappiest moments field and sky spoke to him with a deep and powerful persuasion. But hitherto the emotion had remained in him as a silent ache, veiling with sadness the beauty that evoked it. (Wharton 1911, 36)

The paragraph as a whole is actually reminiscent of something Wharton wrote in the diary she kept about her affair with Morton Fullerton. Like Ethan, she felt frustrated by the lack of understanding Teddy Wharton had for the inner life she took for granted. He didn't understand her sense of humor, her taste in art, or her perception of beauty. In Fullerton, however, she found a man whose rich inner life matched her own. "How often I used to say to myself, 'No one can love life as I do, love the beauty and the splendour and the ardour, and find the words for them as I can' . . .

> And then the day came—the day has *been*—and I have poured into it all my stored-up joy of living, all my sense of the beauty and mystery of the world, every impression of joy and loveliness, in sight or sound or touch, that I ever figured to myself in all the lovely days when I used to weave such sensations into a veil of colour to hide the great blank behind. (Dwight 148).

Ethan has experienced a similar veil that has kept his own inner life hidden from Zeena. Interestingly, it's not just his inability to share his thoughts with his wife that makes him sad, but that this inability is associated specifically with the natural world and serves to make Ethan even lonelier. In the symbolism of the Prologue the cause for this is society's expectations. Ethan would not have chosen the life of a farmer for himself, perhaps becoming an engineer or pursuing a more scientific occupation that was hinted at by the narrator. Instead of reveling in the beauty of nature, then, Ethan is saddened by the vast loneliness and his isolation within it—that is, until Mattie's arrival.

> He did not even know whether any one else in the world felt as he did, or whether he was the sole victim of this mournful privilege. Then he learned that one other spirit had trembled with the same touch of wonder: that at his side, living under his roof and eating his bread, was a creature to whom he could say: "That's Orion down yonder . . . and the bunch of little ones—like bees swarming—they're the Pleiades . . ." (Wharton 1911, 36-37)

Again, Ethan's love for Mattie is mixed with the idea of his possessing her, "at his side, living under his roof and eating his bread." But Wharton also makes sure to juxtapose this with a symbolic reminder to the reader, as this is the second time that the constellation Orion has been mentioned.

In their annotations to the Norton Critical Edition of *Ethan Frome*, editors Kristin O. Lauer and Cynthia Griffin Wolff make an important connection between the mythical figure of Orion and the character of Ethan Frome:

> Orion, handsome, mythical giant hero killed (probably for jealousy) by the fierce and vengeful Artemis, goddess of the hunt, whom he served. Orion follows the Pleiades, or seven sisters; in mythology, the seven daughters of Atlas. Orion pursued them unsuccessfully until Zeus, king of the gods, made them stars, where Orion still pursues them—persistent and frustrated eternally. (Lauer 12)

The two key elements of this description begin with the way that that Orion was the servant of Artemis, and therefore dominated by a woman, a rough equivalence to the relationship between Ethan and Zeena, though all the reader can surmise at this point in the inner timeline is perhaps it is her illness that eventually drives him away during the day. The second is the fact that while Orion pursued the Pleiades, he was never successful. This is an important factor in understanding the true nature of the relationship between Ethan and Mattie. Orion's ultimate end also foreshadows the end of Wharton's novel. As such, the symbolism of Orion is one that could hardly be accidental, especially when Wharton mentions it twice, as well as using a similar image in her very next novel, *The Reef*: "They seemed, he and she, like the ghostly lovers of the Grecian urn, forever pursuing without ever clasping each other" (Wharton 1912, 28).

The romanticism of Ethan's inner world continues in the rest of the paragraph, with Ethan describing Mattie as a person "whom he could hold entranced before a ledge of granite thrusting up through the fern while he unrolled the huge panorama of the ice age, and the long dim stretches of succeeding time. The fact that admiration for his learning mingled with Mattie's wonder at what he taught was not the least part of his pleasure" (Wharton 1911, 37). Here is Wharton's granite outcropping again, reminding the reader during this reverie that whatever Ethan may be saying about Mattie must be tempered with the knowledge that her thoughts will forever be buried, as the story is told exclusively from Ethan's point of view. The only inking the reader can ever have of her true feelings is through her words—though even those can't be trusted entirely, as the reader has no way to know if they reflect her actual thoughts—and her actions—which tend to be more trustworthy. At one point during their previous walks together she had made an observation about the beauty of nature and Ethan felt "that words had at last been found to utter his secret soul . . ." (38). His soul is, in fact, a secret that Mattie cannot possibly know, and yet somehow Ethan sees this as proof positive of her own secret desire to be with him. In fact, for Ethan, secrecy becomes the very foundation of their relationship. "And there were other sensations, less definable but more exquisite, which drew them together with a shock of silent joy" (37).

This is a telling statement, as Ethan practically confesses that the less definable a sensation is the more exquisite his feelings are. In other words, the more open for interpretation his interactions with Mattie remain, the more he can interpret them in the way he wants, for example, his assertion that these experiences "drew them together with . . . silent joy." While their mutual silence about the joy they are apparently sharing is something he believes has drawn them together, this is a claim that has absolutely no basis in fact at this point in the story. Cynthia Griffin Wolff sees this as part of an overall inability or unwillingness in Ethan to genuinely communicate with Mattie. "If Ethan is not able to talk to Mattie during that walk home from church, the deprivation is more than compensated for by his imagination" (Wolff 172). Elsewhere in her book Wolff actually articulates the reason for this in Ethan's symbolic association with women, though she doesn't make the connection directly. "Even within the suffocating strictures of late-Victorian America, young men were permitted freedoms that were forbidden to young women: sexual liberties (of course); but more important, the right to a "Voice," to authority . . . Initiative, assertiveness, intellectual curiosity, originality, the desire for enlightenment or adventure—all of these were viewed as signs of deviance and danger in girls—and all were utterly forbidden" (xiv). The ability to say what they thought and felt was forbidden to girls by society in the same way it is for Ethan because of his marriage, and in this way his aversion to enlightenment can be seen as reflecting a similar aversion by women in their desire to conform to societal dictates rather than risk bringing about opposition by going against them.

Wharton then returns Ethan to the current timeline within the frame story, with the protagonist spying on Mattie from outside the church window. But despite his partial view, the light from within still tells him everything he needs to know. "As he stood in the darkness outside the church these memories came back with the poignancy of vanished things. Watching Mattie whirl down the floor from hand to hand he wondered how he could ever have thought that his dull talk interested her" (Wharton 1911, 38). This should be Ethan's first revelation, that the vanished moments he interpreted as a relationship may never have existed in the first place, and the fact that Mattie is relatively uneducated and a captive audience for his teaching does not necessarily imply that she shared in his fantasy. Then he realizes that, "To him, who was never gay but in her presence, her gaiety seemed plain proof of indifference," and yet this is a proof he is willing to ignore. But to do that Ethan also must ignore his own earlier description of Mattie as a girl who "ain't a fretter." Because Ethan was only happy in her presence, he assumed the same thing about her. In watching Mattie at the dance, however, this assumption clearly has been a false one, as her gaiety there demonstrates that her happiness when she was with Ethan had nothing to do with him. Ethan actually seems to understand in that moment how he has been mistaken. "He even noticed two or three gestures which, in his fatuity, he had thought she kept for him." Again, her indiscriminate use of gestures that he believed she shared only with him is further evidence of her indifference toward him. And, as it should, "The sight made him unhappy, and his unhappiness roused his latent fears."

It's interesting that Ethan's fears are not about losing Mattie but instead have to do with Zeena. The fact that he has potentially misjudged Mattie means that he might also have misjudged his wife, and in this way the earlier apparent inconsistency in her behavior toward Mattie—from Ethan's point of view—is explained. "His wife had never shown any jealousy of Mattie, but of late she had grumbled increasingly over the house-work and found oblique ways of attracting attention to the girl's inefficiency" (Wharton 1911, 38-39). Because this sentence precedes a lengthy description of Mattie's actual lack of skill when it comes to housework, it's easy to miss the inconsistency in Ethan's words. While he states that Zeena has never demonstrated any jealousy of Mattie, he is unable to comprehend that her dissatisfaction with Mattie's performance is exactly that. Ethan even goes so far as to agree with Zeena's assessment of Mattie's abilities. "Zeena had always been what Starkfield called 'sickly,' and Frome had to admit that, if she were as ailing as she believed, she needed the help of a stronger arm than the one which lay so lightly in his during the night walks to the farm" (39). One can almost see in this single sentence the way Ethan's mind works. His attempt to describe Zeena's behavior toward Mattie actually turns into something else as the girl gradually displaces his wife in his thoughts. The deficiencies that have provoked Zeena's ire—something Ethan should be paying attention to— effortlessly transition into his idyllic walks home from the village with her. But Ethan's delusional rationalizations even extend to Mattie. He describes her as "dreamy" and "forgetful" in explaining her lack of ability, saying that she was "not disposed to take matters seriously," and yet at the same time he is utterly convinced that "if she were to marry a man she was fond of the dormant instinct would wake, and her pies and biscuits become the pride of the county."

More evidence of Mattie's light-hearted nature is presented when Ethan remembers her clumsiness on coming to work for them. "At first she was so awkward that he could not help laughing at her; but she laughed with him and that made them better friends" (Wharton 1911, 39). Again, Ethan interprets Mattie's internal happiness as an implication that her external expression of that happiness stems from feelings for him. Though he continues discussing Mattie, one of the most salient features of his marriage to Zeena comes to the fore:

> He did his best to supplement her unskilled efforts, getting up earlier than usual to light the kitchen fire, carrying in the wood overnight, and neglecting the mill for the farm that he might help her about the house during the day. He even crept down on Saturday nights to scrub the kitchen floor after the women had gone to bed; and Zeena, one day, had surprised him at the churn and had turned away silently, with one of her queer looks. (39-40)

Here Wharton presents the reader with more instances of the gender reversal that is at the heart of the novel. Rather than allow Mattie to make mistakes and become confident on her own, Ethan instead tries to help her in secret as a way of deceiving Zeena about the girl's true abilities. He even goes so far as to sneak out of bed at night to scrub the kitchen floor. One can easily imagine him on his hands and knees, in a symbolic position of submission of the kind that appeared in the stories by Chopin and Gilman. The incident when he is caught churning the butter for Mattie is also indicative of his inability to read Zeena. He describes her as silently turning away with a "queer look," implying that she doesn't really understand what's going on, but it's not difficult to believe that Zeena knows precisely what he's doing and why.

In the same way that Ethan's experiences with Mattie were "less definable but more exquisite," certain of his interactions with Zeena were "intangible but more disquieting." Again, it is the "cloudy meanings" that hold more emotional impact for Ethan—ecstasy with Mattie and fear with Zeena—than the actual experiences themselves. At this point Wharton gives the reader the first scene of dialogue in the inner story as a way of reinforcing this idea. Ethan thinks back to one early morning as he was shaving and getting dressed before going out to work. While the dialogue itself is important, the attendant symbolism in the scene is almost more so. Though Ethan had assumed his wife was till asleep, she spoke in the darkness and startled him. "'The doctor don't want I should be left without anybody to do for me,' she said in her flat whine" (Wharton 1911, 40). Significantly, Zeena's first words in the novel are about her illness. The way Ethan processes this information in his mind, however, is to take it to its natural conclusion. "He turned and looked at her where she lay indistinctly outlined under the dark calico quilt, her high-boned face taking a grayish tinge from the whiteness of the pillow." This image of Zeena in death is something that Ethan will return to again and again in the novel, as it is the only way he can truly be free from his obligation to her as her husband and, in his fantasy, be married to Mattie. At the same time, her words are a threat to the possibility of achieving his dream. When he asks why she would ever be left without anyone to care for her, she responds by saying, "If you say you can't afford a hired girl when Mattie goes." While Denis Eady is only a minor conflict for Ethan within the fantasy world of his dreams, Zeena's assumption that Mattie is going to leave their house is the central conflict of the entire novel.

Ethan goes back to shaving and tries to dismiss her suggestion, insisting that there's no reason Mattie would ever leave. Zeena, however, adroitly brings up the one event that not only would guarantee her departure, but would wound Ethan emotionally at the same time. "Well, when she gets married, I mean . . . I wouldn't ever have it said that I stood in the way of a poor girl like Mattie marrying a smart fellow like Denis Eady" (Wharton 1911, 41). Wharton's tremendous gift for symbolic interpolation is evident in Ethan's reaction to this comment. "Ethan, glaring at his face in the glass, threw his head back to draw the razor from ear to chin." The moment is one of symbolic suicide for Ethan when he draws the straight razor "from ear to chin," as though he is cutting his throat after Zeena mentions the possibility of Mattie getting married to Denis Eady. At the same time, Wharton is able to use this symbolic action to foreshadow the climax of her story where Ethan attempts his actual suicide. Zeena continues the discussion, bringing up the fact that her doctor has recommended the couple hire a girl to replace Mattie. Ethan tries to dismiss the idea that Mattie will ever marry Eady by laughing and suggesting she doesn't like him, and will therefore remain in their service. Though Zeena wants to continue talking about it, Ethan makes a show of looking at his watch and saying that he's late. And it's here Zeena confirms for the reader—and Ethan—that she knows exactly what has been going on, as well as her attendant jealousy.

> Zeena, apparently accepting this as final, lay watching him in silence while he pulled his suspenders over his shoulders and jerked his arms into his coat; but as he went toward the door she said, suddenly and incisively: "I guess you're always late, now you shave every morning." (42)

Ethan's reaction to this is just what it should be. "He had stupidly assumed that she would not notice any change in his appearance" (Wharton 1911, 42). This stupidity on Ethan's part is intensified by the apparent insightfulness of his wife, and as a result her "thrust had frightened him more than any vague insinuations about Denis Eady. It was a fact that since Mattie Silver's coming he had taken to shaving every day; but his wife always seemed to be asleep when he left her side in the winter darkness." Ethan goes on to note how Zeena has the uncanny ability to keep her knowledge of certain events to herself—one is reminded of the butter churn incident—and then waiting until the time is right to spring her knowledge on him. Ethan's uneasy reaction to all of this is another way he symbolizes the women of his day, exhibiting behaviors born of being forced into the narrow limits of a specified role he was expected to adhere to. In summarizing the work of psychiatrist Karen Horney, author Carroll Smith-Rosenbert states that those behaviors include, "free floating anxiety, a deep-rooted sense of inferiority, and an absence of adequate aggression, [meaning] the ability to take initiative, to make efforts, to carry things through to completion, and to form and express autonomous views" (Smith-Rosenberg 1985, 214). Ethan exhibits all of these characteristics in the novel, an ongoing anxiety about what Zeena may or may not know, or may or may not suspect, an inferiority complex that has led him to relinquish the power over his life to Zeena, as well as the inability to confront his wife about any of the things that are important to him. Further, this inferiority of personality can be seen in the way that Ethan refuses to take his knowledge about Zeena to heart, and continues to convince himself that she is oblivious to his behavior.

Just as the earlier description of Zeena's dissatisfaction with Mattie's domestic insufficiencies turns immediately to thoughts of love for Mattie in his mind, thus preventing him from understanding that Zeena knows what he is doing, the same thing happens here after a more blatant demonstration of her perception in mentioning his shaving. "Of late, however, there had been no room in his thoughts for such vague apprehensions. Zeena herself, from an oppressive reality, had faded into an insubstantial shade. All his life was lived in the sight and sound of Mattie Silver, and he could no longer conceive of its being otherwise" (Wharton 1911, 43). His refusal to see the truth about his interactions with Zeena in the past, especially when it is right before his eyes, is then juxtaposed with the current timeline in which Ethan similarly refuses to see the truth demonstrated by Mattie's behavior at the dance. Finally, Wharton ends the chapter on a line that perfectly reinforces the central theme of the entire chapter: "But now, as he stood outside the church, and saw Mattie spinning down the floor with Denis Eady, a throng of disregarded hints and menaces wove their cloud about his brain . . ."

Chapter II

As the dancers begin pouring out of the building, wrapped in their winter clothing, Ethan hides himself from view. The villagers start walking home immediately while the country dwellers ready their sleighs in the barn. Ethan is standing behind a storm door when he hears someone ask Mattie if she is going to ride with them. "Mercy no!" she exclaims. "Not on such a night" (Wharton 1911, 44). This is the first time the reader experiences Mattie in dialogue, and her comment typifies the kind of vague and indirect speech she will use throughout the novel. It's a particularly brilliant character trait that Wharton gives her, as it will allow Ethan any number of opportunities to interpret what she says in a way that conforms to his fantasies. The obvious meaning of her remark is that the night is so clear and beautiful that she wants to walk. But her reference to the night could also mean that she is warm from dancing and wants to cool off on the way home. Equally likely, she could be waiting to see if Denis Eady offers her a ride or, in Ethan's mind, that she is waiting for him.

The next paragraph offers more important symbolism as Ethan waits for Mattie to emerge from the other side of the storm door. "In another moment she would step forth into the night, and his eyes, accustomed to the obscurity, would discern her as clearly as though she stood in daylight" (Wharton 1911, 45). Here is the light/dark symbolism again, but used to slightly different effect. First, Ethan's eyes are "accustomed to the obscurity," meaning he has become used to not understanding what it is he sees. The cloudy meanings have remained that way for him and as a result have become his normal way of experiencing the world. This is reinforced by the fact that the obscurity is no different for him than "if she stood in daylight." In this way Wharton is signaling the reader that Ethan's romantic fantasy is equally as strong in the daylight as it is at night, meaning there is very little, if anything, that will be able to shake his belief in the imaginary world he has constructed for himself. As if to reinforce this idea, Wharton has Ethan provide a specific example. "It had been one of the wonders of their intercourse that from the first, she, the quicker, finer, more expressive, instead of crushing him by the contrast, had given him something of her own ease and freedom; but now he felt as heavy and loutish as in his student days when he had tried to 'jolly' the Worcester girls at a picnic." While in his fantasy about their "intercourse," or relationship, he sees a certain give and take between he and Mattie—his teaching her about the world and her lack of fretting rubbing off on him—there is still the reality of his lack of confidence, "heavy and loutish," that should signal to him a conflict with reality. But instead, because the darkness for Ethan is no different than the daylight, he is able rationalize away the truth and continue to indulge in his fantasy.

While Mattie waits, people continue to leave, until the only other person who remains with her is Denis Eady. Wharton draws his character exceptionally well in the brief scene she has given him in the story, which goes a long way to explaining Mattie's reaction to the young man. He begins by saying, "Gentleman friend gone back on you? Say, Matt, that's tough! No, I wouldn't be mean enough to tell the other girls. I ain't as low-down as that" (Wharton 1911, 45-46). This is a very telling piece of dialogue, as Eady essentially informs Mattie that he has the power to humiliate her by telling the other girls that she had been abandoned by the man who had brought her to the dance." Ethan immediately thinks to himself, "How Frome hated his cheap banter!" which is really beside the point, because it serves to misdirect the reader from the true meaning of Eady's implied threat. "But look a here, ain't it lucky I got the old man's cutter down there waiting for us?" (46). Mattie wonders aloud why he would have brought his father's cutter to the dance when he lives only a short walk from the church, but it's fairly obvious that he wants to take her home when he says, "I kinder knew I'd want to take a ride to-night." The problem is, his attempt at coercion doesn't sit well with her. For Ethan, however, the moment is one heavily freighted with meaning. "The girl seemed to waver, and Frome saw her twirl the end of her scarf irresolutely about her fingers. Not for the world would he have made a sign to her, though it seemed to him that his life hung on her next gesture." In Ethan's fantasy, Mattie's next move will be a definitive sign—the only kind available to him as they are unable to express their feelings openly—as to whether or not she loves him.

At this point Ethan notices that Mattie has stopped looking around for him, content to stand perfectly still while Eady hitches up his horse to the sleigh.

> She let Denis Eady lead out the horse, climb into the cutter and fling back the bearskin to make room for her at his side; then, with a swift motion of flight, she turned about and darted up the slope toward the front of the church. "Good-bye! Hope you'll have a lovely ride!" she called back to him over her shoulder. (Wharton 1911, 46-47)

There are several possible reasons for Mattie turning down a ride with Eady. The most obvious is that she didn't like the way he tried to manipulate her, with his implied threat of telling people she had been abandoned after the dance. She could also be reluctant to accept in case Ethan shows up late. But another possible explanation for her allowing him to believe she is going to ride with him and then running away at the last minute could be an attempt on her part to equal out the power differential between them exposed by his earlier threat. This is an idea used by John Steinbeck in "The Chrysanthemums." In that story a farmer's wife becomes frustrated with a life that has limited her to women's work, and when her husband gets the car out to take her to dinner one night she exacts a small measure of revenge by making him wait for her to get ready. "Elisa went into the house. She heard him drive to the gate and idle down his motor, and then she took a long time to put on her hat. She pulled it here and pressed it there. When Henry turned the motor off she slipped into her coat and went out" (Steinbeck 12). Because Eliza feels powerless in her marriage—whether it's actually true or not—she forces her husband to turn off the car before she goes outside in order to feel some measure of power and control in her life, however small. Of course, there is always the argument that Mattie is just playing hard to get, but that can be discounted when the two have their next interaction.

Eady immediately turns the sleigh around and pulls up next to her. "'Come along! Get in quick! It's as slippery as thunder on this turn,' he cried, leaning over to reach out a hand to her. She laughed back at him: 'Good-night! I'm not getting in.'" (Wharton 1911, 47). Ethan's joy is tempered at this point because Eady is apparently still not going to give up. "He saw Eady, after a moment, jump from the cutter and go toward the girl with the reins over one arm. The other he tried to slip through hers; but she eluded him nimbly, and Frome's heart, which had swung out over a black void, trembled back to safety" (47-48). The "black void" in this case is the devastation Ethan would feel if she were to accept the ride and confirm her desire to be courted by Eady. Given that logic, Ethan naturally believes that Mattie's rebuff of Eady must prove she is in love with him. But the most likely cause for her refusal is something that may not immediately be apparent to modern readers. Accepting a ride with Denis Eady, alone without a chaperone, could have two possible consequences for Mattie. The first is the implication that she has somehow promised herself to the young man. Regardless of her true feelings at this point, not only might that be something she doesn't want others to think but, more importantly, she might not want Eady to think it. The second assumption people could make, especially if she doesn't plan on getting engaged to him, is even worse. The kind of damage this could pose to her reputation can be seen in the story "A Rose for Emily," by William Faulkner, when the title character begins going for Sunday outings alone with Homer Baron.

> Presently we began to see him and Miss Emily on Sunday afternoons driving in the yellow-wheeled buggy and the matched team of bays from the livery stable . . . And as soon as the old people said, "Poor Emily," the whispering began. "Do you suppose it's really so?" they said to one another. "Of course it is. What else could . . ." This . . . upon the sun of Sunday afternoon as the thin, swift clop-clop-clop of the matched team passed: "Poor Emily." She carried her head high enough—even when we believed that she was fallen. (Faulkner 125)

Too many authors, however, make the mistake of not looking closely enough at the interaction between Mattie and Eady in this scene, and so find themselves mired in assumptions that make absolutely no sense. Suzanne F. Fournier provides an example of just such a misinterpretation. In attempting to explain why Mattie isn't interested in Eady she says, "The courtship between Denis and Mattie never materializes, of course, for she wants only to continue living at the farm as an unpaid servant in order to remain close to Ethan" (Fournier 89). *Of course*? Is it really logical in any way to assume, as Fournier does, that remaining an unpaid servant living at the whim of her "employers" is preferable to marrying the young man whom even Ethan recognizes will one day take over his father's store and become one of the richest men in town? The argument makes no sense on its face. Mattie's only way out of her current situation as an indentured servant is to get married. To then go on and assume that the reason she rebuffs Eady is because she is in love with Ethan is equally ridiculous. Ethan is a married man, and as a potential avenue for improving her life he seems hopelessly unsuited. Further, Fournier's suggestion that Mattie prefers Ethan to Eady is undercut by her own explanation of the symbolism associated with Mattie and Ethan. "Wharton assigns her qualities which contrast sharply with his defining traits. In the symbolic shorthand of the novel, Mattie is spring and Ethan is winter. She expresses herself with animation, in song as well as speech, and he moves in brooding silence" (100). Because of this it strains credulity to believe that Mattie prefers Ethan as a possible romantic partner when, in the very seasonal symbolism Fournier constructs, Ethan is already dead while Mattie is just beginning her life. Ultimately, the only logical explanation for choosing her current life over a future life with Eady is not that she has any feelings for Ethan at all, but that she emphatically doesn't love Eady.

Once Denis Eady has finally turned around and headed for home, Ethan quickly catches up to Mattie. Significantly, their conversation takes place, "in the black shade of the Varnum spruces" (Wharton 1911, 48). For Ethan, the darkness symbolizes his inability to understand that, as far as Mattie is concerned, their conversation is nothing more than small talk, and as this is also the first conversation between the two in the text Wharton uses it to set up a pattern that will inform their intercourse throughout the entire novel. When Ethan says, "Think I'd forgotten you, Matt?" his intent is clear. He wants to hear that she is slightly distraught over the fact that he wasn't there to escort her home. Instead, she responds by saying very practically, "I thought maybe you couldn't come back for me." Ethan is indignant at the idea that anything could have prevented him from walking her home, and says, "Couldn't? What on earth could stop me?" As before, the implication is that she means so much to him that nothing could prevent his being with her. But once again Mattie is quite matter-of-fact in bringing things back to reality: "I knew Zeena wasn't feeling any too good to-day." Because Ethan is in the dark about the true nature of their relationship, the dialogue between the two takes on an odd complexion, as though they are actually having two separate conversations. From Mattie's perspective, she is simply making small talk with the husband of her cousin. For Ethan, however, every word from her lips is interpreted in a way that supports his fantasy of shared love between them.

This is also the first discussion of Zeena's illness, a condition that, as will become clearer as the story progresses, increases and decreases in severity according to her level of jealousy. Knowing that Ethan was going out that night to walk Mattie home, Zeena therefore "wasn't feeling any too good." After dismissing thoughts of Zeena, Ethan tries to get back to his real point. "Then you meant to walk home all alone?" (Wharton 1911, 48). What he really wants to know is if she intended to walk home without him. Her understanding of the question, however, is entirely different. "Oh, I ain't afraid!" she says, and laughs. This is another example of the two of them carrying on completely different conversations with each other. To emphasize the fact, Wharton steps in and reminds the reader of Ethan's inability to understand any of this as they "stood together in the gloom of the spruces." Unable to accept her inability to answer him directly, Ethan finally comes out and asks her what he wants to know, namely, what her intentions are with Eady. "If you thought I hadn't come, why didn't you ride back with Denis Eady?" (49). But again, she hears the question in an entirely different way, especially after understanding that Ethan was already there and had witnessed the entire episode. "Why, where *were* you? How did you know? I never saw you!" Remarkably, Ethan seems to understand on some unconscious level that they have not been actually communicating, and yet he is still able to turn this disconnect into a reinforcement of his fantasy by symbolically combining the two conversations in his mind. "Her wonder and his laughter ran together like spring rills in a thaw."

Content for the moment that she has said nothing even remotely positive concerning Denis Eady, Ethan locks his arm in hers and naturally, "fancied it was faintly pressed against her side" (Wharton 1911, 49). He is imagining that she is pulling him close because that's what he wants to believe. The context, however, tells the reader everything there is to know. "It was so dark under the spruces that he could barely see the shape of her head beside his shoulder . . . He would have liked to stand there with her all night in the blackness." Thus Mattie's pressure on his arm has to do only with the treacherous nature of walking on snow and ice in the dark. At the same time, Ethan's desire to remain in the blackness with Mattie shows that he doesn't really want to know the truth. Parallel with the fantasy life of Ethan's desires, is the reality of the symbolism that informs the context in which his imagination plays out. Whatever he might imagine, it is imperative for the reader to stay focused on the specific reactions of those around Ethan in order to accurately assess the true nature of what is transpiring in the story. Mattie takes a couple of steps forward and here Wharton gives the reader another complimentary symbol to go along with the blackness. Mattie pauses, "above the dip of the Corbury road. Its icy slope, scored by innumerable runners, looked like a mirror scratched by travellers at an inn" (49-50). A mirror has the ability to provide Mattie with the means of reflecting on Ethan's words and actions, as a way of understanding what his true intentions are. But since that reflection is "scored" and "scratched" it will not afford her the opportunity. For Ethan, the mirror is also a means of gaining further information, as a reflection of himself, giving him some insight into his inclination for self-deception as well as the true nature of his relationship with Mattie. But he is equally blind.

When Ethan offers to take Mattie sledding the following evening she is at first delighted, and then pulls him close with the remembered fear of something that had happened earlier that evening. At the same time, Wharton uses the opportunity to deliver another foreshadow of the ending of the novel.

> She lingered, pressing closer to his side. "Ned Hale and Ruth Varnum came just as near running into the big elm at the bottom. We were all sure they were killed." Her shiver ran down his arm. "Wouldn't it have been too awful? They're so happy!" (Wharton 1911, 50)

Ethan naturally turns the reminiscence, accompanied by her physical reaction, into further proof of her feelings for him. "The inflection with which she had said of the engaged couple 'They're so happy!' made the words sound as if she had been thinking of herself and him" (50). This is the first of several occasions throughout the story when Ethan tries to see his imaginary relationship with Mattie as somehow mirroring that of the genuine love between Ned Hale and Ruth Varnum. Bolstered by this image, when Mattie suggests that the tree is dangerous and it should be cut down Ethan uses the opportunity to present himself as her protector and thereby make another attempt to gauge her feelings. "Would you be afraid of it, with me?" And just as she had done with his earlier inquiry about walking home alone, she responds quite differently than he had hoped. "'I told you I ain't the kind to be afraid,' she tossed back, almost indifferently; and suddenly she began to walk on with a rapid step" (51). Following this, Ethan has what should be another insight into the disconnected nature of their conversation but, as always, he ignores the implications. "These alterations of mood were the despair and joy of Ethan Frome. The motions of her mind were as incalculable as the flit of a bird in the branches." What Ethan perceives as alteration in Mattie's mood is actually the difference between what he believes she is saying and what she actually says—the "joy" of his fantasy and the "despair" of her reality—and as a result they would naturally be "incalculable" to him. The bird comparison is also an interesting one that Wharton will return to several times more in describing aspects of Mattie's character. Here it reinforces yet again Ethan's inability to know what she is really thinking any more than he would have the ability to predict what branch a bird in the wild is going to fly to next—and at the same time it also reflects the quicksilver analogy of her last name.

Of course Ethan offers an explanation for Mattie's changeability, one that fits neatly within his fantasy and yet also reveals his true thoughts. "The fact that he had no right to show his feelings, and thus provoke the expression of hers, made him attach a fantastic importance to every change in her look and tone. Now he thought she understood him, and feared; now he was sure she did not, and despaired" (Wharton 1911, 51). This is a fascinating description, as both the outcomes of fear and despair are technically negative. While Ethan had contrasted joy with despair earlier when trying to decipher the meaning of her words, he now articulates something much closer to the truth when he says that were she to actually understand his coded professions of love he would fear it. The reason why can be understood by examining his explanation. The most obvious reason for not having the right to express his love for Mattie openly is that Ethan is a married man. Most readers take this to mean that his declaration of love would be unfair to her because he is not free to be with her. As disappointing as that might be, however, it certainly doesn't connote the sense that someone's rights have been violated. A much more satisfying explanation is that revealing his love for Mattie actually puts her in an untenable position if she doesn't return that love, having to live in his house with his wife all the while knowing his true feelings for her. Ethan's despair in that context would be quite understandable. By the same token, if Mattie were to return his love, it is Ethan who would then have to live in perpetual fear of Zeena finding out. Because of this, Ethan happily retreats into the world of cloudy meanings, interpreting meaningful implications behind the otherwise mundane conversation between the two of them, forcing him to place more emphasis on the way she says things rather than what she says.

Though Ethan has twice broached the subject of Denis Eady in order to discern what Mattie's intentions are, the disconnect in their conversation has left him unsure. In addition, the information he has learned from seeing Mattie dancing still haunts him. "To-night the pressure of accumulated misgivings sent the scale drooping toward despair, and her indifference was the more chilling after the flush of joy into which she had plunged him by dismissing Denis Eady . . . the need of some definite assurance grew too strong for him" (Wharton 1911, 51). When he says that she would have seen him if she hadn't gone back for the last reel with Eady, she repeats her earlier question to him by asking how she could have known he was there. The issue for Ethan here is that he hadn't really been paying attention to the conversation she had with Eady, and instead was focused on his own jealousy. As a result, he doesn't realize that Mattie has no interest in the grocer's son. But he simply can't let it go, and this forces him to take a more direct approach with her. "I suppose what folks say is true . . . It's natural enough you should be leaving us." Though Ethan is referring to her getting married, Mattie responds with what in her mind is the only possible reason she would be going. "You mean that Zeena—ain't suited with me any more?" (52). Ethan's misinterpretation of what Mattie's says here is reinforced by yet another reference to the darkness in which all of this is happening, as they "stood motionless, each seeking to distinguish the other's face." Mattie begins by launching into an impassioned defense of herself. She's well aware of her deficiencies, but feels she gets no direction from Zeena as to how she can improve. The reader, on the other hand, already knows that Zeena is far more unhappy with the girl's effect on Ethan than she is with the girl herself. Mattie also understands that her pleas to Ethan are meaningless if the couple is united in their assessment of her, which causes her to add, "Unless you want me to go too—" (53).

Ethan, however, hears something completely different in Mattie's rational assessment of the situation. "Unless he wanted her to go too! The cry was balm to his raw wound. The iron heavens seemed to melt and rain down sweetness" (Wharton 1911, 53). Somehow Ethan has managed to hear in Mattie's statement that she is not in control of whether she stays or goes a declaration that she will only leave if he wants her to. His fears assuaged for the moment, Ethan urges her on toward the farm and Wharton takes time to describe the nighttime landscape. "They walked on in silence through the blackness of the hemlock-shaded lane . . . On the farther side of the hemlock belt the open country rolled away before them grey and lonely under the stars . . . Here and there a farmhouse stood far back among the fields, mute and cold as a grave-stone." In this description Wharton not only reinforces the idea that the two are operating in "blackness," and thus are not really communicating, but adds a symbolic foreshadow of death in the form of the "hemlock" trees that surround them and make even the open country appear "grey and lonely," in addition to farm houses—similar to Ethan's own—that look like "grave-stones." At one point a tree limb laden with snow breaks in the still night and Mattie pulls Ethan's arm closer, which reinforces his fantasy that she shares his feelings for her. But as they approach the front gate the reality of being back at home sets in, and Ethan cannot resist one last reassurance. "Then you don't want to leave us, Matt?" Her response is another example of the two engaging in completely different conversations.

The intent of Ethan's question is to gauge not only her desire to stay at the house but, by extension, to be with him. Her response, on the other hand, deals only with the reality of her situation: "Where'd I go, if I did?" (Wharton 1911, 54). It's important to understand that her words do not mean she actually wants to stay with the Fromes, but rather that she has no choice in the matter. This is an idea that will be repeated at the end of the story, and her response here implies that had she any other options she might very well have considered them. More significant, however, is that being forced to articulate her present position actually results in tears from the girl. Suzanne Fournier goes so far as to see this conversational disconnect in terms of the cruelty that Ethan subjects Mattie to in ignoring the circumstances of her life by focusing on his own fantasy. "Selfishly absorbed in extracting the assurance that Mattie will not marry Denis Eady, he fails to consider the fundamental insecurity of her life. Her reaction to his headless words underscores how fearful and dependent she actually is" (Fournier 87). But it makes sense that Ethan would ignore Mattie's feelings, as he already assumes she wants to stay with him. The result of this mistaken belief is that throughout their conversation Ethan has been capable only of understanding her situation in terms of how it benefits him "The answer sent a pang through him but the tone suffused him with joy." Then he hugs her, which in his mind is a definitive declaration of his feelings for her, but which to her must appear wholly as a weak attempt at consolation.

Just inside the gate is the Frome family graveyard, and as he frequently does upon entering his property Ethan ruminates on the inhabitants within.

> For years that quiet company had mocked his restlessness, his desire for change and freedom. "We never got away—how should you?" seemed to be written on every headstone; and whenever he went in or out of his gate he thought with a shiver: "I shall just go on living here till I join them." But now all desire for change had vanished, and the sight of the little enclosure gave him a warm sense of continuance and stability. (Wharton 1911, 55)

This passage can be compared to one in Chopin's "The Story of an Hour" when her protagonist has a similar change of attitude: "She breathed a quick prayer that life might be long. It was only yesterday she had thought with a shudder that life might be long" (Chopin 1894). Both of these examples deal with the entrapment of the characters, caught in marriages and circumstances for which they see no escape. Chopin's protagonist understands that she finally has a way out when she believes her husband has died. For Ethan, however, the presence of Mattie in his home must be compensation for the misery of his marriage with Zeena and the difficulty of his life on the farm. This is reinforced by Ethan's statement to Mattie that, "I guess we'll never let you go, Matt," and his subsequent thought that, "We'll always go on living here together, and some day she'll lie there beside me" (Wharton 1911, 55).

Wharton does an excellent job, however, of juxtaposing these elements of fantasy on the part of Ethan with a healthy dose of reality for the reader. "He let the vision possess him as they climbed the hill to the house. He was never so happy with her as when he abandoned himself to these dreams" (Wharton 1911, 55). So while Ethan becomes lost in his fantasy, the very words used to describe it alert the reader to their inherent disconnection from reality. By allowing the "vision" to "possess" him and "abandoning himself to these dreams" Ethan seems to understand on some unconscious level that what he is experiencing with Mattie is not real. A similar disconnect from reality takes place in the mind of Emma Bovary, whose story has been shown to parallel Ethan's in a number of ways. Author Ana-Isabel Aliaga-Buchenau has noted word choices used by Flaubert to indicate his protagonist's emphasis on her fantasy world rather than reality.

> Emma thinks or dreams in "pictures" that resemble the images she contemplated in the keepsakes. Her dream of a honeymoon "is a mental picture of driving in the mountains," her dream of an exciting existence in Paris "is a group of neatly compartmentalized images of the different worlds of the ambassadors, duchesses and artists in the capital," and her dream of running away with Rodolphe "takes the form of an exotic travel fantasy." (Aliaga-Buchenau 104)

Wharton uses similar words, like picture and vision. In this instance she solidifies Ethan's disconnection from reality when Mattie stumbles while they are walking and she grabs Ethan's coat to keep from falling. "The wave of warmth that went through him was like the prolongation of his vision. For the first time he stole his arm about her, and she did not resist. They walked on as if they were floating on a summer stream" (Wharton 1911, 55-56). Ethan once again enlists reality as an accomplice in constructing his dream world. Mattie's practical concern is to keep from falling in the dark, and so naturally when Ethan puts his arm around her she is not going to resist. But of course Ethan interprets this as a lack of resistance to his overtures of love, while at the same time Wharton has taken pains to remind the reader that this is merely a "prolongation of his vision."

As the two of them walk past the front of the house the windows are dark, just as they were in the church. But this time the lack of freedom and understanding they symbolize has to do with the domestic circumstances Ethan feels have imprisoned him. Zeena has essentially taken control of his life because of the unthinking way he brought her there in the first place. And the dark windows are accompanied by another reference to Zeena's death as the only avenue that will allow him to escape from his captivity. "A dead cucumber-vine dangled from the porch like the crape streamer tied to the door for a death, and the thought flashed through Ethan's brain: 'If it was there for Zeena—'" (Wharton 1911, 56). This unspoken wish on Ethan's part is followed by a vision of his wife as if she had been laid out for burial. "Then he had a distinct sight of his wife lying in their bedroom asleep, her mouth slightly open, her false teeth in a tumbler by the bed . . ." Wharton had written a precursor to this death wish in a short story called "The Choice" in 1908, three years before *Ethan Frome*. In that story a woman much like

Eric B. Olsen

Wharton herself is married to a man much like Wharton's husband Teddy. He is a self-absorbed bore who has driven his wife into the arms of another man, a friend of the family. Late on the night the story takes place she meets with her lover in the boathouse, and about her husband's death she says, "I wish it always—every day, every hour, every moment . . ."

> I'm not the saint you suppose; the duty I do is poisoned by the thoughts I think. Day by day, hour by hour, I wish him dead. When he goes out I pray for something to happen; when he comes back I say to myself: "Are you here again?" When I hear of people being killed in accidents, I think: "Why wasn't he there?" When I read the death-notices in the paper I say: "So-and-so was just his age" . . . I think of the men who die from overwork, or who throw their lives away for some great object, and I say to myself: "What can kill a man who thinks only of himself?" And night after night I keep myself from going to sleep for fear I may dream that he's dead. When I dream that, and wake and find him there it's worse than ever—" (Wharton 1908, 300-301)

The grim reality for so many women at the turn of the twentieth century was that marriage could be a double-edged sword. In one respect it offered the only real escape from the family home, freedom from spinsterhood and the imposed care for elderly parents. At the same time, most women could not risk turning down a proposal for fear of not getting another one, which resulted in numerous loveless marriages that provided no means of escape at all. The symbol Wharton uses to demonstrate this is wonderfully clever. Ethan and Mattie walk around to the back door, where Ethan explains, "It was Zeena's habit, when they came back late from the village, to leave the key of the kitchen door under the mat" (Wharton 1911, 56). Zeena then, like the men in most marriages, holds the key. Before going into the house Ethan is determined to say something meaningful to Mattie, but now that her need for his support in walking through the night is over, "She slipped out of his hold without speaking, and he stooped down and felt for the key. 'It's not there!' he said, straightening himself with a start" (56-57). This moment emphasizes the fact that Zeena has control over both of them, Ethan in terms of the virtually unbreakable bond of marriage, and Mattie in light of her position as a de facto employee. By withholding the key in this scene Zeena emphasizes the power she wields in both relationships.

Neither of them, however, is in a position to understand the full meaning of the missing key, as the light/dark symbolism once again appears to show their ignorance. "They strained their eyes at each other through the icy darkness.

Such a thing had never happened before" (Wharton 1911, 57). For Mattie, the situation is far more dire than it is for Ethan. In symbolically locking her out of the house Zeena is demonstrating her ability to leave Mattie homeless and destitute, whereas Ethan is able to use the instance to conjure up yet another fantasy of Zeena's death. "Another wild thought tore through him. What if tramps had been there—what if . . . ." But reality imposes itself on the scene when Ethan attempts to look for the key. "Again he listened, fancying he heard a distant sound in the house; then he felt in his pocket for a match, and kneeling down, passed its light slowly over the rough edges of snow about the doorstep." Two elements of this sentence are worth noting. First, the light that Ethan possesses is little more than that provided by a match. It's just enough to infuse him with the fear of something sensed, but without the calm reassurance of understanding. Second, this lack of understanding forces him into a position of submission in relation to Zeena, symbolized by the fact that he is on his knees. Both of these ideas are perfectly encapsulated in the next passage.

> He was still kneeling when his eyes, on a level with the lower panel of the door, caught a faint ray beneath it. Who could be stirring in that silent house? He heard a step on the stairs, and again for an instant the thought of tramps tore through him. Then the door opened and he saw his wife. (57-58)

The dominance of his fantasy over reality actually makes Ethan believe for a moment that there might be someone in the house other than Zeena, that tramps might still be inside, an almost ludicrous thought for the reader to consider. But the tableau drawn at the conclusion of the passage speaks volumes. Ethan is on his knees on the porch, with Zeena towering over him in complete control. She is the one who opens the door, but instead of some imagined sense of opportunity on the other side, all he sees is the reality of his life with Zeena.

The next paragraph is almost Gothic in it's imagery. Zeena stands in the doorway holding up a lamp in one hand, the other clutching a blanket around her shoulders and holding it fast, "to her flat breast." The lack of an ample bosom further associates Zeena with male dominance and control. But Wharton's description of her takes the power that she possesses a step further by making her appearance seem monstrous.

> The light, on a level with her chin, drew out of the darkness her puckered throat and the projecting wrist of the hand that clutched the quilt, and deepened fantastically the hollows and prominences of her high-boned

face under its ring of crimping-pins. To Ethan, still in the rosy haze of his hour with Mattie, the sight came with the intense precision of the last dream before waking. He felt as if he had never before known what his wife looked like. (Wharton 1911, 58)

Wharton's word choices here are magnificent. But the description of Zeena that makes her appear like an ugly hag is also the result of the light she holds in her hand. In this way she is revealing to Ethan the truth of their life together. The end result of this is to dispel Ethan's fantasy in a cruel juxtaposition. The "rosy haze" of his fantasy life with Mattie could almost describe the girl herself, while the reference to waking from a dream to face the reality of Zeena is as accurate a depiction of his life as there can be. At last, Ethan has been confronted with the true nature of his circumstances in a way that he had never quite allowed himself to understand before. The symbolic rendering of that life comes in the next paragraph, as Zeena stands aside while they enter "the kitchen, which had the deadly chill of a vault" (58). Though Ethan may fantasize about the warmth that Mattie brings to their hearth, the narrator's statement about him in the Prologue twenty-four years later to the effect that he is dead and in hell already is far more accurate.

But Wharton isn't satisfied with ending the scene there, and continues to reinforce the idea of Zeena's power and Ethan's submission in their dialogue at the close of the chapter. Ethan tries to joke that she forgot about them, but Zeena says, "No. I just felt so mean I couldn't sleep" (Wharton 1911, 58). As in the flashback sequence from the previous chapter, Zeena's first words here are about her illness. Significantly, Mattie asks if there is anything she can do for her. Other than leaving the house for good, the subtext seems to imply, "No. There's nothing" (59). Inexplicably bolstered by his faulty belief that he and Mattie feel the same about each other, Ethan is reluctant to give in to reality just yet by having her see him go to bed with his wife. But Wharton puts it in such a way that it's clear the power differential is more important to him than the implied sexual nature of the relationship. "To-night it was peculiarly repugnant to him that Mattie should see him follow Zeena." So Ethan decides to stay downstairs in the kitchen for a while and work on his accounts, but Zeena's undisguised ridicule is blunt and to the point. "She continued to stare at him, the flame of the unshaded lamp bringing out with microscopic cruelty the fretful lines of her face. 'At this time o' night? You'll ketch your death. The fire's out long ago'" (60). Ethan then looks over to Mattie, "and he fancied that a fugitive warning gleamed through her lashes. The next moment they sank to her flushed cheeks and she began to mount the stairs ahead of Zeena." In reality, the flushed cheeks indicate embarrassment rather than some kind of imagined warning to Ethan. Ultimately, he realizes the pointlessness of his defiance and gives in to Zeena's authority in the most obviously symbolic way possible. "Ethan assented; and with lowered head he went up in his wife's wake, and followed her across the threshold of their room." Again, Wharton's word choices are perfect. In following in Zeena's wake, she possesses the power while Ethan, his head bowed, is powerless to do anything else but follow the path that she has chosen.

Chapter III

Chapter Three opens with Ethan at work the following morning hauling timber. After a sentence establishing the action, Wharton's next paragraph describes the setting: a crystal clear morning with deep blue shadows in the woods, and snow and bare trees in the distance that look like smoke. She also notes, "the sun burned red in a pure sky" (Wharton 1911, 61). This, of course, suggests the old seafarer's poem, "Red sky at night, sailor's delight; red sky at morning, sailor take warning," which has its genesis in the book of Matthew from the Bible.

> He answered and said unto them, When it is evening, ye say, It will be fair weather: for the sky is red. And in the morning, It will be foul weather to day: for the sky is red and lowering. (KJV, Matthew 6:2-3)

Now that Ethan is in the open air of the "clear as crystal" morning during the daylight, he needs to begin processing the information he learned the night before. "It was in the early morning stillness, when his muscles were swinging to their familiar task and his lungs expanding with long draughts of mountain air, that Ethan did his clearest thinking" (61). Unfortunately, his thinking is anything but clear on this particular morning. "Ethan felt confusedly that there were many things he ought to think about, but through his tingling veins and tired brain only one sensation throbbed: the warmth of Mattie's shoulder against his" (62). As it had during the previous evening, his fantasy about Mattie prevents him from seeing the reality of the night's events. In that scene he had reminisced about the "silent joy" the two of them had shared in viewing the "cold red of sunset behind the winter hills," as well as the expression on her face when she saw him that "looked like a window that has caught the sunset" (37, 38). In both of these instances Ethan emphasizes the other half of the sailor's poem as a way of making Mattie's presence in his life conform to his imagination. And further, the comparison of Mattie's expression to a window symbolizes the freedom and opportunity she represents for him.

With the reality of the red sky now giving him a genuine warning, however, there are several things that Ethan should be wary of. The first is the acuteness of Zeena's perception about him. She had noticed that he was shaving every day, and there is only one assumption she could make for his doing so. Second, Zeena locked the two of them outside, something she had never done before, and what to Ethan had simply been complaints about Mattie's inefficiency are actually signs that Zeena is jealous. But Zeena's jealousy must also be understood in context. She's not necessarily fearful that Ethan will somehow run away with Mattie and leave her destitute. It has more to do with the discontent she experiences in her life with Ethan, a pattern of unhappiness that affected many women at the time. What Zeena resents is Ethan's pleasure at becoming infatuated with Mattie. From Zeena's perspective, if she is going to be miserable in their life together then she wants to make sure Ethan is miserable too. Her way of doing that takes many forms. One is by withholding information she knows will embarrass him when revealed at a later date and her ability to put him off balance by bringing up something he thought she had forgotten. "Once or twice in the past he had been faintly disquieted by Zenobia's way of letting things happen without seeming to remark them, and then, weeks afterward, in a casual phrase, revealing that she had all along taken her notes and drawn her inferences" (Wharton 1911, 42-43). Another is their lack of communication as a couple.

While neither of them is completely isolated physically—Zeena does take trips to see her relatives or the doctor, and Ethan works and interacts with people during the day—they are still very isolated within their relationship. Whatever misery the two of them suffer as a result of being together, they both seem to intuitively understand that talking about it isn't going to improve the basic facts of their existence. And worse, bringing up irritations or arguing about things will not only fail to solve their problems, it will leave them in exactly the same place but even more miserable than they were before. This isolation and lack of communication can be seen when Ethan remembers following Zeena up the stairs the previous evening. "He and Zeena had not exchanged a word after the door of their room had closed on them. She had measured out some drops from a medicine-bottle on a chair by the bed and, after swallowing them, and wrapping her head in a piece of yellow flannel, had lain down with her face turned away. Ethan undressed hurriedly and blew out the light so that he should not see her when he took his place at her side" (61-62). The most significant part of this description is the door closing on the

Eric B. Olsen

two of them, symbolizing Zeena's refusal to allow them to separate or break out of their prison-like marriage. In addition, Wharton's words "closed on them," in conjunction with their going to bed suggest the lowering of a coffin lid. Another demonstration of Zeena's unhappiness is expressed in the way she punishes Ethan with her ill health, which will become more apparent later on.

In bed the previous evening, Ethan's gaze was drawn to the faint glow of light from Mattie's room that made its way underneath his door. But with his door closed and Mattie's closed on the other side of the hall, this insignificant amount of light reflects that his obsession has allowed him little room for true understanding. Instead, he inwardly berates himself for not having demonstrated his affection for her. "Why had he not kissed her when he held her there?" he thinks, even though he had already recognized earlier that night that he had no right to express his feelings to her (Wharton 1911, 62). And yet, on some level he seems to understand this as well. "A few hours earlier he would not have asked himself the question. Even a few minutes earlier, when they had stood alone outside the house, he would not have dared to think of kissing her." Rather than coming to grips with the true nature of their conversation, and seeing with his own eyes that he had been mistaken about her behavior toward him, Ethan's desire to possess Mattie crowds out all other rational thought. "But since he had seen her lips in the lamplight he felt that they were his." Wharton is there, as always, to remind the reader of the fallacy of Ethan's conception of their relationship by bringing in the warning rays of the red sun. "Now, in the bright morning air, her face was still before him. It was part of the sun's red and of the pure glitter on the snow." As it had before, Mattie's continued presence in his thoughts—which the sun symbolically tells him should be a warning, and the glitter from the snow enlightening him about—only serves to reinforce his desire for her.

Ethan's unreliability is also in evidence when he describes Mattie's arrival at the farm. "He remembered what a colourless slip of a thing she had looked the day he had met her at the station. And all the first winter, how she had shivered with cold when the northerly gales shook the thin clapboards and the snow beat like hail against the loose-hung windows!" (Wharton 1911, 63). This contrasts somewhat with his earlier statement that "He had taken to the girl from the first day." In his revisionist thinking he also claims, "He had been afraid that she would hate the hard life, the cold and loneliness," though it's difficult to see why immediately after her arrival he would have cared whether or not she might be unhappy, except for Zeena's sake. More likely he was concerned that yet another miserable soul in the house might be one too many and tip the balance of their existence toward overwhelming gloom. Ethan's reminiscence, however, also contrasts Mattie's personality with Zeena's and

186

provides the reader with another example of Ethan's faulty reasoning. "Not a sign of discontent escaped her. Zeena took the view that Mattie was bound to make the best of Starkfield since she hadn't any other place to go to; but this did not strike Ethan as conclusive. Zeena, at any rate, did not apply the principle in her own case." Ethan wants to believe that when Mattie makes the best of her circumstances it has to do with him rather than because it is simply a natural part of her character. Yet at the same time he doesn't seem to realize that Zeena's discontent is in fact a very specific response to his actions rather than the defect in her character he believes it to be.

Wharton takes time out here to give the reader some important information about Mattie's past. Mattie's father, a cousin of Zeena's, was something of a success in their small corner of the world after he had taken over his father-in-law's prosperous drugstore. As a result of the family's "mingled sentiments of envy and admiration," he was able to induce them to invest their savings with him (Wharton 1911, 63). Upon his death, however, it was discovered that he was penniless. "His wife died of the disclosure, and Mattie, at twenty, was left alone to make her way on the fifty dollars obtained from the sale of her piano" (64). Like many upper middle class women of her day, the education Mattie received was intended to make her cultured and refined—presumably in order to get a husband—rather than prepare her for the realities of the working world. "For this purpose her equipment, though varied, was inadequate. She could trim a hat, make molasses candy, recite 'Curfew shall not ring to-night,' and play 'The Lost Chord' and a pot-pourri from 'Carmen.'" As with everything else in the novel, Wharton's references are extremely well chosen. "Curfew shall not ring to-night" is a narrative poem written by a sixteen-year-old girl, Rose Hartwick Thorpe, about a young woman who risks her life to save her lover from a death sentence to be carried out at the ringing of the curfew bell. "The Lost Chord" is a song composed by Arthur Sullivan, with lyrics by Adelaide Anne Procter. The words concern a woman sitting at an organ experimenting with various combinations of notes. She suddenly hits upon a chord that seems to reach into her soul and take all of her worries away, but she can't remember what keys she pressed and is unable to play it again. *Carmen*, of course, is the opera by the French composer Georges Bizet, about a gypsy woman who gets a soldier to fall in love with her and lures him to his doom. While all of these themes are symbolically present in the novel, their literal use is equally important in demonstrating that, in the words of Lauer and Wolff, "Mattie has no practical skills and only a superficial training in 'proper' feminine culture" (Lauer 26).

Nevertheless, Mattie had made an attempt at working, trying her hand at "stenography and bookkeeping" until "her health broke down, and six months on her feet behind the counter of a department store did not tend to restore it" (Wharton 1911, 64). At this point her relatives took pity on her and gave her a home with them. "But when Zenobia's doctor recommended her looking about for some one to help her with the house-work the clan instantly saw the chance of exacting a compensation from Mattie" (65). In this way she essentially became an indentured servant. As far as Ethan was concerned, he felt that taking Mattie on as a housekeeper despite her deficiencies was as much a benefit to his wife as a burden. "Zenobia, though doubtful of the girl's efficiency, was tempted by the freedom to find fault without much risk of losing her." It must be remembered, however, that this assessment is still coming from Ethan. What the reader also knows about Mattie's arrival is that Zeena did make some provision for her emotional well-being by allowing her to take part in activities in the village. It could be argued that Zeena's criticism of the girl didn't really start until after Ethan became infatuated with her. This is reinforced by what Ethan perceives as Zeena's way of expressing dissatisfaction without actually doing so. "Zenobia's fault-finding was of the silent kind, but not the less penetrating for that." At the same time the reader can see the beginning of Ethan's identification with Mattie as a kindred spirit in the way he views her as a proxy for himself. "During the first months Ethan alternately burned with the desire to see Mattie defy her and trembled with fear of the result." This is another instance of the kind of subtle gender reversal Wharton uses in the novel, reflecting the fact that Ethan is unable to defy his wife because of his intense fear of her.

As summer arrived during the first year Mattie spent with the Fromes, her health began to improve. At the same time, "Zeena, with more leisure to devote to her complex ailments, grew less watchful of the girl's omissions" (Wharton 1911, 65). Or so it seemed to Ethan. Spending more time working during the summer months, "struggling on under the burden of his barren farm and failing saw-mill, [he] could at least imagine that peace reigned in his house." It is entirely possible, however, that peace actually did reign, and that it is only Zeena's later jealousy over his interest in Mattie that he has projected backward in time to color the girl's entire stay with them. As Ethan is forced to admit, "There was really, even now, no tangible evidence to the contrary." But the signs are there, and Ethan's subconscious is desperately trying to reveal them to him. "Since the previous night a vague dread had hung on his sky-line. It was formed of Zeena's obstinate silence, of Mattie's sudden look of warning, of the memory of just such fleeting imperceptible signs as those which told him, on certain stainless mornings, that before night there would be rain" (65-66). The "vague dread" on his skyline Ethan should be paying attention to is the actual warning of the red sun. Wharton then goes on to describe Ethan's reluctance to face the truth as "man-like." And while there is much to that, there is also a feminine quality to his avoidance that is probably more representative of an earlier time, before the modern cliché of women as endlessly eager to talk about problems in their relationships. This can certainly be seen in Zeena's reluctance to engage Ethan directly about anything.

At midday Ethan typically sent his hired hand, Jotham Powell, back home while Ethan delivered the wood to the sawmill by himself. But after Zeena's unusual behavior in locking them out the night before, he is worried that Mattie may end up on the receiving end of Zeena's displeasure—though there is absolutely no evidence from the reader's perspective that this is likely—and so he decides that both he and Jotham will go back home for supper. When they enter the kitchen Mattie is at the stove while Zeena is seated at the table. "Her husband stopped short at sight of her. Instead of her usual calico wrapper and knitted shawl she wore her best dress of brown merino, and above her thin strands of hair . . . rose a hard perpendicular bonnet . . . On the floor beside her stood his old valise and a bandbox wrapped in newspapers" (Wharton 1911, 67). Utterly unprepared for seeing his wife dressed to take a trip, Ethan asks her where she's going. "I've got my shooting pains so bad that I'm going over to Bettsbridge to spend the night with Aunt Martha Pierce and see that new doctor." Apparently this impromptu excursion was not entirely unprecedented, as "Twice or thrice before she had suddenly packed Ethan's valise and started off to Bettsbridge, or even Springfield, to seek the advice of some new doctor, and her husband had grown to dread these expeditions because of their cost" (68). While this is the beginning of the reader's understanding of exactly what is wrong with Zeena, Ethan's immediate reaction is essentially the opposite. "For the moment his sense of relief was so great as to preclude all other feelings. He had now no doubt that Zeena had spoken the truth in saying, the night before, that she had sat up because she felt 'too mean' to sleep: her abrupt resolve to seek medical advice showed that, as usual, she was wholly absorbed in her health." Unfortunately, Ethan has misread the situation entirely.

For Zeena, as it was for many women in her day, illness was a tool, if only an unconscious one, "an unspoken idiom of protest, a symbolic voice for the silenced sex, who were forbidden to verbalize their discontents, and so created a language of the body" (Scull 7). Beyond simply a way of easing her domestic burdens, Zeena adeptly wields her sickness as a weapon in a way that has been implied by Ethan already when he admits that he "had grown to dread these expeditions because of their cost" (Wharton 1911, 68). By forcing Ethan to pay for her medical treatments and medicine, Zeena is exacting retribution of sorts for being trapped in an unhappy marriage. She is also able to extract a certain measure of grudging sympathy from him in lieu of any feelings of love. What

Ethan doesn't understand is that her leaving is not proof of her ignorance of his feelings for Mattie, but the complete opposite. Zeena's jealousy not only takes the form of criticism of Mattie, which is something he is semi-conscious of, but also an increase in the severity of her illness. Because of this, her locking the two of them out of the house was just one way of expressing her disapproval. Going to the doctor is another. But of course Ethan is too caught up in his imagined romance to comprehend any of this.

> Her husband hardly heard what she was saying. During the winter months there was no stage between Starkfield and Bettsbridge, and the trains which stopped at Corbury Flats were slow and infrequent. A rapid calculation showed Ethan that Zeena could not be back at the farm before the following evening . . . He became suddenly conscious that he was looking at Mattie while Zeena talked to him, and with an effort he turned his eyes to his wife. (69, 70)

In finally looking at Zeena, however, he once again imagines her death as "the pale light reflected from the banks of snow made her face look more than usually drawn and bloodless." At the same time, he can't help but reflect on what life on the farm has done to her over the years. "Though she was but seven years her husband's senior, and he was only twenty-eight, she was already an old woman" (70).

It's here Ethan makes a major blunder. Zeena is the one who actually suggests that if he's too busy to take her over to the train station the least he can do is allow Jotham to take her. But while Ethan is staring at Mattie the only thing on his mind is how much time they'll have together without her. Meanwhile, Zeena passive-aggressively rambles on about how she would walk to the train station rather than put him out, and when Ethan can finally tear his eyes away from Mattie he agrees to allow Jotham to drive Zeena to the Flats. At that point everything should have been settled. But instead of leaving it alone his guilt forces him to become far too calculating. "He knew that Zeena must be wondering why he did not offer to drive her to the Flats and let Jotham Powell take the lumber to Starkfield" (Wharton 1911, 70). But Zeena was wondering no such thing, as she had already assumed Ethan wouldn't want to take her and so she suggested Jotham herself. Desperate to come up with something to explain his actions, Ethan says, "I'd take you over myself, only I've got to collect the cash for the lumber," and he knows this is a mistake the instant he's said it. "As soon as the words were spoken he regretted them, not only because they were untrue—there being no prospect of his receiving cash payment from Hale—but also because he knew from experience the imprudence of letting Zeena think he was in funds on the eve of one of her therapeutic excursions" (71). And yet Ethan still manages to delude himself as he observes Zeena at the table. "Zeena made no reply: she did not seem to hear what he had said." Seem, is the operative word, as the remark will come back to haunt Ethan later. For the moment, however, Zeena appears preoccupied with the treatment of her ailments, finishing off her medicine and telling Mattie to rinse out the bottle and use it for pickles.

Chapter IV

The opening paragraph of Chapter Four is another wonderful reminder by Wharton of Ethan's inability to fully understand the actual relationship between he and Mattie.

> As soon as his wife had driven off Ethan took his coat and cap from the peg. Mattie was washing up the dishes, humming one of the dance tunes of the night before. He said "So long, Matt," and she answered gaily "So long, Ethan"; and that was all. (Wharton 1911, 72)

Of course the phrase "that was all" is simply referring to what is literally spoken by the two characters, but the symbolic message it sends is too obvious to miss: there is nothing else between them but friendship. As he looks back at the kitchen before going outside, Ethan can't help but remark on the difference between the kitchen in his mother's day, when it was "spruce and shining," and the way it looks in the present. Still, he notices the sun coming through the window to light Mattie's figure, and the way it made the room "warm and bright." But what he attributes the cheerfulness of the scene to mostly is, "the mere fact of Zeena's absence."

With the cat sleeping on the chair, the potted flowers he had planted for Mattie in the doorway, and his wife no longer in the house, Ethan allows his fantasy full expression.

> He pictured what it would be like that evening, when he and Mattie were there after supper. For the first time they would be alone together indoors, and they would sit there, one on each side of the stove, like a married couple, he in his stocking feet and smoking his pipe, she laughing and

talking in that funny way she had, which was always as new to him as if he had never heard her before. (Wharton 1911, 73)

Again, it is Shakespeare who points out the danger in the use of similes. While the word "like" is typically intended to emphasize similarities, as in "like a married couple," the fact that the two things are merely similar rather than exactly the same means that they are inherently different. In *Julius Caesar*, when Caesar asks the conspirators to have a drink with him he says, "Good friends, go in, and taste some wine with me; and we, like friends, will straightway go together" (Shakespeare 1599, 60). Brutus is struck by the way Caesar's words reflect that the conspirators are only pretending to be his friends, and he responds to this with an aside to the audience in which he says, "That every like is not the same, O Caesar, the heart of Brutus yearns to think upon!" As much as Ethan wants to imagine that he and Mattie are "like a married couple," they aren't, and the comparison only serves to emphasize that fact.

Despite his desire to stay with Mattie as she cleans up, Ethan is motivated even more to get his work done so that he can spend as much time alone with her in the evening as possible. "The sweetness of the picture, and the relief of knowing that his fears of 'trouble' with Zeena were unfounded, sent up his spirits with a rush" (Wharton 1911, 73). Twice in these descriptions Wharton uses the word "picture" to underscore the imaginary nature of Ethan's belief in a relationship between he and Mattie and, as she so often does, juxtaposes that belief with the equally imaginary notion that somehow Zeena has no idea of his feelings. What Ethan doesn't realize is that his rationalizations in regard to his wife are a lot more dangerous than his fantasy about Mattie. The other notable thing about this passage is the quotation marks around the word trouble. Though the word had previously been used to describe the kind of amorphous symptoms associated with hysteria, the usage here is different. What it describes is Ethan's relationship with Zeena, and in that respect its usage can be seen as closer to that of the first sentence in Chopin's "Story of an Hour." Like the emotional trouble that Louise Mallard suffers, Ethan's "trouble" with Zeena is of the same nature, and his fears are far from unfounded.

At this point Wharton gives the reader a little more insight into Ethan's past, his time at school when he was something of a loner, and his delight when other students had befriended him. His return to Starkfield, however, resulted in further entrenching his "grave and inarticulate" nature. After his father's death the farm and the mill allowed him very little time to socialize in the village. And while his mother could be talkative at times, "the sound of her voice was seldom heard," and "the loneliness of the house grew more oppressive than that of the fields" (Wharton 1911, 74). This is the context in which his cousin Zenobia came to nurse his mother during her final days of life, and as a result of which "human speech was heard again in the house. After the mortal silence of his long imprisonment Zeena's volubility was music in his ears." At the same time, Zeena told him that she would take over the duties of the house, leaving him free to do as he pleased when he wasn't working, but this release from his previous feelings of confinement also caused him to misjudge the situation. "The mere fact of obeying her orders, of feeling free to go about his business again and talk with other men, restored his shaken balance and magnified his sense of what he owed her" (75). It was ultimately that exaggerated sense of obligation Ethan felt toward Zeena that prompted him to make a decision he wouldn't have otherwise. "After the funeral, when he saw her preparing to go away, he was seized with an unreasoning dread of being left alone on the farm; and before he knew what he was doing he had asked her to stay there with him. He had often thought since that it would not have happened if his mother had died in spring instead of winter . . ." (76). In this way it was not just the relief he felt when Zeena took over the house, but also the dread of the isolation of winter that had prompted Ethan's proposal.

Though the couple had initially agreed on a plan for their future, they ultimately had very different personalities. After so many years on the farm in Starkfield, Ethan was restless. Like many women of that period, whose reading and education gave them the idea that they could do something meaningful and significant with their lives, Ethan had dreams as well.

When they married it was agreed that, as soon as he could straighten out the difficulties resulting from Mrs. Frome's long illness, they would sell the farm and saw-mill and try their luck in a large town. Ethan's love of nature did not take the form of a taste for agriculture. He had always wanted to be an engineer, and to live in towns, where there were lectures and big libraries and "fellows doing things." [Ethan had an] eagerness to see the world; and he felt sure that, with a "smart" wife like Zeena, it would not be long before he had made himself a place in it. (Wharton 1911, 76)

Had the couple been able to sell the farm right away, Ethan might have made it out of Starkfield. In fact, Zeena made it clear to him from the start that she had no intention of staying there and expected them to move. But in the same way that wives were at the mercy of their husband's wishes at this time, Ethan wound up just as helpless when it came to Zeena as she began to see the benefit in staying. "Purchasers were slow in coming, and while he waited for them Ethan learned the impossibility of transplanting her. She chose to look down on Starkfield, but she could not have lived in a place which looked down on her" (77).

In a way, Zeena's initial scorn of Starkfield, in which the village itself seemed unworthy of her, turned back on itself to the point where the anonymity she would have faced in moving to a larger town was something she was unwilling to accept. Though it's never stated directly in the novel, there's a sense that had Ethan managed to make something of himself in the larger world it would have imposed on her a further anonymity as merely his wife. "In the greater cities which attracted Ethan she would have suffered a complete loss of identity" (Wharton 1911, 77). The way Zeena chose to distinguish herself in the small community she looked down upon was one of the few that were available to women of her day: her illness. "Within a year of their marriage she developed the 'sickliness' which had since made her notable even in a community rich in pathological instances." By putting the word sickliness in quotes, Wharton continues to build on the idea that Zeena's pathology has less to do with physiology than it does with psychology, especially when her behavior before her marriage is contrasted with her behavior after. "When she came to take care of his mother she had seemed to Ethan like the very genius of health, but he soon saw that her skill as a nurse had been acquired by the absorbed observation of her own symptoms." At least that's how it appeared to Ethan.

It's more likely the evolution was the other way around, that her symptoms emerged only after seeing the way they affected others who suffered. Because of this Zeena's illness takes a different form than that of the narrator in "The Yellow Wall-Paper." Instead of the guilt that debilitates the protagonist from Gilman's story, Zeena uses her condition as compensation for the misery of her everyday existence. In describing Zeena when she first comes to take care of his mother Ethan says, "Her efficiency shamed and dazzled him. She seemed to possess by instinct all the household wisdom that his long apprenticeship had not instilled in him" (Wharton 1911, 75). But seven years later Zeena has essentially refused to do any housework at all, and her symbolic protest is even sanctioned by her doctor who, she claims, "says I oughtn't to have to do a single thing around the house" (119). This is yet another aspect of hysteria that was observed by Gilman's doctor, Weir Mitchell. "From the outset, Mitchell understood that his female patients were part of an interactive system in which they were curiously rewarded for becoming ill" (Hororwitz 133). Zeena's reward is not only the ability to avoid the drudgery of housework on the farm but also to use her condition as a weapon against Ethan, and as a way of gaining notoriety in the community.

While in one sense the idea of Ethan as the female figure in the novel seems at odds with the mystery of hysteria and the numerous other maladies that were known to afflict women in that time period—including Wharton herself—the author was also well acquainted with the burdens of a sickly spouse in her own life. Her husband Teddy frequently became ill and was ultimately the reason for her divorce from him after her permanent move to Paris. "Diagnosed with a variety of illnesses since 1902—influenza, gout, neuralgia—he was increasingly prone to depression and intractability . . . With Edith's encouragement, he began to divide his time between resting at the Mount and traveling to various spas in search of cures. Although he found temporary relief from these measures, his condition did not improve. By 1909, it was all too apparent to his doctors that he was suffering from the strain of mental illness which had resulted in the committal and eventual suicide of his father . . . Edith agreed to spend the summer of 1911 with him at the Mount. Her hopes that he would recover in that setting were short-lived, however, and . . . she never visited the Mount again, but sold it in 1912 and obtained a divorce at the start of 1913" (Fournier 18-19). It's no coincidence that her marriage had reached a crisis point and her final attempt to help her husband recover occurred just after the writing of *Ethan Frome*, in the very location where the book was set.

Wharton takes time here for a paragraph concerning the rural form of hysteria she would have been acquainted with from her time in Massachusetts.

> He recalled his mother's growing taciturnity, and wondered if Zeena were also turning "queer." Women did, he knew. Zeena, who had at her fingers' ends the pathological chart of the whole region, had cited many cases of the kind while she was nursing his mother; and he himself knew of certain lonely farm-houses in the neighbourhood where stricken creatures pined, and of others where sudden tragedy had come of their presence. At times, looking at Zeena's shut face, he felt the chill of such forebodings. (Wharton 1911, 78)

But Wharton goes into greater detail in her French short story, providing a cause for this behavior that reached back into the history of the area and the people who lived there. It also provides an explanation for Ethan's decision to go along with Mattie's suicide pact at the end of the novel.

> The bitter and tenacious will that led the first inhabitants of New England to this desert, made their descendants creatures of passion and abnegation. Those strong religious convictions left behind the taste of martyrdom,

and a kind of implacable righteousness that dominates the most violent emotions. But life is too sad and monotonous, and the long legacy of sterile effort and reflexive instinct all too often leads to a deadly sadness, a disgust for life which, even among women and the healthy, sometimes goes as far as melancholy and dementia. (MacCallan 47)

One of the many ironies in the novel is that Ethan's sudden urge to marry Zeena had to do with the life and "volubility" she brought to the house during his mother's illness. And yet after they had married, "she too fell silent" (77). While Ethan blames part of this on the isolation of farm life, he also takes some measure of responsibility for her accusation that he "never listened" to her. "The charge was not wholly unfounded. When she spoke it was only to complain, and to complain of things not in his power to remedy; and to check a tendency to impatient retort he had first formed the habit of not answering her, and finally of thinking of other things while she talked" (78). Ethan's reaction to Zeena's illness and complaints was not an uncommon one, according to Carroll Smith-Rosenberg. "Not surprisingly, the hysteric's peculiar passive aggression and her exploitative dependency often functioned to cue a corresponding hostility in the men who cared for her or lived with her. Whether fathers, husbands, or physicians, they reacted with ambivalence and in many cases with hostility to her aggressive and never-ending demands" (Smith-Rosenberg 1985, 207). Because her married life has been such a dismal existence and her disenchantment began shortly after, the question naturally arises, why did Zeena agree to marry Ethan?

Women were dependent on men in a number of ways at this time, and one of them was in their choice of a husband—though in real terms they didn't have much of a choice at all. A beautiful woman with a substantial dowry could choose between suitors, but she was still limited to those men who chose to pursue her. For most women, however, especially those in rural areas, there were far fewer men available. If a woman had no dowry, or was somewhat ordinary looking, much anxiety resulted from the question of whether she would be asked at all. And if by chance she was, what woman in that position would be bold enough to turn down an offer in the hopes of getting a better one, and in the process perhaps lose any chance at all? According to historian Sara Evans, regardless of the circumstances, after the man had made his selection the success of the marriage was dependent on the woman.

Responsibility for relationships, however, rested primarily on the shoulders of women, who had the most to lose. Male identity and economic security still rested primarily on work, whereas women understood that their

economic security, emotional fulfillment, and social status all depended
on a successful marriage. If they failed to marry, they risked becoming
"dried up old maids." The very epithets used insinuated a new valuation of
the single and presumably celibate life as unfulfilled, worthless, deviant.
(Evans 178)

This was not an enviable position for women to be put in, and it's not surprising
that in many marriages women were forced to find self-fulfillment elsewhere.
Sometimes that took the form of an obsession with her children, running an
efficient home, or other types of domestic employment. It could also include
dressing in clothes and jewelry that made her feel beautiful, participation in
church or society, or charity work and the like.

Zeena, however, had none of these options available to her. She certainly
couldn't turn Ethan down, as she was already twenty-seven when he proposed.
But once married to a poor farmer with no prospects of becoming anything
else, her only avenue to avoid what to her must have felt like a life comprised
of unending chores, was to become ill. And in lapsing into silence, she was
able to punish Ethan by taking away from him the reason he had married
her in the first place. One of the cliché's about Zeena is that she is merely
an unhappy, complaining shrew, intent on making Ethan's life miserable,
and there is some truth to that characterization. But her silence was also a
way of exerting some control over her life that, in many marriages, allowed
women none. Because Ethan had essentially surrendered his male authority
and assumed a submissive role in the marriage, Zeena filled the vacuum by
wielding the power that had been ceded to her. In that context, her silence was
simply another way of exercising one of the only avenues of control available
to her. "At other times her silence seemed deliberately assumed to conceal
far-reaching intentions, mysterious conclusions drawn from suspicions and
resentments impossible to guess. That supposition was even more disturbing
than the other; and it was the one which had come to him the night before,
when he had seen her standing in the kitchen door" (Wharton 1911, 78-79). By
keeping her suspicions hidden, and making judicious use of their articulation,
Zeena is able to keep Ethan in a constant state of anxiety about where the two
of them stand in relation to each other, a situation paralleled by many women
of the time who had no idea how their husbands really felt about them.

Further complicating an accurate reading of Zeena is the fact that Ethan
has already abandoned her in his mind. While he may never have experienced
genuine feelings of love for her, he had done his best to live up to the obligation
that his marriage to her entailed, and the couple had been able to live together
in a kind of negative equilibrium. But all of that changed when his discernable

emotional attachment to Mattie began. While Zeena's apparent manipulation of Ethan and Mattie is certainly cause for the reader to view her unfavorably, it must be pointed out once again that the reader is only seeing her from Ethan's point of view. Helge Normann Nilsen makes a similar observation in her essay on the novel. "Zeena's meanness is very real, but Wharton makes it clear that she cannot really be blamed for securing her own interests, given her situation, with no other means of support except her husband. This is in keeping with the general situation for women at the time" (Nilsen 84). Despite Ethan's negative characterization of them later in the novel, Zeena's actions are really defensive in nature. She clearly understands that Ethan has not been any happier with her than she has been with him, but despite their mutual dislike they did make a commitment to each other. In this way Zeena's decision to bring Mattie to the farm can be seen as an attempt to fulfill her obligation of running the house while still allowing her not to do the work herself, and at a minimal cost to her husband. It was Ethan who disrupted the delicate balance they had achieved, and in that context Zeena's attempts to restore that balance seem perfectly justified.

As he does so often, however, Ethan makes the wrong assumption about Zeena, typically erring on the side of presuming she is ignorant of his behavior or doesn't care. "Now her departure for Bettsbridge had once more eased his mind, and all his thoughts were on the prospect of his evening with Mattie" (Wharton 1911, 79). But Ethan has also told Zeena a lie about collecting payment for his timber. Though he has feelings for Mattie, Ethan has made no explicit expression of them and Mattie not only hasn't responded in kind but more than likely has no idea of them. This creates a further irony in the way that Ethan's unnecessary lie to Zeena actually makes him seem more like an adulterer who is fearful his clandestine affair will be discovered. To avoid being caught in his lie, Ethan decides to see Andrew Hale and ask him for an advance on the timber. His decision is based not only on their business relationship, but the fact that the Hales have been good friends with Ethan's family for a long time. Their house is also one of the few places Zeena travels to infrequently, "drawn there by the fact that Mrs. Hale, in her youth, had done more 'doctoring' than any other woman in Starkfield, and was still a recognized authority on symptoms and treatment." While Hale is a genial man and is initially glad to see Ethan, as he does need logs for his lumber mill, Wharton foreshadows the awkwardness to come when she describes his financial situation. "Though he did a fairly good business it was known that his easygoing habits and the demands of his large family frequently kept him what Starkfield called 'behind'" (79-80). As they sit in Hale's office, Ethan finally gets up the courage to ask him for a small advance.

The man's shocked refusal is essentially what Ethan had expected, but while Hale tries to make light of the situation by joking, it only makes matters worse. "Ethan felt that if he had pleaded an urgent need Hale might have made shift to pay him; but pride, and an instinctive prudence, kept him from resorting to this argument" (Wharton 1911, 81). Because he understands so well the nature of a small community like Starkfied, Ethan has no desire for the villagers to learn even more about his financial situation than they already know. Unlike another closely related literary character, Emma Bovary, Ethan was perfectly willing to live within his means, whatever privation it caused. Ethan was also determined not to explain himself to Hale. Either the man would give him the money or he wouldn't. But then, as he is leaving, Hale seems to reconsider when he says, "See here—you ain't in a tight place, are you?" And for once Ethan's instincts are right on. "'Not a bit,' Ethan's pride retorted before his reason had time to intervene." But it was a good thing his pride overrode his reason, as it is clear it would have caused even more embarrassment when Hale replies, "Well, that's good! Because I am, a shade. Fact is, I was going to ask you to give me a little extra time on that payment." It turns out Hale is building a new house for his son and his fiancé, Ned and Ruth. But it is Hale's final words that are even more painful to Ethan than his refusal of money. "It's not so long ago since you fixed up your own place for Zeena" (82).

These are the words that stay with Ethan as he walks into the village, "and he reflected grimly that his seven years with Zeena seemed to Starkfield 'not so long'" (Wharton 1911, 83). This is the same kind of emphasis on the elasticity of time that was evident when Ethan was walking by the graveyard with Mattie and hoped that they would not only be together for a long time in this world, but for eternity in the next. When Ethan is with Zeena, on the other hand, every year together seems like an eternity. As he walks alone through the village, Ethan continues to think over his situation, accompanied by another symbol of light. "The afternoon was drawing to an end, and here and there a lighted pane spangled the cold gray dusk and made the snow look whiter." This reference to sunlight coming through the clouds is then followed by the appearance of Denis Eady in his father's sleigh. "Eady, in a handsome new fur cap, leaned forward and waved a greeting. 'Hello, Ethe!' he shouted and spun on. The cutter was going in the direction of the Frome farm, and Ethan's heart contracted as he listened to the dwindling bells" (83). What Ethan needs to understand is that Denis Eady is a far more appropriate match for Mattie that he could ever be. He also needs to examine his feelings of jealousy, ones he has absolutely no right to, and the specific way those feelings manifest themselves. At this point in the story Ethan suddenly moves beyond the anger he expressed toward Eady at the dance, in the way that he "positively invited a horse-whipping," and instead he becomes angry with Mattie. Ethan's assumption that Eady is going to visit Mattie is followed by what should have been insight on his part. "Ethan was ashamed of the storm of jealousy in his breast. It seemed unworthy of the girl that his thoughts of her should be so violent" (83-84).

Ethan has undergone a major psychological shift here from just the evening before. When he was observing the dance in the basement of the church his jealousy of Denis Eady was focused on the fact that, in his eyes, the two of them were competing for the affections of the same girl. He exhibited thoughts of ownership toward Mattie, to be sure, but Mattie was still the innocent party in Ethan's eyes. She was the one who had been violated by Eady's insolence. "It was strange that the girl did not seem aware of it: that she could lift her rapt face to her dancer's, and drop her hands into his, without appearing to feel the offence of his look and touch" (Wharton 1911, 34). But on the precipice of their evening alone together in which Ethan has fantasized that, except for the presence of Zeena, they will be like the married couple he has imagined them to be, it is Ethan who now has become the injured party. By allowing Eady to visit her at the farm, Ethan is the one who has been violated by Mattie's infidelity to him. As such, she is now the one deserving of his violent thoughts. Of course Ethan recognizes on some level the inappropriateness of his jealousy, as he is ashamed of it, as well as the fact that he has no evidence of Mattie's betrayal and therefore his jealousy is "unworthy of the girl." But ultimately none of that is enough to make him see the elaborate fantasy he has constructed in order to ameliorate the misery of living with Zeena.

To console himself Ethan then decides to visit the spot in the shade of the spruce trees where he and Mattie had talked the night before. Thus his physical actions mirror his mental state. After the panes of light on the snow give him the opportunity to see the significance of Denis Eady as not just a competitor for Mattie, but as a representative of all young men that Mattie should have the opportunity to choose from, Ethan instead retreats into the darkness and the comfort of his fantasy world. There he sees the shapes of two people and quickly realizes it is Ned and Ruth. "He heard a kiss, and a half-laughing 'Oh!' provoked by the discovery of his presence . . . Ethan smiled at the discomfiture he had caused. What did it matter to Ned Hale and Ruth Varnum if they were caught kissing each other? Everybody in Starkfield knew they were engaged" (Wharton 1911, 84). But in this spot amid the dark shadows of the trees, and the symbolic eclipse of knowledge and understanding it represents, he is easily able to transform what should have been the realization of what Mattie deserves back to his ongoing fantasy. "It pleased Ethan to have surprised a pair of lovers on the spot where he and Mattie had stood with such a thirst for each other in their hearts; but he felt a pang at the thought that these two need not hide their happiness." As has been pointed out many times before, just because Ethan believes in his mind that Mattie shares with him "a thirst for each other in their hearts" doesn't make it so. And given the reality of their conversation the night before, the disconnected nature of Mattie's dialogue and his, the reader has absolutely no basis on which to trust Ethan's assessment that she shares in his feelings of love for her.

Ethan heads back to the farm with his horses and cart, all the while listening for the sound of the sleigh bells that would indicate Denis Eady's return, "but not a sound broke the silence of the lonely road" (Wharton 1911, 85). When he nears the gate and sees light coming from Mattie's room upstairs, he can't help but juxtapose Mattie's optimism with Zeena's negativity. "'She's up in her room,' he said to himself, 'fixing herself up for supper'; and he remembered Zeena's sarcastic stare when Mattie, on the evening of her arrival, had come down to supper with smoothed hair and a ribbon at her neck." This is followed by another confrontation with the residents of the graveyard. One of the older gravestones there used to hold great fascination for him as a child because the name on the stone was his very own. The inscription carved on it states that an earlier Ethan Frome had been married to a woman named Endurance, and they had lived together in peace for fifty years. The inscription is symbolic in a number of ways. The name of the elder Ethan's wife, for one, suggests the state of Ethan and Zeena's own marriage, one that they endure together, with all of its implications of duty and burden. And in the suggestion that the couple lived in peace for all those years, the idea of love is conspicuous in its absence. Ethan's focus, however, as it has been twice before, is on the elasticity of time. "He used to think that fifty years sounded like a long time to live together; but now it seemed to him that they might pass in a flash. Then, with a sudden dart of irony, he wondered if, when their turn came, the same epitaph would be written over him and Zeena" (86). The irony of this thought is that while it may look that way to outsiders in the village, their marriage has been anything but peaceful.

This is also the second of three juxtapositions in a row presented to the reader by Wharton. The first is the innocence and light of Mattie coming down to dinner on her first night at the house, contrasted with Zeena's sarcastic stare. The second is the fifty-year endurance test that his marriage to Zeena represents, alongside the thought that fifty years will "pass in a flash" with Mattie by his side. The third instance is the beginning of a theme that will infuse his entire evening alone with Mattie: Ethan's fantasy of replacing Zeena with Mattie. Since he hadn't heard the return of Eady's sleigh bells

Ethan expects to find his horse in the barn, but it is not there, which makes him happy. Ethan then whistles a tune while bedding down his horses for the night and gives them some extra feed. "His was not a tuneful throat—but harsh melodies burst from it as he locked the barn and sprang up the hill to the house" (Wharton 1911, 86-87). Wharton describes Ethan's whistling as cheerful, but even though Eady was not at the house it doesn't mean that he hadn't been earlier, which accounts for the harshness of the melody mixed with Ethan's happiness that Eady is gone. What happens next, however, is a complete surprise. "He reached the kitchen-porch and turned the door-handle; but the door did not yield to his touch." The closed door is information, and to reinforce the idea that his thoughts about Mattie are wrong Ethan is reminded of the same thing that happening the night before.

> So strange was the precision with which the incidents of the previous evening were repeating themselves that he half expected, when he heard the key turn, to see his wife before him on the threshold; but the door opened, and Mattie faced him. She stood just as Zeena had stood, a lifted lamp in her hand, against the black background of the kitchen. She held the light at the same level, and it drew out with the same distinctness her slim young throat and the brown wrist no bigger than a child's. Then, striking upward, it threw a lustrous fleck on her lips, edged her eyes with velvet shade, and laid a milky whiteness above the black curve of her brows. (87-88)

This initial replacement of Zeena with Mattie will be repeated throughout their evening together, reinforcing Ethan's false notion of a love relationship with Mattie. Ethan goes on to describe what Mattie is wearing, her usual dress, but in place of the bow on her neck from her first night there is a red ribbon woven through her hair. Some scholars have tried to claim that the red ribbon symbolizes Mattie's reciprocation of Ethan's feelings of love toward her. But this doesn't really work. In the context of the entire passage the red ribbon is no different than the bow she wore around her neck on her first night there, which is simply a reflection of her general nature. Ethan claims that, "This tribute to the unusual transformed and glorified her. She seemed to Ethan taller, fuller, more womanly in shape and motion" (Wharton 1911, 88). But the ribbon is not a transformation at all. In fact, the ribbon is simply a reinforcement of the character Mattie already possesses, though one she has had to suppress in Zeena's presence. She is not a "fretter," to use Ethan's word, and her happiness at the dance demonstrated that her joy with Ethan was not a way she behaved especially for him. Even Zeena had remarked how the girl seemed to make the best of things she had no control over. In this way Mattie as a person is really the unusual in the Frome house, and the ribbon is a tribute to herself in Zeena's absence, which would naturally glorify her—just not in the way Ethan has imagined, and certainly not as a specific show of affection for him.

Ethan follows Mattie into the kitchen and the scene is just as he had imagined it that morning, if not better. "She set the lamp on the table, and he saw that it was carefully laid for supper, with fresh dough-nuts, stewed blueberries and his favourite pickles in a dish of gay red glass. A bright fire glowed in the stove and the cat lay stretched before it, watching the table with a drowsy eye. Ethan was suffocated with the sense of well-being" (Wharton 1911, 88). Two things in this description merit closer attention, as they will comprise significant symbols over the rest of this chapter and the following one. The first is the cat. It begins by looking at the Ethan and Mattie with a "drowsy eye," but is soon up and about, weaving its way between Mattie's legs. "Why, Puss! I nearly tripped over you." In this way the cat's purpose is hinted at, to trip up Mattie and, by extension, Ethan on their night together. Throughout the remainder of the chapter the cat will not only symbolize Zeena but stand in for her, almost as though she is still in the house in spirit. The cat, then, is a constant reminder to the reader of the impossibility that Ethan will be able to break his marriage vows, and the wrongness of his interpretation and pursuit of Mattie as an object of affection. The second symbol is the red pickle dish, the significance of which will become apparent later in the scene.

For the moment, though, Ethan is still disturbed by the possibility that Denis Eady had come over earlier to spend time alone with Mattie. As she scolds the cat in an amused way, Ethan could see "laughter sparkling through her lashes. Again Ethan felt a sudden twinge of jealousy. Could it be his coming that gave her such a kindled face?" (Wharton 1911, 89). Because Ethan is unable to understand that Mattie's happy spirit is not due to any external force, but simply resides within her, he now assumes that her present happiness must be due to Eady's visit. When he asks her if she had any visitors, "She nodded and laughed 'Yes, one,' and he felt a blackness settling on his brows." Of course the blackness on his brows reinforces his inability to make sense of almost anything that Mattie says. Then she playfully tells him that the visitor was only Jotham Powell coming in for a cup of coffee, and "The blackness lifted and light flooded Ethan's brain." But this enlightenment only results in the moral imperative to say something about Zeena. "After a pause he felt it right to add: 'I suppose he got Zeena over to the Flats all right?' ... The name threw a chill between them, and they stood a moment looking sideways at each other before Mattie said with a shy laugh. 'I guess it's about time for supper'"

(89-90). Though Ethan may have felt a chill, it's impossible to say that Mattie has had the same feeling as they sit down to eat.

Despite Ethan's attempt to make the evening only about the two of them, Zeena's presence continually makes itself known in the form of the cat. "They drew their seats up to the table, and the cat, unbidden, jumped between them into Zeena's empty chair. 'Oh, Puss!' said Mattie, and they laughed again. Ethan, a moment earlier, had felt himself on the brink of eloquence; but the mention of Zeena had paralysed him" (Wharton 1911, 90). Despite this unwanted reminder of his wife, Zeena continues to intrude upon the evening, and again it is through Ethan's own instigation. "Looks as if there'd be more snow," he says to Mattie. But she can't help but respond with the only implication that possibility holds. "'Is that so? Do you suppose it'll interfere with Zeena's getting back?' She flushed red as the question escaped her, and hastily set down the cup she was lifting" (90-91). It's tempting for some readers to interpret Mattie's flush as having to do with Ethan, but despite the girl's sunny temperament she has already confessed to Ethan her frustration with Zeena's incessantly negative attitude toward her. Any embarrassment she might be feeling from mentioning the possibility of Zeena having to stay longer away from home can only be attributed to her own hope that Zeena will be delayed rather than anything having to do with Ethan. Wharton then associates Ethan's discomfiture at the continual mention of Zeena with the cat. "The name had benumbed him again, and once more he felt as if Zeena were in the room between them. 'Oh, Puss, you're too greedy!' Mattie cried" (91).

This sets up the pivotal moment of the evening for the two, as the cat begins to creep up onto the table while Ethan is distracted by his desire for Mattie.

> The cat, unnoticed, had crept up on muffled paws from Zeena's seat to the table, and was stealthily elongating its body in the direction of the milk-jug, which stood between Ethan and Mattie. The two leaned forward at the same moment and their hands met on the handle of the jug. Mattie's hand was underneath, and Ethan kept his clasped on it a moment longer than was necessary. The cat, profiting by this unusual demonstration, tried to effect an unnoticed retreat, and in doing so backed into the pickle-dish, which fell to the floor with a crash. (Wharton 1911, 91)

Ethan's accidental touching of Mattie's hand causes him to linger over the moment, allowing the cat to break the pickle dish. What at first seems an entirely inconsequential accident contrasts sharply with Mattie's reaction to it. "Mattie, in an instant, had sprung from her chair and was down on her knees by the fragments. 'Oh, Ethan, Ethan—it's all to pieces! What will Zeena say?'" (91-92). But after what amounts for Ethan to holding Mattie's hand, he is finally able to override any concern for what Zeena will think, and good naturedly begins to help Mattie clean up the mess.

It's only then that the significance of the destruction of the pickle dish becomes apparent. Ethan tries to laugh it off by saying Zeena will have to blame the cat, but Mattie knows there is far more to it than that. "Yes, but, you see, she never meant it should be used, not even when there was company; and I had to get up on the step-ladder to reach it down from the top shelf of the china-closet, where she keeps it with all her best things, and of course she'll want to know why I did it—" (Wharton 1911, 92). The immediate realization is that the dish is something precious to Zeena. The fact that Mattie had to go to great lengths to get it down in order to use it means that there is a genuine concern about what Zeena's reaction will be should she find out. "The case was so serious that it called forth all of Ethan's latent resolution." At first Ethan suggests that he simply go into Shadd's Falls and purchase another dish to replace it. But Mattie counters with the fact that the dish is irreplaceable. "Oh, you'll never get another even there! It was a wedding present—don't you remember? It came all the way from Philadelphia, from Zeena's aunt that married the minister. That's why she wouldn't ever use it" (92-93). At this Mattie begins to cry. It's a distressing moment for Ethan, who had imagined something very different taking place during their evening together. He tries to console Mattie, but as they look at the pieces of the dish on the counter he thinks to himself, "It seemed to him as if the shattered fragments of their evening lay there."

In keeping with his character, and Wharton's previous description of his preference to delay the inevitable as "man-like," Ethan naturally opts for deception in dealing with the accident.

> He gathered the pieces of glass into his broad palm and walked out of the kitchen to the passage. There he lit a candle-end, opened the china-closet, and, reaching his long arm up to the highest shelf, laid the pieces together with such accuracy of touch that a close inspection convinced him of the impossibility of detecting from below that the dish was broken. If he glued it together the next morning months might elapse before his wife noticed what had happened, and meanwhile he might after all be able to match the dish at Shadd's Falls or Bettsbridge. (Wharton 1911, 93-94)

What's most important for Ethan at this point is getting back to his imagined evening with the young woman he's in love with. Mattie doesn't ask what he's done when he returns, probably assuming he will take full responsibility for the dish. In Ethan's final misinterpretation of the chapter, he "commands her" to finish supper and believes that she is "completely reassured." The only thing that would really account for this is the way that she "shone on him through tear-hung lashes," which most likely represents her belief that whatever comes of the broken dish will be kept between him and Zeena (94). Naturally, Ethan attributes her reaction to his own imagined sense of power, "and his soul swelled with pride as he saw how his tone subdued her."

The chapter ends on an example of sexual symbolism that is otherwise generally absent from the novel. "Except when he was steering a big log down the mountain to his mill he had never known such a thrilling sense of mastery" (Wharton 1911, 94). The log, of course, is a crude phallic symbol, and its use in Ethan's thoughts is tantamount to a sexual fantasy that Wharton wisely leaves on the symbolic level. While the assumption is that Ethan's imaginary love affair would necessarily include the sexual conquest of Mattie, and therefore is appropriate to the plot, it's overt articulation in the story is entirely unnecessary and ultimately beside the point. In keeping this symbolism at a subtextual level—which can easily be missed, and therefore not risk offense—Wharton masterfully allows for a more complete reading of Ethan's personality while at the same time avoids shocking the casual reader and in doing so taking attention away from the more salient aspects of the story. Author Kenneth Bernard, in his essay "Imagery and Symbolism in *Ethan Frome*," sees in this a concession by Wharton to the morality of the times, "perhaps . . . a reticence or modesty of the author's," when it more accurately reflects a strategic narrative device on her part (Bernard 182). Cynthia Griffin Wolff, on the other hand, sees the absence of overt sexuality as another insight into Ethan's character.

As Wolff astutely points out, Ethan has no fantasies about Mattie that go beyond chaste domesticity. "Even when Ethan is given full rein, even when he can make any imaginary semblance of Mattie that he wants, he choses a vision that has no sexual component. He does not see her as a loving wife to warm his bed in the winter . . ." (Wolff 174). Instead he imagines her making pies, sewing by the fire with him at night, keeping the kitchen "spruce," and no doubt sitting enraptured as he waxes naturalistic, unrolling "the huge panorama of the ice age, and the long dim stretches of succeeding time" (Wharton 1911, 37). Wolff sees an element of irony in this, as "Ethan's dreams of Mattie are not essentially different from the life that he has created with Zeena" (Wolff 174). That's probably overstating the case, however. The world of the rural New England countryside in the 1880s was never going to be a hotbed of overt sexual lust. But the signs are there if the reader knows where to look for them. After Mattie opens the door for him that evening when he's locked out of the house, his physical description of her hints at more than just companionship. "She wore her usual dress of darkish stuff . . . She seemed to Ethan taller, fuller, more womanly in shape and motion. She stood aside, smiling silently, while he entered, and then moved away from him with something soft and flowing in her gait" (Wharton 1911, 88). His mention of the dress, combined with his comment about her womanly "shape and motion" actually implies thoughts about what is beneath that dress, "soft and flowing in her gait" as he watches her walk away from him.

Author Elizabeth Ammons goes even further to suggest that Ethan's proclivity to compare Mattie to nature—wheat fields, enchanted glades, butterflies, and the mist on the moon—"is frankly sexual."

> His imagination turns to nature and the fairy world because the desired sexual experience is for him bound up in a masculine fantasy of possessing woman like some secret place the explorer dreams of claiming for himself . . . But Ethan is an unsophisticated and conscientious man; he does not want to "ruin" Mattie, nor spoil his romantic fantasy by turning their relationship into a furtive backstairs affair. Therefore he never makes love to her. (Ammons 65)

Despite Ammons' contention that this is a "masculine fantasy," it does far more to associate Ethan with feminine ideals in the way it reveals his pursuit of Mattie is less about sex than it is emotional stability and security. Author Linda Costanzo Cahir posits a similar conclusion, that Ethan's ultimate goal is has never been sexual in nature. "Frome does not want the temporary physical satisfaction or the real-world intimacy that a sexual assignation with Mattie would provide. Matters are much more complex with him" (Cahir 223). But Cahir is only half right. While sex is the least of it, it's still a part. Ethan desperately desires the "real-world intimacy" that he imagines Mattie could provide, which he sees as the antitheses of the emotional frigidity he has endured with Zeena. Author Parley Ann Boswell puts it this way, "Wharton's Ethan wants to make *all* kinds of contact with Mattie, who represents the opposite of the woman he lives with: warm, sensuous, and flirtatious" (Boswell 121). Boswell then goes on to demonstrate the larger context in which this idea can be seen as foundational in all of the author's works. "In *Ethan Frome*, as in much of Wharton's fiction, love and sex become oppositional: sex is easy, love is difficult, and to mistake one for the other, to confuse fantasy with reality, is destructive" (122). This sentiment goes to the heart of *Ethan Frome*, as it is Ethan's very inability to separate his fantasy from reality that results in his decision to kill himself rather than endure the rest of his life with Zeena.

Ultimately it is love—an emotion he has never experienced with a woman—that Ethan craves. Whatever sexual fantasies Ethan may or may not have about Mattie, his vision of her has always been as a replacement for Zeena, not as a way to create an entirely different life. Because of that, Wolff's assertion that his fantasies about Mattie are simply "variations on the theme of dependency" raises more questions than it answers (Wolff 174). She seems to imply that Ethan would simply be replacing one dependent, Zeena, with another dependent in Mattie. But in the symbolism of the novel this doesn't hold true. While Ethan is in reality the sole wage earner in the family, he nevertheless behaves as Zeena's dependent. And as the log symbolism and his thoughts of possession make clear, Ethan desires a relationship in which he is the master of the house and Mattie his submissive wife. In that kind of relationship the sexual component is implied. Sexual symbolism in the novel is quite overt, on the other hand, as far as the pickle dish is concerned. Bernard correctly points out that this is the key to understanding what is at the center of the conflict between Ethan and Zeena. But the rest of those symbols as they relate to Ethan's fantasy about Mattie are only important in so far as they serve to enlarge the scope of the reader's overall understanding of him.

Chapter V

With the trauma of the broken pickle dish now apparently over, the two finish their meal. Afterward, Ethan goes out to check on the animals and take a look around the house while Mattie cleans up in the kitchen. On his return Ethan finds "Mattie had pushed his chair to the stove and seated herself near the lamp with a bit of sewing. The scene was just as he had dreamed of it that morning. He sat down, drew his pipe from his pocket and stretched his feet to the glow" (Wharton 1911, 95). With the emphasis on light in this scene, Mattie near the lamp and Ethan by the glow of the fire, Ethan should be contemplating the true nature of his relationship with Mattie, but instead he gives in yet again to his imaginary desires. "His hard day's work in the keen air made him feel at once lazy and light of mood, and he had a confused sense of being in another world, where all was warmth and harmony and time could bring no change." His words here are almost a complete summary of Ethan's character. The light of understanding makes him realize consciously that he is "in another world," a dream state that is not real. At the same time his resistance to change is reflected in his laziness, the desire to replace Zeena in his heart with Mattie and continue living just as he has before, a change requiring no effort on his part. In real terms this is simply a continuation of the passivity he has always displayed in his marriage, but this time it is with the compliant Mattie. What that would mean for him if he were to actually achieve his dream is that his normal, submissive behavior with Zeena would actually be rendered as dominant with Mattie.

The emphasis on the dream-like state of the evening reinforces yet again the fantasy world Ethan has been operating within throughout the entire story. This is symbolized by the fact that he can't see Mattie very well from his spot near the stove. The "warmth and harmony" he seeks, then, is not really possible with her. Ever unwilling to abandon his dreams, Ethan asks her to move over near him in order to force the issue. But reality, however suppressed, refuses to conform to Ethan's fantasy.

> Zeena's empty rocking-chair stood facing him. Mattie rose obediently, and seated herself in it. As her young brown head detached itself against the patch-work cushion that habitually framed his wife's gaunt countenance, Ethan had a momentary shock. It was almost as if the other face, the face of the superseded woman, had obliterated that of the intruder. (Wharton 1911, 96)

Just as it had in the previous chapter, Zeena's presence continues to make itself known during their evening together. First it was the dialogue in which Ethan felt self-conscious about his feelings whenever her name came up, then it was when the cat, acting on Zeena's behalf, occupied Zeena's chair and broke the pickle dish. Here Wharton foreshadows the climax of the tale by having Zeena's face appear out of nowhere as if his wife is purposely trying to destroy his evening alone with Mattie.

Though Ethan believes that Mattie's discomfort proves she is conscious of Zeena's presence as well, it's clear to the reader that she is simply having trouble seeing her work, and she says as much before going back to the table. This is significant because it's the first instance of the light/dark symbolism in which Mattie refers to it directly. "I can't see to sew" (Wharton 1911, 96). The comment, along with her action, is yet another indication of the fact that Mattie has no idea how Ethan feels about her. Ethan gets up a short time later, pretending to tend the fire, and then surreptitiously turns his chair so that he can get a better view of Mattie. But even that subtle subterfuge seems to be disapproved of by Zeena's surrogate. "The cat, who had been a puzzled observer of these unusual movements, jumped up into Zeena's chair, rolled itself into a ball, and lay watching them with narrowed eyes" (96-97). Narrowed eyes, of course, connote suspicion. After an interlude of silence the two begin to make small talk about the weather, when the next church dance will be, and the people of Starkfield, and like everything else that evening it only serves to reinforce Ethan's fantasy. "The commonplace nature of what they said produced in Ethan an illusion of long-established intimacy which no outburst of emotion could have given, and he set his imagination adrift on the fiction that they had always spent their evenings thus and would always go on doing so . . ." (97).

What stands out most in this description are Wharton's warning words to the reader, "illusion" and "fiction," in which she makes it clear that Ethan's fantasy is not real. It also continues to suggest that Mattie is unaware of Ethan's feelings for her. More importantly, however, the reason behind Ethan's behavior is merely a continuation of his thought process the night before, that because has no right to express his feelings to her it "made him attach a fantastic importance to every change in her look and tone" (Wharton 1911, 51). The result of his belief that the necessity for silence on the matter of their love is shared by Mattie, is that Ethan is able to see in her silence a conspiratorial ally in his fantasy, one that "no outburst of emotion" would be able to express as powerfully. Thus he is able to rationalize even her apparent indifference to him as a sign that she somehow shares his feelings for her. All of this fits in neatly with Ethan's frequent reference to continuity as well. It's conceivable that were nothing to change in their household for the next fifty years that Ethan would happily maintain his delusion the entire time, secure in the self-deception that as long as Mattie stayed in their home it implied a shared affection for him, and thus her apparent silence on the subject of their love would be understood as being maintained for the same reason as his.

When Ethan reminds Mattie he was to have taken her sledding that evening she suggests that he must have forgotten. But he assures her it is only because of the lack of moonlight saying, "I didn't forget, but it's as dark as Egypt outdoors" (Wharton 1911, 98). Here is another subtle light/dark reference. In the larger context of their one night alone together, despite the warming light inside the house, the two of them are actually enveloped in darkness, signaling once again Ethan's lack of understanding about the truth of his situation. Instead, he indulges in the belief "that they could go on any other night they chose, since they had all time before them." Mattie laughs with delight when he tells her they will go the following evening, but while it's clearly the thought of sledding that is making her happy Ethan can't help but attribute it to her desire to spend time with him. "It was intoxicating to find such magic in his clumsy words, and he longed to try new ways of using it." Picking up their conversation from the previous evening, he asks if she would be scared to go with him on a night this dark. But she repeats her assertion that she wouldn't be any more scared that he would be. Ethan tries to manufacture a bond between them by saying that he would indeed be scared, and that they are better off in the house together. In doing so, however, Wharton indulges in arguably her most blatant foreshadow of the ending. "I wouldn't do it," Ethan says about coasting on a moonless night. "That's an ugly corner down by the big elm. If a fellow didn't keep his eyes open he'd go plumb into it." Mattie, of course, agrees with him about staying home. "She let her lids sink slowly, in the way he loved. 'Yes, we're well enough here,' she sighed" (99).

At this point Ethan can't take their artificial separation any longer, so he moves his chair back to the table opposite her and makes what to him is an overt attempt at a connection. "Leaning forward, he touched the farther end of the strip of brown stuff that she was hemming" (Wharton 1911, 99). Despite his previous assertion that they shared an "intimacy which no outburst of emotion could have given," he seems determined to inveigle out of her some sort of definitive statement of her feelings toward him. He begins by telling her what he encountered that evening in the village. "'Say Matt,' he began with a smile . . . 'I saw a friend of yours getting kissed.'" But Ethan immediately realizes his mistake. "The words had been on his tongue all the evening, but now that he had spoken them they struck him as inexpressibly vulgar and out of place." The accuracy of this assessment is confirmed when Mattie blushes fiercely and continues with her sewing, unable even to look at him when she whispers, "I suppose it was Ruth and Ned." As she goes about her work Mattie pulls the material Ethan is touching from beneath his fingers without realizing he had even touched it, further symbolizing the true nature of their emotional distance. "Ethan had imagined that his allusion might open the way to the accepted pleasantries, and these perhaps in turn to a harmless caress, if only a mere touch on her hand. But now he felt as if her blush had set a flaming guard about her" (100). The evocation of the danger of flames combined with the light they emit makes this simile a powerful example of the truth that Ethan should be paying attention to.

Still caught up in his fantasy, Ethan's attitude here is one of extreme presumptuousness in taking as a given that Mattie shares the same feelings he does. But now, as he inadvertently pushes her away, Zeena reappears, though unspecified, in an attempt to reveal to him the impropriety of his maneuvering.

> He remembered that the night before, when he had put his arm about Mattie, she had not resisted. But that had been out-of-doors, under the open irresponsible night. Now, in the warm lamplit room, with all its ancient implications of conformity and order, she seemed infinitely farther away from him and more unapproachable. (Wharton 1911, 100)

Here is another example of the house as a symbol of women's oppression. The outdoors, in which men escape to during the day to work, is nevertheless seen as "irresponsible," a recognition not only of the physical freedoms men have, but also an implied exemption from the morality that is inherent in this view of the home. At the same time, the "conformity and order" that women are expected to maintain indoors—and by extension their own behavior at all times—is described as "ancient," thus implying that things have always been that way and therefore must continue to do so. As was demonstrated earlier, the reason Mattie allowed Ethan to put his arm around her was in the context of her unsure footing in the icy darkness. Once they had reached the back porch and stopped walking, she immediately slipped away from him. Therefore what he senses in her now as unapproachable is far closer to the truth.

Just as he had tried to recreate their sledding conversation from the night before, Ethan once again tries to gauge her feelings toward Denis Eady. After Mattie mentions that Ned and Ruth will probably get married in the summer, he notices, "She pronounced the word *married* as if her voice caressed it. It seemed a rustling covert leading to enchanted glades" (Wharton 1911, 100). This is an important passage as it accounts for another of Ethan's misconceptions about her. The suggestion that Mattie will get married is brought up three times in the novel. The first time is by Zeena in flashback, after which Ethan commits his symbolic suicide with the straight razor. The next is by Ethan to Mattie herself during their walk home. On this third occasion Eady isn't mentioned by name because Ethan saw her turn him down after the dance amid a "flush of joy into which she had plunged him by dismissing" the young man. But for Ethan that still doesn't preclude the idea that Mattie might get married to someone else. And yet she demonstrates the same kind of dismissive behavior about marriage that she did when Ethan had mentioned Eady on their way home from the dance. This apparent disinterest in her own possible marriage must be understood in the context of Mattie's character as a whole, not just her interactions with Ethan. "It'll be your turn next, I wouldn't wonder," Ethan says to her. "She laughed a little uncertainly. 'Why do you keep on saying that?'" (101).

The reader has clearly seen that Mattie has no interest in Denis Eady because of his domineering manner and what that might suggest for her future with him. Though there were no doubt many marriages at the time based on mutual respect and love, Mattie senses that neither of those things would be present in their relationship if she were to marry him. Nevertheless, he is only one man, and she is still young. The hope that she will one day fall in love and get married is something she obviously thinks about, as it is really the only possibility she has for making any kind of substantial improvement in her life. In the words of Suzanne Fournier, "An attractive young woman who has been recently orphaned, Mattie has few prospects for an independent existence outside marriage" (Fournier 86). While in one sense the goal of marrying well is typically thought of as an urban, upper-class occupation, it must be remembered that Mattie actually came from that milieu. But even if she hadn't, the cultural imperatives for women were just as prevalent among the rural poor, as Carroll Smith-Rosenberg makes clear. "The desire to marry and the belief that a woman's social status came not from the exercise of her own talents and efforts but from her ability to attract a competent male protector were as universal among lower-class and farm women as among middle- and upper-class urban women" (Smith-Rosenberg 1985, 200). In this light Mattie's seemingly negative reaction to the suggestion that she will get married one day comes from the fact that she is a penniless servant and as such she can't begin to imagine the circumstances that would lead to her achieving that dream. Therefore it's reasonable to assume she doesn't even want to think about marriage right now, and certainly not talk about it, because of the emotional pain it causes her. Ethan, however, is naturally going to interpret her apparent disinterest in marriage as a desire on her part to stay with him. After Mattie asks him why he keeps bringing up the idea of her getting married, Ethan responds by saying he wants to get used to the idea. At that point, given Mattie's desire put it out of her mind, it's understandable she says nothing in return.

Wharton uses another bird metaphor to describe Mattie here. As Ethan watches her sew "he sat in fascinated contemplation of the way in which her hands went up and down above the strip of stuff, just as he had seen a pair of birds make short perpendicular flights over a nest they were building" (Wharton 1911, 101). The pair of birds and the building of the nest is an obvious reinforcement of his marriage fantasy with Mattie, yet the image is also information that should be reminding him he has already made his nest with Zeena while Mattie should be allowed the freedom of a bird to go out and find her own partner. Appropriately, the repetition of the marriage conversation from the night before also brings Mattie back to the same practical concern about why she would be leaving: "It's not because you think Zeena's got anything against me, is it?" And similarly, "His former dread started up full-armed at the suggestion." Mattie now stops her work and looks at him with concern, saying that she thought Zeena had been unhappy with her the previous evening. Ethan makes a blustering retort that suggests he would stand up to Zeena were that true, but by now the reader knows he would do no such thing. She finally asks Ethan if Zeena has said anything to him about her, and when he replies that she hasn't Mattie returns to her old self. "She tossed the hair back from her forehead with a laugh. 'I guess I'm just nervous, then. I'm not going to think about it any more'" (102). This passage does two things. First, removing the hair from her forehead is yet another reinforcement of the idea that Mattie has had no idea what Ethan has been doing all evening in relation to her. Second, her verbal response to things beyond her control, namely Zeena, is similarly reflective of her non-verbal response to the idea of marriage. If there's nothing she can do to affect the outcome, she's going to put it out of her mind.

It's at this point the conspiratorial aspect of Ethan's fantasy reasserts itself. One thing that unites the two of them, in his mind, is that they have a common enemy in Zeena. The result of this imaginary critical mass of confirmation about Mattie's feelings for him throughout the evening is that it intensifies Ethan's emotions to the point where he is finally compelled to make another overt gesture toward her.

> She sat silent, her hands clasped on her work, and it seemed to him that a warm current flowed toward him along the strip of stuff that still lay unrolled between them. Cautiously he slid his hand palm-downward along the table till his finger-tips touched the end of the stuff. A faint vibration of her lashes seemed to show that she was aware of his gesture, and that it had sent a counter-current back to her; and she let her hands lie motionless on the other end of the strip. (Wharton 1911, 102-103)

The "faint vibration of her lashes," just as they had done the night before when he imagined they had warned him not to defy Zeena, now confirms for Ethan her understanding of his action. Naturally, Zeena cannot leave the couple alone and must assert her presence again. "The cat had jumped from Zeena's chair to dart at a mouse in the wainscot, and as a result of the sudden movement the empty chair had set up a spectral rocking" (103). Ethan acknowledges to himself morosely that Zeena will be occupying the chair the next evening, and initially the thought seems to make him come to his senses when he thinks to himself, "I've been in a dream." But it turns out the thought is still part of his fantasy when he adds, "this is the only evening we'll ever have together." Nevertheless, "The return to reality was as painful as the return to consciousness after taking an anaesthetic. His body and brain ached with indescribable weariness, and he could think of nothing to say or to do that should arrest the mad flight of the moments."

The use of the cat to symbolize Zeena is an interesting if obvious choice for Wharton. The author herself, while fond of her small dogs, did not generally like being around animals, and in her diary she made her distaste for cats obvious in this definition she jotted down: "The cat: a snake in fur" (Fryer 190). Throughout the novel, while the imagery surrounding Ethan suggests that he is trapped like a mouse, by his farm, by his marriage, by society in the form of the weather, this is continually contrasted with comparisons of Mattie as bird-like, singing or in flight, or helpless like a butterfly, right up to the end of the internal story. The idea that Zeena is the enemy of the two can be seen in the way that the cat is the natural predator of both the bird and the mouse, or to extend the metaphor further using Wharton's own definition, Zeena is the serpent who—in Ethan's eyes—is attempting to exile he and Mattie from Eden. While Ethan is never really associated specifically with the mouse in the text, it's not difficult to see that symbolism in the way that a mouse can also be trapped as Ethan is on the farm and in his marriage, and in the way that Zeena toys with him, the same as a cat would with a mouse. While Zeena is an enemy to them both, however, it is in different ways. Zeena is not so much trying to catch Mattie as she is trying to get her to fly away. Ethan, on the other hand, is an earthbound creature who must remain at the mercy of his predator.

In his essay on the novel Kenneth Bernard states, "The evening progresses with the greatest of intensity. Every action, every word, even every silence quivers. It is because these apparently innocent actions and words exist in such intensity that they must be scrutinized" (Bernard 182). Ethan's description and actions in the following paragraph demand just such scrutiny because of how easily they can be misinterpreted by the reader. First, Ethan makes the observation that "His alteration of mood seemed to have communicated itself to Mattie" (Wharton 1911, 103). The verb "seemed" is important as it stresses the fact that Ethan cannot possibly know if he has communicated anything at all to Mattie. "She looked up at him languidly, as though her lids were weighted with sleep and it cost her an effort to raise them." Here he can see she is obviously tired and sleepy, and therefore any kind of heightened consciousness that is ascribed to her by Ethan has to be looked at in that context. "Her glance fell on his hand, which now completely covered the end of her work and grasped it as if it were a part of herself." Though Ethan can see her look at his hand, there's no way to know whether or not this is simply a vacant stare in which she is thinking about something else. "He saw a scarcely perceptible tremor cross her face, and without knowing what he did he stooped his head and kissed the bit of stuff in his hold." The fact that her tremor—whatever that might indicate—is "scarcely perceptible" has to raise some doubt as to exactly what it means. By the time he stoops his head to kiss the fabric, however, he has lost eye contact with her and therefore he can have no idea whether or not she is still looking at him. Finally, "As his lips rested on it he felt it glide slowly from beneath them, and saw that Mattie had risen and was silently rolling up her work." Whether or not Mattie understood what Ethan was doing at all in putting his lips to the material is guesswork at best, but an earlier moment when she did something similar without thinking, "insensibly drawing the end of it away from him" is the most likely (99). Author Suzanne Fournier summarizes the moment in a wonderful turn of phrase: "The way he fondles and eventually kisses this material emphasizes the unbroken distance between them" (Fournier 85).

Throughout their evening together Ethan has also continued to exhibit behaviors that reinforce the idea of his ownership of Mattie. These take the form of orders and imperatives in which she apparently conforms to his fantasy through her obedience. After he decides to hide the broken pickle dish from Zeena, he tells Mattie to give it to him, "in a voice of sudden authority" (Wharton 1911, 93). He then says that he "commanded her" to come back and finish their meal, and "swelled with pride as he saw how his tone had subdued her." When he tells Mattie to move over near the stove to do her sewing he says, "Mattie rose obediently" (96). And when he assures her of how safe she would be sledding with him, "he luxuriated in the sense of protection and authority which his words conveyed" (98-99). Yet at the same time, these moments are undercut by ones in which Ethan feels completely the opposite. This can be seen most clearly in a single sentence where the two feelings are juxtaposed: "It was intoxicating to find such magic in his clumsy words" (98). Earlier in the evening when he was trying to force their conversation to conform to his fantasy, Zeena's name kept coming up. "Mattie seemed to feel the contagion of his embarrassment," he thinks at one point, and a few moments later when his wife is mentioned again, "the name benumbed him" (90-91). Then, after Mattie picks up the broken pickle dish, "he followed her helplessly while she spread out the broken pieces of glass" (93). Though in one sense Ethan's imagined sense of power over Mattie can be seen as a particularly male fantasy, in this context it is far more readily associated with the reality of his lack of power in his relationship with Zeena. As a result it more closely resembles the behavior of females in that day who had very little control over their lives and compensated for that lack of control by exerting power over their children, servants, shop clerks and the like.

Ethan's imagined evening of bliss ends on an equally drab note as the two of them routinely perform their nightly functions before going up to bed. Of course Ethan notices the decorative paper on her sewing box that he bought for her, and the two of them move the flowerpots that were another gift of his, but to think that Mattie somehow understands any of this as his subtle way of courting her defies credulity. And as if to punctuate the sentiment, Wharton herself weighs in on a symbolic level. "Ethan put the candlestick in Mattie's hand and she went out of the kitchen ahead of him, the light that she carried before her making her dark hair look like a drift of mist on the moon" (105). Here we have Ethan giving the light to Mattie. Initially this represents his desire to make her understand how he feels about her, but it also simultaneously removes the light from him and once again puts him in the dark as way of maintaining his fantasy. More importantly, the dark hair on Mattie's head symbolizes the fact that she still has no idea of Ethan's intent, and the "mist" that it brings to his mind has the same effect on the moonlight as the cloud does on the sunlight. Finally, there is nothing quite so pathetic— in the non-pejorative sense of the word—as the image of Ethan at the end of the chapter, standing outside his bedroom door after Mattie goes into her room and thinking to himself, "When the door of her room had closed on her he remembered that he had not even touched her hand." Again, the door of opportunity, as it always has for Ethan, shuts him out.

Chapter VI

Chapter Six is relatively brief, and its primary function is to provide suspense for the story in a number of ways. The first has to do with Ethan's behavior the following morning. The reader shouldn't be surprised at all that Ethan not only isn't discouraged by his relatively sedate evening with Mattie, but continues to indulge in his fantasy. "Ethan tried to hide his joy under an air of exaggerated indifference, lounging back in his chair to throw scraps to the cat, growling at the weather, and not so much as offering to help Mattie when she rose to clear away the dishes" (Wharton 1911, 106). Thus Ethan's romantic notions seem to be reinforced by the idea that if he simply behaves as if his life is the way he wants it, that will make it so. What's so fascinating is that he even seems to understand on some level that this can't be.

> He did not know why he was so irrationally happy, for nothing was changed in his life or hers. He had not even touched the tip of her fingers or looked her full in the eyes. But their evening together had given him a vision of what life at her side might be, and he was glad now that he had done nothing to trouble the sweetness of the picture. He had a fancy that she knew what had restrained him . . . (Wharton 1911, 106)

The further Ethan goes on with his fantasy, the more Wharton herself underscores the true nature of his delusion by the word choices she makes. Ethan obviously understands that his happiness is irrational, and he is also perfectly clear as to why. But again Wharton uses the word "vision" to demonstrate that the insubstantial nature of the dream he has for his future also applies to the present. Next she calls his memory of the evening before a "picture," in other words an idealized representation of something rather than the real thing. And finally there is his "fancy" that Mattie knows what he is thinking rather than the reality that she couldn't possibly know. All of which builds in the reader a natural curiosity about how and when this fantasy is going to come crashing down around him.

The next element of suspense has to do with the glue Ethan plans to buy in order to put the pickle dish back together so as to avoid detection by Zeena. The nasty weather outside works against him, however, and the "wet snow, melting to sleet" is yet another version of the weather as a force for societal stability that undermines his dreams. It's interesting to note that most of the descriptions of snow—a white substance, which would ordinarily suggest brightness or enlightenment—take place at night. As such, the snow instead symbolizes the kind of anti-intellectual societal restrictions that are placed on women by men and, by extension, Ethan through Zeena. In fact, the interior story begins at night with the words, "the village lay under two feet of snow" (Wharton 1911, 28). In the Prologue the elder Ethan tells the narrator that he used to be able to recall the "sight" of the Florida sun but now "it's all snowed under" (16). During the storm the narrator calls the falling snow "thickening veils of gauze" and a "smothering medium" and describes its falling as a "thickening darkness," as though the "winter night itself" was "descending on us layer by layer" (19-25). And as the two finally make their way to the back door, it's through a "screen of snow" (26). Walking past the graveyard with Mattie inside the frame story, "the Frome grave stones slanted at crazy angles through the snow" (55). And Ethan says to Mattie he thought the key to the back door "might have fallen off into the snow" (57). As was pointed out in the Prologue, these snow symbols represent the fact that Ethan cannot leave his wife, and as a result there is no way he will be able to strike out on his own. He can't openly pursue Mattie either, because of his marriage, or manage to keep her in the house for the fact that she is Zeena's relative and not his. While the spring and summer provide the means to escape the house during the day, and even provide him an escape to his study during the night, wintertime once again finds him trapped in the kitchen and the bedroom with a woman he despises.

For the moment, however, bad weather in the form of snow and ice allows Ethan to justify taking a break in the middle of the day in order to see if conditions improve. In this way he can send Jotham Powell to pick up Zeena at the train station while he goes into town after delivering the timber. Once Jotham leaves to harness the horses after breakfast, Ethan is left alone in the kitchen with Mattie but just as unable to say anything definitive to her as he had been the previous two days. "Ethan stood looking at her, his heart in his throat. He wanted to say: 'We shall never be alone again like this.' Instead, he reached down his tobacco-pouch from a shelf of the dresser, put it into his pocket and said: 'I guess I can make out to be home for dinner'" (Wharton 1911, 107-108). Mattie acknowledges Ethan, but she is busy doing the dishes and doesn't even turn to him. Of course Ethan hears her singing as he leaves and it's not difficult to imagine he takes it as a sign that she shares in the same joy he does this morning rather than because it is simply in keeping with her character. Ethan's plan for the day goes awry from the start, however. "It was what Jotham called a sour morning for work" (108). One of his horses gets injured on the icy roads, and he has to take time to go back to the farm for a dressing. Then sleet begins to fall, icing up the logs and forcing him to take twice as long loading them as usual. "He thought that by starting out again with the lumber as soon as he had finished his dinner he might get back to the farm with the glue before Jotham and the old sorrel had had time to fetch Zenobia from the Flats; but he knew the chance was a slight one" (109).

After dinner, Ethan takes off before Jotham in order to give himself as much time as possible. He tells Mattie that he'll be back early, and once again imagines that he has communicated with her when "he fancied that she nodded her comprehension" (Wharton 1911, 109). Ethan is only halfway to the village with the wood when Jotham passes him in the sleigh, and this increases the tension even further. Ethan says he "worked like ten" unloading the timber, and then raced to Michael Eady's store to get the glue. But of course nothing goes right for Ethan on this day. Naturally, he only finds Denis and his friends at the store because his father is somewhere else in the village. Ethan indulges in a bit of projection here, as he turns his dislike for the young man into a reason to be suspicious of his friendliness. "They hailed Ethan with ironic compliment and offers of conviviality" (110). Then the suspense builds further as "no one knew where to find the glue. Ethan, consumed with the longing for a last moment alone with Mattie, hung about impatiently while Denis made an ineffectual search in the obscurer corners of the store." In the end, Eady is unable to find any glue. He suggests that Ethan wait for his father to return, but Ethan is compelled to go down the street to Mrs. Homan's to see if she has any. At first it doesn't appear he is going to have any better luck there either. "After considerable search, and sympathetic questions as to what he wanted it for, and whether ordinary flour paste wouldn't do as well if she couldn't find it, the widow Homan finally hunted down her solitary bottle of glue to its hiding-place in a medley of cough-lozenges and corset-laces" (111). By now, however, Ethan has used up a considerable amount of time. He races back to the farm as fast as his overworked horses can take him, continually looking over his shoulder for fear that he will be overtaken by Jotham and Zeena before he can fix the pickle dish.

He finally arrives home and it appears he has made it in time. "The barn was empty when the horses turned into it and, after giving them the most perfunctory ministrations they had ever received from him, he strode up to the house and pushed open the kitchen door" (Wharton 1911, 112). Ethan sees Mattie at the stove cooking, and she runs over to him as soon as he enters the house. Then he brandishes the glue and announces that he needs to get to his work when she gives him the bad news. "'Oh, Ethan—Zeena's come,' she said in a whisper, clutching his sleeve." The two stare at each other for a moment and Ethan is confused because the barn was empty, but Mattie tells him that Jotham had picked up some supplies of his own and had taken them home after he dropped off Zeena. When Ethan asks how Zeena is, Mattie looks away and says she doesn't know, as she went straight up to her bedroom. He assures her that there's nothing to worry about, that he'll come down in the middle of the night and glue the dish together. Then Ethan goes back out to take proper care of his horses. As he is finishing, Jotham comes back with the sleigh and that's when the last of the moments of suspense occur.

From Ethan's point of view the presence of Jotham Powell is something he wants to take advantage of. Since he has no idea what kind of mood Zeena is in, he invites Jotham for supper so that it might force her to be more polite. "But the hired man, though seldom loth to accept a meal not included in his wages, opened his stiff jaws to answer slowly: 'I'm obliged to you, but I guess I'll go along back'" (Wharton 1911, 114). Jotham's refusal comes as something of a shock to Ethan, and so he asks him again, but once again Jotham turns him down.

> To Ethan there was something vaguely ominous in this stolid rejection of free food and warmth, and he wondered what had happened on the drive to nerve Jotham to such stoicism. Perhaps Zeena had failed to see the new doctor or had not liked his counsels: Ethan knew that in such cases the first person she met was likely to be held responsible for her grievance. (114)

Eventually Ethan is forced to go back into the house alone. The scene, he notes, is exactly as it had looked the night before, with the table set, the cat by the stove, and Mattie carrying a plate of doughnuts. "She and Ethan looked at each other in silence; then she said, as she had said the night before: 'I guess it's about time for supper'" (115).

Chapter VII

Chapter Seven, following Zeena's return from Bettsbridge, constitutes the only genuine communication between Ethan and his wife in the entire novel. After taking off his coat and hat, Ethan goes to the bottom of the stairs and calls for Zeena but he gets no answer. Finally he trudges upstairs and goes into their room where he sees her sitting by the window, still in her traveling clothes. "The room was almost dark, but in the obscurity he saw her sitting by the window, bolt upright . . ." (Wharton 1911, 116). The darkness, as well as Zeena's "obscurity," is significant. Because of Ethan's ignorance he is actually walking into a situation he is completely unprepared for. Zeena at the window, however, is in the position of creating an opportunity for herself. This is a very different kind of opportunity than the one available to Kate Chopin's protagonist, whose window looked out on a new spring day. Zeena's window looks out on the gloom of dusk in winter, but it is nevertheless a way out of the predicament that caused her to seek out the new doctor in the first place. In this context her only goals are the restoration of the grim status quo that existed before Ethan's infatuation with Mattie, and to punish him for thinking he could get away with it.

Ethan tells her that supper is ready but Zeena responds by saying she has no appetite. Not knowing what else to say, he suggests she must be tired from her travel. "Turning her head at this, she answered solemnly: 'I'm a great deal sicker than you think.' Her words fell on his ear with a strange shock of wonder. He had often heard her pronounce them before—what if at last they were true?" (Wharton 1911, 117). Having had several symbolic visions of Zeena's death and their implication for his happy future with Mattie, Ethan has to marshal all of his latent concern for her in order not to risk saying something inappropriate. What he manages to say is that he hopes it isn't true. "She continued to gaze at him through the twilight with a mien of wan authority, as of one consciously singled out for a great fate. 'I've got complications,' she said." This is a concept Ethan is familiar with and it's a portentous one, but from his point of view it is still a part of Zeena's general attempt to put her illness at the center of their lives. "Almost everybody in the neighbourhood had 'troubles,' frankly localized and specified; but only the chosen had 'complications.' To have them was in itself a distinction, though it was also, in most cases, a death-warrant."

Once again the idea of "troubles," that vague diagnosis that in Chopin's story so clearly indicated emotional disturbance manifesting as physical symptoms, appears in quotes. Zeena has taken the concept a step further, however, and her understanding of Ethan's infatuation for Mattie has resulted in an attempt to raise his level of guilt by suggesting that she's going to die. But she has no way of knowing her husband's true, inner reaction to the news. "Ethan's heart was jerking to and fro between two extremities of feeling, but for the moment compassion prevailed. His wife looked so hard and lonely, sitting there in the darkness with such thoughts" (Wharton 1911, 117-118). The two extremities are not difficult to discern. On the one hand there is his instinctive concern for a woman who has so isolated herself in her misery that she has become "hard and lonely." On the other hand is his rapturous joy at the thought of her death. Ethan asks if that's what the new doctor has told her, and she replies that any other doctor would want her to have an operation. Ironically, he is somewhat relieved by this.

> Ethan was aware that, in regard to the important question of surgical intervention, the female opinion of the neighbourhood was divided, some glorying in the prestige conferred by operations while others shunned them as indelicate. Ethan, from motives of economy, had always been glad that Zeena was of the latter faction. (118)

But then Ethan makes another miscalculation by attempting to cast doubt on the veracity of the new doctor's findings. "'What do you know about this doctor anyway? Nobody ever told you that before.' He saw his blunder before she could take it up: she wanted sympathy, not consolation."

Zeena responds immediately: "I didn't need to have anybody tell me I was losing ground every day. Everybody but you could see it" (Wharton 1911, 118-119). Then she launches into a defense of Dr. Buck from Worchester and the miracles he has performed in his twice-monthly visits to Shadd's Falls and Bettsbridge. "Well, I'm glad of that," Ethan tells her. "You must do just what he tells you" (119). It's at this point Ethan notices a sudden change in Zeena's demeanor. "She was still looking at him. 'I mean to,' she said. He was struck by a new note in her voice. It was neither whining nor reproachful, but drily resolute." Ethan is almost afraid to ask, but eventually he comes out with it and could not be more dismayed by her answer. "He wants I should have a hired girl. He says I oughtn't to have to do a single thing around the house." In this way Zeena is actually the flip side of the narrator in Gilman's "Yellow Wall-Paper" as she not only feels no guilt about abdicating her domestic duties, but understands full well that in this particular nineteenth-century climate she will have no trouble getting away with it. For a poor famer with little enough money as it is, however, a hired girl is a luxury Ethan can't afford. But Zeena continues, saying how lucky she is that her aunt was able to find a girl to come out to Starkfield, and informs him that the girl is set to arrive the following day.

> Wrath and dismay contended in Ethan. He had foreseen an immediate demand for money, but not a permanent drain on his scant resources. He no longer believed what Zeena had told him of the supposed seriousness of her state: he saw in her expedition to Bettsbridge only a plot hatched between herself and her Pierce relations to foist on him the cost of a servant; and for the moment wrath predominated. (120)

What's so interesting here is that Ethan seems to understand Zeena perfectly. He doesn't believe in the "seriousness of her state" anymore, and sees with new clarity the way she has manipulated her supposed illness just to punish him. Yet at the same time he is completely blind when it comes to the fact that his relationship with Mattie is wholly fictitious and a figment of his imagination. Wharton's reference to Zeena's family and their apparent collusion with her comes from her own conflict with her husband's family as Teddy's mental illness became ever more severe. Like Zeena's family, Wharton's in-laws felt that it was Edith's responsibility to care for her husband and they had no concern whatever about the toll that care was taking on her. In a letter to Morton Fullerton, the author said about her in-laws, "The Wharton's adroitly refuse to recognize the strain I am under, and the impossibility, for a person with nerves strung like mine, to go on leading indefinitely the life I am now leading. They say: 'The responsibility rests with his wife—we merely reserve the right to criticize'" (Fournier 52-53).

Ethan tells Zeena flatly that she should have informed him if she was going to spend money on a hired girl, but she responds that she couldn't have known what Dr. Buck was going to prescribe before she left. Ethan has a wonderful comeback when he says, "'Oh, Dr. Buck—' Ethan's incredulity escaped in a short laugh. 'Did Dr. Buck tell you how I was to pay her wages?'" (Wharton 1911, 120). Throughout their marriage Zeena has been able to maintain her composure in the midst of disappointment, as a way of dominating Ethan, but the closest she comes to losing control is when she confronts him here with what must have been a long-held animosity. "Her voice rose furiously with his. 'No, he didn't. For I'd 'a' been ashamed to tell *him* that you grudged me the money to get back my health, when I lost it nursing your own mother!'" The suggestion is ludicrous, but it also provides a bit of insight into Zeena's character, and demonstrates that she has made her own rationalizations over the years, ones that are almost as unrealistic as Ethan's. Nevertheless, her heightened emotion manages to pull Ethan into the argument as well. "*You* lost your health nursing mother?" he asks incredulously, but she continues to press her case. "Yes; and my folks all told me at the time you couldn't do no less than marry me after—" (121). But at this he finally shouts her down. "Zeena!" The fact that Zeena has no trouble in characterizing Ethan's marriage proposal as obligatory says a lot about her relationship to Ethan as she sees it, and it goes a long way toward explaining her behavior, especially keeping him at arm's length sexually. But this was another common cause for the symptoms of hysteria, one that had ironic consequences for women, as Smith-Rosenberg points out. "The hysteric purchased her escape from the emotional and—frequently—from the sexual demands of her life only at the cost of pain, disability, and an intensification of woman's traditional passivity and dependence" (Smith-Rosenberg 1985, 207).

As much as Ethan is shocked by Zeena's revelations, he is equally disturbed by the manner of their disclosure. "Through the obscurity which hid their faces their thoughts seemed to dart at each other like serpents shooting venom. Ethan was seized with horror of the scene and shame at his own share in it. It was as senseless and savage as a physical fight between two enemies in the darkness . . ." (Wharton 1911, 121). Ethan's perception here is unusually keen. Not only is he in the dark about Zeena's machinations, but Zeena is completely unaware of how happy Ethan would be if she were to die. Author Suzanne Fournier makes an interesting connection between this passage and the conclusion of Matthew Arnold's "Dover Beach" from 1852.

> And here we are as on a darkling plain
> Swept with confused alarms of struggle and flight,
> Where ignorant armies clash by night. (Arnold 167)

But Fournier doesn't seem to understand the full significance of the passage as it relates to the light/dark symbolism in Wharton's novel. She speaks of Ethan's attempt to "combat the darkness" by lighting a candle and "the triumph of the gathering shadows" represented by Zeena, but she never articulates exactly what the darkness is (Fournier 109). What she has missed is the direct association that Arnold makes in the last line of the poem between darkness and ignorance. In this context Ethan and Zeena may be together on the "darkling plain" of their bedroom, but while each of them is "ignorant" about certain things concerning the other, Zeena's position by the window assures that Ethan will be the loser in the contest.

Ethan tries to make some sense of the argument through a symbolic attempt to shed light on things. "He turned to the shelf above the chimney, groped for matches and lit the one candle in the room. At first its weak flame made no impression on the shadows; then Zeena's face stood grimly out against the uncurtained pane, which had turned from grey to black" (Wharton 1911, 121). Initially the candlelight is unable to dispel the darkness from the room, and even when it does it is only to illuminate Zeena's face. Instead of the light predicting or accompanying understanding, here it seems to reflect Ethan's earlier moment of clarity as to Zeena's motives. But the light also has another effect on the room when the window in this context becomes associated with both Ethan and Zeena as the freedom and opportunity it represents turns from "grey to black." In this way the argument actually demonstrates the futility of such confrontations, what Ethan describes as "senseless," because the only thing it serves to accomplish is to make staying together even more unbearable. Regardless of how much and how vehemently they lash out at each other, after the argument is over there is no place for either of them to go. And yet despite this, Ethan recognizes that he is really the only one who has been diminished by engaging in the quarrel.

> It was the first scene of open anger between the couple in their sad seven years together, and Ethan felt as if he had lost an irretrievable advantage in descending to the level of recrimination. But the practical problem was there and had to be dealt with. (121)

This confrontation can also be seen as the beginning of the impetus for Ethan's decision to kill himself at the end of the interior story. Zeena had always managed to keep her dissatisfaction limited to thinly veiled criticism, and as long as Ethan refused to respond, or was able to dismiss her criticism, there was little she could do. But once Zeena has been able to manipulate Ethan into losing his composure by arguing with her, he feels that things could never be the same. She has beaten him in a way that makes his submission to her all the more abhorrent. And yet at the end of it all, it has changed nothing, and the practical considerations that dominate the argument cannot be altered. The only thing left for him to say is, "You know I haven't got the money to pay for a girl, Zeena. You'll have to send her back: I can't do it" (Wharton 1911, 122). But Zeena continues to press her advantage, attempting to playing on Ethan's guilt—though she has no way of knowing that it's actually the weakest part of her argument. "The doctor says it'll be my death if I go on slaving the way I've had to. He doesn't understand how I've stood it as long as I have." Again, Ethan is outraged at this assertion, as Zeena does almost nothing around the house anyway. But he manages to keep himself in check and says he'll just have to do more around the house to help her.

That isn't good enough for Zeena, and she brings up the fact that he has neglected the farm enough already, which is true, and then further suggests sarcastically that he might as well send her to the poor house as there have been Fromes there before. "The taunt burned into him, but he let it pass" (Wharton 1911, 122). As much as she may want to humiliate him, it still doesn't change the fact that he can't afford a hired girl. "I haven't got the money. That settles it." But it's here that Ethan's previous lie comes back to haunt him when Zeena says, "I thought you were to get fifty dollars from Andrew Hale for that lumber." Interestingly, Ethan doesn't even remember the lie at first and blurts out that Hale doesn't pay until the end of three months, though as soon as the words are out of his mouth it all comes back to him, and Zeena reminds him of the reason he gave for not taking her to the train station. It's to Ethan's credit, however, that he makes absolutely no attempt to mollify her with some sort of an excuse. "Ethan had no suppleness in deceiving. He had never before been convicted of a lie, and all the resources of evasion failed him. 'I guess that was a misunderstanding,' he stammered" (123). Zeena then asks if he is going to get the money, and he responds by saying, no. Once again, Zeena says she couldn't possibly have known he wouldn't have the money when she went to the doctor, but regardless of the validity of her point, it still changes nothing. "You know it now. I'm sorry, but it can't be helped. You're a poor man's wife, Zeena; but I'll do the best I can for you." At this even Zeena seems to realize the pointlessness of continuing to argue and for a moment appears to have surrendered to the inevitable.

There's an interesting parallel that should be noted in this scene, between money and illness. In Edith Wharton's emphasis on money throughout the novel, author Ellen Moers sees a particularly feminine trait in nineteenth and early twentieth-century fiction by women, beginning with the work of Jane Austen. "This may be the first obviously feminine thing about her novels, for money and its making were characteristically female rather than male subjects in English fiction" (Moers 67). The particularly feminine concern with how a family was going to survive was not just restricted to European women, as Moers goes on to point out. Many women authors—including Edith Wharton—found themselves responsible for making the money that would sustain their immediate and extended families.

> The father, brother, or husband who could not or would not work, and left the entire or major support of a large household to his womenfolk, was responsible for the writing of many best sellers by American women, and a few masterworks. The literally thumb-crushing labors of Louisa May Alcott were mostly, in this sense, her father's doing; Margaret Fuller derived some spur to literary industry from the marriage into her family (for which she had financial responsibility) of the unemployable Ellery Channing; and there might never have been an *Uncle Tom's Cabin* had the Reverend Calvin Stowe been a better provider for his wife and many babies. (85)

The situation Wharton found herself in during most of her literary career was not much different. From the beginning, "Teddy [Wharton] had no vocation . . . An 1873 graduate of Harvard, he finished his junior year tenth from the bottom of his class with an average of forty-five and showed little aptitude for any subject other than natural history" (Fournier 13). Later on, however, things were even worse as his family's history of mental illness became debilitating for him. "Like Frome, Edith Wharton was manacled to the merest ghost of a mate: every superficial pleasure in her marriage had been lost, and nothing remained except the crude and brutal armature of dependency upon which it had been founded" (Wolff 406). As such, it's no surprise that a heightened consciousness about money and where it was coming from would be present as well in the fiction of these women authors. And yet, in another of the many ironies that surrounded women authors at this time, even those who were responsible for the financial solvency of their families were often looked down upon by their extended families for participating in a profession that somehow seemed undignified. Wharton was no exception. "None of my relations ever spoke to me of my books, either to praise or blame—they simply ignored them; and among the immense tribe of my New York cousins . . . the subject was avoided as though it were a kind of family disgrace which might be condoned but which could not be forgotten" (Banta 84). As a result, "I had to fight my way to expression through a thick fog of indifference."

What's unique about *Ethan Frome* is the way in which Wharton's gender reversal places that financial consciousness in the mind of Ethan rather than Zeena, and by the end of the novel it will be the primary element on which the climax of the story turns. But beyond that obvious use of financial scarcity to force Ethan's decision at the close of the interior story, there is another way in which his gender reversal informs the book as a whole. Ethan is a hard worker, unlike Wharton's husband, and while he is still poor it is not through a lack of effort on his part. When looked at in that way it is actually Zeena's illness that is in effect most like the men described above. It's easy to overlook this fact because society assumes that men are going to work just as Ethan does. But there is also an assumption that women are going to aid in that work, within their limited sphere, as part of their responsibility for the family's well-being. In abdicating her responsibility voluntarily, then, Zeena has become more like the ne'er-do-well husbands and male relatives who forced women into taking on the financial duty for the survival of the family on their own. This is reflected in the scene when Ethan tells Zeena, "You sha'n't lift a hand . . . I'll do everything round the house myself—" (Wharton 1911, 122).

As far as whether or not they can hire a girl, from Ethan's point of view their lack of money is the sole determining factor and as far as he is concerned the argument has been resolved. He begins to turn for the door in order to head downstairs for supper when suddenly Zeena says, "There'll be Mattie's board less, anyhow—" (Wharton 1911, 124). This stops Ethan in his tracks, as he can't believe what he's just heard. "Mattie's board less—?" While he was on firm ground talking about money, he is utterly unprepared for what happens next.

> Zeena laughed. It was on odd unfamiliar sound—he did not remember ever having heard her laugh before. "You didn't suppose I was going to keep two girls, did you? No wonder you were scared at the expense!" He still had but a confused sense of what she was saying. From the beginning of the discussion he had instinctively avoided the mention of Mattie's name, fearing he hardly knew what: criticism, complaints, or vague allusions to the imminent probability of her marrying. But the thought of a definite rupture had never come to him, and even now could not lodge itself in his mind. (124-125)

The fact that Zeena has never laughed in their seven years together is actually quite a chilling revelation. But beyond that there is Ethan's continual shock at the lengths Zeena will go in punishing him, this time through her clear intention to get rid of Mattie and engage the hired girl even though he has refused to pay for her. "I don't know what you mean," he said. "Mattie Silver's not a hired girl. She's your relation" (125). Ethan had assumed that Mattie's position in the house would be secure as, in addition to being a cousin of

Zeena's, she has nowhere else to go, but Zeena will simply not allow Ethan's interest in her to continue. "She's a pauper that's hung onto us all after her father'd done his best to ruin us. I've kep' her here a whole year: it's somebody else's turn now."

Before Ethan can respond Mattie knocks on the door to tell the couple that supper has been ready for some time. Zeena says she's not coming down, and Ethan opens the door and tells Mattie that he'll be along in a moment. But Ethan can't leave until he's confronted Zeena about her callousness toward Mattie. "'You ain't going to do it, Zeena?' . . . He continued with rising vehemence: 'You can't put her out of the house like a thief—a poor girl without friends or money. She's done her best for you and she's got no place to go to'" (Wharton 1911, 126). Zeena counters with the fact that she never intended on keeping Mattie for life, and at this Ethan tries a different tack, suggesting that people in the village will form a negative opinion of her for abandoning the girl. "You may forget she's your kin but everybody else'll remember it. If you do a thing like that what do you suppose folks'll say of you?" What follows is probably the closest thing the reader experiences to Ethan's perception of Zeena as threatening and obscure at the same time when she says, "I know well enough what they say of my having kep' her here as long as I have" (126-127). It's difficult to know what to make of this statement. Zeena seems to be implying that others know of Ethan's interest in Mattie as well, and that people think Zeena has been a fool to allow her to stay because of it. But how could they when Mattie doesn't even know herself? It could also simply mean that people think Zeena has been more than generous to the girl already. Considering Ethan's reaction, however, it's more than likely Zeena isn't talking about the people in the village at all, and her comment is simply a way to convey to Ethan that she knows all about his infatuation. It can only be this last meaning that accounts for Ethan's immediate thoughts, and explains the futility he senses in attempting to resist her. "His wife's retort was like a knife-cut across the sinews and he felt suddenly weak and powerless" (127).

Ethan had planned on pleading with his wife to keep Mattie, but after this he understands that Zeena is not to be denied, and the risk that his true interest in Mattie will be brought out into the open is simply too great. "'You mean to tell her she's got to go—at once?' he faltered out, in terror of letting his wife complete her sentence" (Wharton 1911, 127). Zeena appears to ignore his question and forges ahead, saying the new girl will arrive the next day and so Mattie's room has to be empty for her. But it's here that Zeena has miscalculated. Up until now she has expertly manipulated Ethan in order to maintain the upper hand over him. She has been in control of their relationship from the beginning and has used that power to her advantage. In a way, however, she has panicked this time. Her hasty trip to Bettsbridge and her heavy-handed manner of disposing of Mattie by forcing him to hire a girl has only served to rouse Ethan's latent hostility toward her rather than completely cowing him as she assumed she had done, and as the lengthy internal narrative that follows demonstrates.

> Ethan looked at her with loathing. She was no longer the listless creature who had lived at his side in a state of sullen self-absorption, but a mysterious alien presence, an evil energy secreted from the long years of silent brooding. It was the sense of his helplessness that sharpened his antipathy. There had never been anything in her that one could appeal to; but as long as he could ignore and command he had remained indifferent. Now she had mastered him and he abhorred her. Mattie was her relation, not his: there were no means by which he could compel her to keep the girl under her roof. All the long misery of his baffled past, of his youth of failure, hardship and vain effort, rose up in his soul in bitterness and seemed to take shape before him in the woman who at every turn had barred his way. She had taken everything else from him; and now she meant to take the one thing that made up for all the others. For a moment such a flame of hate rose in him that it ran down his arm and clenched his fist against her. (127-128)

The key element of this description comes right at the beginning when Ethan calls Zeena "evil." While her passive self-absorption and manipulative complaining had been irritating, he still had the ability to be selective in how he responded, when not choosing to outright ignore her. But the idea that Zeena is evil somehow changes her into an active malevolence set on doing him harm. Where Ethan had allowed himself to be controlled before, as a way of keeping the peace, her change to an active rather than a passive force over him has inadvertently roused him to action, symbolized by his clenched fist.

Before he goes, Ethan asks Zeena if she's coming down to eat, and when she says she is going to lie down instead, he leaves. Mattie gets up to serve the meal when Ethan enters the kitchen and says she hopes Zeena isn't sick. Ethan says no, and sits down to the table, but he obviously has no appetite. Mattie, of course, has been oblivious to their argument and continues to do her work with her usual cheerfulness. And of course Ethan continues to interpret this as a reflection on him. "So they were to have one more evening together, her happy eyes seemed to say!" (Wharton 1911, 129). But he can't keep up the façade and finally pushes his plate away and walks over to her. "Ethan, there's something wrong! I *knew* there was!" (130). The next passage is an important one to examine closely. Ethan takes Mattie in his arms, which only intensifies her fear. This is underscored by Wharton when she says he "held her fast there, felt her lashes beat his cheek like netted butterflies." The comparison with a helpless insect caught in a net—however beautiful—reinforces not only the idea of Mattie's lack of power but the fear she is experiencing at this moment. "What is it—what is it?" she demands to know, again, still in a state of alarm. Then Ethan finally kisses her. "He had found her lips at last and was drinking unconscious of everything but the joy they gave him."

It must be remembered that this is a girl who had blushed to the roots of her hair when Ethan merely mentioned Ruth and Ned kissing. Forget for a moment the fact of what her actual feelings may or may not be for Ethan, the kiss itself is perhaps one of the most inappropriate things Ethan could have done during this time period—especially given the fact that he had earlier declared he had no right to even verbalize his feelings. Ethan says, "she lingered a moment" and then ascribes this to his belief that she is "caught in the same strong current" (Wharton 1911, 130). More likely it's the shock of what he has just done, combined with the fact that she still doesn't know what Zeena has said, that causes her momentary paralysis. But that isn't the only important body language to observe. Just as she had done two nights previously, "she slipped from him and drew back a step or two," and the reason for this comes in his description of her as looking "pale and troubled." Mattie doesn't just pull back from Ethan here, but actually steps away from him. Had she truly felt something for him, it would have been far more reasonable to expect her to draw closer to him as a way of assuaging her fears. At this point Mattie's actions do not remotely suggest that she returns Ethan's feelings, but instead that she is completely consumed with thoughts about what is going to happen to her. Author Suzanne Fournier seems to understand this unconsciously, as she sort of backs into the idea while making a point about Ethan. "His sense that he need not explain himself to her is unfounded, as Wharton demonstrates . . . when he embraces Mattie immediately following his defeat at Zeena's hands. *Unaware of his thoughts—or his feelings*—Mattie learns of her fate only after he kisses her to ease his own pain" (Fournier 85). [italics added]

Mattie still has no idea what is wrong until Ethan finally blurts out, "You can't go, Matt! I'll never let you!" (Wharton 1911, 130). In addition to Mattie's actions, the only other evidence that can be used to make a determination about her feelings concerning the kiss is her words, and her response is this: "'Go—go?' she stammered. 'Must I go?'" For Ethan, even after delivering this devastating news, the only thing he can think of is himself. "His head reeled and he had to support himself against the table. All the while he felt as if he were still kissing her, and yet dying of thirst for her lips" (131). And yet the girl still has not reacted to the kiss at all. Before Mattie's next response, there is another reference to the light of understanding when Ethan describes the atmosphere in the kitchen after she asks if she really has to go. "The words went on sounding between them as though a torch of warning flew from hand to hand through a black landscape" (130). The light of the torch is, in fact, a warning to Ethan and one that is far more important than the knowledge that he will be able to do nothing to keep her from leaving. The warning light he needs to be looking at is Mattie's reaction, both in word and deed, to the kiss. Mattie never even acknowledges it, and instead is only concerned with asking, "Ethan, what has happened? Is Zeena mad with me?" (131).

Ethan tries to reassure her that it isn't anything personal against her, and in some respects this is true as Zeena's only goal is apparently to hang on to Ethan at all costs—either that or make sure that if she can't be happy in their life together that he can't either. And since it is Mattie who makes him happy, she has to go. "It's not that." Ethan tells her. "But this new doctor has scared her about herself. You know she believes all they say the first time she sees them. And this one's told her she won't get well unless she lays up and don't do a thing about the house—not for months—" (Wharton 1911, 131). Mattie, however, understands the implications perfectly. "And she wants somebody handier in my place? Is that it?" Wharton says here that the two of them "bowed to the inexorable truth," that there is no way to convince Zeena to change her mind (132). After a few moments of silence, Mattie says "Don't be too sorry, Ethan." This is a remarkable statement, coming as it does after the kiss, because as it has been throughout the entire novel there is no indication whatsoever that she shares Ethan's feelings for her. In fact, she seems more concerned about his emotional state than her own. Ethan groans out, "Oh, God—oh, God," and observes, "her quick lids beating back the tears, and longed to take her in his arms and soothe her." But again there is no sense that she shares his emotional pain when she tells him his supper is getting cold. The real meaning of the tears comes from the answer to the question he asks, "Oh, Matt—Matt—where'll you go to?"

Throughout this scene the reader is struck by the fact that Ethan is the one who is the emotional wreck, reinforcing the idea of the gender switch that Wharton has performed. Despite her need to resort to the tactics of women in feigning illness, it is Zeena who is firmly in control of the relationship, and Ethan who is helpless and desperate. As always, his concern for Mattie and her uncertain future transforms effortlessly in his mind into the ramifications for himself.

Despair seized him at the thought of her setting out alone to renew the weary quest for work. In the only place where she was known she was surrounded by indifference or animosity; and what chance had she, inexperienced and untrained, among the million bread-seekers of the cities? There came back to him miserable tales he had heard at Worcester, and the faces of girls whose lives had begun as hopefully as Mattie's . . . It was not possible to think of such things without a revolt of his whole being. (Wharton 1911, 132-133)

Wharton makes a brilliant juxtaposition here, when Ethan's hatred for Zeena finally inspires him to resist her. "You can't go, Matt! I won't let you! She's always had her way, but I mean to have mine now—" (133). At this Mattie lifts her head and looks toward the hall, and Ethan hears Zeena coming down the stairs.

Throughout the novel the reader has been able to make inferences that Zeena's illness is not real, and here the reader finally has direct evidence of the fact. Zeena comes into the kitchen and sits down in her usual place. "I felt a little mite better, and Dr. Buck says I ought to eat all I can to keep my strength up, even if I ain't got any appetite" (Wharton 1911, 133). Of course she's feeling better, now that she has been able to remove Mattie from Ethan's life, and she eats accordingly, pouring extra milk into her tea, taking a large slice of pie, and giving a scrap of meat to the cat—even telling it "Good Pussy," as though rewarding it for taking her place the previous night. Before she eats, however, Ethan notices she "made the familiar gesture of adjusting her false teeth." If there's a legitimate criticism to Ethan as a literary character, it's his passivity, as demonstrated by this subtle bit of symbolism. This is the second mention of Zeena's false teeth in the novel and it suggests that, in real terms, she is toothless. For all its patriarchal unfairness, Ethan is the man of the family and the only one who earns any money. Were he to simply demand that he have his way there is, quite literally, nothing Zeena could do about it. She certainly couldn't make his life any more miserable and, in a slightly perverted way, it may even have made things better between them.

Author Marlene Springer points out that during his argument with Zeena, after Ethan sends Mattie away from the door, he turns to his wife and says, "You ain't going to do it, Zeena?" (Wharton 1911, 126). The interesting thing about this sentence, which at first appears to be a command, is the question mark at the end. "How different his life would have been," says Springer, "had his tone been an exclamation point of determined resolve. Instead of taking over his life, he relinquishes it to his wife, and she is a master of such psychological warfare" (Springer 51). But, as Cynthia Wolff points out, there is a reason Ethan has psychologically succumbed to Zeena in a way that he finds himself unable to resist. "Within every one of us there lurks a phantom self, not our 'real' self, not the self that the world sees, but a seductive shade that calls to us to passivity and dependency in a sweet, soft voice. Here is the greatest danger—to relax, to let go, to fall pell-mell, tumbling, backward and down. The horror of the void." (Wolff 170) "It is the appeal of passivity, the numbing inertia that renders Frome impotent in the face of real-world dilemmas" (173). The evidence of this is Ethan's lament about Zeena that, "She had taken everything else from him; and now she meant to take the one thing that made up for all the others" (Wharton 1911, 128). During their argument he thinks to himself, "Mattie was her relation, not his: there were no means by which he could compel her to keep the girl under her roof" (127). But why attempt to compel her at all, when he could simply demand that Mattie stay? Even though he has far more power to exert over his circumstances, Ethan refuses to put up a fight. The only explanation for this is that it is in keeping with Ethan's role as a female surrogate.

This is the primary motif, in fact, of the story "The Chrysanthemums" by John Steinbeck. Written in 1934, over a decade after women had won the right to vote, the story deals with the unforced repression of Elisa Allen, the wife of a farmer in the Salinas Valley in California. As the description of her home attests—"the neat white farm house . . . was a hard-swept looking little house with hard-polished windows, and a clean mud mat on the front steps"— Steinbeck has painted the portrait of a woman who has outstripped her energies for housework and is in need of a more challenging occupation (Steinbeck 2). Instead, she devotes her energies to growing flowers, symbolically surrounded by a "wire fence that protected her flower garden from cattle and dogs and chickens." By restricting her talents on the farm to flowers, plants that have only aesthetic value, she unconsciously remains in the symbolic control of societal expectations from the previous century. "A female was groomed for only one thing, to become the perfectly adaptable ornament of her husband's world, and all interests other than self-adornment were actively discouraged" (Wolff xiv). When her husband Henry comes over to talk to her he makes clear his desire to have her apply her talents to greater use. "'You've got a gift with things,' Henry observed. 'Some of those yellow chrysanthemums you had this year were ten inches across. I wish you'd work out in the orchard and raise some apples that big'" (Steinbeck 2). But instead of taking on that new challenge she says, "Maybe I could do it, too," and never does. Though Eliza is only thirty-five, a year older than Zeena, and has clearly mastered her role as a housewife, she is reluctant to embrace a new challenge in which she might fail. Because of that she suffers from the same passivity as Ethan, and

Steinbeck ends the story with the same description of her that Ethan uses to describe Zeena, "an old woman" (13). In submitting to Zeena, however, it is Ethan who has become the old woman.

Wolff's "numbing inertia" certainly makes itself visible in this scene, with Zeena all but delighted in the way that she has been able to manufacture Mattie's departure. No sign of illness affects her now because she's won, and a defeated Ethan can only sit helpless and watch, powerless to make any kind of significant impact on his own life. Symbolically, there's purpose for that, as Steinbeck's story demonstrates, because even women who had the opportunity to do more with their lives in the nineteenth-century were often times reluctant to venture forth into the unknown and preferred instead the comfort of their own oppression—which did not mean they were necessarily happy about it. As Mattie engages Zeena about her trip to the doctor Ethan observes, "She looked straight at Mattie as she spoke, a faint smile deepening the vertical lines between her nose and chin" (Wharton 1911, 134). As baffling as hysteria was for many nineteenth-century doctors, there were also cases like Zeena's in which physicians were dubious as to the true nature of a woman's medical complaints.

> As might be expected, conscious anger and hostility marked the response of a good many doctors to their hysterical patients. One New York neurologist called the female hysteric a willful, self-indulgent, and narcissistic person who cynically manipulated her symptoms. "To her distorted vision," he complained, "there is but one commanding personage in the universe—herself—in comparison with whom the rest of mankind are nothing" . . . Even the concerned and genteel S. Weir Mitchell . . . described hysterical women as "the pests of many households, who . . . in unconscious or half-conscious self-indulgence destroy the comfort of everyone about them." (Smith-Rosenberg 1985, 207)

After supper Zeena stands and puts her hand to her chest. "'That pie of yours always sets a mite heavy, Matt,' she said, not ill-naturedly. She seldom abbreviated the girl's name, and when she did so it was always a sign of affability" (Wharton 1911, 134-135). As was implied before, Zeena has no true animosity toward Mattie—she calls her by her nickname here and doesn't appear to be genuinely criticizing her cooking—it is only Ethan's desire for Mattie that she intends to thwart. When Zeena announces that she's going to get her stomach powders Mattie offers to do it for her, but Zeena says they're in a place she doesn't know about. After she leaves, Mattie begins clearing the table and she and Ethan look at each other. "As she passed Ethan's chair their eyes met and clung together desolately," and then the cat jumps up in Zeena's chair just as it had done the night before (135). This sudden reference to the previous evening is something of a foreshadow of what is to come; in the midst of the trauma of the preceding scene with Zeena upstairs in the bedroom, the pickle dish has been all but forgotten. Ethan tells Mattie he's going to take a look outside and then meets Zeena in the hallway on her way back into the kitchen, "her lips twitching with anger, a flush of excitement on her sallow face. The shawl had slipped from her shoulder [and] in her hands she carried the fragments of the red glass pickle-dish. 'I'd like to know who done this,' she said, looking sternly from Ethan to Mattie" (136).

Neither of them answer, and Zeena continues by saying that the powders she was looking for were hidden in her china cabinet, next to the dish that had been up on the top shelf so that nothing could happen to it.

> Her voice broke, and two small tears hung on her lashless lids and ran slowly down her cheeks. "It takes the stepladder to get at the top shelf, and I put Aunt Philura Maple's pickle-dish up there o' purpose when we was married, and it's never been down since, 'cept for the spring cleaning, and then I always lifted it with my own hands, so's 't it shouldn't get broke." She laid the fragments reverently on the table. "I want to know who done this," she quavered. (Wharton 1911, 136-137).

Ethan comes back in from the hall and tells her that the cat did it, which is essentially true. She looks at both of them again and then Zeena asks the obvious question, how the cat got into the china cabinet. Ethan suggests it was chasing a mouse, as it had been the evening before, but there's just as clearly something wrong with that explanation. "Zeena continued to look from one to the other; then she emitted her small strange laugh. 'I knew the cat was a smart cat,' she said in a high voice, 'but I didn't know he was smart enough to pick up the pieces of my pickle-dish and lay 'em edge to edge on the very shelf he knocked 'em off of.'" This is the first reference to the cat's sex, and another subtle hint by Wharton that in the cat's role as Zeena's surrogate he represents Zeena's true status as the patriarch of the house.

At this point Mattie can no longer keep silent and confesses to everything. "It wasn't Ethan's fault, Zeena! The cat *did* break the dish; but I got it down from the china-closet, and I'm the one to blame for its getting broken" (Wharton 1911, 138). Any previous assumptions Mattie might have made that Ethan would take responsibility are proven false as he seems intent on avoiding that responsibility. Up until now Zeena hasn't displayed any personal dislike for Mattie. In fact, Ethan even suggests earlier in the novel that Zeena perhaps

Eric B. Olsen

enjoyed having her there because she could be critical of the girl without any fear of her leaving. But this changes things dramatically.

> You waited till my back was turned, and took the thing I set most store by of anything I've got, and wouldn't never use it, not even when the minister come to dinner, or Aunt Martha Pierce come over from Bettsbridge—" Zeena paused with a gasp, as if terrified by her own evocation of the sacrilege. "You're a bad girl, Mattie Silver, and I always known it. It's the way your father begun, and I was warned of it when I took you, and I tried to keep my things where you couldn't get at 'em—and now you've took from me the one I cared for most of all—" (138)

Initially, there's an element of what seems like hyperbole in Zeena's speech. Her treasuring of the pickle dish is understandable, to a point. But in castigating Mattie she then goes on to say how she never even used it—ever, for anything—and that it was the one thing in the world that she "cared for most of all." Of course, when she says, "I tried to keep my things where you couldn't get at 'em," it's difficult not to see this as symbolic of Ethan. Finally, Wharton tells the reader, as she gathered "up the bits of broken glass she went out of the room as if she carried a dead body . . ." (139).

This overly exaggerated emphasis on the pickle dish in Zeena's mind is something that demands further examination. The most telling information about the dish actually comes from Mattie, when she says that Zeena received it as a wedding present. The association of the dish with marriage suggests that it is another of Wharton's subtle sexual symbols. The dish is a concave receptacle designed to accommodate pickles, which can be seen as phallic symbols. Even the color of the dish is suggestive of female genitalia. At the same time the earlier reference to the dead cucumber vine on the porch reinforces the idea that at one time Ethan's sex drive was strong and virile like the cucumber, while later in his marriage to Zeena his manhood has been essentially preserved, or pickled. All of this symbolism is reinforced by the fact that Zeena has never used the dish, and supported in the literal story by the fact that the couple has no children. There are two possible explanations for this; the first is that Zeena is unable to have children with Ethan because of some medical issue affecting one or both of them. The second, and more likely possibility, is that they have never had sex at all. Putting aside the literal dish for a moment, this goes a long way toward explaining the tension in their relationship. For author Kenneth Bernard, it is actually the key to understanding the couple. "The sexual symbolism . . . is more significant because without an understanding of it the source of Zeena and Ethan's

240

estrangement and antagonism remains unknown. After all, what *is* the deep gulf that lies between them?" (Bernard 182).

But it's Wharton herself who provides the context for the emotional separation between Zeena and Ethan in the example of her own marriage. "Teddy and Edith's marriage was strained from the beginning by a lack of physical intimacy, however, and within three weeks of their April 1885 wedding they settled into a relationship that was friendly rather than passionate. Her effort to learn from [her mother] Lucretia beforehand 'what being married was like' had been angrily rebuffed, leading her to write years later that her mother's failure to supply her with the simplest information about sexual relations, 'did more than anything else to falsify and misdirect my whole life.' The incomplete nature of Edith's marriage—and its increasingly obvious inequality—would inspire a long series of unsatisfying unions in her fiction" (Fournier 13). What is so interesting in *Ethan Frome* is that, with Zeena's pickle dish symbolizing the withholding of sex, Wharton herself seems to have identified more with Ethan, which again serves to support the idea that it is Ethan who takes on the role of the frustrated and oppressed woman in the novel. Zeena's illness in this regard has provided her with a justification for withholding sex from Ethan throughout their marriage. And yet that also has a parallel in Wharton's life. "For more than a dozen years after her marriage, Wharton suffered a number of debilitating symptoms which left her weak and unable to work for months at a time" (14). In this way Wharton was able to write from both Ethan and Zeena's perspective with authority.

Bernard's essay, in addition to looking at the imagery of the setting and the light/dark symbolism, goes into considerable depth in examining Wharton's use of sexual symbols. As far as the pickle dish is concerned, "The dish has only ceremonial, not functional, use. The sexual connotations are obvious. The fact that the wedding dish, which was meant to contain pickles, in fact never does, explains a lot of the heaviness of atmosphere, the chill, the frigidity. The most intense scenes of the book, the most revealing, center [on] this dish. (Bernard 183) In this context the symbolic meaning of the pickle dish and what it represents, as Bernard says, is obvious. But Bernard also sees the relevance of the pickle dish beginning much earlier, at the end of Chapter Three. "This is the only other mention of pickles in the book. Significantly, it is the last word in the chapter before the one devoted to Ethan and Mattie's night together." (Bernard 183) And yet Bernard's complete understanding of what the pickle dish represents seems limited by the fact that he focuses its meaning exclusively on sexuality, even equating Zeena's barren womb with the landscape, which doesn't really serve a purpose in the overall analysis and leads him to make some rather confusing arguments as a result. For example, in looking at the mention of pickles at the end of Chapter Three he concludes,

> The action might be interpreted as follows: after Zeena has exhausted the possibilities of her medicine for her "trouble," she turns to sex—but she passes on that alternative to Mattie. Mattie may use the jar for pickles if she wishes. The action is a foreshadowing of Mattie's use of the pickle dish. In a sense, Zeena has urged her to that act, for she is abdicating the position of sexual initiative. (Bernard 183-184)

In light of the fact that Zeena is attempting to get rid of Mattie in order to keep Ethan, combined with the fallacious assumption of shared feelings between Mattie and Ethan, this argument is specious at best. Further, saying that Zeena "passes on" her opportunity for sexual relations with Ethan to Mattie doesn't fit with any of Zeena's actions or motivations and makes no sense at all. But to say that she first "exhausted the possibilities of her medicine" and only then "turns to sex" is completely backward, the very opposite of the way that Wharton has drawn her character. The truth is, Zeena has purposely withheld her sexual self from Ethan because of the lack of emotional love between the two that would naturally have resulted in that act, and then turned to medicine as a substitute. Author Dale M. Bauer astutely points out that in Edith Wharton's works this idea is not just limited to *Ethan Frome.* "Zeena is addicted to patent medicines . . . The trick with Wharton is to remember . . . her view of these drugs as the endpoint of her heroines' failure to find sexual fulfillment" (Bauer 2003, 118). This replacement of sex with drugs then becomes a self-perpetuating behavior as Bauer states in an impressive turn of phrase: "Drugs even literalize the metaphorical destruction of sexual intimacy."

Bernard's argument, on the other hand, seems equally abstruse when it comes to the breaking of the dish itself.

> The scene following is a symbolic recognition of the fact that Mattie has usurped her place, broken her marriage, and become one with Ethan, though it was in fact the cat (Zeena) who actually broke the dish. The fact that Zeena never truly filled her place, acted the role of wife, and is herself responsible for the failure of the marriage does not bother her. Ethan is hers, however ceremonially, and she resents what has happened. Her emotion transcends any literal meaning the dish may have, so much so that other implications of the dish force themselves on the reader" (Bernard 183).

Once again, Mattie has not taken Zeena's place, as nothing at all has happened between Mattie and Ethan. Cynthia Wolff makes this point very clear. "At first, Mattie Silver seems different [than Zeena], the embodiment of sexual promise. Yet a careful reader will note that this promise is largely a figment of Ethan Frome's imagination—a longing that is nourished with characteristic silence and a hope that can be sustained because it is never put to any test. (Wolff 405). Because of that fact a far more compelling argument can be made that the pickle dish, while still forcing its obvious symbolism on the reader, is actually representative of the emotional love of a couple that has no use for love within the confines of their marriage. Looking at the dish in this way it's easy to see that Mattie has inadvertently captured Ethan's love—not the promise of sex—a love which should, by rights, belong to Zeena. Dale Bauer comes much closer to understanding this than Bernard by pointing out, "When Zeena calls Mattie a 'bad girl,' she does not mean sexual wantonness but something more generally destructive: Mattie has ruined Zeena's one claim to material pleasure" (Bauer 2003, 137). In looking at love and sex as conjoined, it's more accurate to say it is her one claim to *marital* pleasure that has been symbolically destroyed, even though Zeena has elected not to make use of it. Finally, while Bernard does understand the cat's representation of Zeena in his parenthetical reference, his assertion that Zeena wanted to break the dish—in the guise of the cat—conflicts with her motivation to keep Ethan all to herself.

There is, however, a more persuasive aspect of this last point by Bernard that can be understood by reading it in a slightly different way. The assertion that Zeena "is herself responsible for the failure of the marriage" has already been demonstrated by her withholding of emotion from Ethan, and is reflected in the ceremonial nature of her marriage as symbolized by the unused pickle dish. Therefore her devastation at its destruction actually bespeaks a woman whose emotional ramparts have finally been breached. By refusing to consummate their marriage, Zeena has been able to symbolically keep her emotional life safely on a shelf. The breaking of the dish, however, suggests that she was too late in attempting to get rid of Mattie, and because Ethan has already fallen in love with her, Zeena has been diminished in the process. In that respect author Blake Nevius sees Zeena not just as an object of pathos, but one for whom some measure of sympathy has been purposefully generated by Wharton.

Zeena may not be a sympathetic character, but there is a moment when she makes us forget everything but her wronged humanity. As she confronts the guilty lovers, holding the fragments of her pickle dish, her face streaming with tears, we have a sudden and terrible glimpse of the starved emotional life that has made her what she is. The novelist's compassion can reach no further. (Nevius 128-129)

Of course, Ethan and Mattie are not "lovers"—any more than Zeena's face was "streaming" with tears—and any empathy readers might have for Zeena at this point is unceremoniously yanked out from beneath them when she laughs at Ethan's lie that the cat was responsible for breaking the dish. But there is another way Nevius's observation makes more sense, and that is in the earlier suggestion that Zeena was not initially unfriendly toward Mattie and that there might even have been a sense of sympathy on her part toward the orphaned girl. That Zeena is viewed entirely through the eyes of Ethan, however, tends to disguise that fact, just as Wharton's rendering of the touching scene of Zeena in tears becomes a moot point when she lashes out at Mattie with the intent of punishing her for Ethan's crimes.

In moving beyond the pickle dish as a purely sexual symbol and seeing it as representing love instead, it far more accurately symbolizes the fact that Mattie has aroused that latent emotion in Ethan. Because Ethan and Zeena's marriage was not based on love in the first place, the wedding present is therefore stored away and never used. But Ethan's infatuation for Mattie brings out his love in a way that Zeena was never able to do, symbolized by Mattie unconsciously using the dish during their night together. Zeena, in the form of the cat, cannot allow Ethan's one-sided love to flourish and must therefore break that love by sending Mattie away, symbolized by the breaking of the dish—and reinforced by Ethan thinking that the broken dish represented the "the shattered fragments of their evening," as well as the literal shattering of his fantasy. In this context Ethan's attempt to put the pickle dish back together, arranging it in a way that makes it only appear whole, is also emblematic of his marriage, which it turns out is only a marriage in outward appearance and perhaps was never consummated, all of which is reinforced by the gravestone of the elder Ethan and his wife Endurance and their fifty years of peace together. This is an extremely important point, as it serves to strengthen the view of Ethan as a female surrogate even further.

The societal expectations Ethan must operate under do not really allow him to divorce Zeena any more than most women of his day would have been able to divorce their husbands. Even looking past any obligation he might feel toward her for proposing in the first place, or the fact that her illness has indebted him to her, there remains the oppression of social convention. Divorce still held a tremendous stigma at this time, and with Ethan's inability to sell the farm and seek other work he finds himself as trapped in his marriage as most women were. These societal expectations were earlier symbolized by the weather and the winter landscape that has essentially frozen Ethan within the confines of his marriage, and is reflected in the French title of the novel. While the title for the French edition of the book is said to have been *Hiver* (Winter), it's significant that the initial translation of *Ethan Frome* into French in 1912, published in the periodical *Revue de Paris*, was titled *Sous la Neige* (Under the Snow). But further, the narrator referred to winter in Starkfield as the metaphorical "negation" of life, and because Zeena has refused to consummate their marriage Ethan will be unable to father any children, a literal negation of life. Author R. Baird Shuman sees this element of Ethan's situation in its association with the graveyard next to the house. "Death surrounds Ethan; the graveyard is a constant reminder of death's inevitability; and even as he looks ahead, there is no hope. He is the last of the Fromes. The future of his family, the hope of continuance, has been killed by his marriage to Zeena" (Shuman 92).

Zeena's exaggerated outburst, then, makes far more sense as an emotional one rather than a sexual one, as she not only has never used her love before, but now she will never be able to. Additionally, in the same way that Ethan will never have children to carry on his family name, Zeena will never have the opportunity to experience motherhood, and so the dish carries with it a whole host of associations beyond simply a crude symbol of the withholding of sex from her husband. Their marriage has been frozen in a state of stasis, which was symbolized by the dish being hidden away where nothing could happen to it. But once Ethan has fallen in love with Mattie there is no way he will ever be able to look at Zeena in the same way again, which results in their marriage moving from stasis to a state of destruction, again, symbolized by the breaking of the dish. And while Zeena's destruction of the dish in the guise of the cat makes no sense initially, it does when put in the context of her fear of losing Ethan, not just emotionally but physically. In that circumstance she was forced to destroy their fragile stasis, even though from this point forward neither of them will ever be able to love again. This is the real devastation Zeena suffers in carrying the broken glass out of the room as if it were a dead body, the symbolic recognition that now her love must die with her.

Chapter VIII

The following chapter is brilliantly conceived, as Wharton is able to allow the heightened emotion of Chapter Seven to remain in the background, unchanged, as Ethan places himself in isolation to think through everything that has happened. He begins with the genesis of the room beneath the stairs to which he retreats. The specific details used in describing it suggest that either the narrator from the frame story stayed the night there or gained access to the room at some point, and what he found there accounts for another part of what he is able to piece together of the final chapter of Ethan's story. Ethan says his mother gave him the room beneath the stairs when he returned home because of his father's illness, and he had attempted to turn it into something of a study. He put up shelves for his books and built a bed frame and put a mattress on it, and those, along with the small table, were its only furnishings. "He still took refuge there in summer, but when Mattie came to live at the farm he had to give her his stove, and consequently the room was uninhabitable for several months of the year" (Wharton 1911, 140). When he had gone to bed that night in their room upstairs Zeena said nothing, so he waited until she was asleep and went downstairs to think, beginning with the aftermath of Zeena's outburst.

He and Mattie had looked at each other for a moment after Zeena went upstairs, and then Mattie went back to doing the dishes while Ethan made his rounds outside. When he returned Mattie had already gone to bed, but she left him a note under his pipe and tobacco saying, "Don't trouble, Ethan" (Wharton 1911, 141). In writing this Mattie seems to understand that whatever happens from this point forward, Ethan will still be stuck on the farm with Zeena and so he should attempt to get back to something like the adversarial balance the two had been able to maintain before. But after their heated argument about

Mattie leaving and then the broken pickle dish, it's highly unlikely that things could ever return to the way they had been. Naturally, Ethan uses the note as another in a long line of evidentiary proof of Mattie's love for him and treats it almost like a fetish.

> It was the first time that Mattie had ever written to him, and the possession of the paper gave him a strange new sense of her nearness; yet it deepened his anguish by reminding him that henceforth they would have no other way of communicating with each other. For the life of her smile, the warmth of her voice, only cold paper and dead words!

Once in his room he lights the lamp, then bundles up in an overcoat and lies down on the bed. Though his delusion about Mattie continues unabated, Ethan does seem to understand with greater clarity the true nature of his relationship with Zeena. At the moment he was still a young man, not even in his thirties, and yet all he could see ahead of him was a wasted life.

> Confused motions of rebellion stormed in him. He was too young, too strong, too full of the sap of living, to submit so easily to the destruction of his hopes. Must he wear out all his years at the side of a bitter querulous woman? Other possibilities had been in him, possibilities sacrificed, one by one, to Zeena's narrow-mindedness and ignorance. And what good had come of it? (142)

In looking at Ethan's life as a symbol of the societal impositions placed on women, the gender reversal puts Zeena in the position of robbing him of all the options he had earlier in his life in which he could have created a different future for himself. This resembles the experiences of curious and intellectually minded young girls who suddenly found themselves forced to abandon that intellectual curiosity in order to focus their lives exclusively on finding a husband. In doing so they could only look forward to a life of repression amid "the constraints of a strict society that forbids women to have careers, admit to passion, to seek any life outside the rigid confines of the drawing room" (Springer 30). This was an especially difficult transition for some women, as things had been much different in their younger days, a circumstance author Ellen Moers addresses in discussing the childhood of many women writers at the time.

> In every age, whatever the social rules, there has always been one time of a woman's life, the years before puberty, when walking, running, climbing,

battling, and tumbling are as normal female as they are male activities . . . Little sisters were briefly and tantalizingly the equals of little brothers, sharers of infant pains and pleasures that boys quickly grew out of, but girls clung to despairingly at an inappropriate age. (Moers 130)

Ethan has experienced something similar and has had the same reaction to it. His early dreams when he was a young man, like those of a bright girl's hopes of self-actualization, have been completely crushed by the dominant force in his life in the form of Zeena, with the only result that she had become, "a hundred times bitterer and more discontented than when he had married her" (Wharton 1911, 142). It's then Ethan understands the true motivation behind her behavior. "The one pleasure left her was to inflict pain on him. All the healthy instincts of self-defense rose up in him against such waste . . ." (142). Yet his instincts aren't healthy, and as a consequence they push him instead toward imagining a fantasy life with Mattie that harkens back to his earlier college experiences "when he had tried to 'jolly' the Worcester girls at a picnic" (45).

Wharton indulges in a nice bit of symbolism here as Ethan lies back on the bed to think. "Under his cheek he felt a hard object with strange protuberances. It was a cushion which Zeena had made for him when they were engaged—the only piece of needlework he had ever seen her do. He flung it across the floor and propped his head against the wall . . ." (Wharton 1911, 142). The connotations associated with pillows are that they are soft and yielding, used for comfort and the easing of pain. In that context the connection of the pillow with the fact that it was made for him during their engagement implies that it symbolizes Zeena's ability as a woman to take care of Ethan emotionally. But instead of the comfortable pillow one would expect, it is appliquéd with "hard . . . protuberances." As such, Ethan feels no compunction at all in throwing her pillow across the room, and in doing so no doubt wishes subconsciously that he could do the same to Zeena. The pillow also has associations with the description of Zeena's clothing on the day of her trip. "Above her thin strands of hair, which still preserved the tight undulations of the crimping-pins, rose a hard perpendicular bonnet" (67). And it reflects the way Ethan described her earlier that evening in the bedroom, "so hard and lonely" (118), or after the discovery of the broken pickle dish in which her emotional outburst "left her more than ever like a shape of stone" (139). The rebellion that Ethan feels is reinforced by his anger toward Zeena and his feeling that this response is in "self-defense" to the "evil" with which she is actively punishing him, all of which presages his actions in the last two chapters.

Then Ethan begins to spin out another fantasy, this one based on the experience of a young man who had found himself in a similar predicament.

> He knew a case of a man over the mountain—a young fellow of about his own age—who had escaped from just such a life of misery by going West with the girl he cared for. His wife had divorced him, and he had married the girl and prospered. Ethan had seen the couple the summer before at Shadd's Falls, where they had come to visit relatives. They had a little girl with fair curls, who wore a gold locket and was dressed like a princess. The deserted wife had not done badly either. Her husband had given her the farm and she had managed to sell it, and with that and the alimony she had started a lunch-room at Bettsbridge and bloomed into activity and importance. Ethan was fired by the thought. (Wharton 1911, 142-143).

It's interesting that this is the only time the idea of children is invoked in the entire novel, and Ethan seems to have no issue with it, lending credence to the idea that perhaps Zeena has never wanted to have sex with him. It also subtly suggests a desire to have children with Mattie and all that implies. The success story is a good one, in which both the ex-wife and the husband come out better for having separated. "Why should he not leave with Mattie the next day, instead of letting her go alone? He would hide his valise under the seat of the sleigh, and Zeena would suspect nothing till she went upstairs for her afternoon nap and found a letter on the bed . . ." (143).

Inspired by the story Ethan gets up and gathers together a piece of paper and a pen to write a note to Zeena. It's important to understand exactly what he writes to her, as it will become significant in the following chapter. Ethan says, "Zeena, I've done all I could for you, and I don't see as it's been any use. I don't blame you, nor I don't blame myself. Maybe both of us will do better separate. I'm going to try my luck West" (144). But when Ethan tells her she can sell the mill and farm and keep the money, he finds he can't write any more. "His pen paused on the word, which brought home to him the relentless conditions of his lot. If he gave the farm and mill to Zeena what would be left him to start his own life with? . . . And what of Zeena's fate? Farm and mill were mortgaged to the limit of their value, and even if she found a purchaser—in itself an unlikely chance—it was doubtful if she could clear a thousand dollars on the sale." This gives him another idea, though, that Zeena will just have to go back and live with her family. After Ethan managed to situate himself, he could send her alimony. There's a certain satisfaction in that plan as it is the same fate that Zeena is forcing on Mattie. And then Ethan looks up and spies a copy of an old newspaper that he had folded down to an advertisement for trips out West at "Reduced Rates." But before he can look through the listings he realizes he doesn't even have the money for train fare, let alone anything to live on while he looks for work and a place to live. "A moment ago he had wondered what he and Mattie were to live on when they reached the West; now he saw that he had not even the money to take her there" (145).

Ethan doesn't consider trying to borrow the money, as his property is already mortgaged and so he has absolutely nothing to use for collateral. Slowly the reality of his situation sets in and he describes it in a way that accurately reflects the reality of his life. "The inexorable facts closed in on him like prison-warders handcuffing a convict. There was no way out—none. He was a prisoner for life, and now his one ray of light was to be extinguished" (Wharton 1911, 146). The ray of light here is used in its literal sense, similar to the light at the end of the tunnel that denotes escape. This section of the novel is also the most obvious parallel for the way Ethan represents the reality of married women in the late nineteenth-century. Like them, Ethan has no money, no prospects, and no ability to leave and start his life over. Even without the moral implications of abandoning his wife—which it must be stressed he is perfectly willing to do—he would simply be making himself homeless and destitute were he to attempt to leave Zeena. It's sobering, however, to consider that for women of that day things were even worse. Nevertheless, Ethan's poverty and lack of opportunity are almost identical to that of a woman. Without any money at all, he has no choice but to stay with his wife and suffer her abuse.

The use of the light metaphor at the end of the passage—"his one ray of light was to be extinguished"—is also appropriate, as Ethan still firmly believes in the fantasy that Mattie is in love with him. The ray of light that would have exposed this fallacy on attempting to carry out his plan is also gone—but not for good. As he goes back to the bed and tries to fight back the tears, "a pure moon swung into the blue."

> Ethan, rising on his elbow, watched the landscape whiten and shape itself under the sculpture of the moon. This was the night on which he was to have taken Mattie coasting, and there hung the lamp to light them! He looked out at the slopes bathed in lustre, the silver-edged darkness of the woods, the spectral purple of the hills against the sky, and it seemed as though all the beauty of the night had been poured out to mock his wretchedness . . . (Wharton 1911, 147)

The light of the moon is too weak to influence Ethan, and instead the more powerful metaphor is the "silver-edged darkness." The evocation of the silver edges of a sword is thus combined with the ignorance of darkness to demonstrate how fatal his rationalizations have been and create, in an extremely subtle way, another foreshadow of the ending. Ethan falls asleep, but the next morning he awakes to a dawn reminiscent of the one two days earlier. "He rubbed his eyes and went to the window. A red sun stood over the grey rim of the fields, behind trees that looked black and brittle." He thinks to himself that this is Mattie's last day on the farm, but the red sun brings with it the warning that his conflict with Zeena is far from over.

Later that morning Mattie comes down to begin cooking breakfast and goes into his room. She asks if he's been there all night but he says nothing, then he asks how she knew he was there. "Because I heard you go down stairs again after I went to bed, and I listened all night, and you didn't come up" (Wharton 1911, 148). Though Mattie's statement is certainly interpreted by Ethan as proof of her feelings for him, there's also nothing to suggest that her inability to sleep isn't simply a natural response to her being unceremoniously kicked out by Zeena and a contemplation of the uncertain future that lies ahead of her. Wharton then tells the reader that, "All his tenderness rushed to his lips," and yet Ethan says nothing and does nothing that might confirm or deny her feelings, and merely says that he will get the fire started in the kitchen for her. As he tends to the stove and Mattie goes about her business, he remarks on the normalcy of the scene, and it becomes easier for Ethan to delude himself about the severity of his argument with Zeena the night before. "He said to himself that he had doubtless exaggerated the significance of Zeena's threats, and that she too, with the return of daylight, would come to a saner mood." But the daylight is only going to make clearer Zeena's intent. Here Ethan goes over to Mattie and, repeating the phrase from her note, says, "I don't want you should trouble either" (148-149). Mattie smiles and agrees. He asks if she has seen Zeena yet, and when she says she hasn't he tells her, "Don't you take any notice when you do" (149). It's a friendly conversation, but little more. Mattie is resigned to going and while Ethan may believe differently, Mattie knows better. The previous evening, when Ethan tried to suggest that Zeena might change her mind about sending Mattie away, the girl responded with, "If she says it to-night she'll say it to-morrow" (132).

But Ethan's newfound confidence is shaken when he goes out to the barn. At first, "He saw Jotham Powell walking up the hill through the morning mist, and the familiar sight added to his growing conviction of security" (Wharton 1911, 149). A mist, however, in the same way as a cloud, implies obscurity and thus Ethan is able to convince himself that nothing has changed. Instead of providing consolation, Jotham says to him, "Dan'l Byrne's goin' over to the Flats to-day noon, an' he c'd take Mattie's trunk along, and make it easier ridin' when I take her over in the sleigh." At this the reader finally understands the reason for Jotham's refusal of supper the night before. Clearly Zeena had not only told him that she was getting rid of Mattie, but had made plans with him for her departure. Not wanting to get caught up in a family squabble, Jotham judiciously passed up the free meal. The fact that Zeena had already thought all of this through on her way home stuns Ethan, and Jotham continues. "Mis' Frome said the new girl'd be at the Flats at five, and I was to take Mattie then, so's 't she could ketch the six o'clock train for Stamford." The news is infuriating to Ethan—"Ethan felt the blood drumming in his temples"—and in a rare moment of defiance he tells Jotham that he isn't sure Mattie will be leaving (150). When the two of them finish with the horses and head back into the kitchen, Zeena is downstairs already in "an air of unusual alertness and activity. She drank two cups of coffee and fed the cat with the scraps left in the pie-dish." Again, the association between Mattie's leaving and Zeena's good mood is unmistakable. Zeena even gets up at one point and begins to prune the flowers that Ethan had potted for Mattie. "She rose from her seat and, walking over to the window, snipped two or three yellow leaves from the geraniums. 'Aunt Martha's ain't got a faded leaf on 'em; but they pine away when they ain't cared for,' she said reflectively." Several things become apparent here. Not only is Zeena taking over the flowers that were originally intended for Mattie, but her comment that they haven't been cared for seems an indictment of Mattie's inability to help Zeena regain her health. The further implication is that Zeena was fine in her family's care, and it was getting married to Ethan that made her sick. Ethan, seemingly helpless at this point, doesn't even comment as Zeena discusses plans for Mattie's departure with Jotham and the girl. Finally, after the two women leave the kitchen, Jotham says, "I guess I better let Dan'l come round, then" (151).

Back outside Ethan informs Jotham that he's going into the village and wants him to tell the women not to hold up dinner. "The passion of rebellion had broken out in him again. That which had seemed incredible in the sober light of day had really come to pass, and he was to assist as a helpless spectator at Mattie's banishment . . . He had made up his mind to do something, but he did not know what it would be" (Wharton 1911, 151). Naturally, Ethan sees the episode in terms of his imagined relationship with Mattie. "His manhood was humbled by the part he was compelled to play and by the thought of what Mattie must think of him." While he is walking he thinks of nothing but the girl, and Wharton again gives the reader another comparison of Mattie with a bird. "Once, in the stillness, the call of a bird in a mountain ash was so like her laughter that his heart tightened and then grew large; and all these things made him see that something must be done at once" (152). Unfortunately, what they don't make him see is that Mattie doesn't belong to him, and should not remain a part of his prison-like existence. Mattie is young and should be free as a bird, and it is Ethan's obsession with her that prevents him from understanding this.

The only thing Ethan can think to do is approach Andrew Hale again. Though the mill owner had refused him the first time, he had hinted later in their conversation that he might advance Ethan some money if he was in trouble and there was an urgent need. Ethan wouldn't lie, however, and was going to use the fact that Zeena was ill and the doctor required her to have a hired girl Ethan couldn't afford. While he sees in the act a diminution of his pride, it's interesting to juxtapose this humiliation at the hands of Hale with the way Mattie will view him, rationalizing to himself, "how much did pride count in the ebullition of passions in his breast?" (Wharton 1911, 152). His plan is to go directly to Hale's house before he leaves for work, that way his wife will also be there and since she is aware of Zeena's problems and is sympathetic, she will likely overcome any reservations her husband might have about advancing Ethan the money. Contradicting the assertion of so many Wharton scholars that it is Ethan's supposed "duty" to Zeena that ultimately prevents him from leaving her, the next line makes Ethan's intent perfectly clear: "And with fifty dollars in his pocket nothing could keep him from Mattie . . ." (153). As Ethan reaches the village he sees Hale's sleigh in the distance. "But as it drew nearer he saw that it was driven by the carpenter's youngest boy and that the figure at his side, looking like a large upright cocoon in spectacles, was that of Mrs. Hale." Ethan signals the sleigh to stop and asks Mrs. Hale if her husband is at home. She responds that he is. He wasn't feeling well, she says, and she had ordered him to stay home by the fire to get better. "Beaming maternally on Ethan, she bent over to add:

> I on'y just heard from Mr. Hale 'bout Zeena's going over to Bettsbridge to see that new doctor. I'm real sorry she's feeling so bad again! I hope he thinks he can do something for her. I don't know anybody round here's had more sickness than Zeena. I always tell Mr. Hale I don't know what she'd 'a' done if she hadn't 'a' had you to look after her; and I used to say the same thing 'bout your mother. You've had an awful mean time, Ethan Frome. (153-154)

After Mrs. Hale has driven off, Ethan simply stands and looks after the sleigh as it disappears out of sight. Her comments have been a breaking of the isolation that he usually lives within, and he feels heartened by her sympathy for him. Seeing as how she had talked to her husband about his position already, it didn't seem as if it would take too much pleading to convince Hale to lend him the money. Ethan begins walking again with renewed purpose, but then stops short after taking only a few steps. "For the first time, in the light of the words he had just heard, he saw what he was about to do. He was planning to take advantage of the Hales' sympathy to obtain money from them on false pretences. That was a plain statement of the cloudy purpose which had driven him in headlong to Starkfield" (Wharton 1911, 155). At this point Ethan refuses to go on, as the true nature of his circumstances closes in on him and reveals itself fully. "The madness fell and he saw his life before him as it was. He was a poor man, the husband of a sickly woman, whom his desertion would leave alone and destitute; and even if he had had the heart to desert her he could have done so only by deceiving two kindly people who had pitied him. He turned and walked slowly back to the farm."

Many writers see in his actions here Ethan's major flaw as a character. The fact that he simply gives up and relinquishes any chance at happiness is too grim to believe anyone would willingly accept. The problem, perhaps, is that it is actually too realistic. Fiction, after all, is a place where readers expect characters to take chances, to strive above human frailty and, even if they fail, still achieve a sort of nobility in their attempt. Giving up, on the other hand, hardly seems worthy of being immortalized on the page. Marlene Springer, for example, criticizes Ethan as a character for accepting "circumstances with resignation—refusing, for whatever reason, to look at the variety of moral options to [his] dilemma . . . There is no decisive clarity of desire within Ethan, and he becomes frozen in his nightmare" (Springer 10-11). And yet, once the reader understands Ethan's symbolic place within the novel—as the representative of women who genuinely had no options, moral or otherwise, and therefore actually came to see their desires as immaterial—then Ethan's passivity becomes less of a flaw than it does a recognition of the inherent unfairness in the assumed normalcy of the societal oppression of women. The inability—becoming "frozen"—to change their circumstances was a fact of life for women in Wharton's day, and therefore rather than seeing this as an internal character flaw of Ethan's, it should be viewed for what it really is, a limitation imposed on him from without. Regardless, Ethan's defeat is certainly not the result of a lack of effort on his part.

Both the substance of Ethan's thoughts during the time he was writing his letter to Zeena in the study—"she could go back to her people, then, and see what they would do for her"—as well as his clear intention here— "with fifty dollars in his pocket nothing could keep him from Mattie"— completely undercut the idea that it is Ethan's duty to Zeena that keeps him from abandoning her. Author Blake Nevius is representative of this view when he poses the question he sees occupying "the center of Edith Wharton's moral consciousness as it reveals itself in her fiction: what is the extent of one's moral obligation to those individuals who, legally or within the framework of existing manners, conventions, taboos, apparently have the strictest claim on one's loyalty" (Nevius 110). It couldn't be more clear that it is not any perceived loyalty to Zeena that keeps Ethan in Starkfield, and in that context the implication that he wouldn't have had "the heart to desert her" comes only when he realizes there is no way for him to get the money he needs and is therefore nothing more than a rationalization after the fact. Had Ethan possessed or been able to obtain the money that would have allowed him to leave, he certainly would have had the heart to do it. He knows full well that his wife still has family in the area and, however difficult her life might be, she would be taken care of in some way. Instead it is his own personal integrity— not a perceived obligation to others—that is the key to his capitulation. It is the need for deception that prevents him from going through with his plan. Taking money from the Hales would be tantamount to stealing from them, and that's something Ethan, for reasons of his own, simply cannot do.

One contemporary review of Wharton's novel actually touches on this idea, and in doing so inadvertently connects it with the unconscious conformity to societal expectations that women routinely experienced. In what is easily the most insightful review of her book, from *The Nation*, the anonymous reviewer still sees Ethan's final capitulation in terms of his obligation to Zeena—as almost all criticism does. From there, however, the reviewer also seems to sense that Ethan's collusion in his own imprisonment has less to do with Zeena's power than it does his own internal sense of morality.

> The profound irony of his case is that it required his own goodness to complete her parasitic power over him. Without his innate honesty and his sense of duty he could have escaped her demands and her decrees, refused the money for her nostrums and "doctor books," followed the vision of a new free life "out West." In his submission to obligation and in his thwarted intellectual aspirations he typifies the remnant of an exceptional race whose spiritual inheritance has dwindled amid hard conditions until all distinction is forfeited except that of suffering; but which still indicates its quality, if only by its capacity for suffering. (Lauer 118)

The real "profound irony" is that this review comes so close to articulating what is at the center of Wharton's novel that it's almost heartbreaking to see it take a wrong turn. As demonstrated above, Ethan's "innate honesty" is the key to his defeat, rather than any "sense of duty" he owes to Zeena. When the reviewer says that, "he typifies the remnant of an exceptional race," this is an obvious reference to the destitute progeny of New England's rural Puritan forefathers. But had that phrase been replaced with "he typifies the current state of women," it would have assessed precisely what has made *Ethan Frome* unconsciously resonate with readers for the past hundred years. In situating the seemingly endless capacity for female suffering in the form of a man, Wharton was able to penetrate the hearts of her readers, male and female alike, so that they could finally experience vicariously that terrible legacy of "submission to obligation" and "thwarted intellectual aspirations" shared by generations of American women, even if they didn't know that's what they were experiencing.

Chapter IX

When Ethan returns home he finds Daniel Byrne in his sleigh, waiting by the kitchen door for Mattie's trunk. Ethan goes inside and sees Zeena reading one of her medical books by the stove and asks where Mattie is. "Without lifting her eyes from the page she replied: 'I presume she's getting down her trunk'" (Wharton 1911, 156). Ethan is outraged at Zeena's indifference at the girl having to bring her heavy trunk down the stairs all by herself. But despite her apathetic exterior, Zeena is no doubt pleased at her ability to humiliate Mattie one last time before things return to normal. Ethan races up the stairs, but Mattie is still in her room. He knocks on the door and, in another subtle bit of symbolism, she doesn't answer and he has to let himself in. Ethan had only been in her room once before, but he can remember with precision every personal item that she had there. All of it is gone now, packed away in her trunk, on which she sits crying. "She had not heard Ethan's call because she was sobbing and she did not hear his step till he stood close behind her and laid his hands on her shoulders. 'Matt—oh, don't—oh, *Matt*!" (157-158). The final chapter of the internal story is the one that most readers see as conclusive evidence of Mattie's feelings of love toward Ethan. As such, it's even more important to examine every instance that lends itself to this interpretation and see if those moments truly convey what they are so often assumed.

When Mattie turns around, "She started up, lifting her wet face to his. 'Ethan—I thought I wasn't ever going to see you again!'" (Wharton 1911, 158). Her words here, while perhaps implying something more, are really no different than when she says later in the chapter, "There's never anybody been good to me but you" (175). And just because Mattie was crying, it doesn't mean that she was crying because she wasn't going to see Ethan before she left. It's also important to remove Mattie's dialogue from the realm of Ethan's point of view and look at it objectively in the context of her life. After the death of her parents Mattie had been taken in by relatives who, the revelations by Zeena make clear, didn't like her very much. It's not difficult to assume then that her time there was not very pleasant. In coming to stay with the Frome's, however, Ethan proceeded to bend over backward to help her and the two formed a friendship. As such, it's difficult to believe that a young girl like Mattie would even imagine that their relationship was anything but platonic. Ethan was not only married, but had also done and said nothing that could remotely be construed as an intent to pursue her romantically. So it is in this context that Ethan's embraces—as well as his kiss the previous evening—also must be viewed. "He took her in his arms, pressing her close, and with a trembling hand smoothed away the hair from her forehead" (158). He asks her why she thought she wouldn't see him, and she says Jotham gave them the news that they shouldn't wait on dinner. Then he suggests that she assumed he didn't want to be around during her departure. "She clung to him without answering, and he laid his lips on her hair." The verb "cling," it must be remembered, is Ethan's word, and even though the kiss is an intimate gesture she can't be entirely sure that's what he's doing, nor does she respond to this gesture in any way. Finally, they hear Zeena yell at them from the bottom of the stairs that they need to get the trunk into the sleigh or Daniel Byrne will leave without it.

They let go of each other at this point, as Ethan describes them, "with striken faces," though for Mattie her abandonment is reason enough for her fearful countenance (Wharton 1911, 158). "Words of resistance rushed to Ethan's lips and died there," as he is still unable to find within himself a means of exerting his superiority over Zeena, and in his passivity he reaffirms his position as the submissive partner in his marriage (159). Mattie, meanwhile, dries her eyes and the two of them haul the trunk out to the head of the stairs where Ethan takes over and carries it out to the sleigh. As they pass through the kitchen Zeena again refuses to look up from her reading. Outside, after the sleigh drives off, "Twice he opened his lips to speak to Mattie and found no breath. At length, as she turned to re-enter the house, he laid a detaining hand on her. 'I'm going to drive you over, Matt,' he whispered" (159-160). Mattie says she's pretty sure Zeena wants Jotham to drive her, but Ethan simply repeats his statement and the two go back inside to eat, where the true nature of Zeena's illness is once again revealed at the kitchen table.

> At dinner Ethan could not eat. If he lifted his eyes they rested on Zeena's pinched face, and the corners of her straight lips seemed to quiver away into a smile. She ate well, declaring that the mild weather made her feel

better, and pressed a second helping of beans on Jotham Powell, whose wants she generally ignored. (160)

Knowing what he does now about his wife's illness, watching her during the meal is an outrage. But it's almost as though it actually takes Zeena's glee at Mattie's dismissal to finally move Ethan to defy his wife.

After Mattie begins washing the dishes and Zeena removes herself to study her book again, Jotham gets up from the table and asks Ethan what time he should come over to pick up Mattie. "You needn't come round; I'm going to drive her over myself" (Wharton 1911, 161). At this Mattie blushes, not because she sees it as a gesture of love but because of her expectation of Zeena's reaction, similar to the reason Jotham didn't want to come in for supper the evening before. This is followed by "the quick lifting of Zeena's head. 'I want you should stay here this afternoon, Ethan,' his wife said. 'Jotham can drive Mattie over.'" But Ethan is determined to stand his ground this time. "He repeated curtly: 'I'm going to drive her over myself.'" Even with this, Zeena still has infinite belief in Ethan's weakness, and doesn't even raise her voice when she gives him his orders. "Zeena continued in the same even tone: 'I wanted you should stay and fix up that stove in Mattie's room afore the girl gets here. It ain't been drawing right for nigh on a month now.'" Ethan, on the other hand, has no need to disguise his feelings toward her anymore. "Ethan's voice rose indignantly. 'If it was good enough for Mattie I guess it's good enough for a hired girl.'" Even with this challenge to her authority, Zeena is still unwilling to abandon a technique that has always worked with him in the past. "'That girl that's coming told me she was used to a house where they had a furnace,' Zeena persisted with the same monotonous mildness." But at this Ethan has had enough. "'She'd better ha' stayed there then,' he flung back at her; and turning to Mattie he added in a hard voice: 'You be ready by three, Matt'" (162). Though Ethan doesn't stay to see the fallout, it will be revealed later.

Ethan's anger is foremost on his mind as he goes down to the barn with Jotham to get the horse ready for the trip. Because it is daylight, Wharton uses another element to suggest Ethan's blindness to Mattie's true feelings. "The pulses in his temples throbbed and a fog was in his eyes" (Wharton 1911, 163). Reinforcing this idea, he goes about his business without thinking, his emotions driving him, and it's not until the horse and sleigh are walked out of the barn that he remembers how much this day was like the one when he picked up Mattie a year before at the train station. After driving up to the house he gets out and goes into the kitchen, but it's empty. Mattie's bag and shawl are waiting by the door, but there's no sign of the girl or Zeena. He goes to the foot of the stairs and hears nothing. Then a noise coming from his study causes him to investigate, and he finds Mattie there. She is startled by his unexpected arrival, and asks, "Is it time?" Ethan wants to know what she is doing there and she responds that she was just looking around. It's not until they go back into the kitchen and Ethan picks up her bag that he asks about Zeena. "She went upstairs right after dinner." Mattie says. "She said she had those shooting pains again, and didn't want to be disturbed." The information is almost comical in the way that it clearly demonstrates how Zeena uses her supposed illness. She had been feeling fine that morning and the evening before because she knew she was getting rid of Mattie and there was nothing Ethan could do about it. As soon as Ethan defies her, however, she has a relapse and retreats to her bedroom. Ethan takes no time to consider this because all he can think of now is the fact that Mattie is leaving. "Ethan, looking slowly about the kitchen, said to himself with a shudder that in a few hours he would be returning to it alone" (164).

Ethan puts on a happy face and tucks Mattie into a bearskin after helping her into the sleigh. They are a full two hours ahead of when the train is scheduled to arrive and he plans on taking her for a ride before she has to leave.

> At the gate, instead of making for Starkfield, he turned the sorrel to the right, up the Bettsbridge road. Mattie sat silent, giving no sign of surprise; but after a moment she said: "Are you going round by Shadow Pond?" He laughed and answered: "I knew you'd know!" (Wharton 1911, 164-165)

This is another moment that demands careful scrutiny, especially given what comes later. When Ethan says, "I knew you'd know," what he is referring to is the belief that she understands *why* he's taking her to Shadow Pond. But the only thing that can be said with any certainty about Mattie's remark is that she knows *where* they are going when he makes the turn. "She drew closer under the bearskin," beside him, but that's because of the weather and in no way indicates a desire for Ethan, as he had thought to himself just moments earlier, "His face tingled and he felt dizzy, as if he had stopped in at the Starkfield saloon on a zero day for a drink" (164). The reference to a "zero day" means a day in which the temperature is thirty-two degrees below freezing. At the same time his feeling of being "dizzy," as though he had a drink, belies the fact that he can make any rational judgments about Mattie's actions. For example, he holds her hand underneath the blanket and she lets him, but she makes no direct response to it. In fact, she says absolutely nothing throughout the trip to the pond. When they get there Ethan helps her out of the sleigh. "It was a shy secret spot, full of the same dumb melancholy that Ethan felt in his heart. He looked up and down the little pebbly beach till his eye lit on a fallen tree-trunk half submerged in snow. 'There's where we sat at the picnic,' he reminded her" (166). The "dumb melancholy" of the scene also reflects Ethan's inability to articulate to Mattie what he is feeling, while the fact that the tree is "submerged in snow" symbolizes that the event he is thinking about does not have the actual significance he wants to ascribe to it.

In a lengthy paragraph Wharton describes the church picnic Ethan refers to, one that took place at the pond the summer before. To begin with, the very name of the place, Shadow Pond, symbolically suggests a darkness that has prevented Ethan from understanding the true nature of what transpired there. Even though this was months after she had arrived, and Ethan had claimed in the first chapter that he was taken with her from the very beginning, it's significant that he refused to go to the picnic with Mattie when she asked him. Coming back to the house from cutting wood he was met by some of the people who had attended the festivities and so he decided to stop by for a few minutes. There he saw "Mattie, encircled by facetious youths, and bright as a blackberry under her spreading hat . . . brewing coffee over a gipsy fire" (Wharton 1911, 167). It's doubtful that Mattie had met many people or come to know them well over the few months she had been in Starkfield. And even with the young men flocking around her it would have been understandable, upon seeing a friendly face, "the way she had broken through the group to come to him with a cup in her hand." While they were sitting together on a fallen log she discovered that her necklace was missing, and the boys fell all over themselves trying to find it, but it was Ethan who discovered it in some moss. And then, as if punctuating the fact that very little should be made of the event, he says, "that was all." These are the same words that preceded their evening together when Ethan was leaving for the day.

And yet, even in the dead of the winter snow, Ethan still attempts to manufacture retrospective feelings of love from her on that day. "Their intercourse had been made up of just such inarticulate flashes, when they seemed to come suddenly upon happiness as if they had surprised a butterfly in the winter woods . . ." (Wharton 1911, 167). Ethan's reference to the inarticulateness of their intercourse suggests a decided lack of evidence on which to base the presumption of any kind of romantic relationship. The sudden happiness he mentions is certainly reflective of his own feelings— though perhaps only in retrospect—but can hardly be said to describe Mattie's. He puts his foot out to touch the place he found her locket and she remarks on his keen eyesight. Then he says how beautiful she looked in the hat she was wearing, and she decides to tease him. "She laughed with pleasure. 'Oh, I guess it was the hat!' she rejoined" (168). There is still no evidence here that her conversation is anything other than the normal expression of her natural character. She is not morose in any way, which would certainly be expected if, on the precipice of her imminent departure, she were actually in love with Ethan. *If* she actually knew how he felt about her, and *if* she felt the same way about him, there's no one to hide that fact from now that they are alone together in the woods and she about to leave him forever. And yet despite her silence on the matter that is exactly what Ethan hears. "They had never before avowed their inclination so openly, and Ethan, for a moment, had the illusion that he was a free man, wooing the girl he meant to marry." It's incredibly easy for the reader to be seduced into seeing things from Ethan's point of view, despite Wharton's reminder that this is nothing but an "illusion." What carries much more analytical weight is the way Ethan's interpretation about Mattie's behavior at the picnic is proven later in their conversation to be entirely wrong.

Mattie gets to her feet and tells him that they'd better be going, but Ethan doesn't want to leave yet. "There were things he had to say to her before they parted, but he could not say them in that place of summer memories, and he turned and followed her in silence to the sleigh" (Wharton 1911, 168-169). Ethan's decision to remain mute and Mattie's inability to know how he feels about her is symbolically reinforced by Wharton's description of the setting. "As they drove away the sun sank behind the hill and the pine-boles turned from red to grey . . . The clumps of trees in the snow seemed to draw together in ruffled lumps, like birds with their heads under their wings" (169). The setting sun is accompanied by a loss of light that prevents Ethan from understanding the true nature of his relationship with Mattie, even leaching the color from the scenery as it turns everything gray. To extend that symbolism further Wharton compares the trees to birds with their "heads under their wings" indicating that Mattie, who has been associated with birds throughout the novel, is still ignorant of Ethan's feelings for her. The two make their way back to the Starkfield road and Ethan asks Mattie what her plans are. After a moment she says she'll try to get a position as a sales clerk in a store. Ethan reminds her of how damaging it had been to her health in the past, but she tells him she is much stronger than she was before she came to Starkfield. In a way, their conversation here is reflective of when he asked if she had intended to walk home alone in the dark and she replied that she wouldn't be scared. Ethan asks if there are any of her father's relatives who could help her out, but of course after what he did to them she says, "There isn't any of 'em I'd ask" (170). Then he tells her that he would do anything for her if he could, but he can't. Finally, he is unable to hold back any longer. "'Oh, Matt,' he broke out, 'if I could ha' gone with you now I'd ha' done it—'"

Mattie's response to Ethan's confession requires close scrutiny. In lieu of an actual answer, she reaches into her pocket and pulls out the note that Ethan had written to Zeena the night before, which she found in his study. Ethan, of course, can only respond to this in one way. "Through his astonishment there ran a fierce thrill of joy. 'Matt—' he cried; 'if I could ha' done it, would you?'" (Wharton 1911, 170). Here, at last, is a direct question asked of Mattie about her intention toward Ethan. And yet, even in this context, her response is rather shocking. "'Oh, Ethan, Ethan—what's the use?' With a sudden movement she tore the letter in shreds and sent them fluttering off into the snow" (170-171). It's important to remember that Ethan's note said absolutely nothing about Mattie. His message to Zeena was simply that he was leaving her in order to try his luck out West, presumably alone. And this has to be Mattie's understanding as well. Had she assumed that when Ethan said "if I could ha' done it, would you?" he meant that they would be leaving as a couple and living a life together, there would obviously be some benefit to her in urging him to try as she wouldn't be alone and wouldn't be homeless, and yet she responds by saying, "what's the use?" One interpretation of her remark could be that she is asking what's the use of talking about it since there's no way it can happen. But what she says next demonstrates that this is clearly not the intent of her question. In the first place, her remark is followed by some powerful symbolism by Wharton. When Mattie tears up the note she tosses the bits of torn paper into the wind and thus they become associated with the snow, as though the inability of Ethan and Mattie to escape is a reaffirmation of a social order they are powerless to defy. But even though this action can be read either way, what follows cannot.

For the reader it seems clear that Ethan's desire to leave on the same night as Mattie can have only one meaning, and when he expresses his desire to leave with her it must have confirmed that fact in her mind. And yet her response in tearing up the note is not one of affirmation. This causes Ethan to beg for one. "'Tell me, Matt! Tell me!' he adjured her" (Wharton 1911, 171). But even then she still doesn't answer him directly. Instead, she thinks for a few moments and says, "I used to think of it sometimes, summer nights when the moon was so bright I couldn't sleep." What is so fascinating about this sentence is the pronoun "it." What, exactly, is "it?" For Ethan, there is no question. "His heart reeled with the sweetness of it. 'As long ago as that?'" In his mind there can be no other meaning to her statement than as a confirmation of his fantasy, that she really had been thinking of running away with him as long ago as the church picnic. And her response to his question seems to confirm it. "She answered, as if the date had long been fixed for her: 'The first time was at Shadow Pond.'" But in looking closely at what she is really saying here, Mattie's answer is curiously inconclusive. Her comment manages to pull together for Ethan everything that he has imagined over the past year and so he naturally replies, "Was that why you gave me my coffee before the others?" And yet this is what Mattie says in response: "I don't know. Did I?"

At this point it suddenly becomes clear to the reader that Ethan and Mattie are once again having two separate conversations, just the way they had on their walk home from the dance. There was a hint of this at the start of the trip when Ethan believed she understood why he was taking her to Shadow Pond and yet she had been simply talking about where they were going. Looking back at the church picnic in light of Mattie's responses to Ethan makes her end of the conversation much more comprehensible now. The assumption that Mattie's desire to have Ethan attend the picnic was only to have someone there she knew, can now be confirmed by looking closely at her use of the word "it" when she says "I used to think of it sometimes" (Wharton 1911, 171). Again, the note that Ethan had written to Zeena never mentioned Mattie at all; it only said that he was going away to the West. Thus when Ethan tells Mattie that he wanted to leave with her she takes this to mean that they would both be leaving Starkfield at the same time, but not necessarily as a couple, and presumably heading to different destinations. This is reinforced when Ethan pushes her for an answer about leaving and she says that it's no use. What's no use? The answer to that question is escape. This is the "it" that she had first thought about the summer before, the ability to get away and start a new life somewhere else—not running away with Ethan. The fact that the first time she thought about it was at Shadow Pond is conclusive. She would have had absolutely no idea of Ethan's feelings back in the summer—especially since he wouldn't even go with her—and so her idea of escape would necessarily have been about her alone. The feeling came upon her at that time because she felt so isolated at the picnic among people she didn't know, which is the reason she wanted Ethan to go with her in the first place.

What is conclusive in demonstrating that Shadow Pond has nothing to do with imagined romantic feelings Mattie had for Ethan has to do with the fact that when he mentions she brought him his coffee first as an expression of love for him, she says she doesn't even remember doing it. In this way the moment that, for Ethan, definitively proved her mutual affection for him has an entirely different meaning for Mattie, which is reinforced when she follows that by saying, "I was dreadfully put out when you wouldn't go to the picnic with me" (Wharton 1911, 171). As such, her happiness when he did arrive had far more to do with alleviating her loneliness rather than any romantic notions about an older married man. Given all of that, it's not difficult to see the next part of their conversation as the continuation of a wider understanding of Mattie's words and actions in terms of friendship, a desire to alleviate her loneliness, especially when Wharton prefaces the scene with more darkness. "They had reached the point where the road dipped to the hollow by Ethan's mill and as they descended the darkness descended with them, dropping down like a black veil from the heavy hemlock boughs" (171-172). The descent of the two under the "hemlock" branches is another obvious foreshadow of the attempted suicide to come. More importantly, with the "black veil" of ignorance having descended upon them, as well as their being no prohibition against Mattie speaking from her heart now that she is leaving, the reading of their dialogue at this point can only be seen as a continuation of the two separate conversations they have carried on throughout the novel. Ethan begins by saying, "I'm tied hand and foot, Matt. There isn't a thing I can do," which Mattie hears as either an inability to help her financially or to escape himself (172). Mattie reinforces the idea when she tells him, "You must write to me sometimes, Ethan." This is an oddly dismissive statement for someone who is supposed to be in love, but perfectly reasonable for someone who merely values his friendship.

Ethan responds to the idea of written correspondence with frustration at the limited nature of that communication. "Oh, what good'll writing do? I want to put my hand out and touch you. I want to do for you and care for you. I want to be there when you're sick and when you're lonesome" (Wharton 1911, 172). Though the reader naturally understands what Ethan's intent is here, it's important to see how easily misrepresentative this statement actually is in conveying what he means. He speaks of the utility of writing to her as doing little good, and follows this with a list of things it won't allow him to do, touch and care for her, and to be there when she's sick and lonesome. Touching her simply means that he will be there in person in order to provide the care that a friend would, a hand on the shoulder, and this is reinforced when he also mentions taking care of her when she's sick and lonely. But again, this is an odd thing for someone professing his love to say in its implication that were he actually free to go with her she would still have occasion to be lonely in the context of a love relationship with him. Mattie's response, then, is understandable, when she asks him to assume she'll be all right rather than saying she wants him to be with her too. Of course this prompts Ethan to bring up marriage again. "You won't need me, you mean? I suppose you'll marry!" Ethan is obviously referring to the emotional need for love, but by coupling it with the idea that her marriage to someone else will supersede any need for his presence it makes it seem as if he's talking about need in terms of the financial and emotional support of a friend. Additionally, the mention of marriage is also going to bring up Mattie's latent concern about finding a husband who will not only be good to her but is willing to marry a poor woman with nothing to her name.

She says Ethan's name, here, as a way of getting him to stop, but he plunges ahead. In reference to his mention of her getting married he says something extraordinary. "I don't know how it is you make me feel, Matt. I'd a'most rather have you dead than that!" (Wharton 1911, 172). What can Mattie possibly make of Ethan saying that *he doesn't* know how she makes him feel? The expectation for the reader here is that he would say *she* doesn't know the full extent of his feelings for her—*you* don't know how it is you make me feel—but he seems to be saying the opposite. And with her thoughts already on the seeming impossibility of getting married herself, what does she really make of the word "that" when he says, "I'd a'most rather have you dead than that?" If Mattie's thoughts are in a completely different place than Ethan's, on the hopelessness of finding a future husband and having a family, it's quite possible she hears Ethan's "that" as referring to the absence of those things and so she is compelled to agree with him that death is preferable to her being alone. Then it would naturally follow that she responds by saying, "Oh, I wish I was, I wish I was!" When Ethan hears this he is horrified, as much for the fact that he doesn't want her dead as for the jealousy in his heart that provoked him to mention marriage again. "The sound of her weeping shook him out of his dark anger, and he felt ashamed. 'Don't let's talk that way,' he whispered." Mattie's response to this is fascinating. "'Why shouldn't we, when it's true? I've been wishing it every minute of the day.'" By saying "we" she is referencing the fact that she believes the two of them have been talking about her death, the "it" she has been thinking about all day. Again, with absolutely no intimation on her part that she shares in Ethan's feelings, her wish to be dead can only be related to the fact that she has nowhere to go but back to family that hates her, has no prospect of employment or marriage, and feels that she doesn't have the strength to go on. There's also the possibility that she fears the same thing Ethan does, the "miserable tales he had heard at Worcester, and the faces of girls whose lives had begun as hopefully as Mattie's . . ." which can only be a reference to prostitution (133).

As Elizabeth Ammons points out, once marriage has been eliminated there were very few options in that day for a woman of Mattie's age and inexperience. "She can work in a factory and lose her health; she can become a prostitute and lose her self-dignity as well; she can marry a farmer and lose her mind" (Ammons 71). Ethan himself certainly understands the limited choices and consequences associated with each of them. "Despair seized him at the thought of her setting out alone to renew the weary quest for work. In the only place where she was known she was surrounded by indifference or animosity; and what chance had she, inexperienced and untrained, among the million bread-seekers of the cities? (Wharton 1911, 132-133). The oft-cited work in *Ethan Frome* scholarship by Anna Garland Spencer, *Woman's Share in Social Culture* from 1912, exposes the wide-ranging abuse of single women—which included twelve-hour shifts and a high likelihood of illness or physical mutilation—present in all newly industrialized societies. But for women this was just one aspect of unregulated factory life that negatively affected the health and lives of men and children as well. The most extreme example in American history is the Triangle Shirtwaist Factory fire in which one hundred and twenty-three women and twenty-three men perished as a result of the common practice of locking workers inside the factory so they couldn't take unauthorized breaks. The majority of the women killed in the fire were between the ages of fourteen and twenty-three. Farm life for many young women was not much better physically, and in many ways worse emotionally as the article from *The American Journal of Insanity* previously demonstrated. The irony for many unskilled women of that day was that prostitution, while the most emotionally degrading of options, was also the most well paid. As Marlene Springer points out, "a prostitute could earn in one night what a working woman earned in a week. The hours were shorter—usually from nine in the evening until two in the morning. If the woman lived in even an average brothel, the meals were guaranteed, and she was allowed to sleep in the morning and have her afternoons free" (Springer 74).

Now that it has been established that Ethan and Mattie are speaking together about completely different things, the next exchange of dialogue makes some kind of sense in terms of the ending of the interior story. "Matt! You be quiet! Don't you say it," Ethan tells her, the "it" referring to her desire for death (Wharton 1911, 172). But she responds by saying, "There's never anybody been good to me but you" (173). All along, Ethan's half of the conversation has been narrowly confined to himself and his imagined relationship with Mattie, while she has been talking in a much wider context. To say that he's the only one who has ever been good to her is a reference to her treatment by Zeena, her extended family, and even Denis Eady. And in wishing she were dead, someone who was nice to her would naturally want to find a way to help her kill herself. As such, Ethan's response is rather chilling. "Don't say that either, when I can't lift a hand for you!" In terms of finding a way to commit suicide, Ethan is really the only person who can "lift a hand" for her, and while this is obviously not her intent she almost implies as much when she says, "Yes; but it's true just the same." Ethan, meanwhile, is hearing her words through his belief that they have already openly confessed their love for each other. All of which leads to their arrival in the village and the sight of children sledding. "As they drew near the end of the village the cries of children reached them, and they saw a knot of boys, with sleds behind them, scattering across the open space before the church."

With a complete understanding of the true nature of Mattie's dialogue with Ethan, from this point forward the story takes an ominous turn and everything Mattie says and does can be seen in light of her desire to kill herself. Ethan looks at the sky and, with winter about to break, he notes that the children may not be able to sled much longer after that night. Mattie says nothing in response. Then Ethan mentions that they were to have gone sledding themselves the night before but didn't. Still, she remains silent. When Ethan continues talking, Wharton describes him as "prompted by an obscure desire to help himself and her through their miserable last hour," which is another foreshadow of the climax to come (Wharton 1911, 174). Again, Mattie is eerily quiet as he remarks that they had only gone sledding once the previous winter. The structure Wharton uses in Mattie's response this time is worth noting. "She answered: 'It wasn't often I got down to the village.'" Mattie simply answers, preceded by a colon, as her intent is not really to engage in conversation. And her reference to not getting down to the village also underscores the isolated nature of her life as she sees it. Again, all of this is extremely odd behavior for someone who is assumed to be separating forever from the man she supposedly loves. "They had reached the crest of the Corbury road, and between the indistinct white glimmer of the church and the black curtain of the Varnum spruces the slope stretched away below them without a sled on its length." Though the "black curtain" is on just one side of the slope, it still suggests that Ethan has absolutely no conception of how much Mattie's conversation is disconnected from his own, especially when it is coupled with a reference to the white church and it's information that Ethan repressed while watching her at the dance. "Some erratic impulse prompted Ethan to say: 'How'd you like me to take you down now?'" Unlike her spontaneous laughter at Shadow Pond when she had been able to put aside her thoughts of suicide, now "she forced a laugh," and says there isn't time. But Ethan dismisses the suggestion and tells her to come along with him. "His one desire now was to postpone the moment of turning the sorrel toward the Flats."

Mattie expresses concern that the hired girl at the station will have to wait for them, but Ethan doesn't care, and says that it's better for the other girl to wait than Mattie. "The note of authority in his voice seemed to subdue her, and when he had jumped from the sleigh she let him help her out, saying only, with a vague feint of reluctance: 'But there isn't a sled round anywheres'" (Wharton 1911, 175). Ethan sees one over by the spruce trees, however, and pulls Mattie along with him. "She seated herself obediently and he took his place behind her, so close that her hair brushed his face." Just as it had been during their evening together, Ethan's sense of ownership is evident in the way he views his relationship with her; the "authority" in his voice "subdues" her, and she "obediently" takes her seat on the sled. When Mattie expresses concern about the darkness, Ethan jokes that he can coast down safely with his eyes tied, and the two laugh together. Nevertheless, Ethan is still aware of the truth behind her concern. "He sat still a moment, straining his eyes down the long hill, for it was the most confusing hour of the evening, the hour when the last clearness from the upper sky is merged with the rising night in a blur that disguises landmarks and falsifies distances" (175-176). While obviously describing the physical setting, it's difficult not to see this as a symbolic underscoring of Ethan's lack of comprehension as to the true nature of his conversation with Mattie.

Once Ethan has made sure she's ready, he and Mattie push off and head down the slope. "They flew on through the dusk, gathering smoothness and speed as they went . . . Mattie sat perfectly still, but as they reached the bend at the foot of the hill, where the big elm thrust out a deadly elbow, he fancied that she shrank a little closer" (Wharton 1911, 176). Even now, Ethan is couching Mattie's actions in a way that makes them something he still has to interpret. He urges her not to be scared as they head down the second part of the slope, and when they reach the bottom, "he heard her give a little laugh of glee." Then the two walk back up the slope arm in arm. Again, he asks if she was scared, and she affirms that she wasn't. But there's a subtle difference to her assent this time that suggests a change in her thought process. As fun as the coast down the hill was, it's difficult to believe that her thoughts of suicide are not still with her. What she actually says to Ethan is, "I told you I was never scared with you" (177). In fact, she had never said anything of the kind before. The implication in the two previous instances of asserting her bravery is that she was not afraid on her own, which had nothing to do with Ethan. This change in the intent of Mattie's dialogue is important in light of what Ethan says next. "The strange exaltation of his mood had brought on one of his rare fits of boastfulness. 'It is a tricky place, though. The least swerve, and we'd never ha' come up again. But I can measure distances to a hair's-breadth— always could.'" Mattie agrees that his eyesight was always keen, a reference that seems to go back to his finding her locket, but also suggests an ability to completely control what happens to the sled as he guides it down the hill. Ethan thinks to himself that this is the last time they will walk together, and when he asks if she's tired she replies, "It was splendid!" Then Ethan guesses that the sled probably belongs to Ned Hale and he puts it back where he found it leaning against the fence. Wharton once again lets the reader know that the two of them, next to the spruce trees, were also "among the shadows" (178).

What happens next is the principle spot in the narrative that is used to justify the interpretation that Mattie's feelings for Ethan are the same as his love for her. In fact, it may very well be that this was Wharton's intent while writing the novel. But with the accumulated mass of literal and symbolic evidence prior to this moment, and an understanding of a much broader context for Mattie's words and actions, that kind of reading just seems too out of place at this point in the story. "'Is this where Ned and Ruth kissed each other?' she whispered breathlessly, and flung her arms about him. Her lips, groping for his, swept over his face, and he held her fast in a rapture of surprise" (Wharton 1911, 178). While it may at first seem there is only one reason to account for Mattie's actions here, a completely different reason for her kiss emerges when she says immediately after, "'Good-bye—good-bye,' she stammered, and kissed him again." This, combined with her earlier statement that, "There's never anybody been good to me but you," argues for the idea that this is merely a goodbye kiss with the only person in her life who has ever shown her any kindness. Far from leaving it open to interpretation, however, Wharton then goes on to reinforce this idea by juxtaposing Mattie's actions with Ethan's words. In response to her kiss he says, "Oh, Matt, I can't let you go!" but instead of bringing them closer, Wharton defies expectations yet again with a very pointed use of verb, saying that Mattie "freed herself from his hold." In this way Ethan's desire to hold on to Mattie is not only not reciprocated, but she is described as *freeing* herself from him.

Finally, as she is sobbing, she says, "Oh, I can't go either!" Again, while in a superficial way this would seem to imply that she feels the same way he does, it's important to note that Mattie's is a very different statement than Ethan's. His emphasis, as always, is on himself. The verb "to go," from Ethan's perspective, clearly means *leaving him*. But Mattie's emphasis is actually on the verb itself, the fact that she is being forced "to go" somewhere else. While he says that he can't let *her go*, she doesn't say that she can't *leave him*. Instead, she simply says that she doesn't want to go. In addition, the word "either" at the end of the sentence is a synonym for "also," which further indicates her belief that both of their statements are only about the verb. And all of this makes sense when looked at in conjunction with her decision not to encourage Denis Eady. In that scene her motivation wasn't a desire to be with Ethan, but a desire not to be with Eady. And one can go back even further in the story, to the opening scene at the post office. It wasn't Ethan's desire to pick up his mail that made him go through the effort of hitching up his horse every day, but a desire to escape from the house. Similarly, Ethan's statement here means he does not want her to *leave him*, while her words indicate that it is the place she must *go to* that she wants to avoid, not a desire to stay with him. Ultimately it is the thought of a doomed future on her own that torments Mattie, not a future without Ethan.

While Ethan desperately wants to think of something else to do, Wharton describes the two of them clinging "to each other's hands like children" (Wharton 1911, 178). This is another subtle way of connecting Ethan with Mattie's powerlessness as a female in this time period. Neither of them has the ability to control their own lives in the same way that children are dependent on their parents, a state that also reflects the childlike treatment of the narrator in "The Yellow Wall-Paper." When the church bell rings out five o'clock, Mattie starts to panic because they are already late. But Ethan is determined that she shouldn't leave. When she says, "If I missed my train where'd I go?" he responds with the sobering reality: "Where are you going if you catch it?" They stand silently together for a few moments before Ethan says, "What's the good of either of us going anywheres without the other one now?" (179). Despite his frequent intimations of a relationship between the two of them in which they leave Starkfield as a couple, this is actually the only time Ethan has stated it so directly. Significantly, Wharton says about Mattie that "she remained motionless, as if she had not heard him." She possibly didn't, as the formulation she is making in her mind is revealed by the action she takes next—though more probably Ethan's question is the reason for her subsequent action. "She snatched her hands from his, threw her arms about his neck, and pressed a sudden drenched cheek against his face. 'Ethan! Ethan! I want you to take me down again!'" At first her request confuses him, and Ethan asks where, to which she replies, "The coast. Right off,' she panted. 'So 't we'll never come up any more." Not sure that he fully grasps her meaning, Ethan asks Mattie to explain. "She put her lips close against his ear to say: 'Right into the big elm. You said you could. So 't we'd never have to leave each other any more.'"

Ethan's reaction to the suggestion of suicide is the same as it was earlier. "Why, what are you talking of? You're crazy!" (Wharton 1911, 179). Twice now, in the most vehement manner possible, Ethan has expressed his revulsion to the very idea of suicide, which can only mean that Mattie must take a different tack with him if she is going to be able to talk him into helping her. It must be remembered that while Ethan is hearing all of this for the first time, Mattie has been thinking about it for at least twenty-four hours. She is, in fact, so desperate not to be cast out alone into the world that she does the only thing she can think of to coerce Ethan into agreeing with her plan. "'I'm not crazy;

but I will be if I leave you." . . . She tightened her fierce hold about his neck. Her face lay close to his face.

> Ethan, where'll I go if I leave you? I don't know how to get along alone. You said so yourself just now. Nobody but you was ever good to me. And there'll be that strange girl in the house . . . and she'll sleep in my bed, where I used to lay nights and listen to hear you come up the stairs . . ." (179-180)

This is the only place in the entire story where Mattie seems to be directly professing a desire for Ethan, especially the implication that she will go crazy "if I leave you." But again, taken in context, the true motivation behind this statement must be seen as taking place in within her overall desire to end her life. It is her desperation that has driven her to this, and she can't do it alone. The precise nature of her words here also demands closer scrutiny.

Throughout the final chapter of the internal story of the novel, despite the fact that they are alone and that she will be leaving forever, there is never once when Mattie declares her love for Ethan. In this, the second-person pronoun "you" she uses here is very deceptive. She first declares that she will go crazy if she leaves Ethan. But what is that actually saying? In leaving Ethan she will be alone, homeless and penniless. The misery that will cause could very well prey on her mind and make her feel as if she's going crazy—not being without Ethan. This idea is reinforced when she asks him where she will go if she leaves him. Again, the emphasis is not on being without him but what she will face by herself in the future. Next she repeats the phrase that he is the only one who was ever good to her, which was shown earlier to be merely a statement of fact. Finally, the image of a strange girl in the house occupying her bed is clearly manipulative in nature. What's so telling is that she never attempts to use this manipulation to get Ethan to leave Zeena and run away with her. There's no denying that the couple would face tremendous challenges in attempting to start a new life from scratch, with no money, but if she really was in love with him the reader's expectation is that she would certainly make the attempt to convince him to try. Instead, her manipulation is only used to get Ethan to kill the two of them. She knows Ethan hates his wife and believes that, like her, he may be better off dead. But that's not a very satisfying explanation for forcing another person to give up his life in order to help her end hers, and so making him think that she loves him may be the only way to get him to go along with her scheme. And while it's tempting to suddenly see Mattie's behavior here in a way that is just as cold and calculating as Zeena's, there has been nothing to suggest that in her character throughout the rest of the novel. Instead, it is the desperation of the moment that forces her into this subterfuge.

Author Gary Scharnhorst is the only Wharton scholar to attempt an in-depth look at the character of Mattie, in his essay "The Two Faces of Mattie Silver." And while he winds up making some preposterous suggestions that are in no way supported by a close reading of the novel, his willingness to forego looking at her character from Ethan's subjective point of view makes him one of the only critics to attempt an assessment of their relationship in a truly objective way. Wharton's own emphasis on the narrator's sophistication, and by association his objectivity, he states, "has misled readers into assuming that Mattie . . . somehow loves Ethan as much as Ethan protests he loves her . . . [but] Mattie has no romantic interest in Ethan, save what he imagines" (Scharnhorst 263, 264). Unfortunately, his contention that "Mattie seems a conniving minx who plays on [Ethan's] goodwill in a vain attempt to remain in Starkfield" in order to marry Denis Eady, springs from interpretive assumptions that fail to hold up over the course of the novel (263). Scharnhorst clearly understands the numerous ways in which Ethan's belief about Mattie's interest in him is a fabrication stemming from his desire, and yet at the same time he is unable to completely shake off Ethan's interpretation of what Mattie says and does, twisting her words and actions in such a way that it turns these imagined behaviors into an unconvincing long-term manipulation of Ethan. He sees Mattie's dialogue in this scene as implicitly offering herself sexually to Ethan if he'll find a way to get Zeena to allow her to stay, but that doesn't even fit with his own reading of her pursuit of Eady. Scharnhorst also ignores Mattie's thoughts of suicide over the past day and claims that it is only Ethan's refusal to keep her at the farm that prompts her desire to end her life. The real misstep in looking at the story in this way can be seen in the author's own characterization of the future Mattie faces as suffering the "indignities of homelessness," a rather dismissive view of the true horror of abandonment for a single woman in her day (270). In the end there is simply a much better explanation for Mattie's attempt to manipulate Ethan in order to "use him as her executioner."

Though the preponderance of evidence suggests that Mattie has either not understood Ethan's intentions, or has ignored them because she felt it was morally wrong to encourage him, there is certainly an argument to be made that by the end of their journey Mattie has understood with clarity Ethan's feelings for her. If Mattie had felt morally responsible for Ethan's break from his wife, that could also add to her desire to kill herself, and explain why she had deflected his initial concern when Zeena dismissed her, telling him not to go to any trouble. But if she further felt that Ethan's desire to abandon his wife was as morally reprehensible as her desire to kill herself, then it could be another explanation for the way she urges him forward to embrace a mutual suicide pact with her, especially when leaving his wife could cause the same destruction of his life as she envisioned for herself. Of course Ethan can't possibly know any of this, and sees her request in the only way he can.

> The words were like fragments torn from his heart. With them came the hated vision of the house he was going back to—of the stairs he would have to go up every night, of the woman who would wait for him there. And the sweetness of Mattie's avowal, the wild wonder of knowing at last that all that had happened to him had happened to her too, made the other vision more abhorrent, the other life more intolerable to return to . . . (Wharton 1911, 180)

It's one thing for a person to contemplating ending her own life. It's quite another to be able to convince someone else to end his as well. So it speaks to a tremendous hatred of his life with Zeena that it doesn't take much more than Ethan's perception of Mattie's love to get him to agree.

Author Geoffrey Walton makes an interesting observation about Ethan's decision here. "Though the final act is described as 'some erratic impulse,' one feels that it is the last of a sequence. The last 'coast' down the frozen hill and the suicide pact that fails are a symbolic culmination, very powerfully rendered, of the main theme of head-on frustration" (Walton 88). This is an insightful comment because there is an inevitability to Ethan's decision to commit suicide. The literal frustration he faces with Zeena is simply a symbolic representation of the societal frustrations faced by all women, and in that context his death wish is no different from that of Chopin's protagonists in *The Awakening* and "The Story of an Hour," or the symbolic mental death for the narrator in Gilman's "Yellow Wall-Paper." Like all of those characters Ethan as finally achieved his greatest desire—even if it's only in his mind—and in the same way as Louise Mallard, he can't go back. Ethan's thoughts of spending the rest of his life with Zeena, however, are not nearly as forceful in explaining his decision to kill himself as the thoughts of Wharton's protagonist in the French short story that was the basis for her novel:

> A dark spirit had seized Hart. Life was too cruel and empty. Days and months and years would come too slowly and he would see too much of it. He saw himself growing old on the farm in front of his wife, harassed by her complaints, struggling against the worries of money, and struggling under the icy cold of winter and under the blazing sun of the summer. And

never another ray of happiness would come to light his poor, deprived life. (MacCallan 47)

The key to understanding Ethan's decision to kill himself is not that he is giving up the hope of achieving his dream of finally being loved, because in his mind he has already achieved it. In going back to Zeena, then, he is not so much giving up hope in the future as he is throwing away the love he believes he already possesses.

Before he makes his fateful decision, however, Ethan strokes Mattie's hair and kisses her again, all the while with her sobbing in his arms. He wants to remember the moment, he thinks to himself, and compares it to a seed in winter, which suggests he still does not want to die or that he believes in a life after death. He tries to imagine they are at Shadow Pond together and that it is the summer, but the cold of Mattie's cheek and the train whistle in the background bring him back to the present. Wharton then steps in again to remind the reader that, "The spruces swathed them in blackness and silence. They might have been in their coffins underground" (Wharton 1911, 181). In addition to the symbolic foreshadowing of the death he's considering for both of them, the darkness also suggests that Ethan still doesn't know the true motivation behind Mattie's desire for the two of them to die together. The symbol of the coffins is also a direct reference to the foreshadowing that Wharton had used earlier. When Ethan had passed the graveyard by the house on a couple of occasions, he dreamt of he and Mattie lying together there for all eternity. This is an important part of his decision-making process as he thinks to himself, "'Perhaps it'll feel like this . . .' and then again: 'After this I sha'n't feel anything . . .'" It's not until he hears the horse whinny, impatient to be fed, that Mattie pulls him toward the sled and he follows her. "Her sombre violence constrained him: she seemed the embodied instrument of fate."

Following her orders now, Ethan retrieves the sled and brings it to the top of the slope. Everyone in the village is home eating supper and no one is out. Ethan looks around the deserted streets and then up at a sky swollen with clouds—which again symbolize a lack of clear thinking in the novel—and it's here Wharton presents another subtle foreshadow that also confirms the meaning of the cloud symbol. "He strained his eyes through the dimness, and they seemed less keen, less capable than usual" (Wharton 1911, 181). As they climb onto the sled Mattie takes her same position, seated in front of him, and Ethan behind her. But then he gets off the sled and orders her up. Mattie assumes that he's not going to go through with it and she immediately begs him, "repeating vehemently: 'No, no, no!'" (182). What follows is not exactly an argument, but there are opposing forces at work here between the two of them. Mattie finally asks him why he wants her to get up and he says it's because he wants to sit in front. Again, Mattie balks. She says he won't be able to steer in front, but he says the ruts in the snow will guide them. He asks her again to get up, and again she refuses. There's a grim suggestion in his argument that Ethan wants to be sure if only one of them dies that it will be him. It's not difficult to see that Mattie understands this as well and is therefore just as eager to occupy the front position on the sled. Finally, in answer to her demand to know why, Ethan confirms this reading when he says "'Because I—because I want to feel you holding me,' he stammered, and dragged her to her feet" (182). From Ethan's point of view, "The answer seemed to satisfy her, or else she yielded to the power of his voice" (183). Neither one of those explanations, however, is as likely as the fact that Mattie is concerned he might not go through with it at all if she continues to resist him.

Even then, Ethan isn't completely convinced. He sits in front on the sled with his legs crossed and she climbs on behind him. "Her breath in his neck set him shuddering again, and he almost sprang from his seat. But in a flash he remembered the alternative. She was right: this was better than parting. He leaned back and drew her mouth to his . . ." (Wharton 1911, 183). At this point in the story, as long as he goes through with the suicide, his obsession with kissing Mattie seems to mean very little to her. Either she is simply allowing him to, or it is the price she has to pay to get him to go through with the double suicide. But at no time, once she has seemingly convinced him, does she appear to reciprocate his feelings. She never kisses him back. Wharton's description of their trip down the hill is at once haunting and horrifying. "Half-way down there was a sudden drop, then a rise, and after that another long delirious descent. As they took wing for this it seemed to him that they were flying indeed, flying far up into the cloudy night, with Starkfield immeasurably below them, falling away like a speck in space . . ." Ethan has now been joined with Mattie in the bird metaphor as the two are flying together, soon to be free from the pain and suffering of their earthly existence—but also, significantly, into the "cloudy night" as the representation of ignorance. Once Ethan catches site of the big tree he continues to chant to himself, "We can fetch it," over and over (184). Mattie tightens her grip on him and Ethan corrects the sled when it swerves, aiming them directly at the large, jutting branch of the elm tree.

As the two hurl toward the tree, Ethan continues to recite his mantra that they will be able to "fetch it," along with other phrases that Wharton doesn't specify. Then, suddenly, one of the most remarkable things in the entire novel happens.

The big tree loomed bigger and closer, and as they bore down on it he thought: "It's waiting for us: it seems to know." But suddenly his wife's face, with twisted monstrous lineaments, thrust itself between him and his goal, and he made an instinctive movement to brush it aside. The sled swerved in response, but he righted it again, kept it straight, and drove down on the black projecting mass. (Wharton 1911, 184)

Like the moment two nights before when Mattie's face was obliterated by an image of Zeena's, or even when Zeena's surrogate in the form of the cat broke the pickle dish, it seems that Zeena is omnipresent in Ethan's life. More importantly, however, the laws of physics come into play. When Ethan is bearing straight down onto the tree, the force of gravity is at its greatest. But after swerving to avoid the image of Zeena, his velocity has been reduced as he is coming at the tree from a slightly different angle that has necessarily reduced the force at which they will hit it. He has a final thought as they near the black void of the gigantic limb "when the air shot past him like millions of fiery wires; and then the elm . . ." Author Candace Waid makes an interesting parallel between this last sentence, with its ellipsis before the crash, seeing in Ethan's symbolic quest for death the seeking of freedom and opportunity represented by a door. In this instance, however, "The elm that Frome and Mattie smash into is the door that does not open" (Waid 76).

After the ellipsis there is a break in the text to indicate a passage of time, and in the next paragraph Ethan opens his eyes. "The sky was still thick, but looking straight up he saw a single star" (Wharton 1911, 184). The dim light from the single star, however, is enough to begin the process of understanding what has happened to him. He tries to remember the name of the star but is overcome with fatigue and "the effort tired him too much, and he closed his heavy lids and thought that he would sleep . . ." (184-185). Another ellipsis indicates another passage of time. At this point it is still conceivable that one or both of them has died. But the narrative continues on for another page. "The stillness was so profound that he heard a little animal twittering somewhere near by under the snow. It made a small frightened *cheep* like a field mouse, and he wondered languidly if it were hurt. Then he understood that it must be in pain: pain so excruciating that he seemed, mysteriously, to feel it shooting through his own body" (185). Though Wharton has used bird imagery to describe Mattie throughout the novel—which the words "twitter" and "cheep" evoke here—she changes the imagery to that of a mouse after the crash, and Joseph Brennan sees an important symbolic purpose in Wharton's metaphorical shift. "Since Zeena . . . is consistently associated with and even identified by her cat, this shift from the image of a small bird, the eternal but more elusive quarry of cats, to that of the field mouse, their more defenseless prey, is obviously symbolic of Zeena's final victory over Mattie" (Brennan 352). More specifically, Mattie after the accident has been transformed by her injuries from a bird with the ability to fly away to an earthbound mouse like Ethan, literally trapped on the farm for the rest of her life just as he is.

Finally, Ethan makes an attempt to get up. It's significant that his struggle is associated with the snow that surrounds him. In the symbolism of the winter weather throughout the novel, the snow here has gathered Ethan back into its conforming embrace, not allowing him to die, not allowing him any escape at all.

> He tried in vain to roll over in the direction of the sound, and stretched his left arm out across the snow. And now it was as though he felt rather than heard the twittering; it seemed to be under his palm, which rested on something soft and springy. The thought of the animal's suffering was intolerable to him and he struggled to raise himself, and could not because a rock, or some huge mass, seemed to be lying on him. But he continued to finger about cautiously with his left hand, thinking he might get hold of the little creature and help it; and all at once he knew that the soft thing he had touched was Mattie's hair and that his hand was on her face. (Wharton 1911, 185)

Though she was highly critical of the novelist, author Janet Flanner made an interesting observation about Wharton in connection with the snow in *Ethan Frome*, associating the weather with what she perceived as the author's icy personality. "Mrs. Wharton gave something like immortality to the sadness of snow, which it is likely her nature understood too well. At the age of thirty she was remarked as already cold and handsome. She was then spending her years at fashionable Lenox, where the earth, under the many winters, retains a feeling of ice that no spring can thaw. And the rest is under glass" (Flanner 173). More compelling is the idea that it was Wharton's increasingly onerous marriage that is the real parallel in this final scene. In this way Ethan's struggle in the snow with Mattie lying on top of him reflects Wharton's life as she struggled in her relationship to Teddy and the attendant restrictions society imposed on her in trying to extricate herself from their marriage.

When Ethan is eventually able to roll Mattie from on top of him, it is almost as though her dead weight has become inseparable from the societal oppression represented by the snow, like "some huge mass . . . lying on top of him." Ethan pushes himself to his knees and bends over and caresses Mattie's face with his hands. "He got his face down close to hers, with his ear to her mouth, and in the darkness he saw her eyes open and heard her say his name. 'Oh, Matt, I thought we'd fetched it,' he moaned" (186). The final line of the interior story is beautifully rendered. Ethan hears the horse up at the top of the hill, still agitated because he hasn't been fed. "Far off, up the hill, he heard the sorrel whinny, and thought: 'I ought to be getting him his feed . . .'" (186). Thus, the first thing Ethan thinks of after the accident is his obligation. In a way, this foreshadows the next twenty-four years for him, continuing to live on the farm but unable to work it. It also brings to mind Harmon Gow's statement that he didn't know how Ethan was able to make a living. Finally, there's a tremendous sense of sadness conveyed to the reader in the way that Ethan is mentally able to go right back to his life of misery and suffering as if nothing had happened.

The most obvious parallel in Wharton's experience to the suicide attempt is the sledding accident in Lenox in 1904. More compelling, however, is a letter written by the author that better explains the motivation behind the suicide attempt. The sledding accident in Lenox was just that, an accident, and its outward form is the one that Wharton chose to use in her novel. But the situation she found herself in while writing the story in France, trapped in marriage to a sick husband, unable to write consistently for several years because of her own ill health, and separated from Morton Fullerton, caused Wharton to experience the same kind of isolation that so many other women felt, an isolation that her wealth had tended to shield her from. It is this context in which the idea of suicide rears its head in a letter to Fullerton that makes clear her intense frustration with life.

> This is one of the days when it is more than I can bear— I suppose I ought to qualify that more by an "almost," since I am here and the lake is [over there]—and I *am* bearing it. But just now, when I heard that the motor, en route for Havre, had run into a tree and been smashed (bursting tire), I felt the wish that I had been in it, and smashed with it, and nothing left of all this disquiet but a [stilled heart]. (Fournier 47)

Later, after Teddy began to exhibit the symptoms of his madness to family and friends, as well as in public, Wharton wrote to a friend of hers, "only half joking, that 'a little child could lead me—to suicide!'" (Lee 397).

Epilogue

At the end of Chapter Nine, Wharton once again uses a string of ellipses, this time to indicate a return from the fantasy of the internal story, and thus the Epilogue begins with the reality of the narrator back in the frame story. Unlike her use of ellipses at the end of the Prologue, which of necessity meant that the publisher began the following chapter, Chapter One, on a new page, a problem ensued as a consequence of Wharton not actually naming her prologue and epilogue as such. The result was that when she received a copy of the proofs of the novel from Scribner's she was unhappy that they had decided to simply tack on the Epilogue after the ellipses at the end of Chapter Nine, and she wrote to her editor to explain why that needed to be changed.

> On p. 186 there is a sharp break in the narrative, shown by a double line of dots. On seeing the page proofs I have decided that this is not a sufficient indication of the pause, and interval of time, which must be shown here; and I should like the lower part of p. 186 (after the two rows of dots) to be left blank, and the next paragraph to begin on p. 187. (Lauer 173)

The action of the Epilogue picks up right where the Prologue leaves off, with Ethan and the narrator entering the hallway next to the kitchen and the sound of a woman's voice "droning querulously" from the other side. In the Prologue Ethan invites the narrator in, and this is precisely the point where he returns to the narrative. "The querulous drone ceased as I entered Frome's kitchen, and of the two women sitting there I could not tell which had been the speaker" (Wharton 1911, 187).

The narrator goes on to describe the women, and it says a lot about the effect the preceding twenty-four years has had on the two of them. The first, a tall thin woman with gray hair dressed in a "calico wrapper" who goes to the stove to finish cooking the evening meal, is clearly Zeena. "A tall bony figure," he calls her. "She had pale opaque eyes which revealed nothing and reflected nothing, and her narrow lips were of the same sallow colour as her face" (Wharton 1911, 187). The opacity of her eyes seems the most important element of his description. Clearly, Zeena's real reason for wanting to send Mattie away was not what she had claimed, and after the accident she essentially turned a blind eye to Ethan's infatuation in order to care for the girl. But this isn't necessarily out of character for her, as author R. Baird Shuman has suggested.

> [Zeena's] hypochondria provided her with masochistic satisfaction . . . But when she could become the martyred servant of the sharp-tongued wretch Mattie became after the accident, her masochistic satisfaction found its greatest fulfillment. She could simultaneously feel that she was needed, that she was morally superior, and that she had been sinned against but had the humanity to be forgiving." (Shuman 94)

The other woman is described as "smaller and slighter . . . huddled in an arm-chair near the stove" with the same gray hair as the other, but obviously immobilized in some way as the movements of her head do not seem to go with her body. He describes her as looking "bloodless and shriveled" with "dark eyes" that looked at him with a "witch-like stare that disease of the spine sometimes gives" (Wharton 1911, 188). This is Mattie.

The narrator's description of the kitchen is every bit as grim as the two women occupying it. "Even for that part of the country the kitchen was a poor-looking place . . . Three coarse china plates and a broken-nosed milk-jug had been set on a greasy table scored with knife cuts, and a couple of straw-bottomed chairs and a kitchen dresser of unpainted pine stood meagerly against the plaster walls" (Wharton 1911, 188). Ethan puts on a brave face for his unintended visitor and remarks that the fire must have gone out because it's so cold in the room. Zeena continues preparing the food while Mattie speaks up, complaining that Zeena had fallen asleep and let the fire die. "I knew then that it was she who had been speaking when we entered" (189). Robotically, Zeena brings over the food, which the narrator describes as an "unappetizing burden," while completely ignoring Mattie's complaint. Finally, Ethan introduces them.

> Frome stood hesitatingly before her as she advanced; then he looked at me and said: "This is my wife, Mis' Frome." After another interval he

added, turning toward the figure in the arm-chair: "And this is Miss Mattie Silver . . ." (189)

This is the moment Edith Wharton referred to in her introduction as "the dramatic climax, or rather the anti-climax" of her tale (Wharton 1911, vi). There's an overwhelming sense of irony in this ending, on the order of W.W. Jacobs' "The Monkey's Paw," that conjures up the old adage, "be careful what you wish for; you just might get it." Throughout the novel it had been Ethan's desire for Mattie to stay with him and for him to be with her all his life. In the words of Kenneth Bernard, "this is just about what he achieves by crippling instead of killing himself and Mattie. He did not, however, envision that Zeena would be a necessary part of the arrangement" (Bernard 181). The fact that it was Ethan's romantic desire for Mattie that caused their misery also brings to mind a Bible verse from Jeremiah: "The heart is more treacherous than anything else, and is desperately wicked: who can know it?" (KJV, Jeremiah 17:9). What's so fascinating is the way in which Wharton foreshadows this ending in a number of places. The first time is when Ethan is looking at the headstones in the graveyard as he is walking Mattie home from the dance. "'I guess we'll never let you go, Matt,' he whispered, as though even the dead, lovers once, must conspire with him to keep her; and brushing by the graves, he thought: 'We'll always go on living here together, and some day she'll lie there beside me'" (55). Another happens when they are spending their night alone together. "He set his imagination adrift on the fiction that they had always spent their evenings thus and would always go on doing so . . ." (97).

Beyond that obvious irony, however, is one far more subtle and more cruel. Throughout the novel Ethan's fantasy had been to replace Zeena with Mattie. Mattie had been brought to the farm to take care of the sickly Zeena, and now she is the one who must be cared for, and in that circumstance Ethan has been granted his wish. Author Elizabeth Ammon explains these consequences in terms of her analysis of the book as fairy tale.

The ghastly conclusion Ethan must live with is worse than if Mattie had gone away, married someone else, or even died. The suicide attempt transforms Mattie into a mirror image of Zeena . . . The end of *Ethan Frome* images Zeena Frome and Mattie Silver not as two individual and entirely opposite female figures but as two virtually indistinguishable examples of one type of woman: in fairy-tale terms, the witch; in social mythology, the shrew. (Ammons 66-67)

Ammons goes on to remind readers that, "Shocking as that replicate image may at first seem, it has been prepared for throughout the story" (67). The two most obvious examples of this foreshadowing are when Mattie opens the door for Ethan exactly as Zeena had done the night before, and when Mattie is sitting in Zeena's rocker and Ethan imagines her face has been replaced by Zeena's. In that light the most cruelly ironic of Ethan's lines is one that comes early on in the novel. "All his life was lived in the sight and sound of Mattie Silver, and he could no longer conceive of its being otherwise" (Wharton 1911, 43).

Wharton follows this opening section of the Epilogue with another lengthy ellipsis, this time indicating a time shift and the narrator's return to the boarding house. "Mrs. Hale, tender soul, had pictured me as lost in the Flats and buried under a snow-drift; and so lively was her satisfaction on seeing me safely restored to her the next morning that I felt my peril had caused me to advance several degrees in her favour" (Wharton 1911, 189). Because of his newfound stature, the narrator makes a calculated decision in an attempt to get more information out of his host. He decides that he will keep the details of his visit to himself, initially, and let her reveal what additional facts she knows as a way of increasing his knowledge about Ethan. "I therefore confined myself to saying, in a matter-of-fact tone, that I had been received with great kindness, and that Frome had made a bed for me in a room on the ground-floor which seemed in happier days to have been fitted up as a kind of writing-room or study" (190). Though the note that Ethan wrote to Zeena had been torn up by Mattie, the narrator could have seen the old newspaper folded back to the advertisement for travel to the West, as well as Zeena's protuberant pillow. Mrs. Hale is, of course, duly impressed. "I don't believe but what you're the only stranger has set foot in that house for over twenty years."

Mrs. Hale also casually mentions that, along with the doctor, she herself has made regular visits to see the Fromes, and so the narrator ventures to ask her more.

> I used to go a good deal after the accident, when I was first married; but after awhile I got to think it made 'em feel worse to see us. And then one thing and another came, and my own troubles . . . But I generally make out to drive over there round about New Year's, and once in the summer. Only I always try to pick a day when Ethan's off somewheres. It's bad enough to see the two women sitting there—but *his* face, when he looks round that bare place, just kills me . . . (Wharton 1911, 191)

The narrator had ascribed Mrs. Hale's previous reticence to her unwillingness to gossip for the sake of gossip, but now his recent experience at the Frome's house has somehow earned her trust. "I guessed that if she had kept silence till now it was because she had been waiting, through all the years, for some one who should see what she alone had seen" (191-192). This assumption is based on an earlier observation the narrator has in the Prologue about Mrs. Hale. "It was not that Mrs. Ned Hale felt, or affected, any social superiority to the people about her; it was only that the accident of a finer sensibility and a little more education had put just enough distance between herself and her neighbours to enable her to judge them with detachment" (11). Once he has her talking, the narrator simply agrees with her about how terrible the situation is for the three of them, and this induces her to continue confiding in him.

She begins with a fact that he already knows, that she had been the first to find them, and then adds that Mattie had been brought to her house while Ethan was taken to the minister's.

> They laid Mattie Silver in the room you're in. She and I were great friends, and she was to have been my bridesmaid in the spring . . . When she came to I went up to her and stayed all night. They gave her things to quiet her, and she didn't know much till to'rd morning, and then all of a sudden she woke up just like herself, and looked straight at me out of her big eyes, and said . . . (Wharton 1911, 192)

Mrs. Hale starts crying at this point and says she doesn't know why she's telling him all of this, but she continues anyway. She says that a rumor made it around the village the next day that Zeena had sent Mattie away in order to bring in a hired girl, and it's not difficult to conclude that Jotham Powell was the source of that particular bit of gossip, but Mrs. Hale also states that "I never knew myself what Zeena thought—I don't to this day. Nobody knows Zeena's thoughts" (193). Then she adds another very interesting piece of information. "The folks here could never rightly tell what she and Ethan were doing that night coasting, when they'd ought to have been on their way to the Flats to ketch the train." This actually makes Zeena's pronouncement to Ethan in their bedroom, that "I know well enough what they say of my having kep' her here as long as I have," that much more vague (126-127). It seems clear that no one in the village ever knew about Ethan's feelings for Mattie. Which only makes sense, as it's pretty clear that even Mattie didn't know about them until right before the accident. Though Mrs. Hale suggests that she and Mattie spoke after the girl woke up, there's no indication from the widow that Mattie said anything about her final day with Ethan—further evidence that she had no prior feelings of love for Ethan.

It's here that the contention there was no reciprocation of Ethan's feelings by Mattie actually seems to be reinforced by Wharton herself. The narrator says, "Mrs. Hale paused a moment, and I remained silent, plunged in the vision of what her words evoked" (Wharton 1911, 194). This sentence brings back very strongly the idea of just how fictional the narrator's story inside the frame actually is. According to Cynthia Griffin Wolff the facts in evidence throughout the Prologue—Ethan's accident, his parents' deaths, Zeena's illness, etc.—are the only "real" truth contained in the entire novel. "To these facts the various members of the town will all attest—and to *nothing more.* Everything that the reader can accept as reliably true can be found in the narrative frame; everything else bears the imprint of the narrator's own interpretation" (Wolff 161). This includes the Epilogue as well. As Wolff points out, "Even at the end of the narrator's vision, in the concluding scene with Mrs. Hale, Wharton is scrupulously careful not to credit the vision by giving it independent confirmation . . . the narrator elicits nothing that he has not already known" (161-162). This is fascinating to consider, as it would have been very easy—and is perhaps even assumed by casual readers—to believe that the information found in the Epilogue accepts to a certain degree that there was a love relationship between Ethan and Mattie. But it doesn't. What Wharton was able to do in this respect is what so many great writers have been able to do: put the reader in the place of the protagonist without the reader's knowledge. When readers make the assumption all the way through the interior story that Mattie is in love with Ethan, they are actually sharing in Ethan's fantasy.

But the most remarkable thing about the accident, in terms of the reaction by the villagers, is the seemingly miraculous recovery of Zeena.

When she heard o' the accident she came right in and stayed with Ethan over to the minister's, where they'd carried him. And as soon as the doctors said that Mattie could be moved, Zeena sent for her and took her back to the farm . . . Zeena's done for her, and done for Ethan, as good as she could. It was a miracle, considering how sick she was—but she seemed to be raised right up just when the call came to her. Not as she's ever given up doctoring, and she's had sick spells right along; but she's had the strength given her to care for those two for over twenty years, and before the accident came she thought she couldn't even care for herself. (Wharton 1911, 193-194)

Of course readers are perfectly aware of the nature of Zeena's strength: the fact that she was never really sick in the first place. And again, Wharton's sense of irony is on full display. Zeena had imagined that however desolate and loveless her life on the farm with Ethan would be, at least she wouldn't have to submit to the drudgery of the woman's work that society expected her to do. And yet, after the accident, she not only had to resume taking on the normal household chores but had to play nurse to the woman who had stolen the affections of her husband.

One of the elements of the ending that is sometimes obscured in the Epilogue, with its emphasis on Mattie's injuries, is the physical effect the accident had on Ethan. This is because the detailed description of Ethan happens back at the very beginning of the novel, in the Prologue. While contemporary commentators failed to see in Ethan's injuries the emotional crippling that happened to so many women in America's Victorian era, there are glimpses of isolated elements in that overall symbolism that emerge on occasion in later criticism, not unlike Wharton's own "granite outcroppings." One of these comes from Wharton scholar Candace Waid. "In becoming a mutilated and crippled man, he also seems to become the barren and infertile woman. Ethan Frome himself represents the failure of fertility and the insistent barrenness described throughout the novel" (Waid 75). Waid also sees in the broken pickle dish a reflection of the childless state of the couple, as well as a foreshadow of the accident which will render Mattie childless as well. But the most devastating aspect of the entire affair, according to Mrs. Hale, is the emotional toll that the episode has taken on the three prisoners trapped on the Frome farm.

> It's pretty bad. And they ain't any of 'em easy people either. Mattie *was*, before the accident; I never knew a sweeter nature. But she's suffered too much—that's what I always say when folks tell me how she's soured. And Zeena, she was always cranky. Not but what she bears with Mattie wonderful—I've seen that myself. But sometimes the two of them get going at each other, and then Ethan's face'd break your heart . . . (Wharton 1911, 194)

This is probably the most interesting aspect of the story for the narrator, imagining what the emotional rift was between the two women that could have had such a tortuous effect on Ethan. As the widow says, "I think it's *him* that suffers most" (Wharton 1911, 194). It also explains several curiosities present in the Prologue. When the narrator says that it looks as though Ethan is "dead and in hell" already, the torment of what he brought upon the three people in his house explains that. It also makes sense, then, why Ethan would go through the tortuous ritual of harnessing his horse every day to go to the post office when there is rarely anything there for him to pick up. The escape he seeks is not from Zeena's illness, but the tension between Zeena and Mattie. Finally, there is the narrator's assumption that Ethan had been forced to stay in Starkfield because of the injuries he sustained in the smash-up. That is followed by Harmon Gow's sardonic chuckle and his response, "That's so. He *had* to stay then." But it wasn't Ethan's injuries that necessarily forced him to stay, it was his obligation to the two women whose lives he had ruined. In that light the most damning of the comments from the Prologue that must be reassessed is when Harmon Gow had said, "Most of the smart ones get away," and the narrator's response indicated his belief that Ethan was one of the smart ones. Looking at Ethan's repeated failure to avail himself of the "revealing rays of light," all the while allowing his fantasy to cloud his judgment, and with his refusal to look at the reality of his situation as well as Mattie's actual responses to him, it could be argued after all that Ethan was not one of the smart ones.

The final element from the Prologue that makes its way into the Epilogue is the symbolism of the Starkfield winters, a brutality and isolation that is only intensified after the accident. "'It's a pity, though,' Mrs. Hale ended, sighing, 'that they're all shut up there'n that one kitchen. In the summertime, on pleasant days, they move Mattie into the parlour, or out in the door-yard, and that makes it easier . . . but winters there's the fires to be thought of; and there ain't a dime to spare up at the Fromes'"" (Wharton 1911, 194-195). At last Mrs. Hale concludes her story by telling the narrator of a day shortly after the accident when it was thought that Mattie would die, and how she wondered out loud at the time if it wouldn't have been better if Mattie had. "I said it right out to our minister once, and he was shocked at me. Only he wasn't with me that morning when she first came to . . .

> And I say, if she'd ha' died, Ethan might ha' lived; and the way they are now, I don't see's there's much difference between the Fromes up at the farm and the Fromes down in the graveyard; 'cept that down there they're all quiet, and the women have got to hold their tongues. (195)

This final epitaph about the lives of the three main characters in the novel is one that would be echoed a few years later by Edgar Lee Masters in his *Spoon River Anthology* as well as in Thornton Wilder's *Our Town* from 1938, and certainly places Edith Wharton solidly in the top tier of American authors. But as the last line of the novel it is also a fitting end to *Ethan Frome*. At a time when women did not have the right to vote, did not have the right to own property, did not have the right to keep the wages they earned, and for many not even the most basic right to speak out for what they believed, Wharton's novel powerfully reflects the living death that so many women were subjected to in her day.

Critical Reception

In her literary biography of Wharton, author Grace Kellogg makes the crucial distinction between the reception of *Ethan Frome* by critics as apposed to its reception by the author's audience. As far as this last group is concerned, she says, "The reading public accepted it without question.

> From East Coast to West, from the Canadian border to the Gulf of Mexico, it was read and reread, discussed, passed from hand to hand. Its power, its moving simplicity, its dreadful and pitiful tragedy spoke direct to the heart. Nor was its acceptance a thing of popular whim. *Ethan Frome* lives today and will continue to live, one of the few books which triumph over time and custom. (Kellogg 159)

As far as critics were concerned, however, "it aroused a very different reaction." One of the difficult things to escape in reading much of the contemporary criticism surrounding *Ethan Frome* is the abundance of negative adjectives used to describe the book. "Cruel, compelling, haunting" said the *New York Times Book Review* on the novel's initial publication, while words like "pessimistic," "bleak," "terrible," and "hideous," were used by other reviewers, all as an attempt to grapple with what was commonly felt to be Edith Wharton's heartlessly cruel treatment of her characters. Because so many reviewers simply couldn't get past the shocking implications of the ending, they found themselves praising Wharton's writing on the one hand while decrying her apparent inhumanity to her characters on the other.

But all of those assessments of the novel also assume a reciprocal love affair between Ethan and Mattie, which would tend to reinforce the idea that the purpose of the work is little more than the cruel twist of fate that comes after the unsuccessful suicide. The opinion offered by the *Saturday Review* is typical of this outlook.

> Having read the story, we wish we had not have read it. The error is in the end. There are things too terrible in their failure to be told humanly by creature to creature. Ethan Frome driving down with the girl he loved to death—here there is beauty and a defiance of the misery of circumstance which may sadden, but uplift, the reader. But these lovers could not die. They must live horribly on, mutilated and losing even the nobility of their passion in the wreck of their bodies. (Lauer 120)

For this reviewer Wharton's climax is not the noble self-sacrifice of *Romeo and Juliet*, one that leaves readers hopeful in their sorrow through the promise of a future in which the strife between two families has ended. The disappointment expressed in so many reviews arose from what was perceived to be missing from Wharton's story: a reason for all the suffering.

Even years later—and sometimes decades—critics were still unable to fully grasp what purpose Wharton had in keeping Ethan and Mattie alive. The opening paragraph of Alan Henry Rose's essay from 1977 gives about as good a summary of this widespread critical opinion as there is.

> The apparent pointlessness of the destruction the protagonist suffers in Edith Wharton's *Ethan Frome* often has disturbed readers. Lionel Trilling, for example, sees the work as, "a facetious book, perhaps even a cruel book." Irving Howe describes it as, "a severe depiction of gratuitous human suffering in a New England village." Marilyn Lyde finds, "no element of justice in the catastrophe." The harshness of this novel sometimes has been accounted for as Wharton's response to the sentimentality she saw as typical of New England fiction, or as an especial case of the need to inflict "punishment," as Jo McManis suggests, upon her characters for the author's own transgressions. (Rose 423).

For Rose, as it was for other critics, the answer seemed to lie in Wharton's apparent disconnect from her subjects. Instead of the upper-class society to which so many critics acceded her expertise, they refused to likewise grant her true knowledge of the Western Massachusetts people she spent her summers among. And yet like so many of those other critics, Rose would hit upon the right interpretation but for the wrong reason. His contention that "the dark fate of her New England characters stems from their contact with Wharton's unexpected vision of the most destructive of forces underlying American society" is exactly right (424). But his Freudian assertion that this destructive force is "the incestuous relationship . . . which serves as a gauge of the incapacity of moral growth," is startlingly off the mark (425, 428).

Another way critics and reviewers attempted to make sense of the story was by turning to Greek tragedy as a convenient parallel with which they could compare the novel. The review in the *New York Times* said, "The present grim tale of a bud of romance ice-bound and turned into a frozen horror in the frigid setting of a New England winter landscape is conceived in the remorseless spirit of the Greek tragic muse" (Ochs, 65). *Chicago Tribune* reporter Ella W. Peattie was far more complementary about the novel overall, but concluded her review by saying, "It doesn't sound like pleasant reading, you will say, [but] it really is a great book. Perhaps it is the best thing Mrs. Wharton has ever written. It is at any rate as relentless as a Greek drama" (Peattie 8). Though the reviewer for the *Boston Globe* went on to point out, "It is not the swift tragedy of death, but the slow, grimmer tragedy of life and decay" (Editor 10-11, 5). Book review editor Una H.H. Cool, however, writing in *The San Francisco Call*, made it clear that *Ethan Frome* was "worse than any Greek tragedy, for it is set in our own country and our own time—today—and its horror is so real it leaves a physical pain" (Cool 7). While this assessment of the novel is closer to the truth than many of them realized—as the misery of many married women seemed fated by the rigid societal structure that controlled their lives—the fact that Wharton had so ably disguised the plight of women in the form of Ethan led many of them to come to the wrong conclusions as well. According to Suzanne Fournier, "From this perspective, Wharton's portrayal of the ruined lives left to Ethan and Mattie [and Zeena] after the crash becomes an indictment of conditions in the remote villages of New England" (Fournier 118). In fact, just two years after its publication author Edwin Björkman was able to take this idea and turn the novel into a communal plea for the kind of social safety net that wouldn't be realized until FDR's New Deal during the Depression.

> *Ethan Frome* is to me, above all else, a judgment on that system which fails to redeem such villages as Mrs. Wharton's Starkfield. I am not now preaching socialism in the narrow sense . . . I am pleading merely for the extension of certain forms of social cooperation or coordination . . . Those who dwell in our thousand and one Starkfields [have] fallen into their hapless positions by no fault of their own. And though helpless now, they need by no means prove useless under different conditions . . . Social effort should be employed in making those hillsides fruitful once more. (Björkman 297-298)

In the late twentieth century scholars had no trouble transforming this idea from an economic argument to one of gender. At that time Wharton's novels and stories had become an early cornerstone of feminist literature and, as such, authors were able to identify and explicate the numerous symbols that represented the societal restrictions placed on women in Wharton's time. Dale M. Bauer's essay, "Wharton's 'Others:' Addiction and Intimacy," is probably one of the best summaries of the way these arguments typically played out. "In *Ethan Frome*," he says, "[Wharton] sees womens' illnesses as part of the country's 'pathology,' a word she uses twice in describing Zeena's connection to other women who had turned 'queer'" (Bauer 2003, 137). This is certainly the case, as the pathology of patriarchal expectations in Wharton's day was the primary cause for the wide variety of symptoms observed in the diagnosis of hysteria. Bauer then goes on to deal with Mattie, in the way that her paralysis at the end of the story is symbolic of the restrictions placed on all women in Wharton's day. "Mattie's spinal injury is even culturally symbolic: it is a broken will, a fate for women who oppose the patriarchal script but fail to rewrite it." The problem with focusing exclusively on Zeena and Mattie in a modern feminist context, however, is that it doesn't lead anywhere, which Bauer is eventually forced to admit. "Wharton provides no alternatives to the cultural conflicts between Victorian domesticity and modern sexuality. She can point to this conflict, dramatize it, but not quite resolve the ambivalence it stimulates."

The problem isn't Wharton's, however, it's society's. For readers in her day the problems of her female characters were easily dismissed: Zeena was a wicked witch who was punished by having to take care of Ethan and Mattie for the rest of her life, while Mattie was a foolish girl who was deserving of her fate after trying to steal another woman's man. Wharton's real success was in moving so far beyond these obvious examples that even modern feminists couldn't see it. In writing her novel in this way, Wharton's achievement was also in keeping with Theodor Adorno's belief that great art isn't about solving the questions of the day, but presenting them in such a way that the audience is able to see them from an entirely new perspective. "A successful work . . . is not one which resolves objective contradictions, but one which expresses the idea of harmony negatively by embodying the contradictions, pure and uncompromised, in its innermost structure" (Adorno 32). The success of *Ethan Frome* is that the title character does exactly what Adorno suggests: he is able to embody the "pure and uncompromised" contradictions of the oppression of women precisely because he is not a woman. Instead of confronting this oppression head on by making her protagonist a woman—and thus eliciting immediate resistance from her male audience in the process—Wharton was able to "express the idea of harmony negatively"—that is, in the opposite way, by making her protagonist a man.

Once the true nature of the story is understood through close reading, *Ethan Frome* takes on a whole new level of meaning and significance. Rather than seeing the characters as individuals who are suffering because of their desperate struggle to escape their circumstances, the novel is really a commentary on the variety of ways in which women were oppressed in nineteenth-century America and how little sense it made. Ironically, while Björkman viewed this societal oppression in economic terms, his analytical justification matches perfectly with the gender switch in Ethan that he was unable to see.

> Mrs. Wharton never refers to it in plain words [but] the tragedy unveiled to us is social rather than personal. It is so overwhelming that the modern mind rebels against it as a typical specimen of human experience . . . As it is, and because that social aspect asserts itself so irresistibly, we are led into almost overlooking what those crushed lives must have meant to those living them . . . we are here instinctively moved to "shake off" the thought that Ethan and Matt and Zeena are individual sufferers. They become instead embodiments of large groups and whole strata; and the dominant thought left behind by the book is not concerned with the awfulness of human existence, but with the social loss involved in such wasting of human lives. (Björkman 296-297)

Because they are women, the "wasting of human lives" that Björkman senses "instinctively"—though not the right one—is more obvious in the way it manifests itself in the characters of Zeena and Mattie. Zeena married Ethan out of desperation, the fear that she might never get another offer, and her unhappiness turned itself into an illness that she used to exact a measure of retribution in order to compensate for her misery. Mattie represents the upper middle class notion of grooming women only for marriage, and when her parents died it left her utterly unprepared to take care of herself. As Elizabeth Ammons points out, "The fact that Wharton cripples Mattie, but will not let her die, reflects not the author's but the culture's cruelty . . . Mattie Silver has not been prepared for an economically independent life. The system is designed to keep her a parasite or a drudge, or both" (Ammons 71). But both of these views of women were common at the time and their plight easily dismissed by a predominantly patriarchal society. What's unique about the character of Ethan is that he represents the silent suffering of the majority of women who were trapped in a system they could not even recognize. Like

Eric B. Olsen

Charlotte Perkins Gilman's narrator, Ethan accepted his place and did his best to make it work, but couldn't see that he was on the losing end of an accepted way of life that was inherently unfair to him.

The success Wharton achieves in conveying this idea to the reader's unconscious comes from her use of the narrator and the skill she demonstrates so effectively in his telling of the internal story. Author Stuart Hutchinson makes it clear just how effective Wharton's narrator is at suspending the reader's disbelief—and in the process their cultural filters—to make the internal vision seem just as realistic as the framing device. "In *Ethan Frome* [the narrator's vision] is not a problem Wharton shows any interest in. To the contrary, so *un*problematic is the prose . . . so authoritative its account, that we lose all sense of a characterized first-person narrator (and, therefore, of the possibility of subjectivity or partiality) as we engage with it" (Hutchinson 222-223). Elizabeth Ammons takes this idea even further in suggesting that the narrator actually represents an idealized version of Ethan. "He serves as a surprising double for Ethan. Young and well educated, he is the engineer that Ethan hoped to become, until a series of women blighted his world. To impress the parallel, they also have in common their compassion for animals, their interest in pure science, and fond memories of a trip to Florida each of them has taken" (Ammons 74). In this way of looking at the story it is actually a more sophisticated version of Ethan, rather than Ethan himself, who narrates the inner story. All of the frustration and misery that he endures is thus presented in the same way that it was for women, an immovable force that Ethan is unable to overcome. Tellingly, there was no parallel for the narrator in the real lives of women of this time, unless it is Wharton herself and other female authors like her. And in that respect the narrator can be seen as functioning in Wharton's novel, in his role as Ethan's voice, like Charlotte Perkins Gilman's narrator in "The Yellow Wall-Paper," obsessed with discovering a secret that he knows is important but can't quite seem to understand.

Like many of the women of his day—and just like Zeena—Ethan also married out of the fear of being alone. Because this necessarily limited his choices, he wound up tied to a spouse who not only didn't love or respect him, but felt compelled to abuse him in order to compensate for her own feelings of dissatisfaction. Like many of the women of his day, Ethan had no way to earn enough money to change his life, and found himself trapped financially as well as emotionally. And because of this financial scarcity—even more severe for women who, legally, owed any wages they earned to their husbands—divorce was not a viable option either. Over the long term, this prison-like existence resulted in an emotional torture that is symbolized in Ethan's eventual physical injuries. And as with Ethan, the only escape for many women at this point was the world of fantasy. Unfortunately, this could lead to a distorted view of the world that resulted in any number of self-destructive decisions by women who deluded themselves into thinking there actually were viable extra-legal means to happiness—bad decisions that were typically encouraged by men who had little to lose in the bargain. This sort of moral ruination is symbolized in Ethan's physical destruction, stemming from a decision made as a result of an inaccurate understanding of Mattie's true feelings for him. Again, there is clearly a parallel between the male protagonist of Wharton's novel and the female protagonist in *Madame Bovary.* Van Meter Ames made this connection in his book on the *Aesthetics of the Novel* back in 1928. *Ethan Frome,* he said, "recalls Flaubert's *Madame Bovary,* which is taken as the fixed point in criticism in the technique of the novel. But while [Wharton's technique] is interesting, technique is a trivial matter compared to the native genius of an author, [her] zest and gusto, sympathy, imagination and sheer creative power" (Ames 192). Like Emma Bovary, it is Ethan's fantasy world—for him a shared love with Mattie—that is his undoing.

Admittedly, this way of looking at the novel can be a challenge for many readers who have become heavily invested over the years in the idea of the novel as a love story gone wrong. Edith Wharton herself, however, left no definitive statement as to Mattie's true feelings, and so her intent can only be inferred. The single piece of writing that comes the closest to addressing this is the foreword she wrote for the dramatization of the novel by Owen and Donald Davis shortly before her death. Though all of her characters were changed significantly by the Davis's, the major difference between the book and the play is that throughout the play both Ethan and Mattie openly profess their desire for one another in a very unambiguous way. About the characters in the play, Wharton says, "I imagine few [novelists] have had the luck to see the characters they had imagined in fiction transported to the stage without loss or alteration of any sort, without even that grimacing enlargement of gesture and language supposed to be necessary to 'carry' across the footlights. I should like to record here my appreciation of this unusual achievement, and my professional admiration for the great skill and exquisite sensitiveness with which my interpreters have executed their task" (Wharton 1936, viii).

While it seems clear from this statement that Wharton agreed with the way in which the Davis's had portrayed her characters, it doesn't really address the way they made overt Mattie's return of Ethan's feelings toward her. And even Wharton's praise for the Davis's characterizations can't really be taken at face value, as it's difficult to imagine that she would have had any other choice. Wharton's purpose for having the play adapted for the stage in the first place was a purely financial one, and as such it would have made no sense for her to undermine its success by sharing her true feelings about its deficiencies. That's what makes the first part of her statement about this process so interesting. Prior to praising the Davis's for their characterization, Wharton makes a more general comment about dramatic adaptation as a whole. "It has happened to me, as to most novelists, to have the odd experience, through the medium of reviews or dramatizations of their work, to see their books as they have taken shape in other minds: always a curious, and sometimes a painful, revelation" (Wharton 1936, viii). This statement seems to imply that, despite whatever happiness she may have professed about the rendering of the characters, their severe alteration along with the change in the story as a whole suggests that it is still very different from the one she had written, and therefore it's not too difficult to imagine that she might not have been as happy with the adaptation as she professed. Even so, this hardly seems definitive either way.

Much more convincing is the original French version of the story Wharton wrote in 1907. This is the generally acknowledged starting point for the novel, and it is immediately apparent upon reading that this is essentially the same story using similar characters. And yet there is one significant difference. Unlike the novel, the short story opens with the acknowledgement that the Ethan character and Mattie have already confessed their mutual feelings for each other, and the recognition of what this has done to their formerly familial relationship. "At each word, now, they felt the weight of the chains they had forged by confessing their love" (MacCallan 41). Unlike Ethan's giddy prospect of a night alone with Mattie in the novel, when the Zeena character leaves for the night Hart can't trust himself to be alone in the house with Mattie and spends the evening in town to avoid acting on his emotions—and perhaps being caught in the act by his wife. What this means, then, is that the ambiguity present in the novel was not an accident. It was not "a reticence or modesty of the author's," as Kenneth Bernard and others have suggested (Bernard 182). Instead, Edith Wharton made the deliberate decision to disguise the true nature of Mattie's feelings for Ethan in the novel, and cloak Ethan's understanding of them in uncertainty. In every other respect, the novel is almost identical to the story. The only things missing from the shorter work are the debilitating sled ride and the narrator. But since everything else is the same, the change from Mattie's collaboration with Hart in the story to the opposite with Ethan in the novel has to be considered significant.

At the same time, the only real argument for a love-story reading of the novel is a biographical one, the implication that the relationship between Ethan and Mattie in the novel mirrors the one between Edith Wharton and Morton Fullerton in real life. But there are significant discrepancies that undercut this interpretation. Though they had met in early 1907—and Wharton would not write her sketch until later that spring—her letters during that same period demonstrate that she had very little to say about him other than he was an interesting acquaintance. "Your friend Fullerton . . . is very intelligent, but slightly mysterious, I think" (Benstock 170). It would not be until October of that year, well after she had written the original short story, that Fullerton stayed in Lenox with Edith and Teddy. Only then did she begin a new diary devoted to him, and the two would not consummate their affair until the following year. A further problem in attempting to read the facts of her life into her fiction is that *Ethan Frome* shows Wharton was writing from both sides of the affair. While she clearly experienced being tied down to an invalid in the same way that Ethan did, she was also the female being pursued by a married man. In this way Wharton's own behavior toward Fullerton in early 1908 seems to mirror the enigmatic Mattie. "He would soon complain to her that he had no idea how she really felt about him . . . Fullerton wanted her to express her feelings and demonstrate her affection for him. Was she toying with him, 'amusing' herself? he would soon ask. She answered him in a letter, explaining that theirs was a 'fugitive' relation, which inhibited her" (176, 179).

In spite of that, Wharton's primary identification is still clearly with Ethan, which is evident in the entries she made about Fullerton in her diary. Shortly before their affair commenced, she wrote of the two sitting together in her apartment. "The moment was 'exquisite.' She had 'the illusion . . . of a life in which such evenings might be a dear accepted habit" (Benstock 181). These are very similar to the words describing Ethan's night alone with Mattie. "The commonplace nature of what they said produced in Ethan an illusion of long-established intimacy which no outburst of emotion could have given, and he set his imagination adrift on the fiction that they had always spent their evenings thus and would always go on doing so" (Wharton 1911, 97). In another entry in which Wharton writes of a night spent at the theater with Fullerton, she says about the two of them, "I felt for the first time that indescribable current of communication flowing between myself and someone else—felt it, I mean, interruptedly, securely, so that it penetrated every sense and every thought" (Benstock 180). Again, this is reminiscent of the moment Ethan touches the material Mattie is sewing during their night together. "She sat silent, her hands clasped on her work, and it seemed to him that a warm current flowed toward him along the strip of stuff that still lay unrolled between them" (Wharton 1911, 102).

While none of these explanations comes close to being definitive in arguing Wharton's intent was that Mattie returned Ethan's affection toward her, the novel itself is quite definitive in showing Wharton was reluctant to state Mattie's desire outright, and in refusing to do so it allowed her to

Eric B. Olsen

unconsciously render the plight of so many women of her day in the character of Ethan. Though in certain respects it seems logical to assume that Wharton felt Mattie harbored similar feelings of love toward Ethan, as most readers do, the problem is that the reader is then left with the reticence of Ethan as a character that pales in comparison to Mattie's lack of explicit articulation. Even if one assumes that Mattie's silence is in keeping with the expectations for behavior in those days—just as Wharton's was toward Fullerton early on—which would necessitate Mattie keeping her feelings hidden, that still doesn't seem to adequately explain the abundance of symbolism the author used, the complete disconnect between Mattie's words and actions, or how Ethan could have possibly guessed that they objectively indicated a mutual love. Even at the end of the novel after it became clear to Mattie what Ethan's feelings for her were, she still refused to declare similar feelings for him in an unambiguous way, and used her manipulation of his feelings only to get him to participate in the suicide pact rather than make even a single attempt to get him to consider running away with her.

In the end, what can't be ignored is the fact that if *Ethan Frome* is really nothing more than a love story gone horribly wrong then all of the negative criticism leveled against the novel about Wharton's cruelty toward her characters must be correct. And the issue with that way of looking at the novel, as it has been for so many critics over the past century, is that there is simply no logical purpose for the suffering of her characters. Even Cynthia Griffin Wolff, whose psychological biography of Edith Wharton is otherwise excellent, remained baffled by that aspect of the story.

> The novel invites us, in effect then, to ask the reasons for Ethan Frome's tragic failure to find that fulfillment (even as the narrator obsessively asks these questions). What did he do wrong? Was he condemned by the very components of his past—the family into which he was born, the community in which he was reared? Or did he, somehow, select his lot? Of course the novel does not fully answer such queries . . . (Wolff 403)

In seeing Ethan as misreading Mattie's feelings, however, the novel persuasively answers all of them. With Ethan serving as a symbol for the need of nineteenth-century women to fantasize as a way of coping with their lives, it gives the novel a purpose by demonstrating how illogical the subjugation of women was in that day. It also powerfully demonstrates the ultimate incongruity of the consequences for oppressed women in the way those consequences manifest themselves in the character of a man.

What is so absolutely fascinating in reading the novel in this way is how critics themselves seemed to have understood all of this at an unconscious level while at the same time finding themselves unable to articulate it directly. To begin with, critics first had to see the novel as more symbolic than literal in order to make some sense of the ending. The idea of the preference for a symbolic reading of *Ethan Frome* over a literal one can be seen, ironically, in criticism waged against the novel by Bernard DeVoto shortly after the author's death. The British critic saw in Wharton's story a surfeit of expert literary technique that he felt tended to obscure the humanity in the characters, with the novel essentially the opposite of the kind of fiction written by New England authors like Sarah Orne Jewett or Mary E. Wilkins. "*Ethan Frome* is a model of literary technique but it is not a transcript of human experience; it is a 'well-made' novel done with exact calculation and superb skill, but it is not an exploration of or comment on genuine emotion" (DeVoto iv). DeVoto's criticism, which argues that there is something lacking in the avoidance of a slavish attention to the details of the lives of the characters, is then the natural starting point for suggesting that Wharton's novel must be something other than that.

The best argument for why this should be seen as a positive instead of a negative attribute comes, once again, from Cynthia Griffin Wolff, who is able to address the true nature of the kind of local color fiction that Wharton impolitely characterized as "seen through rose-colored spectacles" in the works of "my predecessors, Mary Wilkins and Sarah Orne Jewett" (Wharton 1934, 293). As Wharton had previously claimed in her introduction to *Ethan Frome*, it "bore little except a vague botanical and dialectical resemblance" to the life she had known there (Wharton 1911, v). Wolff agreed with this assessment.

> If we remove the accidents from a writer like Sarah Orne Jewett . . . what will we find? . . . We read of early-morning blueberries, and succulent fresh fish, of hot tea and cold milk, and of long, chilly, dreamless summer nights. The disruptions in such a world are few (and they often come as unwelcome invasions from the world outside), but peace has been purchased at the price of passion. There is no rage, and the climax of sexual fulfillment has been indefinitely suspended. (Wolff 178)

The reality is, had Wharton "breathed life into daily experiences" as DeVoto had wished, it would have diluted the message that is at the heart of the novel, what the narrator in the Prologue calls the "negation" of life that was a woman's lot in the nineteenth-century. And again, it's only the inability of male—and, it must be said, female—critics to understand how these women's issues are exemplified in Ethan's miserable existence, that keeps them from seeing *Ethan Frome* as a masterpiece in a way that they could never have imagined.

Another criticism that makes a similar point comes from Alfred Kazin, who stated unequivocally, "the world of the Frome tragedy is abstract" (Kazin 81). And while this is absolutely true, again, he makes the point for entirely the wrong reason. Kazin's intention was to suggest that Wharton was too distant from the real people of rural New England, despite her summer residences there, to render them accurately, and like Björkman he sees the work in economic terms—Kazin's specific argument, that Wharton's treatment of her characters was based on her hatred of the lower classes, is one that is best ignored. Yet also like Björkman, in doing this he comes incredibly close to articulating the very issue for women that the book really represents. "Ethan . . . is spiritually superior and materially useless. He has been loyal to one set of values, one conception of happiness, but powerless before the obligations of his society" (81). While Kazin sees this as a flaw in a similar way that Trilling does—Ethan is weak, but it's Wharton's fault—he also misses the true implication of his own words. As a result of marriage laws women actually were "materially useless," but through no fault of their own. They adhered to society's values and ideas of success not because they thought they were right but because women were, in fact, "powerless before the obligations" of patriarchal society. All of which does tend to make *Ethan Frome* an abstract story. The struggle that Ethan goes through is not really with Zeena at all but against the societal expectations that oppressed him the same way they did to the women of his time. The review of the novel in the *New York Times* makes a similar point in criticizing both Wharton and the novel. "She never shows life as it is, as the great novelists do, but as an aspect or view of life—the reflex of life on the writer if you will—which colors all things with some mastering mood of him or her" (Ochs, 65). Again, the charge that Wharton was not attempting to duplicate life is correct, but for the wrong reason. This is yet another negative response to the author's move away from realism without understanding why, or understanding what she was actually able to achieve by doing so.

A further attempt to grapple with this apparent contradiction comes from Geoffrey Walton, who also comes tantalizingly close to understanding the true nature of the symbolism of the novel, ironically, by trying to eliminate it altogether. The obvious reason the kind of overt societal restraint that appears in Wharton's other work seems to be absent in *Ethan Frome* is because *Ethan Frome* is an entirely symbolic novel. So because he doesn't see it, Walton tries to jettison the idea completely. "It is a tale of gratuitous and unavoidable frustration of natural impulses, of revolt, and of suffering. There is again no social conflict; human and inanimate environment seem all one" (Walton 86). The irony here is that Ethan's environment *is* the social conflict. As demonstrated earlier, the winter snow is representative of the social restrictions placed on individuals. Zeena, in her role as society's oppressive imposition on the will of her spouse, "has become both the supreme product and, for Frome, the ever-present representative of that environment, a silent brooding power from which he cannot escape" (86). Again, this is a perfect description of the way that the environment in *Ethan Frome* is able to symbolize the same inescapable power that kept women imprisoned within the confines of their marriages by a society that viewed them only as dependents. In Walton's mind, "it is all too primitive to be called social rebellion," but that's finally the point (87-88). *Ethan Frome* is not about disobeying one's family, one's ethnic group, or even one's social class. In reality it is the ultimate example of social rebellion because it is about rebelling against *the entirety of society's assumptions* . . . and losing.

But by far the most fascinating attempt to deal with the symbolic nature of *Ethan Frome* and the unconscious power that it conveys to the reader comes from author Grace Kellogg. Her rather convoluted argument begins by refuting the notion that Wharton's time in Lenox gave her any insight at all into the lives of the "hill-people" she had written about so eloquently:

> There is no record or least likelihood that Mrs. Wharton ever spent any summer—or week or a night—under a village roof anywhere in New England. Even from the daily life of Lenox The Mount stood in the main remote and aloof. Nor was Lenox village, with its comfortable modest affluence, fringed with pretensions of elegance, in any way representative of the back country . . . To know the Berkshire back country at all would have meant living in it long enough to penetrate its inner life and attitudes—a difficult achievement. Those meager homes, those introverted hard lives, were shut jealously and suspiciously away from the city-bred outsider whose friendliest interest would be taken for patronizing curiosity. (Kellogg 160, 163)

Kellogg goes on to claim that Wharton's only mistake was in attempting to defend herself in print and argue that she actually was writing from personal knowledge. But when Blake Nevius suggests that her setting needs no more justification than that of any historical novelist—citing Marsha Davenport's *The Valley of Decision* as evidence—Kellogg even balks at that. "Mr. Nevius seems to have made an unhappy choice of example to buttress his argument . . .

Those two bulky volumes are a splendid spectacle. They glitter and flash and gleam; they blaze with color. But like too many historical pageants they are for looking at. They do not draw one into a life re-created in the pages . . . The truth is that Mrs. Wharton is one writer who preeminently had to know her material" (162).

So here is an apparent paradox. Kellogg claims on the one hand that Wharton in no way was drawing from personal experience during her residence in the Berkshires when she wrote *Ethan Frome*, and yet at the same time argues that Wharton could only write from personal experience. "There is a mystery," Kellogg admits, "about this novel. For half a century it has nagged at us. For half a century critics have pecked away at it, trying to come at the moment of truth" (Kellogg 165). But the blame for the mystery she places at the feet of Wharton herself. "The controversy would have died down, in all probability, if Mrs. Wharton herself had not kept it alive . . . It would have been much better if she had retired into a dignified silence . . . But that was the one thing Edith could not do: retreat under attack" (163). Kellogg's suggestion—"that handy expression found so useful by many a prosecuting attorney"—is that *Ethan Frome*, as so many critics have insisted, is not really a New England story at all, and at the same time that Wharton could only have written it from her own experience.

> I suggest that the copybook situation [Wharton's original French short story] had vaguely linked itself with a familiar folk tale from Brittany—or perhaps the Basque country—or some Alpine village . . . not when, on a day long past, Edith Wharton saw a squalid back country farmhouse in the Berkshires, but on a motor drive along a mountain road in France when, high above a tiny village clinging to the rugged slope, she glimpsed a solitary dwelling and conceived the isolation of winter within it. (168)

Kellogg posits that Wharton may have been reluctant to submit a European story to her publisher and so she simply transposed the setting to New England. "There was no sin in such a transplanting," says Kellogg. But the result, "produced a changeling, one of those eerie creatures a little dislocated from the environment with something of an elfin otherworldliness about them that disconcerts the observer. The critical world sensed this wrongness and it made them uneasy" (168). And like every other critic writing about the way *Ethan Frome* produces an effect of feeling that can't be articulated, Kellogg comes to the perfect conclusion but for the wrong reason: "Once we accept this theory of the transplanted story everything that has puzzled and disturbed us falls into place." It's true there is a changeling at the heart of *Ethan Frome*, but it's not the setting, it's the main character. Men and women both, who had become inured to the inherent unfairness and inequality that was an inescapable part of women's lives at the turn of the twentieth century, were able to sympathize with Ethan's plight, and recognize in it a suffering that could have only one purpose, in the words of Lionel Trilling, "to shake us with the perception of social injustice, to instruct us in the true nature of social life" (Trilling 1956, 40).

It seems fitting that perhaps the best assessment of Edith Wharton's achievement in writing *Ethan Frome* comes from one of the least persuasive writings about her work. While author Gary Scharnhorst makes an essentially unsupportable argument in his essay on Mattie Silver, he nevertheless was able to characterize the true nature of Wharton's novel more accurately than any other writer. His summation explains not only the way Edith Wharton was able to demonstrate the illogical nature of female oppression in the character of Ethan, but also the way Ethan's reaction to that oppression in creating an imaginary love relationship with Mattie destroyed an entire family in the process. "*Ethan Frome* is a sad naturalistic tale set in a stark New England village, but it is a story of tragic love only in the most superficial sense. It is also an experiment in point of view that has misdirected readers with narrative sleight-of-hand for nearly a century" (Scharnhorst 270).

The year before she died Edith Wharton wrote—and not without some measure of dismay—of her reaction to a critic who expressed the belief that *Ethan Frome* was the one work of hers that would remain popular after the rest of Wharton's oeuvre had been forgotten. "His reference to me . . . was to the effect that that *Ethan Frome* had some chance of surviving, though everything else I had written was destined to immediate oblivion. I took the blow meekly, bowed but not broken . . . Perhaps the lecturer was right" (Wharton 1936, vii). Two years earlier, in her autobiography, she had already expressed frustration with the praise heaped on the novel—to what can obviously be assumed she felt was to the detriment of her later works. "I am far from thinking *Ethan Frome* my best novel and am bored and even exasperated when I am told it is" (Wharton 1934, 209). Interestingly, this quote is often misunderstood to mean that she didn't like the book at all, as this 1950 newspaper account attests: "Mrs. Wharton wrote some 40 books. The best seller of the books available at present, though the author was reported to have disliked it, is the novel *Ethan Frome*, published in 1911" (Editor 6-50, 3). But that's not at all what Wharton was saying. Her issue was with the idea that *Ethan Frome* was her only great work, which implied that some of her works she valued more would necessarily be overlooked as a consequence.

One of the harshest critics of the book at the time of its initial publication, Elizabeth Shepley Sergeant, was unimpressed with Wharton's bleak picture of rural New England life, and was very vehement in her belief that *Ethan Frome* did not show life at all, but was instead a "literary copy of it," which would ultimately reveal its lack of artistry over time.

> Wait till you are old! That is a New England counsel, but just wait! Then "The Queen's Twin," and the "Dunnet Sheperdess" [two stories by Sarah Orne Jewett] will still be full of living human poetry and truth and the salt-sweet scent of high coastal pastures, and Ethan Frome will be rotting in his grave. (Lauer 125)

While Edith Wharton is not the beneficiary of the hindsight modern readers are allowed, there is some measure of satisfaction that can be had in the knowledge that while *Ethan Frome* has been taught in public schools in America for nearly a century and remains one of the author's most popular novels, "The Queen's Twin," and the "Dunnet Sheperdess" are virtually unknown today. In 1934 writer O.O. McIntyre gave this astute assessment of the book, which essentially says it all: "Edith Wharton's *Ethan Frome* is about the second best story ever told by an American. No. 1, of course, is *Huckleberry Finn*" (McIntyre 8).

The *Ethan Frome* Legacy

Even before Edith Wharton's death in 1937 *Ethan Frome* had attained a cultural significance that demonstrated it was already firmly rooted in the popular consciousness. A 1924 news story from New Hampshire with a cruelly ironic twist naturally brought to mind for the reporter an equally tragic tale set in the same vicinity. "Edith Wharton, who gave the world the New English tragedy in her book, *Ethan Frome*, could return to the same atmosphere and find a plot in a recent incident in New Hampshire . . . Elizabeth Ruth Dart and Louis W. Rollins, New Hampshire orphans, who loved and married and then were cast into jail . . .

> They were abandoned to the care of an orphan asylum when they were infants. Elizabeth was adopted by one family and Louis by another. They took the names of their foster parents and, living in nearby communities, grew up together and became lovers . . . Recently they married. Then from the past came evidence that they were children of the same mother. And they were imprisoned in Portsmouth as the law forbids consanguineous marriages. (Grimm, 4)

Though the situations are entirely different, there is something in the lingering suffering of Ethan and Zeena and Mattie that brings to mind the suffering that Dart and Rollins would be forced to live with the rest of their lives. The writer finally goes on to give an epitaph that is equally worthy of the ending of Wharton's novel. "Even the court must realize the futility of the law in heaping further punishment upon these children, broken upon the wheel of life . . . Pity and projection are all that human charity and justice can give them."

Eric B. Olsen

Ten years later, in a newspaper self-help column from 1934 titled "Friendly Counsel" by Caroline Chatfield, a husband wrote in to ask advice about his sickly wife.

> Dear Miss Chatfield: I am married to a complaining woman who is not satisfied with anything. She complains of her health. It is better than mine, yet while I work she lies in bed and groans, and leaves the housework for me to do when I get home in the evening. She spends all I earn on doctors and medicine and never gets any better . . . What is a man to do when a woman won't get out of bed? (Chatfield 14)

Miss Chatfield's advice centered on getting the wife out of the house. "Show her what a good time you could have together if she would make the effort to go around with you." Barring that, however, "If she won't budge out of bed, go out in the evening occasionally and leave her by herself." Then Chatfield warned him against showing her sympathy and suggested he point out unfair the situation is for him. Finally, she ended with this piece of advice: "Buy a copy of *Ethan Frome*, written by Edith Wharton, and read it aloud to her. There is a life-size picture of her in that book."

It is also interesting to observe the effect the ending of the book had on some readers, in which it became for them the wintertime version of *Jaws*. But instead of staying out of the water for fear of sharks, people were staying off the slopes for fear of a nasty elm tree waiting at the bottom. "I blame myself for what happened to Astra and me," said columnist Susan Ager in 2006. "Once upon a time I loved sledding, I guess. What child doesn't?

> But a few years ago I read Edith Wharton's bleak classic *Ethan Frome*, first published in [1911]. It climaxes with two would-be lovers aiming their sled toward an elm tree, hoping it would kill them and unite them in the afterlife. Instead, the woman is paralyzed, Ethan is left lame and bitter—and his wife must take care of them both. I decided no good can come on steep snowy hills. (Ager 41)

But sure enough, like Quint and Brody and Hooper setting out on the water in the Orca, Ager went against her better judgment to go coasting with her ten-year-old niece. And just as in Peter Benchley's potboiler—and Steven Spielberg's popular film—danger was waiting for them. "The flying sled flung us off and our faces collided with the icy snow and even through my bulky coat I could feel my huge body sliding right over Astra's head. I ended up with a two-inch scratch on my cheek . . . Astra's face was scraped all over, as if someone had dragged her down a long, carpeted hallway." But there were no broken bones and tragedy was averted, and in giving the girl a terrific tale to tell when she returned to school, "I was reminded again of one of life's happiest ironies: Bad times can make the best stories."

Because the novel has been taught for decades in junior and senior high schools across the country—by teachers who obviously have little idea what is really in Wharton's work and to students far too young to make sense of it—*Ethan Frome* was bound to come in for some good natured ribbing, if not outright ridicule over the years. Most of these comments are not very complimentary, as they paint the enforced reading of the story in terms nearly as excruciating as Ethan's life after the smash up. In a novel by Brock Clarke, a faux-autobiography called *An Arsonist's Guide to Writers' Homes in New England*, the main character, Sam, makes it his mission to destroy all that American readers have held dear in his neck of the woods. Reviewer Connie Ogle, however, posits that the loss of *Ethan Frome* might not be as great as some of Sam's other destructions. "OK, maybe nobody loves Edith Wharton's tiresome sad sack; anyone forced to endure that wretched novel in eighth grade might applaud Sam when he kicks a copy of the book. 'In doing so I imagined I was striking a blow on behalf of its many unwilling, barely pubescent readers'" (Ogle 49). But one of the best comic summaries of the novel comes in this Dave Barry-like send up by Amanda Mitchell from 2008. "*Ethan Frome,* by Edith Wharton:

A man laid up in a small, snow-bound New England town winds up staying with the most depressing man on the planet. Thrill as Ethan almost wears the pants in his family, almost cheats on his wife, and almost finds some happiness in a cold, cruel world. You will almost finish it. (Mitchell 13)

A real *Ethan Frome* oddity, however, is a piece of music written by New York composer Josef Alexander called the "New England Overture." The music premiered in St. Louis, played by that city's symphony orchestra on February 12, 1943, and apparently left much to be desired.

The concert began with a "New England Overture" by Josef Alexander, one of the Massachusetts group of composers. According to the program notes, this music was inspired by a reading of Edith Wharton's *Ethan Frome.* What sounded like brittle orchestration and a wholly inexpressive melodic line was undoubtedly Mr. Alexander's way of translating irony into music. The audience met this unpromising work with an indifference you could cut with a knife. (Sherman 5)

Given that review, it's no wonder Alexander's composition has never been recorded commercially. But what may be a surprise is how much more music Wharton's novel has inspired. An *Ethan Frome* ballet made its appearance thirty years later in Connecticut, with Allan Miles staging what he called a "dramatic ballet" for the Connecticut Valley Regional Ballet Company. First choreographed in 1970, Christopher Neilson was the composer of the piece entitled *The Silent Cry of Ethan Frome*.

Shortly after Edith Wharton's death another New York composer, Frederick Woltmann, began composing the first opera based on *Ethan Frome*.

> Woltmann had long wanted to write an opera on the Edith Wharton novel. He had set sail in 1937 for France to speak with the authoress, but while on board was informed of her death. Asked for assistance, the Academy directors sent him to the literary executor, who said it was fine with him (and would have been with Wharton), but Woltmann first had to obtain dramatic rights from Owen Davis and his son Donald, who had gotten these rights from Wharton. The composer had some difficulty with Davis; finally, by late December 1939, he obtained them. In 1938-1939 Woltmann arranged the libretto and designed the scenery but the opera never came to fruition. (Olmstead 34-35)

The composer did manage to write an overture and two scenes worth of music, and would perform them on occasion, usually as piano pieces in support of a vocalist. But this was just one of several operas that have been based on *Ethan Frome*. The next was by Douglas Allanbrook, a lyric opera for five voices composed in 1955. Aaron Copeland had initially promised to have the opera produced in New York, but when he went on to other things Allanbrook shelved the manuscript. It wasn't until nearly fifty years later that Allanbrook's son rescued the work and after several performances it was commercially recorded in 1999. Another mention of an *Ethan Frome* opera came in 1973, composed by Ottawa University music professor William Kloster, but there is no real record of it having been performed other than in a couple of newspaper articles about the work's premiere at the Kansas State Teacher's College music teachers convention. More recently, composer Caryn Block wrote a three-act opera of the novel that premiered in 2012. A final humorous coda to this musical outpouring came about after *Ethan Frome* had been made into a film in 1993, when an unwitting columnist made this comment after recounting the grim tragedy of the story for his readers: "*Ethan Frome* may yet be unfinished. It sure ought to be an opera" (Swindell 27).

Ethan Frome on the Stage

One of the earliest dramatic presentations of *Ethan Frome* was a performance in 1913 by students attending the Lawrence University's School of Expression in Appleton Wisconsin. Anne Mitchell's one-act adaptation divided the story into three scenes, "Scene 1—The Forboding, Scene 2—In the Absence of Zeena, Scene 3—The Catastrophe" (Ryan, 4). Twelve years later a group of college students from USC presented another dramatic performance of the novel in the spring of 1925. The students were members of a group called "The Players' Guild of Metropolitan College, University of Southern California" (Andrews, 21). The playwright, John Baxter Rogers, called his adaptation *The Elm*, and appeared himself in the starring role as Ethan. His co-stars were Margaret Goodyear and Beatrice Hanning. Of course college productions like these were completely unauthorized by Wharton, but then they were never intended as moneymaking ventures and so there was very little motivation for the author or her publisher to pursue legal action, especially considering the bad press it would engender. Another student adaptation was written the following year and appeared in the February issue of the Columbia University magazine *Morningside*.

> Ferrice Fraser has done an excellent dramatization of Edith Wharton's *Ethan Frome*. The action and suspense are kept up throughout the short play, and the whole thing runs smoothly without the accustomed groaning of machinery that is audible in most patchwork adaptations of current novels. It is not only readable, but would probably lend itself very well to action. (Blumberg, 3)

It would not be until 1936, just a year before the author's death, that the first authorized dramatization of *Ethan Frome* made it to the professional stage. What's so curious is why it had taken that long for the project to materialize. Wharton herself had worked on an adaptation of her short story "The Joy of Living" with playwright Herrmann Sudermann, which was brought to the stage by producer Charles Frohman in 1902. Though the play ran for less than a month, Wharton was well aware of the financial potential of turning her works into Broadway productions. Her next collaboration was with Clyde Fitch on *The House of Mirth* in 1906, but it was also short lived and closed in just a few weeks. Nevertheless, Wharton was working in good company. "Fitch and the play's producer Charles Frohman were among the ruling elite who controlled the commercial U.S. stage providing popular stars in often effective but ephemeral plays" (Anderson 157). Another major production, this time of *The Age of Innocence*, was much more successful, playing for over two hundred performances in 1928-29. The circumstances surrounding *Ethan Frome* were much different, however, for a couple of reasons. In the first place, this wasn't the first time she had been approached about producing a theatrical version of the story, but "lingering concern for her characters is borne out by the number of times she refused to entertain requests to adapt the novel. Protective of the novel for more than two decades, she rebuffed a series of producers and playwrights attracted by the dramatic qualities of the work" (Fournier 124). The second reason had to do with money.

One of the unintended consequences of Edith Wharton's move to Europe was that the sales of her books gradually began to decline, especially during the early part of the Depression. With a large extended family to support, Wharton continued to look to the theater as a way to generate badly needed income. In 1934 she sold the rights to her novella *The Old Maid*, which was concluding a successful run on Broadway during the adaptation process of *Ethan Frome*, going on to earn a Pulitzer Prize for playwright Zoë Akins in 1935. In terms of other works that could be converted into a theater piece, *Ethan Frome* was an obvious choice, as its brevity and limited locations seemed to be ideally suited for the stage. Further, a fairly negative review of the book in the *New York Times* in 1911 ended with this thought: "There are dramatists who do not write for the theatre and so pass as novelists. It seems to this reviewer that Mrs. Wharton belongs properly to the last classification and that *Ethan Frome* is the proof of it" (Ochs, 65). And even Scribner's own advertisements for the novel frequently quoted a review from the *New York Evening Sun*. "So absorbing is the book that you want to read it at the sitting. You can read it that way with the result that the total impression is as vivid as on going away at the close of the performance of a great play" (5).

In a similar fashion as the spontaneous creation of those earlier college productions, it appears that Wharton was not the one who initiated the process. Instead, a playwright from Santa Barbara, California, named Lowell Barrington Christ, who used the pen name Barrington, set about writing a stage version of Wharton's novel. Whether he ever contacted Wharton to get permission is unclear, especially as he went on to obtain a copyright, but with Wharton's reluctance to allow the novel to be adapted he was probably working on his own initiative. In the copyright entry from June of 1934 his work—which he titled *The Silent Women*—was described as a play in three acts with a prologue and an epilogue. It was at that point that Barrington sent his completed adaptation to New York producer Jed Harris. Harris liked the treatment and passed it on to Wharton in Paris, who agreed with him. But Wharton was also savvy enough, or perhaps greedy because of the success of *The Old Maid*, to instruct Harris to find a big-name playwright to do a rewrite in order to generate the kind of income she was looking for. Her first choice was Owen Davis. Davis had been tremendously successful on Broadway with his literary adaptations, including F. Scott Fitzgerald's *The Great Gatsby* in 1926, and *The Good Earth* by Pearl Buck in 1932, though it was his original story, *Icebound*, that won him the Pulitzer Prize in 1923. In a 1936 interview Davis himself tells the story this way:

> A year ago last August, a long-distance call from Jed Harris asking me if I thought I could make a play out of Mrs. Wharton's novel started the chain that ended with the production of *Ethan Frome*. Something of a task it turned out to be. There had been a dramatization by Lowell Barrington, and we all agreed that Mr. Barrington had at least a claim on us of being the one who brought the idea to Mr. Harris' attention. (Sedgwick 20)

Davis agreed to rewrite Barrington's play and brought in his son Donald to help him work on the adaptation. "Donald and I turned over our first draft to Mr. Harris in about three months and he received it with flattering enthusiasm" (Sedgwick 20). In his autobiography, *My First Fifty Years in the Theatre*, however, Davis makes some patently false claims about Wharton's novel. "It was the story of something that happened twenty years before and none of the characters, either of the book or of the play, told any of it" (Davis 1950, 136). While it is technically true that the narrator tells the bulk of the inner story, they are Ethan's thoughts, and there is plenty of dialogue throughout the novel. Davis then goes on to say that Wharton had given her characters, "no voices at all . . ." and despite the tragic nature of the story, "nowhere in the book was there a record of a single angry word" (137). This is also untrue, as Ethan and Zeena exchange angry words in at least one scene. The only likely explanation for this description of the book is that Davis was primarily remembering the Barrington version of the story rather than Wharton's original, especially when he makes the claim that, "What Zenobia had said, and what Ethan had said, was . . . always in the words of some neighbor who was repeating it, [and] Mattie was only told about" (137). This description of the story, which bears absolutely no resemblance to Wharton's novel, might also account for the significant changes in character that appeared in the Davis's adaptation. Nevertheless, after Jed Harris sent the first draft to Wharton in France, she agreed to go ahead with the project.

In the December 1, 1934 contract that was worked out between the parties Wharton retained fifty percent ownership over the property while Barrington and the Davis's split the other half, an agreement that also allowed the Davis's to use anything in the Barrington version they wanted—which, again, seems to be significant. The project was announced eleven days later, and Harris already had an actress in mind to play Mattie, though it would be a year before the play went into production. "Ruth Gordon is to have the lead in *Ethan Frome*, the new Owen and Donald Davis play which Jed Harris will produce" (Soanes 19). Harris was also said to have spent a good deal of time working on the play with the Davis's, though Donald primarily, according to his father.

> Jed Harris, I think, is one of the most able editors of playscripts in the world . . . He and Donald devoted many hours a day to careful revision and elaboration of character drawing, brutally hard work in which I bore very little share, partly because of other work I had to do, but more, I think, because Donald's careful and honest method of playwriting seemed to me to offer more promise than my own in this particular occasion. (Sedgwick 20)

Harris had an interesting cast in mind that was referenced six months later in June. "That mystery man of the theatre, Jed Harris . . . is expected back from Hollywood most any day now to begin work on *Ethan Frome*, the Edith Wharton novel which Owen and Donald Davis have dramatized and which Harris would have done last year had he been able to assemble Willard Robertson, Ruth Gordon and Beulah Bondi for the leading roles" (Mantle 6-35, 66). The only problem was that Harris was unable to get Robertson—or anyone else for that matter—to actually commit to play the part of Ethan, and by November he decided to temporarily call off the project. "Partly because of the difficulty of finding a suitable leading man, strange as that statement may seem, Jed Harris has decided not to produce this season, at least, the play called *Ethan Frome*, with which it was expected he would make his way back to the theater. Instead, he has gone to Hollywood, where he may do picture work for a time" (Shaw 12).

With Jed Harris out of the picture Owen Davis persuaded Max Gordon, who had been so successful in the late twenties with *The Jazz Singer*, to produce the play. Gordon had actually fallen on hard times after the Depression hit and was making a substantial comeback in the mid-thirties when he brought *Ethan Frome* to the stage. By November Gordon was attempting to lure Pauline Lord out of retirement to play Zeena, and in addition to Ruth Gordon he was looking at James Bell as a possible Ethan. In December Gordon finally had his lineup set, beginning with Guthrie McClintic as director. McClintic was a logical choice to helm the project as he not only had directed Wharton's *The Age of Innocence* in 1928 but also *The Old Maid*, which had just finished it's run of over three hundred performances in September. The production starred Raymond Massy as Ethan, Ruth Gordon as Mattie, Pauline Lord as Zeena, Tom Ewell as Denis Eady, and Francis Pierlot as Jotham Powell.

> The earlier *Ethan Frome* rehearsals were at the Martin Beck. There, under the towering arch of the *Winterset* bridge, was the Frome kitchen: a pine table, a few straight chairs . . . One uncovered light wrapped the handful of actors in the sullen shadows of a Vermeer . . . It was a prophetic vision of the production which came into being four weeks later on the stage of the National Theatre. (Sedgwick 23)

The show first played to preview audiences at the Garrick Theater in Philadelphia in early January of 1936, and then moved to Broadway a short time later, opening on January 21, 1936 at The National Theatre, where it ran for nearly a hundred and twenty performances over the next four months. As had been the case with *The Old Maid*, the Davis's version of *Ethan Frome* was a tremendous hit and Wharton, who "kept an eye on the bottom line . . . monitored carefully the $130,000 earned in royalties and box-office returns" from the two plays (Anderson 157). Meanwhile Wharton's publisher, Scribner's, purchased the publishing rights to the play in late 1935 and put it out in book form the following January to capitalize on the play's opening.

In his review of the preview in Philadelphia writer Linton Martin emphasized the story and setting more than he did the performances by the actors. "The stage version carries with it a bleakness that gets into the bones. This is due to a degree to the atmospheric fidelity of Jo Mielziner's settings, with rooms that look as though they had really been lived in for years, and snow which causes shivers as impressed playgoers declare they can hear it crunch under the actors' feet" (Martin 57). The effect is not surprising, given Ruth Woodbury Sedgwick's opening paragraph in her story on the play for *Stage* magazine. "'I want it real,' said Guthrie McClintic at one of the early rehearsals of *Ethan Frome*. And real it is . . . It provides, for those in whose blood since 1620 has lived the austere beauty of America's frontiers, an experience as fundamental as going home" (Sedgwick 20,22). But Martin's review also repeats some of the inaccuracies surrounding the writing of the play that were no doubt perpetuated by Owen Davis himself, as they appeared in his autobiography the same way fifteen years later. "For one thing, they had no direct dialogue to 'lift' from the novel to stage, for readers will recall that that Mrs. Wharton's entire story was told in the second person [sic] by a visitor who met Ethan twenty years after the narrated events" (Martin 57). Finally, Martin goes on to make the interesting suggestion that, "Perhaps the play may be enjoyed better by those who have not read the novel, because of the surprise of the ironic ending, in the results of an intended suicide pact that missed fire, leaving worse than frustration as its aftermath."

Burns Mantle of *The New York Daily Post* had good things to say about the play after it moved to New York and opened on Broadway at the National Theatre. "Owen Davis is New England born and knows both the country and the characters that Mrs. Wharton drew so truthfully out of it. Raymond Massy, playing the titular character . . . has feeling for and knowledge of the Ethan he plays superbly. Given as aid to these, such consummate emotionalists as Pauline Lord for the unpleasant part of Zenobia Frome and Ruth Gordon for the lighter but equally intense part of Mattie Silver, and the story becomes a dramatic reality of the first quality" (Mantle 1-36, 47). Mantle eventually went on to list the play as one of his ten best for 1936. Arthur Pollock of *The Brooklyn Daily Eagle*, however, was not nearly as impressed. He called the play "dignified, honestly and simply realistic and, with its many changes of scene, a little monotonous . . . This stage *Ethan Frome* is a workmanlike production, having all the merits that can be asked of good reproductions and the perhaps unavoidable defect of seeming a warmed-over dish" (Pollock 13). He nevertheless recommended the actors and the play as a whole, stating, "It is an excellent production, an excellent cast, a grim, old-style entertainment." In general, the reviews from across the New York area were positive and after the show ended its run at the National it went on the road a few months later to equally glowing reviews.

The play opens on a set showing the back of the Frome house in the wintertime, with the narrator from the book and Harmon Gow there to ask Ethan if he'd be willing to drive the narrator over to the power station in Corbury since Denis Eady's horses are sick. The description of Ethan as he comes out of the house is essentially the one from the novel, and what is called a prologue to the first act is a condensation of Wharton's Prologue. It's actually a fairly clever piece of writing, as Gow delivers all of the pertinent information from Wharton's Prologue and peaks the narrator's—and the audience's—interest at the same time. In fact, parts of the entire adaptation are impressively rendered. Things that Ethan only reminisces about in the narration are fully developed on the stage in a way that wouldn't even be attempted in the filmed version sixty years later. At the same time, however, the love relationship between Ethan and Mattie is so blunt as to render everything that is unconsciously powerful about the novel meaningless. And while the Davis's also manage to get a lot of Wharton's symbolism into the stage directions, that's not something the audience is going to experience or understand. As happens with so many literary adaptations to the stage, there is no subtlety, no room for interpretation at all, and as a result it virtually turns the play into a different story.

Act One begins with a true deviation from the novel, the action starting in early spring and the Davis's expanding on episodes only referred to in the book. It must be said, however, that the skill involved in doing so is admirable. The opening scene has Ethan bringing wood into the kitchen and cutting kindling by the fireplace. Zeena makes her way in a short time later complaining about the window in the spare bedroom. After she continues to complain, Ethan puts down his hatchet and runs upstairs to fix the window while Zeena pours herself some tea and sits down to read her medical catalogue. Ethan returns a minute later and goes back to his work without having said a word to his wife the entire time. It's a nice way of demonstrating Ethan's explanation of this dynamic in the novel: "When she spoke it was only to complain, and to complain of things not in his power to remedy; and to check a tendency to impatient retort he had first formed the habit of not answering her, and finally of thinking of other things while she talked" (Wharton 1911, 78). When Zeena asks him directly for something in the catalogue, however, he replies shortly, without turning around, "How'd I pay for it?" (Davis 1936, 19). Then she intimates that something is wrong with their milk cow, but Ethan knows exactly what her intention is and says he's not going to sell it.

Ethan further implies that he has cattle he is raising, though that is strikingly at odds with the novel. In Wharton's story, while the Fromes could possibly have a milk cow, Ethan seems far too poor to purchase feed for animals during the winter, which is why he makes his living selling timber from his property instead. Zeena continues to complain about her health, as well as the fact that Ethan never listens to her, and how the doctor says she should have a hired girl to help her around the house. Ethan thinks for a moment and then asks why she sent Jotham Powell up to the train platform. He thought she had sent him there to pick up some medicine for her, but now Ethan presses her and Zeena admits to him that Mattie Silver is coming. "No she ain't!" Ethan shouts. "If I told you once—I told you fifty times I won't have her here—I won't have nobody here! And I won't have you whinin' and moanin' for doctorin' and . . . hired girls with my cattle out there starvin' to death!" (Davis 1936, 23-24). This is also a significant departure in character for Ethan who, despite his desire to ignore Zeena, seems easily goaded into emotional outbursts. At the same time, Zeena's implacable nature in the novel is transformed into an infuriating passive-aggressive mock innocence that makes Ethan's impassioned retorts seem more than justified. After pretending that she wants to do everything she can to help her poor relative, she finally reveals, "And bein' my cousin—course we won't have to pay her wages" (24).

Denis Eady turns up a moment later with Mattie's trunk, and Ethan does everything he can to get him to take it back to the train station. But when Denis says he would need to get paid, that puts an end to the discussion. After he leaves, Ethan goes back to chopping kindling while Zeena delivers a lengthy monologue disclosing some of Mattie's backstory, in addition to complaining about how she herself has no clothes, can't eat, and will most likely die soon. By the time Jotham arrives with Mattie, Ethan is almost relieved because it will get Zeena to stop talking. Mattie knocks on the door and enters, saying hello to Ethan, who barely acknowledges her. Then Mattie addresses Zeena and happily blathers on about everything she can think of. Zeena tells her she'll have to start right away, as she has her shooting pains, and Mattie is happy to do so. Unlike the dour character from the book, Jotham actually laughs at Mattie's behavior even after Ethan tries to shame him into silence. In fact, in the play he is something of an instigator, teasing Zeena and doing whatever he can to create tension between she and Ethan. Mattie demonstrates her ineptitude right away when she can't find the supper dishes, and so Ethan serves up the stew himself. Despite his grim demeanor—and Zeena's vocal disapproval of Mattie's lack of skills—Ethan does warm to her by the end of the scene, smiling and saying, "Well—she ain't a fretter, anyhow!" (Davis 1936, 47).

The second scene of the first act begins less than a year later, outside the church at the dance that opens the internal story of the novel. In the play, however, there is no place for Ethan to hide, and so he must interact with nearly everyone who exits the church. One of the fascinating things that emerges from his conversation with Ed Varnum, Ruth's father, is that Ethan actually sold him the milk cow back in the spring so that Zeena could buy her medical equipment. This is the first moment when Ethan's character is undermined by his actions, and the beginning of the audience's suspicion that he might be far less inclined to stand up to Zeena than the first scene would suggest. He then goes on to ask Varnum if he can buy the cow back, but is refused. It's a moment as embarrassing for the audience as it is for Ethan. The Davis's use the exiting villagers to convey the substance of what is happening inside through their dialogue. They tell Ethan that Mattie is having another dance with Denis Eady, and that the young man will probably bring her home. Then Ethan pulls back further into the shadows as Ned and Ruth come outside and kiss. Another major change happens when Eady suddenly emerges from the church to ask if he can take Mattie home and Ethan refuses his request.

Eady is still pleading with him when Mattie comes out, but then Ethan says it's her decision. While she sends Denis on his way, she has no qualms about expressing her displeasure at Ethan's manipulation. "If I'd knowed you was goin' to be put out about it—I wouldn't never've waited for that last dance, Ethan" (Davis 1936, 66). Ethan says he isn't put out, but immediately begins walking away from her. Downstage they each turn a different direction. Mattie wants him to go her way, but he refuses, and they end up going their different ways as the curtain comes down.

The third scene begins with Ethan halfway home. Mattie suddenly appears at his side and asks him not to be angry. Again, he denies he is. She intimates that the only reason she passed up the ride with Eady is because she knows Zeena makes Ethan walk to get her, and she didn't want him to walk home alone. Ethan then tells her that he doesn't really mind the walk, and in fact he's getting to like it. Then the two of them sit on a fallen log and talk about Zeena, the fact that they don't have time for making conversation at the house, and about Ned and Ruth's near fatal sledding accident. But their dialogue when he asks her if she wants to go sledding with him seems much too pedestrian. By now the audience has also become painfully aware of the extreme child-like nature of Mattie's character, especially when compared to her character in the novel. It's actually Ethan who suggests that she wouldn't need to be scared if she rode with him. When Ethan begins naming the stars, she gushes like she's five years old and her naiveté is fairly disconcerting. He tells her tales from the novel, about going to school in Worchester, and visiting Florida, but when she begins going on about the accident of birth her dialogue seems strangely out of place.

> MATTIE: Ain't it funny the way things go now when you just stop to think about 'em? Just supposin' my father hadn't've married Zeena's cousin . . . why I most probably wouldn't've been born at all! *Then thoughtfully.* Still 'n all . . . I don't knows I'd mind that!

> ETHAN: Some people might . . . I'm kind of glad myself . . . bein's that's why you're here. (Davis 1936, 82)

The purpose for this particular dialogue is that it accomplishes two things. First it confirms more directly what was only hinted at earlier: Ethan's interest in Mattie. The second thing it does is to suggest Mattie's indifference to her own existence.

Eric B. Olsen

Mattie goes on to tell him about the difficulties she experienced working in a mill and how her health has improved since moving to the farm. Then Ethan says that it's natural she'll be leaving them, but without his internal thoughts from the novel their dialogue goes back and forth without a clear understanding that he's talking about her getting married. As in the book, she assumes it will be Zeena's dissatisfaction with her that will ultimately end her employment, and then complains that Zeena doesn't give her any direction about how to improve. He tells her not to worry, that no one's going to get rid of her, then he finally gets around to suggesting she'll get married one day. "Why, who'd want to go and marry me?" (Davis 1936, 85). The underlying sentiment is the same as in Wharton's novel, but in saying it aloud it makes it seem as if it's more Mattie's failing as a woman than merely her circumstances—though as far as her dialogue in the play goes, that's not far wrong. All subtlety goes out the window, however, when Mattie comes out and says that nobody's rushing to marry her and Ethan responds by telling her that he would, if he could. "That's interestin', ain't it?" she says. "Maybe you would, Ethan . . . but nobody else . . . anyhow you couldn't." But Ethan is still compelled to tell her, "No, I don't guess I could . . . But I mean, if I could . . . I would" (86). At this point any resemblance to Wharton's novel is gone. Ethan has made it clear to Mattie that he wants to marry her, and she knows it. She even finds it "interestin'," which is also completely out of character for a late nineteenth-century woman to consider, much less suggest out loud. The conceit of the play, however, is that the frame story is contemporary— "It was back in 1910 when Ethan and Mattie fell in love" (Sedgwick 20). But there's not that much difference between the two periods, and the whole scene seems far more in keeping with the time the play was produced rather than when the interior story was set. Mercifully, the curtain finally comes down on the third scene.

Scene Four opens on the same set outside the Frome house as the Prologue, but this time at night. Ethan and Mattie are still talking about the stars as they approach the back door. Then Mattie asks Ethan about the people buried in the graveyard next to the house. Again, all subtlety is abandoned when Mattie blurts out, "Ethan, don't you ever want to get away from here" (Davis 1936, 90). But she doesn't wait for an answer and goes on to read the tombstones, including the one with the elder Ethan Frome and his wife Endurance. It's here where Ethan recounts the death of his parents, and how Zeena came to take care of his mother at the end of her life. Strangely, it's Mattie who suggests that if she never leaves them she'll be buried there alongside him. Finally Ethan goes to look for the key, and is alarmed to find it missing. Mattie helps him look for it but is equally unsuccessful. Then a light begins to glow in the house and becomes stronger just as Zeena opens the door for them. She says she felt too mean to go to sleep and the two of them enter the house, which concludes the first act.

Act Two opens on Ethan and Zeena's bedroom the following morning. Ethan is shaving while Zeena lies in bed coughing. She teases him about whistling and the fact that he has been shaving regularly the past week, but unlike the novel he seems fairly impervious to it. Zeena makes a big deal of how cold it is, and for comedic effect gets dressed in stages, retreating back under the covers after donning each layer. Ethan finally tells her that she should just stay in bed all day, but Zeena complains that Mattie isn't adept enough to keep the house running on her own. "I have to work twice as hard now's I ever did before—that's what's ailin' me . . . followin' her around . . . showin' her . . . watchin' over her . . ." (Davis 1936, 106). It's here that Zeena begins to intimate Mattie will have to go, that in the end she's not worth having around. When Ethan says she's crazy for thinking that way, Zeena gets incredibly upset at the questioning of her sanity. In fact, she begins crying at that point, as though she's on the verge of an actual breakdown. When Mattie comes up to say breakfast is ready Zeena complains that she still feels a chill from the night before, after having to go downstairs and let the two of them in the house. Ethan had lied to Zeena earlier, saying that he had been talking business with Ed Varnum to explain why it took he and Mattie so long to get back from the church, but when Mattie suddenly confesses that they were late getting home because she had stayed to dance with Denis, Ethan is stung by his own embarrassment and quickly leaves the room.

With Ethan gone, Zeena keeps Mattie in the room to talk about Denis Eady. She intimates that because his father owns the grocery store he would be a good catch for her, and says that she can invite him over on Wednesday evenings if she wants. Unlike Mattie's distaste for Eady in the novel, which can only be surmised, here Mattie comes right out and says it. "Why—gory— what ever put that idea into your head, Zeena! And I never thought of him that way at all! I don't like *him!*" (Davis 1936, 116). Then, to the audience's horror, Mattie begins recounting Ethan's conversation with her the night before, about how he said he would marry her if he could. By the end of it Zeena is sitting up rigid in bed, and her stare is enough to frighten Mattie. As the girl nervously tries to take Zeena's breakfast tray and straighten her pillow, she winds up accidentally spilling coffee all over the blankets. Yet maddeningly, through it all, Mattie will not stop talking. In fact, this aspect of Mattie's character combined with her childish behavior was so noticeable that the reviewer for the *Harrisburg Telegraph* called her a "likeable little moron" (Stackpole, 19). Angrily, Zeena gets up and starts taking down her travelling clothes, and when Mattie tries to help her Zeena suddenly lashes out in a terrifically symbolic moment that is as much about Ethan as it is about her other possessions. "Don't you never touch none of my things. You hear me! You keep your hands off my things! An' don't forget that as long as you live!" (Davis 1936, 120). Finally Mattie leaves, and at the curtain Zeena begins getting dressed.

The second scene of the second act begins in the kitchen with Ethan eating breakfast as Mattie rushes down from upstairs. Ethan asks for more coffee but Mattie is in a state, hurriedly getting out the washtub in order to clean the soiled bed blankets. He gets up to help her pump water and stoke the fire, but when he asks what Zeena said to her Mattie tells him she said nothing. After Ethan instructs her to ignore half of what Zeena says, Zeena suddenly appears in the kitchen fully dressed for traveling. She sits at the table to have her breakfast, all the while ignoring Ethan's questions as to where she's going. She finally tells Mattie to ask Jotham to hitch up the sleigh before she deigns to inform Ethan of her plans. When she tells him she's going to Bettsbridge to see the new doctor Ethan reminds her that they don't have the money, as well as the fact that she already spent money on medical equipment that she still doesn't know how to use. Nevertheless, she informs him that she plans on spending all of their money to see the doctor because she is in so much pain. Her passive-aggressive manipulation of Ethan, telling him how sick she is and that she doesn't have the strength to walk into the village or she would, seems to be more of the reason he doesn't want to take her than his desire in the novel to spend that time with Mattie. But Zeena goes even further, as it's she who suggests that Ethan get Hale to pay him early for the timber, which in essence will force him to humiliate himself by begging so they won't starve. When she says she'll be staying the night, Ethan and Mattie look at each other, and for no apparent reason Zeena is pleased about this. Then she leaves, but before the curtain falls Mattie encourages Ethan not to be ashamed to ask for the money from Hale.

Scene Three opens on the same set, as night begins to fall. Mattie is preparing supper, and has retrieved the red pickle dish from the top shelf of the cupboard where Zeena keeps her medicine as Jotham Powell enters from outside. When Ethan comes downstairs he asks Jotham if he brought the cider that Andrew Hale gave him, but instead of Ethan's obsession to spend the night alone with Mattie from the book, the hired man is almost pressed into staying by the two of them. During their meal Ethan says he received twenty dollars in feed for the cattle from Hale. Mattie offers Ethan pickles from the red dish and he comments that he's never seen it before. When Mattie says Zeena never uses it, Jotham jokes that she must not like pickles and the three laugh. The subtle sexual symbolism is rather humorous. Mattie has also made a desert, something rare for the house, but when Jotham comments that he can't see why Zeena complains about her it causes a bit of tension in the room. After drinking some cider Jotham leaves the two alone. While Mattie cleans up, Ethan comments on the snow that's coming down and remembers that he was going to take her sledding that night. Ethan sits by the fire and smokes his pipe, while Mattie helps him off with his boots and gets his slippers from the hall. But the moment becomes a little too intimate for him and he abruptly pulls his foot away from her and they stand up facing each other. "Matt! Matt . . . that was real nice of you . . . an' I didn't mean to complain . . . I guess, I just ain't used to . . . any one . . . doin' for me . . . an . . ." (Davis 1936, 162). He offers to help her clean up the kitchen but she tells him to sit back down. Nevertheless, he reaches for a stack of dishes at the same time that Mattie does, and when she pulls her hand back it's she who knocks the pickle dish off the counter and breaks it.

Here the dialogue returns to what it was in the novel. Mattie becomes panicked at the idea of Zeena finding out she broke the dish. Ethan tries to comfort her by saying that he'll buy another one, but Mattie tells him it was a present from her aunt—not a wedding present, though. What this accomplishes is to tie in the breaking of the dish with the scolding Zeena gave Mattie that morning in the bedroom. "Oh, Ethan . . . she hates me so! And she told me never to even touch anythin' of hers . . .! She hates me, Ethan . . . I'm scared of her!" (Davis 1936, 164). Ethan is reluctant to touch Mattie at this point, but he has her sit down and puts the broken pieces of the dish together up on the shelf. He says he'll get some glue the next day and that will give him a few months to find a new dish before Zeena notices. Inexplicably, Mattie is the one who tells Ethan not to worry, and immediately sits down to start sewing. Then Ethan says something strange. Throughout the day he has never intimated at all that he was looking forward to their night together—certainly nowhere near the single-minded obsession his character exhibits in the novel. And yet the Davis's have him say at this point, "I been lookin' forward a lot . . . all day, I ain't been thinkin' about a thing . . . but this evenin' . . ." (167). Mattie says it's been the same for her, and after few moments she puts down her sewing and asks him to tell her what Zeena had said to him about her that morning. But Ethan reminds her that they weren't going to worry, and she agrees.

The two comment on the weather some more, with Ethan hoping the snow delays the train for another day and Mattie telling him he shouldn't be thinking things like that. Then she goes on and on about working in the shoe factory, and finally utters a line that it's difficult not to imagine eliciting a burst of laughter in the theater. "Do you think I talk too much?" (171). Of course Ethan says she doesn't. Mattie looks at the clock a short time later and is amazed to find it is already time for bed. Ethan naturally wants to prolong the evening but she seems oblivious to his desire and puts away her sewing. He begs her to stay and she does for a while, but he doesn't have the words to tell her what he's feeling and she doesn't possess the intelligence to figure it out. Finally Mattie says goodnight and heads for the stairs, leaving Ethan alone in the kitchen gripping the back of Zeena's rocker, bringing the play to the end of the second act.

Act Three opens in Ethan and Zeena's empty bedroom the following evening, with Mattie seen across the hall in her room. Ethan goes into his room and she follows him, asking if he remembered the glue. He feigns ignorance at first, to tease her, and then says he did remember. As he begins washing in the basin, Ethan tells Mattie to open the package, but there are two on the bed and the first one she opens contains a pink pincushion he bought for her at the widow Homan's store. In the other is the glue, and she takes both of them out of the room. The two had planned on putting the pickle dish back together before supper, but sleigh bells are heard offstage and Mattie rushes back in to tell him that Zeena is home already. Before Mattie has the chance to leave the room, Zeena suddenly appears in the doorway. She doesn't say a word, but goes to the window and sits in a chair while Jotham brings in her suitcase. Ethan, relieved to see Jotham, invites him to stay for supper again but as in the novel the man ominously refuses. When Mattie says that the food is ready Zeena announces she will not be eating and Mattie goes back downstairs. The dialogue between the two then proceeds essentially as it does in the book, with Zeena saying the doctor wants her to have a hired girl. Ethan implies that she isn't right in the head if she thinks they can afford it, and once again she warns him never to say that. Then Zeena calls for Mattie, asks to be brought some food, and accuses the girl of eavesdropping.

After Mattie brings the food and leaves, Ethan closes the door and tells Zeena matter-of-factly that he simply doesn't have the money to hire a girl. Here the decision the Davis's made earlier undercuts the moment as it appears in the novel. Zeena says accusingly that she thought Ethan was going to get cash for his timber from Andrew Hale. The problem is, that was Zeena's suggestion, not Ethan's. As such, he has nothing to feel sorry for, and yet Ethan still behaves as he does in the book, apologizing for the misunderstanding. Ethan says again that they just can't afford it, when Zeena suddenly turns the tables on him. "Oh, I figured I wouldn't take no chances countin' on you . . . so 'stead of buyin' myself a lot of medicines I been needing real bad . . . I paid the girl a half a month in advance out of the cow money and give her a dollar extry like I said" (Davis 1936, 199-200). When Ethan says it doesn't matter, and he wants her to get the money back, that's when Zeena muses that they won't have to pay for Mattie's board anymore. His reaction is just as it is the novel, arguing she can't turn out a relative because people will think ill of her. But she also repeats the ambiguous threat that she knows what people are saying already and this seems to frighten Ethan. Zeena has been eating her supper the whole time, and when she finishes she calls for Mattie. She announces that she needs her stomach powders, which she is going to hunt for downstairs, and also that Ethan has something to tell her. Then she leaves the two of them alone. Mattie rambles on for a while before Ethan can tell her that the new doctor has convinced Zeena to hire a girl to take her place. Ethan says he doesn't want her to go, but Mattie is too struck by the news to understand his meaning. Then Zeena begins yelling for them to come to supper as the curtain falls.

Scene Two of Act Three takes place in the kitchen the following afternoon, with Mattie sitting alone and dressed for travel. Jotham comes in to pick her up—delivering the news that Ethan probably won't be back—and he heads upstairs for her trunk. After he leaves the room Ethan comes in, much to Mattie's relief. She comments on the fact that he spent the night downstairs and, when asked, says she hasn't heard Zeena say anything all day. Zeena's use of her illness to punish Ethan is much less defined in the play, but there is one hint to it here, when Ethan says sarcastically that Zeena doesn't let much trouble her and Mattie responds, "No, she don't and that's a fact, Ethan . . . not when she ain't a mind to" (Davis 1936, 213). Ethan intimates that he has some sort of plan, but then Jotham comes down with the trunk. Zeena's instruction to send Mattie's trunk ahead to the train station angers Ethan and he tells Jotham that Mattie may not be going after all. Then Zeena appears in the kitchen to finalize the schedule for Mattie's departure, and also insist that the girl clean her room before she leaves. It's here that the Davis's alter Mattie's character yet again by having her actually get angry. When Zeena looks over at the geranium by the window and implies that Mattie has done a poor job taking care of it, Mattie has suddenly had enough.

> MATTIE: *Furiously . . . and with the ready tears suddenly welling up.* I don't care, Zeena . . . I don't care . . . what you say else about me. That geranium I been tendin' every day regular's clockwork . . . and you can't say different 'cause it ain't so. (218)

Mattie races up the stairs in tears while Jotham delights at the whole thing—which only serves to remind the audience that this change in his character would have made him want to stay the night before rather than leaving the way he does in the novel. But when Ethan finally stands up to Zeena and refuses to help him with the trunk, Jotham does decide to slip out before a fight ensues. Ethan tries to argue that it's wrong to evict Mattie, but

Zeena counters with the fact that he argued against bringing her to the farm in the first place. Then she confronts him with her knowledge that he has been helping Mattie do the housework instead of his work on the farm, and accuses him of "gettin' to be a regular old woman," the single unconscious reference to Ethan's symbolic gender switch (Davis 1936, 221). At this Ethan tells her he's had enough, that he wants to go out West and will leave her the farm. She can continue to run it with Jotham and he'll send her money, or she can sell it and keep the profits. But Zeena wants to know what she'll live on in the meantime. Selling the cattle would be an obvious place to start, but in the play Ethan doesn't have an answer. When he suggests that he could get an advance from Andrew Hale, Zeena tries to shame him, saying that he would just be taking advantage of their friendship. Apparently this is different for her than asking him for money for her medical bills. Still, it is another significant change from the novel, with Zeena acting as Ethan's conscious rather than Ethan's own integrity preventing him from taking Hale's money.

Defeated, Ethan sits at the table while Zeena calls Mattie down from upstairs and decides to go through her suitcase. Just then the sleigh arrives to take the trunk to the train station. Denis Eady has agreed to take it, along with Mrs. Hale, and the two of them come in to say hello first. Reluctantly, Ethan takes the trunk out to the sleigh and their guests leave with it. Jotham Powell comes in next, ready to take Mattie, but Ethan says he is going to take her over himself. Zeena wants Jotham to wait outside, but he is eager to see what happens between the two. Zeena tells Ethan she wants him to stay and fix the stove in Mattie's room, but he refuses. At this Zeena feigns an attack and says she needs the stomach powders that she decided not to take the night before. Of course, in looking for them she finds the pickle dish. She wants to know what happened, and Ethan lies and said the cat broke it. But Zeena makes the same remark as in the book, that the cat wouldn't have been able to put the pieces back together on the shelf. To this Ethan bluntly replies that he doesn't care about her dish. Mattie, however, can't take the tension anymore and confesses, opening herself up to the same abusive castigations that Zeena delivers to her in the novel. Then Zeena takes the broken pieces upstairs and Ethan and Mattie leave as the scene comes to a close.

Act Three, Scene Three, opens on the crest of the same hill where the two talked on the way home from the dance. They stop to rest and Ethan points out to Mattie that they can see the spot where they attended the church picnic at which he found her missing locket. When he asks what she is going to do she says she'll probably go back to working in the mill. He finally manages to tell her that he would go with her if he could, and asks if she wants that too. She says there's no use and, as in the book, he asks again in order to get a direct answer. Mattie's response replicates that from the novel, saying she used to think about "it" on summer nights, and then the Davis's abandon Wharton's subtle narrative when Ethan says, "I guess I was thinkin' a lot about you . . . right from the first, Matt" (Davis 1936, 242). The majority of the dialogue is still from the book, with Ethan saying he's tied hand and foot, and Mattie saying he can write to her. And when she says she wishes she were dead Ethan has the same reaction, telling her to stop talking that way. Then they hear the shouts of children and stop to watch them sledding. Ethan reminds her that this was the night they were to have gone coasting together. Mattie is worried about catching the train, but Ethan is adamant, and finally she pulls his face down to hers, kisses him, and says goodbye. Then she tells him she wants to go down and have him run into the big elm. She uses the same line about a new girl occupying her bed and Ethan says, "I can't go back there . . . I can't go back to that place never again!" (249).

So Ethan finds the sled and gets it ready for them to go down the hill. In an interesting twist on the attempted suicide, Mattie seats herself in front and Ethan tells her to get up. But instead of having her ride behind him, he has the two of them lay side-by-side together facing down the hill. "We're goin' down head first and together . . . holdin' each other tight!" (Davis 1936, 250). Mattie asks Ethan if it's going to hurt and he responds by saying,

ETHAN: Don't be a scared, Matt . . . it ain't goin' to hurt . . . it ain't goin' to hurt at all . . . we're goin' to fetch that elm so hard we won't feel anything at all . . . exceptin' only each other! (251)

At the precipice of the slope Ethan says Mattie's name twice, and she tells him to hold her tight, and then they push off and disappear. As the curtain falls and the lights dim the only noise that can be heard is the rush of the sled down the hill.

The sled is heard once again as the curtain comes up on the Frome's kitchen. The Epilogue takes place twenty years later, the same night that Ethan took the narrator to the train station in the Prologue. Zeena can be seen rocking in her chair by the stove, visibly older. When she hears Ethan's sleigh pull up, Zeena rouses herself and puts some milk on the stove to heat. The lame and grizzled Ethan enters the room and she sits him at the table. He has an engineering magazine that the narrator loaned him, but the only thing Zeena cares about is that he collected the dollar. Ethan assures her he did. Then a high-pitched voice is heard calling Zeena's name and she leaves for a moment. When she returns from the hallway she is pushing a paralyzed Mattie in a wheelchair. As she is wheeled in front of the stove Mattie complains that

Zeena has hurt her, but Zeena says she's been taking care of her the same way for twenty years and leaves to attend the milk on the stove. "I wish you hadn't," Mattie says. "I wish you'd let me die. Why didn't you let me die that night they carried Ethan 'an me in here!" (Davis 1936, 259). Then Mattie complains that she's cold, and Ethan struggles to his feet to get her a blanket. But Mattie doesn't want him near her. Then she asks him brutally if he isn't ever going to die. "The Fromes're tough I guess," he says, sitting back down. "The doctor was sayin' to me only the other day—'Frome,' he says, 'you'll likely touch a hundred'" (260). And with that the production comes to a close.

Despite the positive contemporary reviews, the thing one notices most of all in the Davis's adaptation is the significant change in the characters from Wharton's book. It's an aspect of the story that did not go unnoticed by Henry James scholar Leon Edel, who wrote to Wharton shortly after the production's New York opening.

> While the play was "beautifully mounted, winter scenes crisp and white against deep blue-night backgrounds, and interiors scrupulously conveying the atmosphere of the New England farmhouse," the principal characters, "have been arbitrarily altered. Mattie Silver has been turned into a giddy young girl, fluttery and insipid. Contrasted with her, Zeena emerges mature, dignified, and even sympathetic to an audience alienated by Mattie's excessive exuberance. Ethan is weak, indecisive, robbed of much of his stature and nobility." The play was, he felt, "yours and yet not yours." (Fryer 183)

New York drama critic Irving Hoffman, however, was apparently unsparing in his dislike for the production and said as much in his review for the *Hollywood Reporter*. Hoffman was an eccentric figure in the Broadway theater circle who wore thick glasses and had little tolerance for artistic pretension. But his scathing review of *Ethan Frome* was too much for Max Gordon, and after the producer was compelled to contact Hoffman's publisher he found himself on the losing end of the critic's acerbic wit.

> Hoffman's scalding and witty reviews are the freshest written. His blast at Max Gordon's play, *Ethan Frome*, moved Gordon to squawk to Hoffman's boss about permitting a review by a man who didn't see well. "I may not see very well," Hoffman said, in a reply that sort of settled the argument, "but there's nothing wrong with my nose." (Wilson 7-45, 4)

Nevertheless, the play spent over two years on the road after its Broadway run had finished, and throughout the nineteen-fifties and sixties, the Davis version of *Ethan Frome* was a staple of college and community theaters around the country. But the Davis's liberties with the story, as this description of the material by *New York Times* writer Mel Gussow on the occasion of the play's 1982 revival attests, fared less well with modern audiences.

> The 1936 Broadway dramatization by the father and son team of Owen and Donald Davis is less an adaptation than a play based on an original work. As such, it suffers both when it departs from Mrs. Wharton and when it tries to emulate her . . . The story is told in straightforward, chronological order, starting with the arrival of Mattie in the Frome household. The invented dialogue varies from the understated to the obvious, and moments that in the novel are impacted with portent— such as the accidental smashing of Zeena's favorite pickle dish—become melodramatic when seen on stage. (Gussow)

There have been a number of other dramatic adaptations of *Ethan Frome* in the years since Edith Wharton's death, all of which demonstrate the difficulty of translating a story that is primarily introspective into one that is exclusively verbal in nature.

Raymond Massy and Ruth Gordon were reunited in 1940 for a radio production of a truncated version of the play for the Texaco Star Theatre, broadcast nationally on June 19th. In this abridgment of the Davis play Margalo Gillmore was cast in the role of Zeena. Interestingly, Bette Davis had been scheduled to appear in a version of the play on the Lux Radio Theatre six months earlier, and this announcement appeared in newspapers at the time: "Bette Davis insisted on *Ethan Frome* as her vehicle when she was booked to co-star with Spencer Tracy in the Radio Theatre program of Jan. 8. The booking marked the first time these two Academy Award players were signed for a joint broadcast" (Ferris 5). Instead, the two stars appeared in a broadcast of *Dark Victory* that night, a version of the Bette Davis film that had been released the previous year. In 1947 Raymond Massey returned to the radio airways, this time with the original Zeena from the stage, Pauline Lord, and Mary Anderson as Mattie. The program was produced by the Theatre Guild on the Air and broadcast on May 25th. Again, the actors were working from the Owen and Donald Davis script. The same production company tapped Massey for the role one more time in another airing of the hour-long adaptation of the play four years later on May 20, 1951. His co-stars this time were Shirley Booth as Zeena and Pamela Brown as Mattie. Two years later, Best Plays

327

aired a version of the Davis play on September 13, 1953 with Geraldine Page as Mattie, Karl Weber as Ethan, and Evelyn Varden as Zeena. John Chapman was the host of the program, and acted as the narrator, though more on the model of Thornton Wilder's *Our Town* than the one in Wharton's novel.

The earliest televised version of the play came in 1940 in a half-hour condensation directed by Donald Davis in New York City and broadcast locally by NBC on January 5th. It wasn't until late 1959 that another televised version of the play was announced, this time to be broadcast nationally, produced by David Susskind as an episode of the *DuPont Show of the Month*. Initial publicity had Geraldine Page appearing as Zeena instead of Mattie, and Richard Boone as Ethan. But when the show finally aired on February 18, 1960, the two-hour broadcast starred Sterling Hayden as Ethan, Julie Harris as Mattie, and Clarice Blackburn as Zeena. Blackburn, it turns out, was something of a last-minute addition to the cast. "Geraldine Page was supposed to play it first, but withdrew to go on the road with *Sweet Bird of Youth*. Kim Stanley was signed for it next, but got into a disagreement over the interpretation of the character and withdrew. With rehearsals drawing perilously close, Clarice was called in to read for the part at the last minute and was accepted" (Stern 4). The director of the episode was Alex Segal, who had a long career in televised dramatic productions, and would go on to direct Lee J. Cobb in *Death of a Salesman*, and George C. Scott in *The Crucible*. Also in the cast was Charles Tyner in the crucial role of Jotham Powell, Jack Betts as Denis Eady, and Arthur Hill as the narrator. The bulk of the program was broadcast live, though some portions had been filmed earlier in order to facilitate scene changes and the like.

The screenplay, written by Jacqueline Babbin and Audrey Gellen, was essentially a modified version of the Davis's play and as a result Donald Davis eventually filed suit against DuPont and producer David Susskind for copyright infringement. Davis had paid close attention to the broadcast because a year earlier, when Susskind was looking for properties to televise for DuPont, he actually approached Davis to see about acquiring the rights to the play. But Davis's conditions didn't sit well with the producer, so he decided to bypass Davis and go directly to the estate of Elisina Tyler. Tyler had acquired the executorship of Wharton's literary works after the author's death and had acted in the place of Wharton in rights negotiations involving the Davis's play. Since her recent death in 1957—and before the executorship had passed on to her son William—requests had to go officially through her estate. In doing so Susskind discovered that Tyler had previously sold the rights to the Davis's play to Warner Brothers, which CBS had purchased in 1958, and so it turned out the television studio already owned a screenplay of the story that had been written by Helen Deutsch, which Suskind promptly gave to Babbin and Gellen to rewrite. Unfortunately, that screenplay was also simply another version of the Davis play. What Susskind and CBS soon realized when they looked at the specific terms of Tyler's contract with Warner Brothers is that all CBS really owned was the right to televise any film that had been made of *Ethan Frome* by Warner Brothers, but not the right to broadcast an independent production of the story. Since no film by Warner Brothers had ever been made, even had Babbin and Gellen written an entirely new screenplay they still would have been in violation of Warners original agreement with Tyler and, by extension, Donald Davis.

The suit was based on the fact that Helen Deutsch had adapted the Davis's play, and Babbin and Gellen had then gone on to repeat the process. What's so fascinating is that Susskind actually went ahead and purchased the rights to the story of *Ethan Frome* independently from Tyler's estate to avoid the copyright implications of using Deutsch's script as part of the Warners contract. But instead of commissioning an entirely new screenplay, Susskind instead instructed Babbin and Gellen to make enough changes to their version of the Davis-Deutsch script to avoid a lawsuit. The court, however, ultimately found those changes unconvincing, as Judge Wilfred Feinberg made clear in his ruling.

> I have compared the Davis play with the kinescope of the television show, as well as with the transcribed audio portion of the broadcast. Despite several additions, the overall impression is that, in the majority of instances in which the television show dramatized something that Davis had dramatized, it did so in the Davis manner. The labors of Misses Babbin and Gellen to take Davis out of the television show after being asked to do so were too little, too late and too transparent. In almost every instance, their "changes" amounted to mere paraphrasing, inversion of dialogue, or substitution of one insignificant object for another. But paraphrasing is tantamount to copying in copyright law. Defendants did not successfully remove the original, protectable features of the Davis play from the television script, and defendants are therefore liable for copyright infringement. (Feinberg 622-623)

Judge Feinberg ultimately found in favor of Davis despite the fact that, in his words, "the defendants have hurled a barrage of contentions" to counter Davis's claim (615).

That legal fallout, however, wouldn't happen for several years, and at the time of the telecast the program was considered a major success. AP writer

Cynthia Lowery called "Edith Wharton's New England tragedy . . . an exciting production . . . and [a] rewarding 90 minutes," while TV columnist Harriett Van Horne praised its adherence to the original novel (Lowery 6). "How satisfying it is to see a well-beloved novel come to life on the small screen with even approximate fidelity . . . In the minor episodes where it became unfixed, the liberties taken were understandably if not entirely forgivable" (Van Horne 22). Reporter John Crosby was equally impressed with the performances. "Julie Harris played Matty [sic] with her accustomed sweetness and sureness of touch. It is the sort of role she was almost predestined to play and play well. The big surprise was Sterling Hayden, who was tremendously moving and marvelously well controlled as Ethan Frome . . . Clarice Blackburn as the hypochondriac wife [performed] with splendid savagery and intensity through an extremely difficult, complex, and very rewarding role" (Crosby 16).

It's interesting that the few mixed reviews focused on the screenplay as the weak spot in the production. "Adapters Babbin and Gellen have done a good job capturing the bleak, uncompromising aura of this rural tragedy," said the editors of TV Key. "They haven't been nearly as fortunate in capturing its character" (Editor 2-60, 18). TV columnist Charlie Wadsworth was even more blunt.

> Adaptation of *Ethan Frome* last night proved to be disappointing for the same reason, or reasons, as many other television adaptations: You cannot bring the meat or the vital descriptive material of classic novels to light on video in a prescribed number of minutes . . . What you have left was this: Great acting performances with a plot that was lost on the television screen. Yet some very stirring moments. This was one of the times which a fine cast could catch up and portray on the screen some of the moments in which the adaptation of the script was unable to provide. (Wadsworth 48)

Overall, however, the high praise for the show proved well deserved when the Emmy announcements were made that May. *Ethan Frome* was nominated for best dramatic production and Julie Harris was nominated for best actress.

Twenty-five years later, in the mid-1980s, a plan was put into place by a Northeastern theater troupe, Shakespeare & Company, to convert the barn on Edith Wharton's former property in Lenox, Massachusetts, The Mount, into a theater with the goal of staging a production of *Ethan Frome* there every year during the summer. A decade after that, one of the more fascinating theatrical productions associated with the author came about as a benefit to raise money to restore The Mount. This was the one-woman show by Tony-award winning actress Irene Worth called *A Portrait of Edith Wharton*.

Standing against an understated set that conjures up an aristocratic library (which, Wharton wrote, in most houses she knew, were really "book dumps"), Worth reads from Wharton's autobiography, her novels and, yes, even that pornographic fragment—which is, in fact, an elegant piece of writing. In Worth's commanding voice, Wharton's incisive, pungent prose animates the space with great theatrical force. When she reads from *Ethan Frome*, she uses a New England accent, which underscores the cruel humor that links the book to Wharton's more urbane writing. (Kissel 58)

The show premiered on Broadway in January, and was presented in various other cities around the country throughout 1994, receiving mostly positive reviews everywhere it played.

It was also around this time that *Ethan Frome* fell out of copyright and into the public domain, and this prompted the appearance of several new theatrical versions of the novel. One of the first was by Dennis Krausnick in 1995. In fact, Krausnick directed his version of the story for Shakespeare & Company at the Lenox, Massachusetts theater at The Mount during the 1996-97 season. Krausnick's play names the narrator Winterson—fairly obvious symbolism, though also very similar to Wharton's own character named Winterman from her 1910 short story "The Legend"—and attempts to replicate the Prologue in a more thorough way than had been done by the Davis's. Another adaptation of the story was written for the stage by Gary L. Blackwood in 2001, though it apparently wasn't produced until 2017 by a Vermont community theater. In Blackwood's version Ned Hale is alive in the Prologue—as he is in the 1993 film—and assumes the Harmon Gow role of getting the narrator interested in Ethan. Blackwood's innovation was to use the frame story as the narrative center of the piece and then frequently shift the narrative as Ethan thinks back to the past during the journey when he takes the narrator to the train station. This required that a separate cast be used to represent the younger Ethan, Mattie and Zeena in the flashback sequences.

The most recent major stage production of *Ethan Frome*, this one written by Laura Eason for the Lookingglass Theater group in Chicago, debuted in 2011. Eason used a minimalist set design like the ones often used in performances of *Our Town* or *The Fantastiks*.

Rather than attempting realistic sets, the production, designed by Dan Ostling, consisted of a skeletal, sculptural suggestion of the Frome house, while the sledding was staged in a stylized rather than realistic way, with Ethan and Mattie leaning toward each other on a spinning platform, turning ever faster, as a film of the bleak landscape played over them. (Anderson 164)

Chicago Tribune critic Chris Jones was less than impressed by the play's initial production, and his disappointment focused primarily on the lack of attenuation by the actors who he felt were too fearful of turning their characters into caricatures. Eason's adaptation does what most do, and provides an overt love relationship between Ethan and Mattie. Jones also felt the narrator was a bit too intrusive, as he stays onstage for the entire production, "looking a little awkward and, well, in the way. He has a few too many straight-from-the-narrative lines about Ethan Frome . . . that doesn't feel necessary" (Jones 86).

Ethan Frome on the Screen

The earliest thoughts about rendering *Ethan Frome* for the screen came during the silent era. According to Wharton biographer Hermione Lee, "there was talk of a film of *Ethan Frome* in 1920, with Lionel Barrymore" (Lee 594). A few years later a young James Agee, writer, budding film critic, and aspiring screenwriter and director, put forward an idea for the project in a letter to fellow author and film critic Dwight MacDonald dated June 26, 1927. It's a fascinating insight into a way of looking at the story that is probably closest to Edith Wharton's conception because of the absence of dialogue in silent film. But taking that idea even further Agee hints later in the letter that, inspired by Murnau's *The Last Laugh*, he also would have tried to produce the film without title cards at all.

> I have a wild desire to direct *Ethan Frome*, and the first thing I thought of was my first and final shots. Do you know the story? Mrs. Wharton compresses it into a very few days and builds her background into the story. I'd begin with the death of Ethan's mother—an oblique shot, from near the ground, of a coffin being lowered into a grave—a lap dissolve—becoming a shot from the coffin lid with rain blurring the lens and the light above telescoping into a small rectangle. The four walls of the grave, rough-dug, slipping slowly upward with cut roots sprawling out. Camera moved upward, out of the grave, swings in behind the crowd, catching in profile the heads of Ethan and Zeena. Then the camera swings on up the hill—with the group at the grave crumbling away in the rain and snow—swerves over a semicircular sweep of New England country and comes to rest on the Frome farmhouse . . . (MacDonald 13-14)

In beginning the film this way Agee necessarily forgoes the presence of the narrator, which would have been of little use anyway in a straightforward, chronological telling of the story. But more than just that, it seems that Agee would have completely reimagined the story in order to turn it into a kind of Gothic descendent of Hawthorne and Poe. Most indicative of this is his desire to perfectly capture the final words of Wharton's novel in a way that no other dramatic production has ever been able to do.

> At the end, Ethan, Zeena and Mattie in the kitchen on a winter night. Mattie sitting very straight. Zeena hunched near the fire, Ethan leaning against the fireplace. Make the composition obvious enough to be remembered. Then a lap dissolve into three grave-stones—two crazily leaning, one straight between them. Night—snow sifting over them. Then a series of dissolves, 6 or 8 of them, first fast, then slowing down to a stop, with the gravestones half-buried in the snow. (MacDonald 14)

One can only imagine what Agee would have done with scenes like Zeena coming to the door with the lantern, or the final coast into the tree. It probably wouldn't have been an issue getting the rights to film the story either, as Wharton had actively pursued Hollywood's interest in her works as a way of making money. "She did not want to be in any way involved with them, and was not an enthusiast for the new cinema, but she could see that her novels were promising material for the movies" (Lee 594). In fact, Metro Pictures had already produced a silent version of *The House of Mirth* in 1918.

Two years later, in the wake of the Pulitzer Prize for *The Age of Innocence*, her royalties for the work, "included a contract for a silent movie of the novel, with Warner Bros., for $9,000—at which point Wharton became aware that 'fillums' of her books could become a good source of income . . . 'I have always thought "The Age" would make a splendid film if done by someone with brains—and education!' she wrote" (Lee 594). A film version of *The Age of Innocence* was eventually made by Warners in 1924, while a year earlier Famous Players-Lasky had mounted a production of her novel *The Glimpses of the Moon*. In the sound era her novel *The Children* was made into a film by Paramount in 1929, starring Fredric March and called *The Marriage Playground*, and *The Age of Innocence* was remade in 1934 by RKO with Irene Dunne and John Boles. Also in 1934, Universal made *Strange Wives* from her story "Bread upon the Waters," and a version of *The Old Maid* based on the dramatization by Zoë Akins went in front of Warner Brothers' cameras before the decade was out. In 1940 actress Ruth Gordon, who played Mattie Silver on Broadway, was asked about appearing in a possible film version of Wharton's

Ethan Frome, but she expressed concern about the wisdom of filming that kind of story while the country was still suffering from the effects of the Great Depression. "No," she said, "not now. They haven't any right to film *Ethan Frome*. It's too tragic, too morbid. No one has the right to picture or portray unhappiness in times like these" (Tucker 6). That same year Bette Davis had expressed her desire to do a radio-play version for the Lux Radio Theatre but it fell through, probably because the Texaco Star Theatre had acquired the services of Raymond Massy and Ruth Gordon from the original Broadway production for their radio adaptation.

Finally, though the contracts wouldn't be signed until four months later, Louella Parsons announced Hal Wallace's acquisition of *Ethan Frome* for Warner Brothers in October of 1941.

> *Ethan Frome*, considered by many to be Edith Wharton's finest novel, has been purchased by Hal Wallace for Bette Davis . . . [Bette] has been urging Warners to buy it for her for a long time. Interesting that Bette will have Raymond Massey as her acting partner in . . . the role he played on the stage . . . No one understands the character of the New Englanders better than Bette who comes from Massachusetts and who has spent much time in New Hampshire and Vermont. (Parsons 10-41, 13)

It's likely that what Wallis actually purchased for Warners was an option on the property. But the studio's intent to pick up that option was confirmed by Jack Warner who, in another article by Parsons, announced in late December his choice of producer for the picture. "According to Jack Warner himself—and he should know—there isn't the slightest chance of Robert Lord, producer of *One Foot In Heaven* and Warners saying au revoir. Why Bob has four pictures scheduled for him, Jack says, one of the most important being *Ethan Frome*, Edith Wharton's novel bought for Bette Davis" (Parsons 12-41, 12). Parson's report was confirmed by Edwin Schallert a month later in the *Los Angeles Times*.

> Extraordinary among stories that are resurrected is *Ethan Frome*, which in all probability will serve Bette Davis as her next starring subject. Many know this Edith Wharton novel, done on the stage some six years ago. Its longevity is astonishing, because the original book issued away back in 1911. Against the hard-bitten New England snow setting is unfolded a story of fervid love which ends in disaster. It will be a strong event for Miss Davis. (Schallert 1-42, 44)

This would not be the first time Bette Davis would star in a Wharton film for Warners, however, as she had played the lead in their production of *The Old Maid* in 1939.

In the deal that was made with Elisina Tyler—Wharton's literary executor—Warners purchased the rights not only to Wharton's novel, but both the Davis and Barrington versions of the play. Screenwriter Waldo Salt, who would go on to win two Oscars late in his career—for *Midnight Cowboy* and *Coming Home*—reportedly wrote the first draft of the screenplay in March. Then Helen Deutsch, whose later literary adaptations for the screen would include *National Velvet*, Rudyard Kipling's *Kim*, and *King Solomon's Mines*, completed a draft of the story shortly after. Though there's no way to know what the Salt script looked like, the screenplay Deutsch wrote was based heavily on the Davis's play—as Donald Davis's successful lawsuit confirmed later—and this was the version that was subsequently shown to the actors. At the time, Raymond Massey and Bette Davis were the obvious choices for Ethan and Mattie. There's no way to know precisely why the project was shelved initially, but it was probably due to the unavailability of Massey at the beginning of World War Two. According to Louella Parsons, Ida Lupino was also briefly considered for the role. "Six months ago Bette was dying to do this play with Raymond Massey, who played it on the stage. But along came the war, taking Massey to Canada—and along came *Mr. Skeffington* for Bette. So now it's Ida who will face the camera in *Ethan Frome*" (Parsons 3-43, 23). Hedda Hopper, on the other hand, made no attempt to disguise her enthusiasm for this particular development. "Hurray, hurray! Ida Lupino is getting that good part in *Ethan Frome*" (Hopper 3-43, 24).

But there was another actresses being considered for the film after the property was first acquired, Joan Crawford, who joined Warners in 1943 when her contract at MGM wasn't renewed. "One of the main reasons I went to Warners," said the actress, "is because they owned the rights to *Ethan Frome*. I wanted very much to play in that picture" (Considine 166). The move to Warner Brothers was just the latest development for Crawford, however, as she had designs on the property even while she was still at MGM. An article from July of 1941 stated, "She has two more years to go on her contract. During that time she wants to do the Edith Wharton-Owen Davis *Ethan Frome*, despite the fact that everybody says it's depressing" (Chapman 37). Crawford had Gary Cooper in mind for the title role and of course assumed she would play his love interest, Mattie. Interestingly, the actress she thought would be perfect to play opposite them as Zeena, was Bette Davis. Crawford also wanted to use director Edmund Goulding, who had been so successful with Davis on *Dark Victory*, and suggested he approach Davis about the project, but the director wanted nothing more to do with Davis after working with her once, and refused. "That was my dream," Crawford said later. "When I brought it up to Jack Warner, he suggested I move slowly, because he said Miss Davis also had her heart set on the property, but in the younger role" (Considine 166). It's difficult to imagine that Warners would have put those two stars together in the same film, even if Crawford had been willing to play Zeena, which is why it appears that the studio was actually using the threat of Crawford to manipulate Davis.

On June 13, 1943 Hedda Hopper announced that Warners had decided to put Crawford in the film. "Joan Crawford certainly didn't waste any time after she'd received Metro's permission to do an outside picture. She was seen lunching at Warners, and I'm told she'll do *Ethan Frome* for them [even though] it was bought for Bette Davis" (Hopper 6-43, 20). This news resulted in a flurry of activity in the papers the following week denying the report, which makes it appear that Crawford had never really been in serious contention. On June 22nd Parsons scotched the rumors that either Ida Lupino or Joan Crawford would star in the film and the studio confirmed that Davis was still their first choice. She also reported that Davis was adamant about appearing in the film and that a new producer had been assigned to the project. "Don't let anybody tell you that Bette Davis isn't going to do *Ethan Frome*, and that Joan Crawford will take her place. Jack Warner has handed it to Henry Blanke to produce and it may precede *The Corn Is Green*" (Parsons 6-43, 7). The reason for Warners' initial statement about Crawford became apparent just a week later when George L. David made the following announcement: "As the result of conferences here [in New York] between Jack L. Warner, executive producer, and Bette Davis, now on vacation, the Warner Bros. star has been handed a new deal with the studio. The length of the contract and the number of pictures the star will make were not revealed . . . Starring roles in *Mr. Skeffington*, *The Corn is Green*, and *Ethan Frome* already have been announced for her" (David 8). Finally, a week later, Hopper was forced to reverse herself. "Joan Crawford's first for Warners won't be *Ethan Frome* but *Night Shift*. She's hoping to get Humphrey Bogart as a consolation prize" (Hopper 7-43, 14).

In mid July Warners announced it was attempting to hire Gregory Peck for the film but by the end of 1943 *Ethan Frome* still hadn't been made, even though it continued to be named as an upcoming project for Bette Davis. Then in January 1944 Warners had Hedda Hopper stir the pot again when she suggested Crawford might be back in the mix, though the information was really an attempt to clarify Crawford's desire to play Zeena rather than Mattie. "Most people think Joan Crawford would like to get *Ethan Frome* away from

Bette Davis and do it herself, instead of which Joan really wants to co-star in it with Bette, she to play the wife" (Hopper 1-44, 6). In August the film was still on Warners' slate of projected projects, and by the fall of 1944 Parsons reported that it was Bogart who was now incomprehensively attached to the film. "[Bette Davis] stars in *Ethan From* as soon as she finishes *Stolen Life*, and it's interesting that Humphrey Bogart will be her costar. Two of Warners top people in the popular Edith Wharton novel is news" (Parsons 9-44, 9). And yet it seems clear that Warners was already thinking about backing away from Davis at this point when that same day their favorite rumormonger Hedda Hopper reported about the 36-year-old actress, "Bette Davis wants to play a 17-year-old in *Ethan Frome*, for which Andrea King has already tested" (Hopper 9-44, 10). Nevertheless, all through the winter of 1944-1945 a number of articles claimed that Jack Warner was intent on having Davis and Bogart star in *Ethan Frome*.

In March of 1945 Warners was still trying to keep up pubic interest in the film. First came an item about unsuccessful location scouting for the project. "Warner Brothers were unable to find snow in Stowe for scenes in the film *Ethan Frome*. Vermont is having one of its earliest springs in many years" (Editor 3-45, 11). Then later that summer this anecdote appeared about producer Henry Blanke:

> To the office of one of Hollywood's best known doctors, the other day, came producer Henry Blanke, for his annual check-up. "Working hard?" asked the doctor. "Night and day," replied Blanke—and forthwith launched on a 30-minute condensation of *Ethan Frome*, the book he is readying for production. At the end of the half-hour, the doctor donned his hat. "I'm sorry, Mr. Blanke," he said, "but I'm due at the hospital. You owe me nothing—but here's 80 cents—my admission fee for *Ethan Frome*! (Fidler 6-45, 14)

On the heels of that story came Hedda Hopper's announcement that Bogart was now out. "Now I know why Warners are rushing *Ethan Frome* for quick production. Looks as if their big three—Bette Davis, Joan Crawford, and Paul Henreid—would go into it" (Hopper 7-45, 11). But apparently producer Henry Blanke had other ideas for Zeena, specifically Agnes Moorehead who was on contract at MGM. "[Metro] may also be surprised that Henry Blanke wants [Moorhead] for the Pauline Lord part in *Ethan Frome*. I hope she gets it" (Hopper 9-45, 23). Then in October, Hopper added a new twist to the plot. "Bette Davis usually gets what she wants, and let me be the first to say she should. Now she wants Henry Fonda for *Ethan Frome*. That's as perfect casting as I've come across in many a day. But I don't think she'll get around to it until sometime in January" (Hopper 10-45, 22). A few weeks later a press release by the studio confirmed that Jack Warner had indeed assigned the project to Fonda, as his first film after returning from the service. It wasn't until November that Hopper announced Warners had turned down Agnes Moorehead for the role of Zeena.

In 1945 a third screenwriter was said to be working on the *Ethan Frome* screenplay for Warner Brothers, Thames R. Williamson, who would also work uncredited on *Mildred Pierce*, which won an Academy Award for Joan Crawford. At the beginning of the year John Dall's name was floated as a possible lead in the picture, and it was also revealed that earlier Robert Alda had lobbied for the role but lost out to Fonda. In January 1946 Edwin Schallert confirmed that *Ethan Frome* was on Bette Davis's schedule, but a few months later Sheilah Graham reported that the actress still hadn't decided which part to play. "Bette Davis thought of playing the old wife in *Ethan Frome* but reconsidered in favor of the part of the young niece. She said she was afraid of being typed as a character actress—'and I'm not that old yet,' says Bette" (Graham 3-46, 4). Then in April of 1946 a director was finally announced for the project, the German Curtis Bernhart, who directed Bette Davis in *A Stolen Life* and would go on to direct many of the star's other late forties films for Warner Brothers. Fonda was still assigned to the lead role and a tentative schedule was set for September 1946. At the same time a fascinating look at the script changes to the story emerged that showed how the studio was attempting to deal with the downbeat nature of Wharton's original ending while at the same time addressing the deficiencies of the Davis's stage play.

> The Davis-Bernhart partnership was so successful it will be continued at Bette's request in *Ethan Frome* and in *The Life of Sarah Bernhardt*. "In *Ethan Frome*," said Curt, "the wife is a hypochondriac on a farm in 1905. Her ailments eat up her farmer-husband's profits. A niece is called in to help. Bette is the niece. She and the farmer—Henry Fonda—fall in love without a word of love passing between them. The wife finds out, and sends the niece away—but the husband goes with her." (Graham 4-46, 59)

After *A Stolen Life*, however, Davis went on to film *Deception* with Paul Henreid, and in July she said that *Ethan Frome* would be her next project.

That May a new actress was tested for Zeena, Mildred Natwick, who was only three years older than Davis. But the project was officially put on hold yet again in August, and the reason given this time was that both Davis and Bernhardt had other commitments. The following month the public learned what Davis's commitment was when she announced she was pregnant and wasn't going to work again until six months after the baby was born. That also gave Henry Fonda plenty of time to appear in a play on Broadway. "Bette Davis has postponed the start of her *Ethan Frome* until the following year because Henry Fonda, her leading man, is planning to work in a New York play when he finishes *A Time To Kill.* And when Bette finishes her picture, *Deception*, she will take a long rest, either at Laguna or in New Hampshire" (Graham 9-46, 18). At this point the picture wouldn't be able to get underway until at least the winter of 1947-48, not only because of Davis's pregnancy but because the studio wanted to shoot exteriors on location. "*Ethan Frome*, also on the Davis schedule, is believed to be definitely a winter enterprise, because of the fact that the company wants to shoot the feature on the actual terrain" (Schallert 11-46, 12). In October Sheilah Graham resurrected Agnes Moorehead as playing Zeena to Davis's Mattie, even though she had already been turned down for the role a year earlier.

As 1946 dragged into 1947 there was little real news about the project. In March Sheilah Graham once again reported that Agnes Moorhead was scheduled to play Zeena. After Davis's daughter was born, the reports had her going into *Ethan Frome* as her first picture back. But by the time summer rolled around Graham disclosed that the star was still having meetings with her director and hadn't decided what her next project would be. "Bette Davis is ready and rarin' to get back to work again. Over the weekend she conferred with Curt Burnhardt on her next picture. It's a toss up between *Ethan Frome* and *Sarah Burnhardt*. Bette is quite a gal. Most mamas want a little bit longer before resuming their careers" (Graham 6-47, 8). In October there was talk that Davis was reaching out to Raymond Massey again to see if he'd be interested in reprising his Broadway role, and only a month later it was said she was thinking of Glenn Ford as a possible Ethan. At the same time, Joan Crawford suddenly came back into the picture. "Joan Crawford and Bette Davis both want to star in *Ethan Frome* at Warners," Graham announced. "It has been on Bette's schedule for a long time but she had delayed production. Now Joan has read it and wants it" (Graham 11-47, 15). Finally, in December, Hedda Hopper passed on word from the studio that signaled the beginning of the end for the project. "*Ethan Frome* has been shelved temporarily. The studio considers it too moody for the times" (Hopper 12-47, 30).

By January of 1948 Henry Fonda was off the project and Davis had expressed interest in a new leading man. "Bette Davis has put in a bid for David Farrar, famous [British] star, to be her leading man in *Ethan Frome*. Bette was supposed to do this one with Henry Fonda, but he will be tied up for a long time, he hopes, in his stage play, *Mr. Roberts*" (Graham 1-48, 14).

Following a month off in which Davis recuperated after a bout with the flu early in the year, the studio apparently scheduled her to begin work on the film in March. According to Louella Parsons, the picture had a new director as well. "Bette, who again is feeling tip top, goes into *Ethan Frome* March 1st . . . What makes Bette so enthusiastic about doing *Ethan Frome* is that Edith Wharton's novel will be directed by Bretaigne Windust. She's enthusiastic about the way he handled [*Winter*] *Meeting*" (Parsons 2-48, 12). Sheilah Graham, however, was not so optimistic when she reported on a dispute between Davis and the studio over casting. "Bette Davis and the Warner boys are in a tizzy because they want her to play the middle-aged lady—the best role by the way—in *Ethan Frome*, and Bette is insisting on playing the young girl. Looks as if the movie will be shelved" (Graham 3-48, 19). And yet just a month later the studio announced that they had gone ahead and signed David Farrar for the lead. After finishing work on *June Bride* in late July, Davis headed back to New Hampshire and was rumored to be taking along a second unit film crew for shooting exteriors on *Ethan Frome*, though actual location filming wouldn't begin until the winter. But reporter Edith Gwynn had access to sources that said otherwise. "Warners have cancelled the deal whereby David Farrar, the English actor, was to come here to play opposite Bette Davis in *Ethan Frome*. We have a private hunch, based on a lot of reliable information, that this picture won't be made at all!" (Gwynn 61)

By August the writing was on the wall. Early in the month reporter Hugh Dixon declared, "Forget about *Ethan Frome*. Warner Brothers have shelved the proposed Bette Davis vehicle because the subject matter's too grim and unpleasantness isn't very profitable at the box-office these days" (Dixon 5). Then Hedda Hopper confirmed the fact a day later: "Bette Davis has one more picture to do at Warner's before her contract is up. *Ethan Frome*, which was scheduled for her, has been canceled" (Hopper 8-48, 22). And yet late in August articles continued to appear proclaiming Davis was still making the film and that the studio was intent on filming exteriors on her farm in New Hampshire. But that information is likely to have come from Bette Davis herself rather than the studio. According to Davis biographer Lawrence J. Quirk, the actress never wavered in her enthusiasm for the project. And despite continued rumors of Joan Crawford's participation, the property had essentially been promised to Davis. Throughout 1946 Warners had done screen tests for the film, but the one person she couldn't get to green light the production was studio head Jack Warner. "Warner was hesitant about the project—not only was it a period drama and he hated 'costume stuff,' but the theme seemed too drab and downbeat to be good box office. To Davis's frustration, he refused to go ahead" (Quirk 332-333). By November of 1948 nothing had changed when Sheilah Graham summarized the impasse in an article titled, "Bette Davis vs. Studio, Row Looms Over Ethan Frome." The article began with an apparent disagreement over casting. "Bette Davis is insisting that she play the young girl in *Ethan Frome*. The studio bosses want her to play the middle-aged aunt, which is the stronger role actually" (Graham 11-48, 7). But that issue was almost beside the point. "Truth to tell, the studio would prefer to junk the whole picture because of its somber theme. Sounds like more fireworks when Bette returns [to Hollywood] next week."

Over the years the property became an obsession with Davis, and apparently the cause for much of her antagonistic behavior on the set of *Beyond the Forest* in 1949. "[Jack] Warner just thinks *Forest* would be less expensive than *Frome*," she said in an interview at the time. "He wants something trashy and cheap that he thinks will sell to the lowbrows" (Quirk 345). In May the status of the project still seemed to be in flux and, according to Graham, with the possibility of an entirely new cast. "Gregory Peck, with two pictures to make at Warners, looks set for *Ethan Frome*. And from where I sit, it looks like Jane Wyman will co-star with him. This will interest Bette Davis, who has wanted to make this movie for a long time" (Graham 5-49 11). But in June of that year Davis was still reportedly intent on making the picture. And while her new contract stipulated that she only needed to make one picture a year, she told Louella Parsons in July that she would make an exception if Jack Warner decided to go ahead with *Ethan Frome*. Then later that month Davis announced she was breaking her contract with Warner Brothers and would not be making any more films for them at all. Once Davis left the studio there was little she could do about the project, as Warners owned the property. In August the speculation as to who would inherit the project began. "With Bette Davis and Warner Brothers agreeing to professional divorce, it's odds-on that Bette's arch rival, Joan Crawford, will win the top role in *Ethan Frome*" (Fidler 8-49, 10). In September Davis told Sheilah Graham that she had seen no less that twenty-two different versions of the screenplay for the film. Finally, in December of 1949 it was announced that another actress would officially be taking over the role. "Jane Wyman falls heir to *Ethan Frome*, Edith Wharton's novel which was bought some years ago for Bette Davis and which was intended as Bette's big picture for 1950 . . . This and many other stories originally bought for Bette will go to Jane" (Parsons 12-49, 25).

But Bette Davis never let go of the idea of doing the picture. In March of 1950 she said it was the one picture that she would go back to Warner Brothers to make.

"They have one thing I want, and that is *Ethan Frome*," she declared. "I was scheduled to do it, but it was called off when I got pregnant." . . . "I can't understand why it was passed by . . . *Ethan Frome* has a beautiful love story." . . . She told of finishing her last scene at Warners at three o'clock one morning. Someone suggested she ought to take something with her as a memento of her long association with the studio. "I'd like to steal up to the front office and take the script of *Ethan Frome*," she answered. (Thomas 13).

That same month, however, Jane Wyman was confirmed as Jack Warner's choice for the role of Mattie. At that time Gregory Peck was still assumed to be playing opposite her, while a new actress was being considered for Zeena. "Due to her Academy Award victory Mercedes McCambridge is very likely to play the role of the wife in *Ethan Frome* at Warners, which will star Jane Wyman and probably Gregory Peck" (Schallert 3-50, 11). Wyman made it clear that she was unhappy about the prospect of working with McCambridge, though, and in July the actress bowed out of consideration to be in the film. Reports in April said that Kirk Douglas had been given the script for the film, but no reporter believed he would actually do it. Then in May of 1950, Charlton Heston's name was suggested as a possible co-star for Jane Wyman in the picture, and a few months later it was announced that he had been signed to play the role of Ethan. But tired of the problems with both Wyman and Heston, in September Warners once again pulled the plug on the whole venture. "After the flareup between Warners and Hal Wallis over getting Charlton Heston, the former have decided to shelve *Ethan Frome*. The news should also quiet Jane Wyman and others who have been plugging for this classic drama ever since Bette Davis left the lot" (Manners 16).

Warner Brothers' lack of interest in *Ethan Frome* was not a rumor this time, as Warners set about selling the property to Stanley Kramer at Columbia in August of 1951 and thereby washing their hands of it completely. It's no surprise then, that once Bette Davis caught wind of the sale she lobbied heavily to be in the film, though she had altered her stance on the role she had fought over so bitterly with Warners. "Bette Davis is more than interested in Stanley Kramer's purchase of *Ethan Frome* from Warners. They bought it for Bette, then shelved it when she insisted on playing the young niece instead of the better role, that of the middle-aged aunt. Now she wants to play the aunt!" (Graham 9-51, 11). Two weeks later she shared the results of her efforts with Hollywood reporter Erskine Johnson. "A tip-top movie queen came right out with it and informed me that she's been turned down for the part she has wanted to play for a decade. The star: Frank outspoken Bette Davis. The picture: *Ethan Frome*, purchased from Warners by Stanley Kramer . . . 'Mr. Kramer said he did NOT want me. Not any part of me: this after 10 years of wanting to play it'" (Johnson 14). Davis's interview came on the heels of an utterly bizarre announcement by Stanley Kramer of his intention to reassemble the original 1936 Broadway cast for the film. Raymond Massey was already forty-years-old when he played the part on stage and would now be fifty-five. Ruth Gordon, playing the twenty-year-old Mattie would be fifty-five as well, while Pauline Lord, the oldest of the bunch, would be sixty. A far more realistic choice for Mattie emerged at the end of the year, when Geraldine Brooks announced her desire to play the part.

But Bette Davis wasn't ready to give up just yet, and in 1951 she even made tentative plans for a Broadway revival, probably in the hopes of forcing Kramer's hand. "Before *Ethan Frome* becomes a movie, there is a likely chance that City Center may get the stage version, as a sort of preview, with Bette Davis, Gary Merrill and Dorothy McGuire in the roles originally played by Pauline Lord, Raymond Massey and Ruth Gordon" (Walker 45). But the play was never produced. The only news in 1952 about the project was that Kramer was still looking for actors to be in his film. Then in early in 1953 he said the lineup he had in mind was Arthur Kennedy as Ethan, Julie Harris as Mattie, and Shirley Booth as Zeena. While Harris had apparently lobbied Kramer for the part, Sheilah Graham was still indulging in some wishful thinking as far as Davis's participation. "Producer Stanley Kramer called Julie Harris in Pittsburgh to inform her of her Oscar nomination. At the end of the call, he said, 'If there's anything I can do for you in Hollywood, let me know.' 'There is,' said Julie, 'just make me the girl in *Ethan Frome*.' Now, if only Bette Davis would play the old lady" (Graham 2-53, 15). A year later in 1954, the only mention of the film in the papers actually suggested the possibility that Davis would be in Kramer's picture, and Glenn Ford was once again mentioned as the lead. In 1955 Davis continued her quest for the part, but there was no mention of Kramer's ownership of the property or participation in the project. "Bette Davis during her press conference disclosed that she . . . is also still interested in *Ethan Frome*, though she said, 'Now I will probably have to play the wife role,' which is the more mature feminine lead" (Hotchkiss, 61).

But there was no news about the project for the rest of the decade, and with Kramer's project halted Julie Harris eventually decided to appear in a televised version of the stage play in 1960. The success of that production once again spurred Bette Davis into action a few years later, and resulted in a 1963 announcement that read like something from twenty years earlier. So much so, in fact, that columnist Mike Connolly didn't realize his amusing mistake. "Bette Davis and Curtis Bernhardt are preparing a TV replate (a special) of *Ethan Frome*. He directed her in the movie version years ago. But Bette, who played the young girl in the original, will play the older doll this time" (Connolly 6). In a time before VCRs Connolly's gaff is understandable, especially since any cursory check back through clippings from the 1940s would have assured him that the film must have been made. It wouldn't be until April of 1968 that news of the project resurfaced, this time in a cryptic line in a column by Jack Bradford: "Edith Wharton's 1911 novelette, *Ethan Frome*, after four attempts, will make it before the cameras later this year" (Bradford 19). But there was no follow up the rest of the decade and no information as to who was supposedly producing it.

It's no surprise that the next mention of *Ethan Frome* is associated with Bette Davis yet again. Ten years after her planned television version failed to materialize, the actress—who was sixty-five at this point—hinted at another possible Broadway revival. "Bette Davis, visiting backstage at *Seesaw*, said she might return to B'way in *Ethan Frome*. Henry Fonda and Liv Ullman were mentioned, too. (Wilson 11-73, 28). As late as 1977 Davis was hoping for more than Broadway, and told Wayne Warga she was "still determined to do a picture she has wanted to make for 30 years: *Ethan Frome*.

> Back then I wanted to play Mattie. Now I'll play the wife. Henry Fonda would be a perfect Ethan. I begged [Gary] Cooper to do it but he was making *Sergeant York*. Then, when he was ready I was pregnant. I think Liv Ullman would be perfect as Mattie. I even called her and told her so. I told her 'You're the great big star. You've got it made.' She's going to read it and I'm trusting she'll want to do it. (Warga 385)

In numerous interviews the actress gave late into the year in conjunction with her Lifetime Achievement Award from the American Film Institute, Davis continued to express her desire to make the film. In June Maggie Daly went so far as to announce that William Wyler had agreed to come out of retirement for Davis to direct the project. "The remaining problem: Getting a producer and company to do the film" (Daly 54). But the problem proved to be an insurmountable one. A year later Davis was still talking about the project in interviews, though she was now nearing seventy. Davis worked regularly in films throughout the nineteen seventies and early eighties, but in 1983 she suffered a series of strokes after an operation, and her dream of filming *Ethan Frome* finally came to an end.

It wasn't until 1986 that the idea of making an *Ethan Frome* movie was revived for a new generation and actor William Hurt, who was riding high after a series of successful films, was chosen to play the title character. "There have been many attempts to translate *Frome* from printed page to screen, and producer Michael Fitzgerald says he feels he has the knots all worked out and expects to have the story before the cameras in late spring" (Beck 90). Fitzgerald's project was to be one of many films of classic novels that appeared on movie screens in the late eighties and early nineties. Author Parley Ann Boswell sees the proliferation of films based on Wharton's work—and by extension other authors—at that time naturally taking shape for a couple of reasons. The first was because of the affinity filmmakers had to "these artists who had worked during the previous fin de siècle. Their backward glance resulted in a remarkable number of movies based on long-neglected or difficult texts" (Boswell 111). Second, the approach these modern filmmakers were taking to classic literature was necessarily more sophisticated than their predecessors. "By the last decades of the twentieth century, profit might still be the primary motive for movie studios, but the process by which studios chose literary adaptations had changed. Unlike the movie moguls of the early years, contemporary producers and filmmakers were most likely credentialed and trained in their craft," giving them a unique ability to adapt "complex narratives and experimental fiction." While the fact that Fitzgerald signaled his attempt to make the film while Columbia still owned the property in the late nineteen-eighties supports Boswell's contention to a degree, the much more obvious and overwhelming reason for the resurgence in filming literature from the turn of the twentieth century is because those works were entering the public domain *en masse.*

Money was clearly a factor in choosing to film stories that could be adapted to the screen with limited expense compared to the cost of commissioning an original screenplay. In addition, the classics came with their own built-in name recognition and a convenient literary tie-in to help promote the new pictures. Ultimately, nothing came of Michael Fitzgerald's attempt to film *Ethan Frome,* but by the time the novel entered the public domain in 1990, the property was fair game for anyone who wanted to bring the story to the screen. That's when Lindsay Law, the producer of the *American Playhouse,* rushed in to put together his own production.

> More widely known that most of the other classics serving as source material for Hollywood, the novel "has had a very strange history" where movies are concerned, said producer Lindsay Law. Several earlier attempts fizzled. Long in the hands of Columbia Pictures, the property came into the public domain a year and a half ago, and immediately attracted the attention of a number of producers, said Law, adding, "We were getting extremely nervous." But Law managed to dive in first. (Pristin 216)

Compared to the $30 million that was spent on Martin Scorsese's version of Wharton's *The Age of Innocence* that same year, the PBS production of *Ethan Frome* was a relative bargain. "Wharton's tale of a love triangle, was made on the usual American Playhouse budget of $2 million. Because the book is in the public domain, no rights fees were involved. And with a cast whose biggest name is Liam Neeson, talent costs were held down" (Beale 141). While Neeson was not a major star at the time, he and his co-stars, Joan Allen and Patricia Arquette, would gain substantial reputations in the years to follow and make the casting something of a coup in retrospect. But keeping costs down was a matter of course for the company because of the sheer number of productions they were undertaking annually.

> *American Playhouse* provides PBS with twelve programs a year, which makes it the nation's most prolific independent film outlet . . . Law depends on [financial] partners on particular films, private investors and *American Playhouse*'s own profits, which, because it is non-profit, must be plowed back into moviemaking. Some productions are released in theaters before being broadcast on PBS. (Weber 27)

A screenplay adaptation was commissioned in 1991 from Richard Nelson, whose previous work for the production company had been *Sensibility and Sense*—nothing to do with the Jane Austen novel. "I wrote the first draft of a screenplay of Edith Wharton's novella, *Ethan Frome,* for the director, Trevor Nun. The film is to be a co-production between US and UK film companies to be shot on location in the US next winter (the story needs a great deal of snow)" (Nelson 1991, 32). But along the way British television director Trevor Nun was dropped from the production and another British television director, John Madden, was chosen to helm the project.

> Following location scouting in New York, New Hampshire, and Maine, producer Stan Wlodkowski discovered Peacham, VT, a small town subject to the state's "strict zoning and environmental controls [that] ensured that the land and buildings . . . remained virtually untouched" for nearly one hundred years. After the town voted to allow filming there, a defunct farm in Peacham, "uninhabited since the early 1900s," was found for the Frome residence. Madden stated that shooting inside the small farmhouse caused many difficulties but ultimately gave the film a sense of claustrophobia that aided the narrative. (Kallevang)

Filming took place in Peacham in February of 1992, though by all accounts it turned out to be a difficult shoot.

> When scouts for the American Playhouse production of Edith Wharton's novel *Ethan Frome* set out looking for a location last year, they were looking for one key ingredient: snow. That's what made the Northeast Kingdom, which has one of the highest snowfalls in New England, ideal for the production. But winter never has been easy in the Northeast Kingdom. Nor is making a film . . . The crew has logged about 20 car accidents driving on the slippery roads between locations in Peacham, Groton and Bellows Falls. An ice storm on the fourth day of shooting made the crew's drive to Bellows Falls a four-hour nightmare. Not surprisingly, the shoot has fallen a few days behind in the 37-day schedule. (Killinger 25)

Post-production work on the project took place during the remainder of 1992, and the film was scheduled to open in U.S. movie theaters in January of 1993. That date was pushed back, however, in order to avoid putting Liam Neeson up against Al Pacino's performance in *Scent of a Woman* at Oscar time. Eventually, it appeared in theaters in March.

The film opens on the crest of a snowy slope, which turns out to be a road. While the credits roll a figure can be seen making his way out from the camouflage of trees behind him. It is the bent and limping figure of Liam Neeson as Ethan Frome. He makes his tortuous way in tattered clothing past the camera and in the background a train appears and pulls up to the platform. It seems that screenwriter Richard Nelson was, from the very beginning, intent on violating all of the things about Wharton's novel that were so important to the story, the most obvious and offensive the complete destruction of the character of the original narrator. Nelson apparently neglected to read Wharton's introduction, or if he did he chose to ignore it. Wharton herself makes it perfectly clear how vital the role of the narrator in the novel is, and more than that, the way in which that character is essential to creating the realism of the inner story.

> It appears to me, indeed, that while an air of artificiality is lent to a tale of complex and sophisticated people which the novelist causes to be guessed at and interpreted by any mere looker-on, there need be no such drawback if the looker-on is sophisticated, and the people he interprets are simple. If he is capable of seeing all around them, no violence is done to probability in allowing him to exercise this facility; it is natural enough that he should act as the sympathizing intermediary between his rudimentary characters

and the more complicated minds to whom he is trying to present them. (Wharton 1911, viii)

But the first thing one notices about the character of the narrator, as Nelson has reinvented him, is that he is a fool. He is played for comedic effect—exactly the opposite of the role he should have in the story. "In Wharton's novel, Frome's story is recounted to an electric company employee temporarily assigned to Starkfield, rather than a minister. 'We gave him a stake in the story' said director John Madden. 'He's young and passionate but not terribly experienced'" (Killinger 25). The choice of occupations wasn't necessarily a bad one, and in a way fairly inspired, unfortunately the characterization is all wrong for the story. Secondly, at the end of what constitutes the Prologue in the novel, Nelson does precisely what Wharton said would be wrong in telling the story of these particular characters: "I might have sat him down before a village gossip who would have poured out the whole affair to him in a breath, but in doing this I should have been false to two essential elements of my picture: first, the deep-rooted reticence and inarticulateness of the people I was trying to draw, and second to the effect of 'roundness' . . . produced by letting their case be seen through eyes as different as those of Harmon Gow and Mrs. Ned Hale" (Wharton 1911, viii). But what Nelson in fact does, is to have Mrs. Ned Hale "[pour] out the whole affair to him in a breath."

The opening of the film proper cuts to the interior of the train with Tate Donovan playing the narrator, Reverend Smith. At first he's oblivious to everything around him and doesn't even hear the ticket taker announce that they are in Starkfield. When he gets off of the train he spies Frome walking along the road and then becomes so fixated on the figure that he doesn't hear Stephen Mendillo as Ned Hale—who has already died at this point in the novel—yelling his name. Smith slips and nearly falls and Hale can only shake his head at the fact that he has no boots. As Hale and Smith travel in Hale's horse-drawn cart they pass Ethan walking along the road, which makes absolutely no sense. In the book the narrator first sees Ethan at the post office, after he had ridden there in his buggy. It's also clear in the novel that the train platform is miles away from the village. What possible business Ethan could have hobbling along the road from the platform to the town is never even addressed, which is especially puzzling considering that in the book his farm is on the opposite side of the village from the train station, and even more incomprehensible when he is seen to still own horses and a wagon later in the film.

The next scene is like something from a Jane Austen novel, fabricated entirely by the screenwriter. Smith is holding court in the parlor of the Hale's home, so emphatic in his idealism that it shows him to be completely out of touch with the nature of his parishioners. His expressions of outrage about the dire poverty of people living in the tenements of Boston to a people barely scratching out a living from the earth is similar to the hypocrisy of the Christian housewives in Harper Lee's *To Kill a Mockingbird*, who are absolutely heartbroken over the living conditions of the primitive Mrunas, and yet refuse to help poor blacks living in their own town. At the same time, every mother in the village with a daughter of marrying age is in attendance in the hope of foisting her child on the unsuspecting minister. When Pastor Smith finally has the opportunity to see Ethan close up the following day, the scene is again in direct opposition to Wharton's narrator who respects the man's privacy in the same way as the rest of the men there. In the film Smith blunders right up to Ethan and introduces himself. Ethan is forced to give him his last name and then departs. But unlike the respect the narrator witnesses from the men in the novel, in the film they act almost embarrassed to see Ethan, which seems out of character for the citizens as Wharton had drawn them. Further, there's a sense that the villagers know about Ethan's feelings for Mattie and how they led to the botched suicide, something they couldn't possibly have known, and that's what their embarrassment stems from.

Later Smith rants to his hosts, Ned and Ruth Hale, about the apparent lack of concern that the men at the post office exhibited toward the unfortunate Ethan, but the couple is almost equally embarrassed by the reverend's behavior. Because of this, any "sophistication" in the way that Wharton developed her narrator simply doesn't exist in the film. Instead it is the people of Starkfield who appear far more wise and composed when compared to Smith, a city slicker who has no conception of the way his behavior appears to them. Rather than the intellectual curiosity of Wharton's narrator, who becomes obsessed with a man in whom he recognizes a certain nobility of spirit in spite of his injuries, Reverend Smith behaves like a colonial master who demands as his right to be informed about a person he can only perceive of as an object of pity. Thus it is Smith who takes it upon himself to walk out to the Frome farm and ask Ethan to chauffer him around to the various homes in the county to visit with his parishioners. In this way, rather than the great favor that Ethan winds up doing for the narrator in the novel, Smith's hiring of Ethan becomes an act of charity.

At the other extreme, one of the areas in which the film excels is in the characterization of Ethan and Zeena. Much of the credit for that must go to the actors, Liam Neeson and Joan Allen, who tend to be exceptional in whatever roles they take on. "Neeson's account is indeed of award caliber," said columnist Larry Swindell, "and is well-matched by the work of Joan

Allen and Patricia Arquette" (Swindell 27). The elder Ethan has just the right amount of brusqueness and impatience with Smith to set him apart from the naive minister. Ethan agrees to take him around, and after picking up Smith's personal belongings at the train station he lifts out a volume of the *Scientific American* from one of the crates and looks at it with affection while Smith is inside visiting with his parishioners. It's here that the screenplay jumps right to the snowstorm, on their first day together, and when Ethan's wagon gets stuck the two men are forced to retreat to Ethan's farm to wait it out. Of course the storm in the film lacks the eerie menace of the curtain of blackness that descends upon the characters in the novel. It is also the only real instance in the film where the weather asserts itself at all, though Parley Ann Boswell still sees in this a connection with Wharton's novel in the way that weather in the film seems to accidentally mirror the oppressive symbolism of nature in Wharton's story. "In the film, Ethan feels most entrapped outside on the cold, white landscape . . . In opposition to the whiteness of the exteriors, the dark interior of the house becomes the site of Ethan's dream world" (Boswell 153). They first go into the kitchen where Ethan pours them some coffee. Of course, when the nosy Smith hears coughing in the other room he immediately gets up to investigate, but Ethan informs him sternly that he can sleep in the kitchen, implying that the rest of the house is off limits. Again, screenwriter Richard Nelson is compelled to violate the character of Wharton's "granite outcroppings" by having Smith inform Ethan that in sitting in the home of his neighbors they opened up to him and told him "their whole life story" (Nelson 1993). Smith's implication is clear: he wants Ethan to tell him his life story on the presumption of "easing his burden." It's actually quite insulting, especially when Ethan suggests to the minister that some people prefer to be left alone.

But Smith's ignorant and insulting behavior apparently knows no bounds when he delivers a sermon to his church members the following Sunday as a way of coercing them into telling him everything he wants to know. It's especially ironic when he quotes from the Bible saying, "I understood as a child. I thought as a child," and that he saw "through a glass darkly," as Smith seems an especially ignorant and childish character (Nelson 1993). He speaks of faith, hope, and charity, from I Corinthians, emphasizing that the greatest of them is charity, but this is just a thinly veiled admonition to the churchgoers to ignore the wishes of the Fromes and barge their way into their lives in the guise of easing their presumed loneliness. Of course his propaganda campaign works on Ruth Hale. Nevertheless, she does manage confront him with his own ignorance at the same time. As he tells her what he believes the Fromes need she interrupts, saying, "Who knows what Mr. Frome needs, Mr. Smith? Who can presume to know a thing like that?" In his petulance, Smith actually tells her at this point that he should probably return to Boston because of his assumption that the people of Starkfield just aren't charitable enough to those in need. And after finally wearing her down she makes it her mission to set him straight, telling the reverend the whole sordid tale.

The interior story begins with the funeral of Ethan's mother, as mourners trudge through the snow carrying the coffin from the house to the graveyard. In the house afterward, while Joan Allen as Zeena efficiently takes care of things in the kitchen, it comes out that Ethan had just begun to study engineering at Harvard and that he intends on selling the farm in order to get back to his studies. But throughout the day it is also evident that Ethan is smitten with Zeena, as he can't stop looking at her. Allen has a radiant charm throughout these early scenes, though knowing the story it's not difficult to see the calculation beneath that charm. After the mourners have left, Ethan tells Zeena that she doesn't have to go, but she claims she sees no reason to stay now that his mother is gone. There is also an early intimation here that something is wrong with her when she has a coughing fit during the scene, though Ethan ascribes it to working all day without eating. Later Zeena is seen trying to wrestle her trunk down the stairs by herself—something that isn't in the original novel—which makes a nice parallel to later in the story when she makes Mattie do the same thing. The fact that she has wedged the trunk in the staircase so tightly that even Ethan can't budge it is a wonderfully humorous and endearing moment between the two, something lacking in Ethan's grim account of their marriage in the novel

But suddenly Katharine Houghton's voice-over as Ruth Hale is heard on the soundtrack and it seems particularly intrusive at this point in the film, especially when nearly everything she says has already been conveyed visually. Worse yet, this is followed by a return to the frame story, with Ruth and Reverend Smith walking through the snow as children sled down the hill in front of them. Ruth points out the big elm tree and says, "That's where it happened," followed by Smith's reply, "What happened?" (Nelson 1993). Then the film cuts back to a sickly Zeena in bed five years after their marriage, and Ruth continuing with her superfluous narration. Zeena shows Ethan a letter saying that Mattie Silver is coming to work for her. As in the book, there's an element at the beginning of Mattie's presence in their home that Zeena sees as positive. "Well, she don't cost anythin' 'cause she's a relative," she tells Ethan. "She might be someone to talk to." There's also a nice hint of Zeena's purposeful hypochondria when Ethan starts complaining that he doesn't want Mattie staying in his old room because that's where his books and desk are. Zeena launches into a coughing fit at this point that immediately shuts down his argument. Then later, when he begins packing up his books and his map of Florida, Zeena suddenly appears with a smile on her face saying how good she feels just knowing she's going to be getting some help.

The next scene has Ethan at the train platform picking up Patricia Arquette as Mattie. It's Ruth who provides Mattie's backstory. Of course Ethan is not happy with the situation, as Mattie appears just as sickly as Zeena at first and therefore promises to be of little help. Then Ruth says a year went by—which is a significant change in the story as Mattie's stay with the Fromes in the novel is contained within a single year—and still Mattie isn't much better at the housework than she was when she arrived. From there the scene shifts to the church dance that opens the interior portion of the novel. At the same time Ruth's narration tells the audience that another entire year has gone by, one in which Mattie proceeded to get better at her chores and recover from her illness. Thus it has been two years Mattie has been with the couple rather than one, enough time for Ethan to have figured out well in advance how he felt about her. While Ethan trudges through the snow to the church, at the dance Jay Goede as Denis Eady looks longingly at Mattie. Liam Neeson does a nice job at conveying with his expression what obviously can't be articulated in voiceover. On approaching the church window he is delighted and happy looking at Mattie, but as he sees her continue to dance with Eady his expression changes to one of seriousness and then sadness as he finally turns away and runs to help Ruth Varnum and Ned Hale who have had an accident sledding. This is an event that is only mentioned by Mattie in the book, but here Ethan carries Ruth back into the village while the dancers pour out of the church, Eady with his arm around Mattie.

Later Eady walks Mattie back into the building, and then tells her he can give her a ride home. Unlike his character in the book, in the film Eady seems a very nice young man who is clearly infatuated with Mattie. Ethan hears the conversation and says he'll meet her at home, but after the next cut Mattie is seen walking beside him. This is a very different take on the material in the novel, one in which Ethan seems resigned to keep his feelings to himself while Mattie appears to be pursuing him. Ethan suggests the two of them go sledding, and she seems delighted at the prospect. But when he mentions that Denis Eady must have asked her, she says, "Why would I go anywhere with him?" (Nelson 1993). One perceives a modern sensibility at work here, imposed upon a time period in which Mattie would have felt compelled to be far more circumspect in expressing her feelings, especially in a time when she would have been keenly aware of the possibility of any marriage proposal. Mattie's the one who spots Orion in the sky, and as the two sit on a fallen log it almost looks as if she's going to kiss Ethan. But this is just part and parcel of Richard Nelson's screenplay, in which there's no subtlety to Mattie's behavior whatsoever. On a technical level, there's also no way to replicate the complete darkness that is such a frequently recurring symbol throughout the novel. By comparison, the film seems almost bathed in light throughout, even in the scenes shot at night.

The next morning the camera pushes in on a bottle of strychnine on a shelf in the barn. This is another element of the film that is entirely invented by Nelson. Ethan has the poison in order to kill a fox that has been getting into the chicken coop, all of which is a foreshadow of it's primary purpose later in the film. George Woodard as Jotham Powell shows up and the two men go off to the wood lot while Mattie prepares a meal. The next shot, up in Zeena's bedroom, begins with the top of her dresser covered with bottles of medicine. When Mattie comes into the room with Zeena's tea she gets distracted and proceeds to spill it all over. The two argue and then Zeena suddenly smells Mattie's meal, which has caught on fire in the oven downstairs. In Wharton's novel Mattie was never very good at housework, but she did improve over time. In the film she is positively inept, though the implication is that her absent mindedness has been caused by her obsession with Ethan—a significant reversal from the book. As the four characters sit around the kitchen table, it's Mattie who blurts out that Zeena is leaving to visit her aunt in Bettsbridge. Mattie is also the one who seems to be mentally calculating what Zeena's absence will mean for her rather than Ethan. Richard Nelson does make a nice change to this scene when he has Jotham Powell essentially force Ethan into the lie about collecting money from Andrew Hale. At first Ethan says he won't be able to accompany Zeena on her trip because he needs to deliver logs to Mr. Hale, which makes sense, but then Jotham Powell volunteers to do it for him. So next he says that Hale is eager to get his lumber right away because of the house he's building for Ned and Ruth, but when Jotham begins to contradict him Ethan is forced to interrupt him and make up the excuse about collecting money, which is something Jotham can't do. Therefore it's precisely because of the prospect of his collecting money that when Ethan volunteers to take her to the train station, it's Zeena who suggests that Jotham Powell can do it. Finally, after Zeena leaves, Ethan looks back at the house to see Mattie standing in the doorway as she virtually offers herself up to him.

The scene at the lumber mill goes essentially as it does in the book, with the exception of the ending. Dennis Meinter's character, Andrew Hale, doesn't say that he was going to ask Ethan for an extension but does imply that he would be willing to loan him money if it was an emergency. Then Nelson adds another scene that wasn't in the book, Ethan's visit to Michael Eady's story to buy a present for Mattie, where Denis asks Ethan to give a hair ribbon to her as well. That night at dinner Mattie appears to have no trouble whatever putting a meal together. Interestingly, when the cat jumps up on Zeena's rocker and Ethan makes a playful joke about it keeping the seat warm, it's Mattie who nearly scowls at the mention of her name. The entire scene seems to reverse the roles that the two characters occupy in the book. Mattie is the one who seems displeased that Zeena will be back the following evening, while Ethan is the one who is happy and good-natured. Mattie is hyper-attentive to Ethan's needs during the meal, and even makes another disparaging comment about Denis Eady. At one point she cries when he compliments her cooking, saying she hasn't been complimented in over a year. Throughout supper her dewy-eyed gaze remains focused on Ethan, and Ethan is the one who seems clueless as to why. She mentions her piano playing, and even sings for Ethan, and she seems so overwhelmed with sexual tension that it eventually manages to spill over onto Ethan.

When the cat finally jumps up on the table and breaks the pickle dish, the editing makes it appear as if Mattie can't tear herself away from fantasizing about Ethan in order to go into a panic. But then she finally does. Later the two of them finish their evening together with Mattie sewing and Ethan smoking his pipe. It's here that Ethan gives her the present he bought for her, candy, as well as the hair ribbon Denis Eady asked him to give to her. She thanks him for the sweets, but is especially taken with the ribbon and immediately goes to the mirror to put in on. Ethan is almost embarrassed to say it, but finally confesses that the ribbon was from Eady, and so of course Mattie decides not to put it on after all and goes back to gushing over the sweets. Unlike the novel, when Ethan walks over to the table and touches the material she is sewing, Mattie's eyes are riveted to his hand and the expression on her face is one of delight, then he pulls it to his lips and she stops to watch him. At the top of the stairs before bed, she tells him about her time in school and recites a bit of "Curfew shall not ring to-night." Impossibly, Ethan finishes the stanza for her. Sure, he's been to Harvard, but the moment feels entirely manufactured. Then the two of them go to their respective rooms, but as Mattie begins undressing her door suddenly swings open and Ethan walks in. Breathlessly, the two kiss and the music swells symbolizing that they have sex.

For author Linda Costanzo Cahir, this is the tipping point in a film that was already struggling to maintain a connection with the novel's underlying power. "The movie aspires to depict scenes just as they appear in Wharton's novel. This tenaciously faithful adherence to Wharton's novel makes its one plot alteration seem even more jarringly odd and radical: Ethan Frome and Mattie Silver consummate their love in Frome's farmhouse one evening" (Cahir 222). Cahir sees this as pandering to audiences who can't conceive of anything other than what they're used to, what they've been trained by

Hollywood to expect, so Madden and Nelson give them "soft-hued lamplight, openmouthed kisses, and gentle sex" (223). In defending this change, however, author Parley Ann Boswell goes back to Wharton's novel, arguing that it is perfectly in keeping with Ethan's character. "During the scene where he and Mattie are sitting together after supper on their one night alone, Wharton suggests that he wants to touch Mattie so much that he aches. He may crave companionship, but he also yearns for more. Wharton's descriptions of Ethan suggest his sexual excitement" (Boswell 121). But Boswell is really overstating the case. Of primary importance to Ethan in the novel during this scene is the idea of a "long-established intimacy which no outburst of emotion could have given," and the "fiction that they had always spent their evenings thus and would always go on doing so . . ." (Wharton 1911, 97). As with the many women Ethan represents in the novel, the need for love is paramount. Once that has been achieved, sex is essentially a given. It is a necessity, to be sure—as demonstrated by the way Ethan craves to touch Mattie—but it is a byproduct of love, not the initiating factor.

For Boswell this makes little difference. To her the defining act of the novel is the suicide pact that fails. "Had Madden's version of *Ethan Frome* ended differently from Wharton's, Ethan and Mattie's sexual encounter would have violated the integrity of Wharton's story. However, both versions conclude with the same grim scene of Ethan, Mattie, and Zeena in their frozen hell together" (122). This argument doesn't really work, though, because it is based on the assumption of a mutual affection between the two characters in the story that, as has been demonstrated above, is already a violation of the integrity of Wharton's novel. Boswell goes on to say, "Reading Wharton's novella, we understand that Ethan is a dreamer whose love for Mattie might be fantasy but whose yearnings and desperation are real. Whether Ethan and Mattie have been intimate makes no difference" (122). But it does, as it's that very element of "fantasy" that is so key to the power behind the original novel. Undercutting this idea reduces the story to little more than a tragic romance that, as history has shown, has contained enough to captivate the conscious mind of readers for a century but, as Madden's film also demonstrates, is not enough to keep the subconscious mind from losing interest. For Cahir, this is simply evidence of filmmakers who are "either too unpracticed or too distrusting of an audience's capacity to follow depths of meaning to explore Frome's aching intricacies" (Cahir 223).

The film then cuts to the next day—Rachel Portman's film score connecting the two scenes—with the two of them riding happily together through the woods in the sleigh. Eventually they wind up at Eady's store together. There are only a few customers inside and for the most part they ignore the couple—except for Denis Eady, who at first is genuinely pleased to see Mattie. But she treats him cruelly, and makes it perfectly clear that she has nothing but disdain for him. After he proves ineffectual at finding glue for Ethan, he asks Mattie if she received his present and she thanks him rather dismissively. In the novel Eady was arrogant and a potentially domineering husband, but one of the things Nelson does in the screenplay is to turn him into a very sympathetic character. Unfortunately, the screenwriter also significantly altered Mattie's character, and not for the better. In addition, the consummation of the relationship between Ethan and Mattie removes all of the suspense that had been built into this part of the story by Wharton. When the two of them arrive home in high spirits and are told by Jotham Powell that Zeena has already arrived, their joy vanishes. What follows, presented as a sort of noble struggle between Ethan and Zeena in the book, suddenly turns into something unseemly that manages to diminish both of their characters.

Ethan's confrontation with Zeena in their bedroom is rendered fairly accurately. The most significant difference is that Zeena, rather than playing her winning hand with finesse, launches into a heated argument the moment the issue of money comes up. And in the same way that the characters of Ethan and Mattie are significantly altered, this only manages to undercut the evil, calculating quality Zeena had maintained throughout Wharton's novel. It does have the ironic effect of softening her in the film, though, turning her into a more sympathetic character, but that only makes what Ethan and Mattie are doing to her that much more repugnant. Unlike the book, when Ethan comes downstairs it now appears that Mattie has heard the entire argument through the thin walls of the house. And later during dinner, when the three of them are sitting around the table, instead of Zeena relishing the victory she has achieved, she glowers at Ethan in anger. After Zeena goes in to get her stomach powders later and finds the broken pickle dish, she screams at the two of them instead of the measured incredulity that informs her actions in the novel. Finally, at the conclusion of their confrontation, Ethan is shown racing out to the barn to chase away the fox. There's a sense that what Nelson was going for in the screenplay is that the violence with which Ethan poisons the animal and nails its dead body to the barn the next morning is an outward expression of the inner emotion he feels toward Zeena—a more demonstrative version of throwing the pillow across the room.

That night after Ethan goes up to his room he finds Zeena asleep, then he steals into Mattie's room. Here Mattie says something that is probably the closest thing in the film to her character in Wharton's original short story when she tells him they shouldn't have sex because Zeena will need him after she's gone. Ethan hears Zeena cough in the other room, but doesn't return, and he and Mattie have sex again while Zeena lies in her room staring pitifully from beneath the covers listening to them. The next morning an exasperated Zeena unpacks Mattie's entire trunk on the pretext of looking for things that she is trying to steal. What Mattie has stolen, however, Zeena is not going to find packed among her personal possessions. At dinner Zeena claims to have been awakened the previous night by the sound of the dying fox, but the more subtle implication is that she really heard the two of them having sex. Her inability to confront her husband directly makes her seem almost as averse to the truth as Ethan is in the novel—though in a way it certainly seems more realistic. All Zeena can do while the men are eating is complain, and she gives Jotham the task of taking Mattie to the train station and picking up the hired girl. Nevertheless, after she sits down to eat Zeena miraculously has her appetite back now that Mattie has to go. Unlike her measured speech in the book, as Ethan goes to upstairs to help with Mattie's trunk Zeena yells at the top of her voice that she wants him to fix the stove. Again, this contrast with Zeena's passive-aggressive refusal to show emotion in the novel is notable, as it further serves to soften her character.

Ethan takes Mattie's trunk out and puts it on Daniel Byrne's sleigh, and then goes into to the barn. There he discovers Mattie on her knees with the bottle of strychnine. As she pours the crystals into her hands Ethan shouts and runs to keep her from ingesting them. She does, however, have time to inhale, which in reality would have been enough to keep her in bed for several days at least. But this is simply the payoff for the two earlier scenes when Ethan used the poison to kill the fox. Nelson's intent here seems to be to establish Mattie's desire to kill herself so that it doesn't come as such a surprise the way it does in the novel. Ethan wrestles her to the ground and washes off her hands as Mattie screams that she wants to die. It's also here that Nelson finally gives the viewer a real taste of the Zeena that readers of the book know and love. Zeena is seen climbing the stairs while Mattie is heard screaming and crying in the background. When she reaches the top of the stairs Zeena pauses, and a barely perceptible smile crosses her lips before she goes into her room. Actress Joan Allan explained in an interview what she felt was the motivation of her character, as well as her role in the overall story.

So much is unspoken, especially in terms of when Zeena realizes what's going on, and when Ethan and Mattie start to know that. It's very intricate, and though not a lot happens in the piece [in terms of physical action], a lot does "happen" in a way. This was a departure for me, since I've never played the "bad guy" before, but I kept on saying on the set, "She's just unhappy and misunderstood. That's all." She was just a fabulous character to work on, and with so much depth, it was like working on a stage role. There was a lot to her. (Bobbin 231)

After the aborted suicide Ethan marches into their bedroom and announces that he's taking Mattie to the train station himself. Just as in the novel, where the scene plays out in the kitchen, Zeena is reading one of her medical books. It's unfortunate that, despite a look of disappointment on her face, Zeena doesn't have the opportunity to demonstrate again that her illness is not real. She does manage to punish Mattie by leaving her with nothing, giving her only enough money so that, along with every penny she has saved, she will be completely broke after purchasing her train fare.

Ethan takes Mattie in the sleigh to the top of a hill with a breathtaking view overlooking a river and then, reluctant to go on, he gets out so he can talk to her. This is where the story of the man who leaves his wife appears, but there is one subtle difference to it. Much has been made of the apparent morality that prevents Ethan from leaving Zeena in the novel. But a close reading of Wharton's story actually reveals that if Ethan had possessed enough money he would have left her. There's no denying that Ethan is a weak and timid character in the novel, but to have him say as he does here, "Fifty dollars. I'm goin' to save it up," makes him appear even weaker in the film, especially when he implies that it would be wrong to leave Zeena with nothing (Nelson 1993). Mattie agrees, but both she and the audience know he'll never be able to save the money. Once the two get into Starkfield they stop at Eady's store again, another invention of Nelson's. Ethan is determined to buy her a proper gift this time, one the equal of the hair ribbon Eady had given her. Mattie, however, has no desire to interact with other people who might be inside. When they enter, Eady is much more wary and observant than he was the first time, especially after he sees Ethan stroke Mattie's cheek. Ruth Varnum and her mother are also in the store and their awkward conversation makes it clear that they don't know what to make of the couple. Ruth's mother delivers the dialogue that Mrs. Hale had spoken in the novel about how she sympathizes with Ethan for what he's had to go through with Zeena. But the sentiment is lost on him as he is completely consumed by his passion for Mattie. He eventually buys her a hair comb and Eady painfully wraps it for her. Then the two quickly leave the store.

After putting the comb in her hair, Ethan says that they're going to go coasting like he had promised. And it's clear from his face—despite Mattie's desire to get to the train station on time—that he's not taking no for an answer. Ethan finds a sled and, after asking her if she wants to take the big run, they climb to the top of the hill and head back down together on the sled. Mattie squeals with delight as they speed down the slope, screaming as they pass the big elm, and then agrees when Ethan wants to go down again. Delighted with each other at the bottom of the second run, they hear the church bell and it brings them back to reality. Then they kiss again. In another major deviation from the book, when Mattie asks him to take her down a third time so that she will never have to leave the hill, Ethan says nothing. The rationale for this probably has to do with her earlier suicide attempt, but he still seems incredibly acquiescent to his own impending death. Mattie is also very compliant about getting on the back instead of the front, and after another kiss they take no time to think about what they are doing before they push off. There are no screams of delight this time, and director John Madden does a nice job by filming the sequence in slow motion, set to Portman's evocatively mournful music. The waiting horse and the children climbing the hill with their sleds are intercut at normal speed. Then the ruined sled is seen flying in the air by itself and the two bodies come to rest in the snow at the base of the tree as the children run back to the village for help.

From there, the film cuts to the latter-day Ethan, seen from behind laboriously trudging up the hill through the snow to his house. At the same time the voiceover by Ruth Hale returns, telling Reverend Smith that she was the first to reach them, and that Mattie was brought to her house. The camera cuts to she and Smith, outside in the snow in front of their horse-drawn sleigh watching Ethan, and she urges Smith to walk the rest of the way to the Frome's. A latch is heard on the soundtrack behind a black screen, and the door is opened from the inside. Ruth says hello to Ethan and essentially invites herself in on the pretext of visiting Zeena. Ruth walks through the kitchen with the Reverend following, and the two go on into the living room where she sits down with Mattie. Smith initially mistakes her for Ethan's wife, before Ethan corrects him and introduces Zeena sitting in the corner. When he then introduces Mattie, she turns her head and reveals a face that has been badly scarred from the accident. Smith is suitably horrified and, if it's even possible, humbled. Misreading the situation as he always does, however, he tries to open the curtains, and when Mattie turns her head in pain Zeena tells him they prefer it dark. Ethan won't even look at the man. Ruth and Smith are next shown walking back to their sleigh, and Ruth tells him not to say anything. Then they both look back at Ethan before turning and heading down the hill. After a close up on Ethan's scarred face, he is shown walking around the corner of the house and the camera cuts to a long shot of the farm as the end credits begin to roll.

A hint of the problems associated with the project came in December of 1992, before it was theatrically released, in the form of Liam Neeson's unhappiness with the way the film had been edited. "Actor Liam Neeson and Harvey Weinstein, Miramax Films honcho, got into it good at a Monday screening of *Ethan Frome* for a test audience in Manhattan. Neeson started howling about cuts. Weinstein loudly defended them. Four-letter words all around. 'Tempers did flare,' confessed Weinstein. 'But we worked it out'" (Speers 76). Originally scheduled to open in January, the film's release was pushed back to March, but word of mouth about the film's deficiencies when it finally arrived in theaters resulted in a small audience and a short run. Reviews for the film were decidedly mixed, with many reviewers unwilling to see the success of the acting as compensation for a poorly executed screenplay. For every reviewer who gushed over the film—"This artful movie is as carefully crafted as a haiku poem. With *Ethan Frome*, thoughtful filmgoers have something to see" (Russell 35)—there were just as many who were brutally off put by its apparent failures—"*Ethan Frome* the movie is almost as dead as Edith Wharton the person, who wrote her novelette in 1911 and hasn't been with us for 55 years" (Mannweiler 40). Columnist Michael Price's headline was typical of the critical consensus that fell somewhere in the middle: "Blizzard of boredom buries 'Ethan Frome'" (Price 25). In his review he goes on to say, "All-'round capable performances help alleviate the tedium—Joan Allen in particular, as the distant-cousin wife who has made Ethan Frome's life a hell on earth—and the cinematography is nothing short of lovely. It's the writing and directing that make this adaptation a less-than-exhilarating experience."

Roger Ebert did as well as any of his colleagues in articulating the real problem with the film. "As a novel, *Ethan Frome* can grow on you because of Wharton's quiet passion. This movie version, however, doesn't find a cinematic equivalent of Wharton's style, trusting that the story and the acting will interest us. The problem is the story, simply as a story, is a forlorn and cheerless morality tale. We drag our feet on the way out of the theater or make unkind jokes about poor Ethan" (Ebert 47). Ebert, as had so many critics of the novel, almost understands what's wrong without really quite getting it. *Ethan Frome* works as a novel because of its ability to tap into the reader's subconscious and—in the words of Lionel Trilling—"to shake us with the perception of social injustice, to instruct us in the true nature of social life and to dispose us to indignant opinion and action" (Trilling 1956, 40). While there are films that can do the same thing, they don't do it in precisely the same way as literature, something Ebert clearly understands. "The overall tone of the movie, directed by John Madden, is reverent—too reverent . . . Madden doesn't give us a reason to see the movie instead of reading the book, and *Ethan Frome* is a very long slog through grim pastures" (Ebert 47). Ebert's complaint that the story as a story isn't very interesting is really the key. As a simplistic tale of love gone wrong—and an ironic punishment that seems monumentally out of proportion to the sin committed—the film does suffer from the same criticism leveled at the novel on its initial publication. What made the novel so inexplicably powerful with readers is what it was actually saying about the plight of women, symbolically disguised as Ethan, a quality that Wharton herself seemed to recognize when she said of critics, "They don't know *why* it's good, but they are right: it *is*" (Lauer 84).

There were certainly a number of critics who enjoyed the film for various reasons, and it must be said that there is something mildly compelling about it, but that probably has more to do with Edith Wharton's story than anything intrinsic to the film. By removing the viewer's uncertainty about Mattie's feelings, and destroying the true function of the narrator in the novel, it resulted in what author Linda Costanzo Cahir has called the "pedstrianization of Frome's complexity" (Cahir 223). In the end, she has been the most adept at summing up the overall problem with this filmed version of *Ethan Frome.*

> It is not the tampering with Wharton's text that is objectionable . . . many great literature to film translations are the product of radical alterations to the parent text. Here it is the film's supercilious manner, in all its prurient, dumbing-down transparency that is so unfortunate. John Madden's *Ethan Frome* takes wine and turns it into water. (Cahir 223)

In comparison, one only has to look at the filmed version of Charlotte Perkins Gilman's "The Yellow Wall-Paper" from BBC television that aired a year earlier to understand what Cahir is talking about. That production, regardless of the assessment of its artistic success or lack thereof, made substantial changes to the story in order to create something meaningful in its own right. Author Janet Beer states the project's goals in that regard: "picking up, emphasizing and developing themes, tropes and structural devices in order to build the story into a substantial drama which reverberates with wider signification" (Beer 1997, 197). But that is something screenwriter Richard Nelson either wouldn't, or couldn't, do. By reducing Wharton's novel to a straightforward forbidden romance with no subtlety whatsoever, he removed the powerful undercurrent of Ethan's mistaken fantasy and left viewers with what writer Cahir describes as the "bleakness of mediocrity" (Cahir 221).

One of the remarkable things about the film is that when it finally appeared on television in November of 1994 it received rave reviews. Apparently television critics operate using a different set of criteria than their cinematic brethren. The only real explanation given for this disparity came from columnist Larry Swindell on the occasion of the film's appearance on video a year earlier. "The new release from Touchstone Home Video may well have a more bountiful existence than its theatrical film. Tragedy plays better in the living room than comedy does, and *Ethan Frome* bears this out: intimacy is a plus, and one or two people at home can respond to it as well—surely better—than in an almost empty theater" (Swindell 27). Another, less tangible, reason for the film's success on television could be that in the interim Liam Neeson had become a major film star as a result of playing the lead in Steven Spielberg's *Schindler's List*.

Ethan Frome in Literature

One of the earliest references to *Ethan Frome* in literature came in 1919 with the short story "Leave It to Lydia," by Frank Lapham, first published in *All-Story Weekly*. The story is about a young man named Hal Hammond who has been away at Oxford for the past six years and after graduation returns during the winter to his small hometown. Shortly after his arrival he is told his father is set to marry Hal's childhood sweetheart, Lois, and for everyone's sake Hal tries to pretend he doesn't have feelings for Lois anymore. Early on in the story Lois invites her friend Lydia to stay with them and, not being convinced of the sincerity with which Lois has become engaged to Hal's father, she comes to see for herself what is going on. She immediately sizes up the situation and becomes determined to marry the father herself, so that the two young people will be able to be together again with a clear conscious. Her plan begins, interestingly enough, by trying to make everyone think she is in love with Hal.

Lois commandeers Lydia and Hal go coasting with her one moonlit evening. After two runs down a treacherous but exhilarating road Lois suggests they go again, and that she ride in front steering the bobsled. For Hal, the ending of Wharton's novel suddenly comes to mind.

> Despite an accompanying sense of the absurdity of the thought, there flashed on him, clear and terrible, the story of Ethan Frome: where Ethan and the girl he loved, overwrought by their hopeless yearning, had sent the sled on which they were coasting into a tree at the foot of a fearful declivity. (Latham 294)

When the rope gets caught beneath one of the runners, a similar fate looms for the protagonist. "Before he could reach around her to grasp the wheel, the bob, at a terrifying angle, shot up the steep incline that bordered the road. They shuddered to a halt, and, for a sickening instant, hung—and then with an ominous crash the heavy sled went over." No one is seriously hurt, however, but Hal nearly gives his true feelings away in his concern for Lois and decides to leave for the city the next day. Lydia's plan works a little too well, however, when Lois gets jealous of her, but before she can divulge her plan to Lois she must first secure the affections of Hal's father. As the title suggests, Lydia eventually triumphs and the story concludes with an ending worthy of Jane Austen.

In Elenore Meherin's serialized 1924 novel *Chickie*, the protagonist—the ambitious typist Helen Bryce, also known as Chickie—uses another man to finally spur the man she loves into action. In forcing his hand it comes out that Barry has been reluctant to pursue Chickie because of his financial situation, which he compares to that of Ethan Frome. But watching Chickie go out time and again with the wealthy Jake is more than Barry can stand, and he eventually confronts her with the truth. In Chapter Eighteen, after finally maneuvering Barry into confessing his love, "She reached her hand to him, shutting her lips hard against a frantic, happy cry." Barry has learned of Chickie's ploy and wants to know if it's true. When she nods yes, he begs her not to kiss Jake anymore. "She wouldn't meet the pleading in his voice: 'Oh—I've plenty, you know. And you've wanted so few this last moon.'" By this time Barry has had enough of her intrigue.

I wonder who's cruel now? Chickie, can't you see things are pretty hard? If I had the money he has—Lord! do you think we'd be stalling around like this? It's just what we were talking of the other night—that in *Ethan Frome*, you think it was terrible for them. What's the difference? I tell you, it's terrible for us! We can't take a sleigh and dash ourselves to death down a hill. But when I sit here and watch you, that's what I'd like to do—throw everything up—" (Meherin 5)

Of course this is exactly what Chickie wants to hear. "He drew her to him: 'What are we going to do, Chickie?'" But she won't let him get away from her now. "'Years and years to talk, Barry! After that, years and years to love!' He kissed her. His lips were cold. He said: 'Chickie, you're beautiful today.'"

While the retelling of *Ethan Frome* on stage and screen has focused primarily on attempting to replicate Edith Wharton's novel, later uses of the work have reimagined the story from Zeena's point of view. In her 1969 collection of poetry entitled *Love Poems*, Anne Sexton wrote about a fall she took down the stairs in her house that resulted in a lengthy hospitalization. "The Break" recounts the misery she suffered after breaking her hip. She begins with the shock of the break itself, the ride to the hospital in an ambulance, the humiliation of having her dress cut off in the emergency room, and then the brutality of the operation. With poetic concision Sexton conveys the intensity of her bad attitude and negative feelings during her post-op recovery period with the evocation of Wharton's novel. "Please don't touch or jiggle my bed. I'm Ethan Frome's wife. I'll move when I'm able" (Sexton 24). Author Joanna Gill's lengthy essay connecting the two works reveals that the life of Sexton herself was as dramatic and tragic as any literary creation. But Gill's argument, which centers on the attempt to tie the "smash-up" of Wharton's novel to "the break" in Sexton's poem, is perhaps a little too ambitious. While Gill finds an abundance of things in the poem that apparently connect Sexton's narrator with everyone in the novel—including Wharton's narrator and Ethan's mother—the overt comparison Sexton's narrator makes between herself and Zeena seems to be the only meaningful one worth exploring. In stating directly, "I'm Ethan Frome's wife," it seems clear that this is where the analytical imperative lies.

There are plenty of lines in the poem that do seem to resemble elements of the novel associated with Zeena, and so it seems only logical that these should be the ones singled out for close study. In describing the break that happened during the fall, Sexton's narrator says the accident resulted in, "splintering up the hip that was merely made of crystal . . . So I fell apart. I came all undone" (Sexton 23). It's not difficult to see a parallel here with the shattering of the pickle dish in Wharton's novel, especially in the way that it is followed by Zeena's tears and emotional outburst, suggesting her own falling apart. Gill, on the other hand, seems too focused on connecting this to Ethan and Mattie's suicide attempt. The "reference to her 'splintering up' as she falls down, and later to coming 'undone' and being tied 'up,' mimic the literal action of *Ethan Frome*: as Mattie and Ethan start their final descent down the icy hillside . . ." (Gill 15). Perhaps, but what does that have to do with Zeena? Even more incomprehensible, however, is Gill's willingness to abandon the direct comparison altogether and instead claim that, "The place of the pickle dish is taken, in Sexton's text, by a bouquet of desiccated roses" (17). While there are similarities between the two, this is merely one of a barrage of examples Gill serves up that are never able to find a thematic center.

The very first stanza of the poem, on the other hand, perfectly captures the association between the pickle dish and Zeena's unused emotion of love.

It was also my violent heart that broke,
falling down the front hall stairs.
It was also a message I never spoke,
calling, riser after riser, *who cares / about you, who cares* . . . (Sexton 23)

The only real substitution necessary to analyze the poem in terms of its associations with *Ethan Frome* is that the narrator's broken body symbolically represents Zeena's pickle dish. This is an easy assertion to defend as Edith Wharton makes the very same comparison in the novel: "gathering up the bits of broken glass she went out of the room as if she carried a dead body . . ." (Wharton 1911, 139). Seeing the pickle dish as representing Zeena's emotional state in the first line of the poem, "It was also my violent heart that broke," is a wonderfully vivid reference to Zeena's own heart which, being denied love, has only hatred left to fill it. The third line, "It was a message I never spoke," is also reflected directly in Wharton's novel as well, when Ethan says of her after their marriage, "Then she too fell silent" (77). Finally, there is the brutal pathos of Zeena's sense of abandonment—primarily emotional, but nearly physical— in the last line of the stanza, "*who cares / about you, who cares . . .*" But Gill attempts to expand the meaning of the poem to include nearly every aspect of *Ethan Frome* and all of its main characters, when keeping the emphasis on the narrator's own assertion, that she is, in fact, Zeena, makes for a much more compelling comparison between the novel and Sexton's poem.

Another direct connection between Zeena and Sexton's narrator comes after the operation, when the narrator goes on to complain, "And now I spend all day taking care of my body, that baby. Its cargo is scarred" (Sexton 24). Because she is confined to her bed, Sexton's narrator seems to understand that the all-consuming focus of her life is the same as Zeena's obsession with her own illness. But there's even more that can bolster this argument in the biographical implication that Sexton herself may have brought about the accident on purpose, and yet Gill fails to connect any of that with Zeena's hypochondria. Gill also missteps when she tries to connect the narrator's comparison of her body to that of a baby by claiming it represents both Ethan's mother, her "regression from matriarch to infant," as well as Mattie after the crash, her "vivacity and blossoming sensuality wither[ing] to a child-like dependency" (Gill 15). But this misses the point entirely, that the healing of the broken bones within her body is similar to the care and attention that pregnant women must take with their unborn children. One of the most interesting lines in the poem is when Sexton's narrator makes a connection between her physical injury and a similar emotional injury, "And the heart too, that cripple, how it sang once. How it thought it could call the shots!" (Sexton 24). This neatly connects the scarred cargo from the previous quote—though literally referencing her broken hip—with the more direct reference to her crippled heart here. In the same way, Zeena's heart "sang once," but after the breaking of the pickle dish and the realization that she will never be loved in her lifetime her heart will forever be "crippled" as well. Even the narrator's assertion that her heart thought it could "call the shots," fits nicely with Zeena's attempt to control and manipulate Ethan during their marriage.

Gill attempts to explain, midway through the essay, her lack of focus on Zeena by claiming a certain ambiguity in the narrator's reference to being "Ethan Frome's wife," which she argues comes from Sexton herself. In the Crenshaw Lectures the author gave she apparently asked her audience, "What do I mean by Ethan Frome's wife?" but Gill omits Sexton's answer. She then tries to bolster this apparent ambiguity with more of her own:

> It's not clear whom this label signifies: the woman Ethan loves, the woman he is married to, or the woman / women for whom he is responsible. The ambiguous identification may be read as simultaneously meaningless (it is not certain who is the referent) and profoundly meaningful (in that it reveals and confirms the identification, even interchangeability, between the two women). (Gill 19)

The reason Gill tries so hard to makes this argument is painfully clear. Despite her assertion that, "as I have suggested, we may read Sexton's speaker's affinity as being with Zeena Frome," this artificial ambiguity gives Gill free reign to articulate "a far more complex and mutable series of identifications" that then allows her to make connections to anything and everything in the novel. Ultimately, there is no ambiguity, and Gill's essay demonstrates the danger of analysis that goes too far afield of the text. Unless one assumes the narrator of Sexton's poem symbolizes Mattie in her disabled condition at the end of the novel—which doesn't work at all—it's obvious from the abundance of evidence in the rest of the poem that Sexton's use of "Ethan Frome's wife" as a reference means only what the words themselves mean: Zeena.

It wasn't until almost thirty years later that the next significant reference to *Ethan Frome* in literature occurred. In the fall of 1996 a short story by author Gina Berriault called "Zenobia" appeared in the winter issue of the *Threepenny Review*. This brief story is a first person response by Zeena Frome, all alone in her old age, to Edith Wharton herself. "One can't outlive God but I have outlived you, and I say to you where you lie in your tomb, far across the ocean in a foreign land: Edith, you shall never forgive yourself for wronging me" (Berriault 33). Where most commentators tend to puzzle over the apparently inexplicable punishment meted out by the author to Ethan, few have gone beyond that to examine in any detail the obvious burden Zeena must bear in caring for both Ethan and Mattie the rest of her life—though it's not difficult to see how that omission might be a result of feeling she is deserving of her punishment. Berriault, however, clearly disagrees, and imagines a life for Zenobia Pierce that goes beyond her portrayal in the novel as a bitter shrew. "Recollect, Edith, how I was in the time when I was still a very young woman, before I ever met him, how my own eyes saw myself . . . My face some thought austere, but kindly so, and my hair was black and shown in lamplight and firelight, and my hands were long and gentle . . . Before I ever knew Ethan Frome, before I ever knew he was on this earth, there was good in me" (Berriault 33).

Berriault also recognizes the fact that Ethan's viewpoint in Wharton's novel is not an accurate representation of the woman, and is very blunt in recounting the hints the novelist provides about Zeena's true character, especially as it relates to Mattie's presence in the Frome home.

> When I asked Mattie Silver to come to this house and help me with the chores, it was not just for my sake, it was for her sake, too. She had no mother or father and was in poor health. Recollect, Edith, that she blossomed while she was here, and recollect I urged her to go down to the dancing in the church basement where she could meet a young man who'd fall in love with her and make her his wife, and recollect I urged her to go to picnics in the summer with other young people around her. (Berriault 33)

Because the novel is told from Ethan's viewpoint Wharton typically doesn't get credit for this information about Zeena. Instead, it is the vision of the wicked witch that remains in the minds of readers. "But how shamelessly, Edith, you made the most of my meanness! You made my hair sparse and tangled and gray, and my body thin as a rake, and my eyes lashless, and my neck scraggy, and you took away my teeth, every one, [and] you gave me asthma, and that was further proof of my bad nature, like God's punishment of me." Zeena goes on to call Ethan a coward, essentially saying that she can hardly be blamed for her husband's faults. And yet she freely admits, had he and Mattie died, that she would have taken the blame upon herself. But when the two of them arrived back at the house, broken in body and spirit, "why then I saw that I was not to blame. I saw it was their fate and I saw it was my fate to care for them."

Zeena is under no illusion as to why she was treated the way she was by the author. "I sit in my gray wrapper that's ages-thin, ages-old like a dead bird's feathers, at this greasy table where you sat us down together, the three of us, your beloved Ethan and your darling Mattie and your dread Zenobia" (Berriault 33). Zeena goes on to consider what she would have done had the two of them run off together, prefaced by her visit with a young painter one summer while she was alone on the farm before Mattie's arrival. The young man, already deep into his work, smiles at her when she approaches and asks if he can take the liberty of painting her mill. "Oh take the liberty and ask afterwards! I liked that, it amused me" (34). And her response to Ethan leaving with Mattie and abandoning her, she decides, would have been the same. "Oh take the liberty! . . . I would have packed my satchel and my portmanteau and climbed aboard a train bound West." The story ends on a surprisingly powerful note, as Zeena tells Wharton that her only fault was caring too deeply for the man she married. "Your heart was moved by what had befallen him . . . my own heart was moved by him for the rest of my days." "Zenobia" was eventually collected in a book of the author's stories called *Women in Their Beds*, published in May of the following year and which was incredibly well received. Gina Berriault was not only awarded the Pen/Faulkner Prize for her collection, but the National Book Critic's Circle prize and the Rea Award for the Short Story as well.

The last major appearance of *Ethan Frome* in literature came shortly after Berriault's story, in October of 1996, with the publication of *Zeena*, by author Elizabeth Cooke. In the early nineteen nineties the floodgates opened on the co-opting of characters from classic novels as those novels continued to enter the public domain in great numbers. *Scarlett*, by Alexandra Ripley, the continuing story of Scarlett O'Hara from Margaret Mitchell's *Gone With The Wind*, was one of the first to be published in 1991. This was followed by Susan Hill's *Mrs. deWinter* two years later in 1993, the sequel to *Rebecca* by Daphne du Mauier. But the most famous of these literary hijackings was *Wicked*, by Gregory Maguire in 1995, the story of L. Frank Baum's Wicked Witch of the West from *The Wizard of Oz*, which went on to become a Broadway musical in 2003 and is still being performed as of 2018. And there are dozens of others that have appeared since, including *Zeena*.

There is much to appreciate in the novel, though it's questionable just how successful it is overall. Cooke adopts Wharton's structure beginning with an untitled Prologue set in 1904 on the night of the storm after which the narrator is brought inside to stay overnight at the Frome house. But right from the start Cooke dramatically alters the character of Zeena as Wharton had conceived her. The Prologue is a maze of time shifting narration that is difficult to summarize, but perfectly understandable to anyone who has read the original novel. Zeena is in bed with her husband and awakened by the sound of Mattie whimpering. She recalls that the first time she heard that sound, when Mattie was brought to the house after the accident, she thought it had come from a wolf outside—and one has the sneaking suspicion that the fox from the *American Playhouse* film version might be the inspiration for that. Unable to sleep in the present, she thinks back to her childhood and Cooke has her illness beginning then, though that doesn't really fit with the way Wharton had conclusively demonstrated Zeena's illness wasn't real. Cooke deals with Zeena's apparent vigor during the time she was taking care of Ethan's mother as an aberration, an energetic episode in the house further enhanced by her delight at being married to Ethan. "In November's first cold and dark days, Zeena'd found her blood racing in her veins, and when she peered into the looking glass, she saw her own clear eyes dancing with life. Her marriage to Ethan . . . Who'd have guessed her journey into these hills to look after his mother'd turn out as it did?" (Cooke 4). Again, this rings false, even given the small amount of background present in the novel, though she does admit things had changed by the time winter set in without really saying why.

When Zeena's thoughts return to that morning she claims that Ethan had been taking the narrator to the flats all winter, when it had only been a week in the novel. She does, however, mention the cause for Ethan's employment as resulting from Denis Eady's sick horses. That brings Zeena back to the fact that there is a stranger in the house downstairs, in Ethan's study, a room she says he hasn't been in since the accident. When Zeena recounts the narrator's entrance into the kitchen, Cooke invents some dialogue that demonstrates a verbosity Wharton's characters were unlikely to indulge in—especially the narrator, who sounds more like Reverend Smith from the film than Wharton's extremely astute and respectful engineer. Mattie's whimpering in the present initiates more bitter thoughts from Zeena about having to care for her and Ethan, and hatred for the girl, especially given that she knew all along they were in love with each other. She thinks back to the time when Harmon Gow came to tell her about the accident, and her belief that he seemed a little too pleased to be doing so. But the real impetus for the novel emerges from a statement of Zeena's that slips out when she is talking to Mattie. "I'm the one with the secrets," she says. "You don't know what he done to me before you come here" (Cooke 8). As she heads down the stairs to take care of Mattie in the present, Cooke uses Wharton's sparrow imagery in the description of the girl when she first arrived, and this is followed by Zeena's malevolent thoughts about wanting to smother her the night she came home after the accident.

From there the narrative shifts back to 1873, Chapter One, to Zeena's childhood home and her mother and father. Her mother had been a faith healer, not really a charlatan but a religious woman who used the folk wisdom of the era to minister to the sick people of Bettsbridge. The oldest child in the family, all of Zeena's siblings had died in childbirth, finally taking her mother with them when she was only ten. From then on she assumed the chores of her absent mother, cared for her distraught and silent father, and finds herself seventeen years later a spinster. Thin and sickly, she has no prospects for marriage either. When her father receives a letter from Zeena's aunt saying that one of her cousins is sick, her father tells her she must go and take care of the woman, Ethan's mother. Most impressive in the novel is the way the descriptions of the setting and the events of Wharton's novel are woven into the story. Zeena arrives in Starkfield shortly after and is at first dismayed by its isolation. But Ethan is strong and she senses in him something different from the other men like him she's known. Still, in among all of the specific elements from the novel—like the gray cat that Ethan already owns—is the uncomfortable characterization of Zeena as Cooke has imagined her. Her insistence that she's there just as a "healer," for example, makes her seem a bit mentally unstable—the exact opposite of the cold and calculating Zeena from Wharton's book.

Their first conversation, in fact, in the kitchen on the night of Zeena's arrival, is not only radically different from Wharton's conception but also rather disturbing:

> Would he understand that she was a spinster because of her calling? That she wasn't just come to do housework, to relieve him of his responsibilities to his mother? . . . Zeena held her hands in the air, palms up. "I can do it with these hands," she whispered, realizing as she spoke that this was the reason she'd come . . . Zeena felt God's calling her to this point in time . . . "I mean to bring her back," she voiced. (Cooke 38-39)

This is certainly a departure from Ethan's memory of Zeena's role in the house after she arrived. "Zeena seemed to understand his case at a glance. She laughed at him for not knowing the simplest sick-bed duties and told him to 'go right along out' and leave her to see to things" (Wharton 1911, 75). Though it's definitely subtextual, there's a sense in Wharton's novel that Zeena knows exactly what she's doing with Ethan, and that his subsequent "magnified . . . sense of what he owed her" might not have been entirely accidental. Cooke does emphasize Zeena's obsession with her health, her interest in medicines and treatments that might alleviate her condition, but again, given Wharton's careful revelation of her character in the course of the novel, this simplistic connection to the original story seems almost prosaic.

When Ethan tells her about going to college and working in Florida, it reminds Zeena of her own desire to get away. "Zeena wanted to tell Ethan of her dream of going to Springfield . . . It was why she had to bring Ethan's mother back. If she could go to Springfield with this new healing to her credit, why, there's no telling what direction her life might go" (Cooke 53-54). And yet this also seems slightly at odds with Ethan's statement in Wharton's novel that, "She chose to look down on Starkfield, but she could not have lived in a place which looked down on her . . . In the greater cities which attracted Ethan she would have suffered a complete loss of identity" (Wharton 1911, 77). After asking Ethan why he doesn't just take his mother and go somewhere else, he lapses into silence and Zeena exhibits even more bizarre behavior, becoming paranoid about almost everything. First, it's Ethan himself. "Ethan Frome was no better [than her father]. He'd tricked her, is how she saw it. Told her about going to Florida . . . led her to believe she could speak the truth . . . but instead she'd discovered otherwise" (Cooke 68). The same thing happens the following day. Waking up and looking outside on a sunny October morning, Zeena comments on the fact that the warm colors of the leaves in late fall are only a distraction from the brutal winter ahead. Then she connects that idea to the seemingly joyous occasion of a birth she attended that went horribly wrong and ended in the woman's death. "That's what an October day'll do, Zeena thought, as the gray eased from the sky, replaced by pale blue. It would be a beautiful day, but she would take no pleasure from it. No sense in giving in to such trickery" (Cooke 60). Portrayed in this manner, Zeena's character is more like the demented Addie Bundren from William Faulkner's *As I Lay Dying* than the calculating woman Edith Wharton created. This connection between childbirth and death, however, does one very nice thing for the story in that it creates a credible reason for Zeena to resist having children with Ethan. "Babies're life threatening, is all she'd thought. Too many babies took too many mothers' lives. And then the babies, they died too" (95).

Zeena's physical struggles with Ethan's mother are typical of any attempt to care for someone with dementia but she soldiers on, convinced that she can cure the woman as a way of honoring the memory of her dead mother— and inflating her own ego in the process. Cooke indulges in an incredible amount of detail in her writing, which is interesting to a point, but repeated accounts of washing the mother's feet or observing Ethan's uncouth way of eating soon become occasions for impatience on the part of the reader. Edith Wharton's genius in telling Ethan's story was in allowing the narrator to tell it from his more sophisticated sensibility. *Zeena*, on the other hand, is all Zeena all the time. Cooke also tries to parallel the presence of Denis Eady in Wharton's novel by inventing in a love interest for Ethan in the form of the oldest Varnum daughter, Rebekah. Zeena had already noticed something in Ethan that attracted her in a general way, but the presence of Rebekah seems to bring out the same sense of ownership in Zeena that Ethan had exhibited toward Mattie in the book.

"Hello," the girl called, coming closer and stopping, looking all around. "I guess Ethan's at the mill?"

Zeena shook her head. "The woodlot," she said, feeling irked that this girl was looking for Ethan . . . Now she stepped to the door and looked up at Zeena who could see she was more than a girl; she was a young woman . . ." (Cooke 78-79)

This scene is followed later that day by more specific thoughts on Zeena's part about a life with Ethan. "Zeena tried to work on the shawl, but her eyes kept returning to Ethan . . . As strong as [his hands] looked, there was a surprising gentleness to them. So many men, their hands stiffened at the touch of a baby. Ethan's were hands that would deftly change a diaper. They would be tender with a woman, they'd . . . She shook her head. Foolishness, she told herself" (85).

In addition to the disturbing character changes in Zeena are the equally puzzling changes in Ethan. In Wharton's novel he could be inarticulate at times, but he still seemed very clearheaded when speaking with others. In Cooke's version, however, Ethan is almost mute, which gives him the air of a stuttering clod rather than "the most striking figure in Starkfield." When he comes into the kitchen one evening to talk to Zeena she has to repeatedly prompt him to get him to say anything. Finally he shows her a picture of Florida. Then later, after he pathetically pouts over his lost dream, he gets up and heads for the stove. "He reached out and lifted a stovecover with one hand. Zeena saw what was coming. She lunged at his arm, but it was too late; the picture was gone, sizzling into nothingness" (Cooke 65). But this makes no sense at all, as Ethan still had grand plans at this point in Wharton's novel, and even felt as if Zeena might be an aid to achieving them. He might be sad about the prospect of losing his mother, something Cooke goes overboard with throughout the novel, but with his mother gone there will be absolutely nothing to keep him in Starkfield. In Cooke's novel he acts as if he's already been married to Zeena for seven years. More puzzling, Rebekah Varnum actually tells Zeena at one point that Ethan will never move from the farm, even though the reader knows full well that seven years later he will have every intention of lighting out for the West with Mattie. In that context the defeatist attitude Cooke saddles Ethan with in her version of the character makes absolutely no sense. "I saw you walk down toward the graves tonight," he says morosely to Zeena. "I'll never be more'n them. I am them, don't you see? And nothing, not technological school, not Ma living, not your telling me what to do's going to change it" (128).

Once Zeena learns that Rebekah Varnum is not interested in Ethan romantically, she decides she likes the girl, especially given the concern she shows for Ethan's mother. Jotham Powell, on the other hand, turns up a third of the way into the story and Zeena takes an instant disliking to him from the moment he first invites himself for dinner. Lawyer Varnum even stops by halfway through the story with a letter from Zeena's father. After only a week of being at the farm, however, Ethan's mother finally dies. In the meantime there have been growing signs of Zeena's interest in Ethan. On the night of his mother's death, Ethan leans close to Zeena but she isn't really sure why. After he pulls away, "Her knees had turned to trembling, and his arm, where she held to it still, was shivering ever so slightly, but 'Don't think on it,' she whispered, though she wasn't sure whether she meant Cousin Beatrice or the fact they'd almost kissed" (166). The death of her Aunt, Ethan's mother, does destroy her belief in herself as a healer, and a life ahead as a spinster with no healing powers looms large. The one positive result of this is that it releases her from the delusion that she is a healer and her character improves from this point on. Ethan, however, seems like someone completely alien from Wharton's novel. He's a sad, hulking, man-child who can barely speak two syllables in a row without lapsing into silence and wandering off. Nevertheless, Ethan does manage to squeeze out a marriage proposal after the funeral, and Zeena accepts.

The next morning the two discuss moving to Florida in the spring, and after Ethan tells her about the opportunities and the better weather, she finally agrees. Later they ride into the village and get married in the minister's office rather than the empty church, then return home that afternoon. Because she's never experienced feelings like this before, Zeena is willing to forego her paranoia and embrace the future. "The unfamiliar sensation of love . . . Zeena feared it, but now, simply because of how she was feeling, what once she'd viewed with disgust she now saw with a hunger to know" (Cooke 229). Yet after all of the anticipation, her wedding night could only be described as a major disappointment. Their brief, painful sex, for Zeena, has inadvertently started her period and in the following days Ethan stays emotionally as well as physically distant from her until it is over. But their sex is no less painful the second time, and no less brief. Ethan cries afterward, but Zeena is the one who really needs comforting. The first truly believable moment between the two doesn't happen until two thirds of the way through the novel. Zeena begins to understand that, even though Ethan married her, he doesn't really love her. They have sex at night—or at least he does—but they share no intimacy whatsoever.

She comes to feel her own yearning for him less and less. In her mind is the memory of the nights before. It isn't just the pain it causes her. She has the dim sense it could be otherwise. But how to make it so? . . . The moments in which a man and his wife are most tender and close are to her the most brutal and distant. She lies awake into the night. Finally she sinks into a bitter sleep. (243).

The result of this emotional disappointment is the pain in her back that had frequently cropped up since her arrival in Starkfield—and that she had been able to keep in check—now begins to debilitate her.

In embracing the desire to have what she saw other women enjoying, and the societal expectation that she would have that simply by virtue of being married, Zeena has gone against her own instincts and now finds herself trapped in a loveless marriage on an isolated farm that brought with it lots of work but little comfort. "The days were filled with hard work starting before sunrise and ending when they collapsed into bed at night and Ethan turned to her and she felt the pain again" (Cooke 245). Zeena still clings to two hopes, however, first that the two of them really will be able to escape to Florida, and the second that she will be able to have Ethan's baby. "There was one comfort. She would carry a child and birth it and then she would have what she needed. Then she would be somebody." Cooke has Ethan take Zeena into town to go coasting one evening, even though she fears losing the baby she hasn't told him about yet. There's also a dance going on in the church basement, setting up the regular events that will appear in Wharton's novel. Zeena enjoys sledding in the dark with Ethan, perhaps a bit too much, as the last time they go down the hill she flies off into the snow, and that night she has a miscarriage. From this point on the twists come fast and furious all the way to the end of the novel. Rebekah calls on Zeena the next day, desperate because she's become pregnant. So Zeena has Ethan take her into town to ask the Varnums to let her stay with Zeena's Aunt Martha in order to have the baby in secret. But while they are at the Varnum's Zeena accidentally witnesses a meeting between Ethan and Rebekah. "It came on Zeena then like a cold wind that Ethan loved Rebekah. And then she knew: The baby, it's Ethan's" (292).

By the time the true climax of the story arrives the whole thing feels to the reader like completely different characters living completely different lives than the ones Wharton had written. While having Ethan fall in love with Rebekah could have worked—though he still couldn't ask her to marry him because he wasn't good enough for her family—the Ethan in Cooke's novel that slept with her is decidedly not the Ethan from Wharton's novel. That Ethan actually believed in love. What Elizabeth Ammons said about

Ethan and his relationship to Mattie holds even more true about a woman like Rebekah in whom he could have seen a potential wife: "Ethan is an unsophisticated and conscientious man; he does not want to "ruin" Mattie, nor spoil his romantic fantasy by turning their relationship into a furtive backstairs affair. Therefore he never makes love to her" (Ammons 65). Edith Wharton's Ethan is a man who refuses to borrow money from a friend—even though he would have paid it back, and then some—in order to make a new life for himself. And though he hated Zeena, he never begrudged what he owed her as her husband. Cooke's Ethan, on the other hand, is nearly unrecognizable in the context of Wharton's novel. The day after his wedding, "He just went about his day, heavy limbed, plodding, his shoulder sloped as ever, with not so much as a word about how things'd changed" (Cooke 249-250). At the end of the novel Zeena decides not to reveal what she knows to Ethan, even though he has become aware that Rebekah is pregnant. But it does result in her complete emotional withdrawal from him. "She would not give Ethan a child. She would not let him turn to her in the night. No one would fault her for it. They would say she was too old. They would say, Zenobia Frome, she done her best by him" (299).

When the narrative returns to the present, 1904, Zeena is still poised at the top of the stairs, and as she goes down to tend to Mattie she naturally contemplates killing her again. But despite her desire, it is an act with which she would never be able live with herself. It's also interesting the way that Cooke picks up on the "querulous" nature of the injured Mattie at the end of Wharton's novel and turns her into an evil character who torments Zeena, almost daring her to kill her. "You can't even hurt me," she says at one point, to which Zeena responds, "'What about me? You ever think on what you done to me?' Mattie barked a laugh. 'Maybe you never thought what it's been like to be me, beholden to you and your meanness for every thing'" (Cooke 316). But Zeena can't hold back after that and finally spits out, "'It'd been better if you'd'a died.' Again Mattie laughed. 'You ain't the first. I thought it myself a thousand times.'" When Mattie goes on to say how the people of the village think of Zeena as an object of pity for staying and taking care of them, it's all Zeena can do not to tell her what Ethan did to Rebekah. Finally, Zeena simply calls Mattie evil, and though Mattie tries to turn it back on Zeena, she's had enough. Later that day, after Ethan returns from taking the narrator back to the village he finds Zeena dressed for travel again. But this time she's not coming back.

Reviewer Francesca Stanfill from the *Los Angeles Times* recognized the primary difference in the writing style between Wharton's novel and Cooke's prequel. "The language here is more homespun than the severe classical tone of Wharton's traveler-narrator, for it is always through Zeena's country eyes and the rough cadence of her voice that we revisit the desolate New England story and its web of tragic disappointments and love affairs" (Stanfill 211). The review is mostly positive, though the shortcomings of the novel are obvious even to Stanfill. "Occasionally Cooke veers toward a sentimentalism and an elated, rather than elegiac, view of love that might have made Wharton wince." There is also the dubious nature of the potentially happy ending for Zeena that Wharton would not have liked either, but from Stanfill's point of view can be justified because, "After the unrelieved gloom and starkness of the story, the reader can hardly object to the meager ray of sun that Zeena Frome, in this version at least, seems to merit." Stanfill says the attempt at telling the story from Zeena's viewpoint "works well" and that Cooke has rendered her "an astonishingly sympathetic character." All of which is true, up to a point.

There's no escaping the fact that what Cooke has tried to do is to rectify what was thought to be missing in the original work, to create a legitimate justification for Ethan's suffering. By turning his fantasy with Mattie into something real—which is certainly the implication after what he has done to Rebekah—Cooke has placed a romantic flaw at the center of the man. She has tried to create a desire in him that he can't control, a willingness to use and abuse women: first getting Rebekah pregnant, then marrying Zeena under false pretenses, then finally destroying Mattie's life by offering her a love she could never have and bringing about the desire to kill herself. There is some power in telling the story this way, it must be told, and Cooke is gifted in her way at rendering the everyday tasks of life on the farm. But in the end her story is a different story, a different Zeena, and a different Ethan that, however similar the trappings of their lives, are so distant from the original characters as Edith Wharton imagined them that they are nearly unrecognizable. One film reviewer called the *Amerian Playhouse* version of *Ethan Frome* an "honorable failure," and that is probably the best way to sum up Elizabeth Cooke's novel (Swindell 27).

Appendix

One of the alternately fascinating and frustrating aspects of any study of *Ethan Frome* is the original version of the story Edith Wharton composed in 1907 in order to improve her conversational French. It's fascinating, of course, that it exists at all—despite Wharton's contention that she lost it—surviving in a small, black composition book. Elisina Royall Tyler, the literary executor of Wharton's estate, eventually made the copybook public in 1952. The text, transcribed and corrected in its French version, appeared along with a detailed account of those corrections by W.D. MacCallan in his article for the *Yale University Library Gazette* that same year. "In the transcription of the manuscript which follows, all of Mrs. Wharton's corrections have been accepted and, of the tutor's corrections, those which concern only points of grammar and orthography or minor changes in vocabulary and phrasing have also been incorporated into the text" (MacCallan 38). MacCallan's brief introductory comments then go on to outline what he considers the major differences between the French short story and the novel that Wharton wrote four years later. The frustration for the casual scholar, however, is the lack of an English translation of the story.

Where this frustration becomes most vexing is in looking at the works of biographers who have either relied on explanations of the text by others, or who have actually read the original French and have been biased in their interpretation in favor of the way the story plays out in the novel. Biographer Cynthia Griffin Wolff is probably the worst in this regard. She begins by stating that the opening lines of the story show Hart and Mattie "are lovers and that Mattie has been asked to leave Hart's home" (Wolff 157). But that's a major misreading of the first paragraph—especially puzzling considering she transcribes the entire first paragraph in French in her book. It's true that the two have declared their love, which is made clear a few paragraphs later, but Mattie has not been asked to leave yet. The reference to leaving is Hart's fear that she will want to leave because of the awkward position their declaration puts her in, and so he assures her that he will behave himself and try to resume their former familial relationship in the hope of keeping her from going. It's similar to the reason addressed in the novel when Ethan says, "he had no right to show his feelings" to Mattie.

Wolff goes on to say that the narrator of the story is omniscient but, just as with the central story of *Ethan Frome*, that's not quite true. The only character whose thoughts are ever shown is Hart, making the viewpoint third person limited, just like the novel. As such, the use of the plural pronoun "they" when describing the feelings of Hart and Mattie are still from Hart's viewpoint. Worst of all, however, Wolff attributes Hart's decision to stay away from Mattie on their night alone to the fact that he is "embarrassed and timid," and says that he "stays at a local tavern until he returns late in the evening rather tipsy" (158). This is a complete mischaracterization of the story, as no such thing ever happens. Not only is Hart not embarrassed and timid, he knows full well that he will act on his feelings for Mattie with his wife out of the house—and he doesn't want to get caught in the act. He also doesn't go to a tavern; he goes to the minister's house for supper. After staying there as long as he dares, he then goes to visit a friend in the village and doesn't leave until it becomes clear he has overstayed his welcome. It is only on his way home that he stops into the drugstore and has *one* shot of whisky, which he instantly regrets. And while it warms him up and gives him courage on the way home, he is completely sober by the time he gets there.

The story has been available to the public in its French version since 1952, so it's unclear as to why it hasn't been given a more careful analysis, especially considering it is such an important part of the creation of *Ethan Frome*, which even MacCallam admits. "It is something that should be examined by anyone contemplating a detailed study of Mrs. Wharton's work" (MacCallam 39). My attempt at a translation, however, should not be considered in any way definitive, as it was merely an exercise I went through in order to ascertain exactly what the major underlying differences were between the two versions—and I was actually gratified to learn how similar the two stories really are. While I did the best I could, given my limited translating skills, the goal was never to create a faithfully artistic rendering of Edith Wharton's story in English. And while MacCallam dismisses the notion that the story has any artistic merit at all—"intrinsically it has little interest; the style is bad, the descriptions seem dragged in, the character of Mattie lacks definition, and the ending is unsatisfactory"—I heartily disagree (39). It is actually quite an elegant piece of writing.

The lack of inherent interest that MacCallam suggests is obviously one that goes beyond its fascination as the genesis for *Ethan Frome*, and this might account for his apparent disinterest in providing the reader with an English translation. But there are some incredibly satisfying descriptive elements and characterizations in the story, as well as an overall concision that is reminiscent of Kate Chopin—who was also fluent in French. As far as the unsatisfactory nature of the ending, the story was never intended to end the way it does because Wharton simply stopped writing it, as she makes clear in her article about the novel. "The French version of *Ethan Frome* . . . ploughed its heavy course through a copy-book or two; then the lessons were interrupted and the Gallic 'Ethan' abandoned, I forget at what point in his career" (Wharton 1932, 78). But even with that, there is a case to be made that the story really doesn't need any more exposition. And while Wharton's own reference to the "heavy course" the story made suggests her own assessment of it as a work that is beneath her usual artistic level, it is nevertheless an interesting piece of fiction in its own right. In the end, I felt that there has been a sufficient misreading and neglect of the story for English speakers that, regardless of its deficiencies, having any translation was better than none at all, and that fact alone accounts for its inclusion in this volume.

The French Precursor to *Ethan Frome* (1907)

I

"You're right . . . I can't do anything for you . . . but don't leave me, my darling. I'll be reasonable, you'll see . . ." he stammered, realizing that to keep things from going any further and to ease the pain of the words they had exchanged, the only way forward was to bravely resume his role as elder brother.

Without answering, she continued to walk beside him to the lake, which shone under its layer of snow like a meadow surrounded by trees. Then they climbed silently through the dark woods, where the jasper trunks of the beeches seemed detached from the dark bark of the hemlocks, and then a moonbeam, slipping through its light, brought out the spectral paleness of a bouquet of birches.

As they sank together into the shadows, Hart had to brace himself to keep from losing his courage. The woods were too full of memories. It was there that, in the summer, Mattie sometimes took refuge from her work, and when he returned from the sawmill in the evening he would find her seated on a wooden bench that he had built for her from a larch. And now he felt that if they left this place he would never get those sweet hours back.

"Stay a moment—don't go back yet," he implored.

"It's getting late . . . We have to get back."

"What does it matter how late we are? She went to bed hours ago!"

"We could wake her up—and tonight she was complaining about her headache."

The mere mention of Anna's name conjured up a fresh sense of embarrassment. He knew there was no need to rush, however, as these nocturnal walks that they took together in the rustic American countryside were followed by his wife's retreat to her bed, before which she would put the key of the door under the doormat.

There was nothing to fear out in the woods: it was themselves, not Anna whom they feared. But both of them were still ashamed of the feelings that arose from hearing her name. At each word, now, they felt the weight of the chains they had forged by confessing their love.

"Let's go back," Hart said sharply.

They returned to the house, which slept shuttered against the black background of the pines; but as Hart bent to remove the key from its hiding place, the door suddenly opened.

He raised his head and saw his wife standing above him, lean and shivering, on the threshold. The oil lamp she held in her hand illuminated from below her pale, tired face and washed out her features, throwing macabre shadows over her cheekbones, burying her eyes in their sockets, bringing out the blue hollows of her temples, and gave to her face, stripped now of its distinctness, the threatening appearance of a ghost.

"Oh! What are you doing, Anna? Why aren't you lying down?"

"I was waiting for you," she said, stepping back to let her niece and Hart inside.

"But why? What for? You knew we were going to come back late," he said, becoming more and more embarrassed.

"I know that. You always come back late. But I couldn't sleep. I have a headache."

"Oh, Aunt, I shouldn't have left you alone!" exclaimed Mattie, with self-reproach.

"This is the first time you've ever thought about it," Anna replied dryly.

She had put the lamp on an old mahogany console, the only remnant of the beautiful furniture brought from England by Hart's ancestors, but this lone bit of elegance was lost against the backdrop of the ugly wallpaper and the narrow staircase covered with worn, threadbare carpet.

Hart lowered his head under the gaze of his wife's cold, enigmatic eyes.

"Do you want to sit down while I go find the doctor?" he asked sheepishly.

She emitted a strange laugh. "At this hour? Don't you know it's past midnight?"

And that was all. Without uttering another word she took up the lamp again, climbed the stairs, and returned to her room where the flaming stove exhaled a heavy and unhealthy heat. Hart followed her.

II

They had sworn to themselves that what had happened would not change their respectable familial relationship, but it seemed as if fate took pleasure in tormenting them.

The next day Anna's cousin arrived, with whom she enjoyed talking about her physical ailments. Her cousin was also a big believer in drugs, had a penchant for quack doctors, and was an avid researcher of new remedies. The cousin said she was actually frightened by how thin Anna was, and by the symptoms she took such pleasure in detailing to her; and she advised an immediate visit to one of Worcester's doctors. It was difficult to get Anna to go, as she was afraid of the cold and the jostling of the train ride; but she could not resist the temptation to consult a new expert. Already she had spent large sums on these trips, and more than once Hart had had to borrow money to support it; but how could he avoid giving in to the demands of a sick woman?

Afraid to be alone with Mattie, he offered to accompany his wife; but the latter reproached him with this useless expense, pointing out to him that she was not anxious for him to waste on a pleasure trip the money with which he was so miserly when it came to her health.

Knowing that she would be away for only two days, he resigned himself, not daring to propose to Mattie that she stay with one of their neighbors, since this approach could have aroused malevolent suppositions.

In the summer, he would have remained at the sawmill, pretending to have extra work to do; but in winter this was an excuse he couldn't use. He returned home after taking his wife to the station; and while he was letting his horse rest and putting the sled back his heart filled with joy at the thought of the sweet evening he was going to spend alone with Mattie, in this house so full of humiliating and painful memories.

But suddenly another thought came to him. He remembered Anna's strange face when she opened the door at midnight and frankly wondered if she suspected his love for Mattie, and if this sudden departure for Worcester was only a trick of a jealous woman. His heart froze as he thought she might come back unexpectedly, hoping to catch them in a trap. And the fear so overtook him that, instead of returning home, he walked back to the village and asked the pastor for supper, on the pretext of business that needed to be addressed in the evening with the "selectmen." He lingered on in the rectory, playing with the children, talking politics with the pastor; then he took his leave and went to the house of one of his colleagues. There he chatted endlessly, until the whispers of his guests reminded him that they were not very happy with this late visit. Then he excused himself awkwardly, and took the road back to the farm.

The moon was dark, veiled by clouds, and he groped his way through a black night that seemed to vibrate with cold. Suddenly his blood warmed at the sight of the drugstore, which was still sending shafts of yellow light out from its front window onto the deserted street. He decided to stop by, and found some friends there still sitting around the big tin stove. But something in Hart was so cold he couldn't get warm: the heat of the stove burned his skin without heating it. So he passed almost shamefully into the back shop, where they sold whiskey, though even the smuggled brandy he drank once burned his throat as it went down. A very sober man, accustomed to drinking only water, he hastily swallowed the glass of whiskey that was poured out for him and left the shop, already regretting what he had done.

But as he walked he felt his heart expand and newly warmed blood flowed into his veins. Why was he still afraid to go home? What a fool he'd been to imagine that his wife was coming back! He was no longer gloomy, but it was that swallow of alcohol that had given him courage, and also, it seemed to him, clarity of spirit. He thought tenderly of Mattie, who was probably waiting for him, already worried that he had not come back. Perhaps he would find her at the door, the lamp in her hand, just as they had found Anna the night before. And he had a very clear vision of Mattie's face, illuminated from below like the other, but made more rosy, more precise, by the caressing reflection of the flickering light, with the golden spirals of hair blending into each other, and the golden tones of her forehead, and the deep blue of her eyes soaked with shadow. He saw her so alive, so close to him, that all his blood flowed back out of his heart, and he was afraid again, more afraid than before.

But why? He had already sacrificed his life to a sickly woman just to maintain a scruple of honor. How could he imagine for a moment the thought of doing harm to that poor child, without resources and without a future, whom he alone could by his friendship guarantee safety against the harsh realities of life? He felt that a word could perhaps restore the shaken confidence of that poor loving heart, so deprived of happiness, and this conviction restored all his resolution.

His hands clenched, his chest constricted by the cold, he continued on to the farm. A thin ray of light escaped through the ill-fitting shutters, and as he put his foot on the first step of the porch stairs he heard the creaking of a bolt, and Mattie opened the door, the lamp in her hand.

At this sight, the blood rushed back into Hart's head.

"Ah, you're finally home," she said, her tender voice a little fearful.

Without answering he took the lamp from her, so as to quickly erase the rosy and luminous vision that his thoughts had evoked—then he said to her, in a rather gruff tone, "Go to bed, child. I have to work tonight."

Two days later Anna returned, delighted by her journey, and especially with the fact that the new doctor had found her sicker than she thought she was.

She had spent a lot of money: twenty dollars for the consultation, ten for drugs, and five for an "electric band" that she had to apply to her forehead to protect herself from neuralgia, and he wondered how he was going to find a way to pay for it at the end of the month. In the winter, when the sawmill was idle, he had barely enough money to keep the house running, and any additional expense dragged him to the depths of debt, the remedy for which he had great difficulty in extracting from his father's property.

But that wasn't all. The doctor had stated that Anna's poor health was being aggravated by the housework, and that she needed a maid . . . "But a real one, you understand—a strong and hardworking girl, who would be available at all hours, and to whom I would not hesitate to entrust the most tiring tasks . . ." And she glanced at Mattie, who was listening, her head down, with a slight quiver at the corners of her mouth. She had gone to great trouble for her aunt, however—even though she had not been trained for this work, and often, no doubt, she had misunderstood her instructions.

Hart listened, stupefied. How was he going to pay the wages of a servant? And how was he going to feed another person? He certainly didn't enjoy seeing Mattie work for his wife, but he consoled himself by saying that he was compensated in the way she turned his house into a home, and gave him a real family. But now—?

His wife was still talking. "I have no doubt, my dear Mattie, that you are delighted to see yourself delivered from this chore, which I could see how displeasing it was for you. And I've talked about you to my cousin. Maybe we'll find you a job in Worcester, perhaps as a shop lady . . . Finally, I'm sure you understand that first of all I have to think about my health . . . I owe it to my husband, to myself . . ."

Anna was getting rid of her, then! From jealousy, out of simple egotism? He had no idea what it could be, and perhaps she didn't even know herself. He only felt that his wife had pierced him through the heart. He felt a sudden dizziness. His eyes dazed, his head buzzing, he fled from the house and took refuge in the stable, where the old farm horses tramped in front of their feeders, in the thick, warm atmosphere exhaled from their heavy bodies.

How many times had Mattie come to join him here, bringing a handful of carrots for the horses, and whose soft strokes had caressed them with her little hand, reddened by work! Anna was afraid of animals, and despised the toil of the countryside. But every corner of the farm evoked Mattie's presence . . . And now she would never be back! And all of the charm and poetry she had given to the bitter life of a laborious country farmer, everything would go with her! From now on he would see nothing but the hard and ungrateful side of his work, for she had been the only one to share with him the exquisite ache of its rustic and mysterious attraction. No heart would feel with his the wild splendor of the winter nights, nor would it thrill to the solemn beauty of the sunrises that were seen during the harvest season from the high alpine meadows, suspended on each side between river and mountain.

And where would she go, what would become of her? He knew well that it wouldn't do to put much faith in Anna's visionary plans, as she was never very worried about the well-being of others, and frightened by the idea of her own threatened health. As for Mattie's relatives in Worcester, they were poor people without any financial support, and they had neither the power nor the will to be concerned with Mattie's future. Forced by circumstances, then, she would no doubt return to the idea of marrying Lee, that conceited braggart who, loving initially its momentary freshness, would soon tire of the responsibilities of marriage.

III

Anna remained intransigent.

At Hart's first words, she gave him such a strange look, so full of cold irony that he no longer dared to oppose her will. He certainly feared nothing from her himself, though he had hoped he might have set off a spark of violence in her which would have allowed him to break her spell; but how to provoke such anger without risking compromising Mattie? If the poor girl had to leave, the least he could do is protect her against the malicious remarks of Anna, and it would keep her from attributing her dismissal to the actions of a jealous woman.

He therefore submitted, still stunned by the unexpectedness of the blow, and at a loss how to get out of the impasse in which he was struggling.

Two days later the new maid Anna hired sent word that her trunk could be picked up at the nearby station, and that she would arrive there herself the next day. As it was very beautiful out, and a thin layer of new snow had filled the ruts in the snow and formed a smooth surface on the roads, Anna proposed that Hart go with the big sled-cart to look for the maid's trunk and collect some other parcels that had been in the station for a few days.

"At the same time you can take Mattie's trunk; and tomorrow you can take her to the station when the other girl arrives.

The station was eight or nine miles from the farm, and in the winter supplies were brought up which were delivered from time to time to the neighboring towns. Hart decided to go at once. Since Mattie had to leave, it was probably best that he see it as a good thing that she was going away. He felt that she was suffering from staying, now that Anna did not want her anymore.

"Is your trunk ready?" he asked, as Anna left the room.

"It will be done soon. When do you plan to leave?"

"As soon as we have dinner." Without looking at her, he added: "Do you feel like coming with me?"

She hesitated, then decided quickly. "I don't mind." And a flood of redness infused her pale cheeks.

An hour later they left, the humble trunk of Mattie's loaded on the cart behind them. Anna's farewell had been preoccupied, indifferent. She was cooking an herbal tea that the doctor had recommended to her, and asked her husband to bring her a poultice from the pharmacy and a special medicine she had read about in the newspapers, which seemed to suit her case.

Once on the road, Hart and the girl were silent. The winter landscape hung all around them in its glittering whiteness, cut out in places by the black woods, and covered by an intense blue sky, like an inverted cup of enamel, and in the middle of that sky the sun was like a large hole of pale and blinding light. They left the village behind them, made their way to the valley, and passed by the sawmill, which overlooked its little river caught in the ice, under the snowy branches of the hemlocks.

As they both stared at the big motionless wheel, Hart said abruptly, "You'll never come back to fetch me from here anymore."

"No," she said, in a voice filled with uncertainty.

"I'll be alone, always alone . . . everywhere alone!"

She did not answer, and they fell silent again.

Suddenly he began again, pushed by a dull jealousy.

"You'll probably marry Lee, won't you?"

"Oh, that, never!" she cried.

"Why not?"

"I don't know—we'll see . . ."

And then he felt that his whole body was shaking with tears.

"Mattie—my poor Mattie—life is too painful . . ."

"Oh, yes," she stammered out in a sob.

He suddenly wrapped his arm around her, pulled her against him, and kissed her trembling lips.

"What are we going to do, my love? How will we live without seeing each other?"

"I don't know . . . I don't know . . ."

She pulled away from him, and buried her face in her hands.

He would have liked to speak, to express to her all his tenderness and his despair; but a sense of generosity held him back. Since he could do nothing for her, since her love could be for her only a source of misery and suffering, it was better to be silent, to stiffen against this last assault of the senses and the heart.

The bitter and tenacious will that led the first inhabitants of New England to this desert, made their descendants creatures of passion and abnegation. Those strong religious convictions left behind the taste of martyrdom, and a kind of implacable righteousness that dominates the most violent emotions. But life is too sad and monotonous, and the long legacy of sterile effort and reflexive instinct all too often leads to a deadly sadness, a disgust for life which, even among women and the healthy, sometimes goes as far as melancholy and dementia.

Since he had felt his mouth still wet with Mattie's tears, a dark spirit had seized Hart. Life was too cruel and empty. Days and months and years would come too slowly and he would see too much of it. He saw himself growing old on the farm in front of his wife, harassed by her complaints, struggling against the worries of money, and struggling under the icy cold of winter and under the blazing sun of the summer. And never another ray of happiness would come to light his poor, deprived life.

Arriving at the station, he unloaded Mattie's trunk and hoisted the other parcels onto the cart. Then they returned.

Both were silent, but Mattie leaned against him, and it seemed to him that even through the rough fur of her cloak he could feel the warmth of her small, frail and delightful body. She had lowered over her forehead the folds of the white woolen scarf around her head, and he saw only the faint line of a cheek burnt by the cold.

Then an overwhelming desire came over him to look into her eyes one last time.

"Look at me, Mattie," he said softly.

She lifted her head, and her face seemed bruised, as though emaciated by cold and pain. On her anguished eyes the eyelids fluttered like wings of swallows beating the ground before the storm; then, with great effort, she looked him in the face.

"What are you going to do when you get there?" he asked.

"I don't know . . . I'll work."

"Sometime later, maybe we'll see each other again?"

"Perhaps."

"Do you have friends in Worcester, at least some acquaintances?"

"No. But what does it matter?"

And suddenly he saw in her eyes that tremendous disgust for life that was compressing his own heart.

"Is it going to be very difficult for you?"

"Yes, very difficult."

He lowered his voice. "You know, if you want—"

"No, no—that's not what I want! That's not what I want!" she exclaimed violently.

"But if I did—"

"Then I'd kill myself! And I'd be happy to do it!"

Their eyes met, burning with the same dark desire. Hart was frightened.

"That's madness! Don't talk like that . . ."

"Why not? I'm tired of life. My childhood was miserable. I've only been happy here. And I don't have the courage to start over again."

"You're still young—you'll make yourself a new life."

"Oh, don't tell me that!" she said, with a note of despair. Her face was suddenly transformed, consumed by pain, and the slender, pink bow of her mouth was stretched in a dry, hard line above her small, willful chin. In her features she expressed all the deep anguish of the long line of women who, for two hundred years, had worn out their lives and devoured their hearts in the narrow and gloomy existence of the American countryside.

"But I can't let you go this way . . . I'll leave my wife and go with you, or whatever you want . . ."

"Never, never, do you hear me? When my father died it was she alone who offered me a place to live. You're not happy together—and it makes you unhappy, I know it—but if you leave her to marry me, what humiliation for her, what infamy for me!"

Sources

Adorno, Theodor. *Prisms*. 1967. MIT Press, 1983.

Ager, Susan. "Sled story hits bottom, then shoots back up." *The Detroit Free Press*, Mar. 9, 2006.

Aliaga-Buchenau, Ana-Isabel. *The Dangerous Potential of Reading: Readers & the Negotiation of Power in Selected Nineteenth-Century Narratives*. Taylor & Francis, 2004.

Ames, Van Meter. *Aesthetics of the Novel*. 1928. Edwards Brothers Inc., 1966.

Ammons, Elizabeth. *Edith Wharton's Argument with America*. University of Georgia Press, 1980.

Anderson, John Dennis. "Stage Adaptations of Wharton's Fiction." *Edith Wharton in Context*. Laura Rattray, ed. Cambridge University Press, 2012.

Andrews, Harry E., ed. "Guild To Stage Play." *The Los Angeles Times*, Apr. 28, 1925.

Angelou, Maya. "I Know Why the Caged Bird Sings." *Poems*. Bantam, 1986.

Arnold, Matthew. "Dover Beach." 1867. *The Portable Matthew Arnold*. Viking Press, 1949.

Bacon, Francis. *Bacon: Selected Philosophical Works*. Hackett Publishing, 1999.

Balzac, Honoré de. *Physiology of Marriage*. 1829. Johns Hopkins University Press, 1997.

Banta, Martha. "Wharton's Women: In Fashion, In History, Out of Time." *A Historical Guide to Edith Wharton*. Carol Singley, ed. Oxford University Press, 2003.

Bauer, Dale M. *Edith Wharton's Brave New Politics*. University of Wisconsin Press, 1994.

Bauer, Dale M. "Wharton's 'Others:' Addiction and Intimacy." *A Historical Guide to Edith Wharton*. Carol Singley, ed. Oxford University Press, 2003.

Beale, Lewis. "Female authors get Hollywood treatment." *The Philadelphia Inquirer*, July 26, 1992.

Beck, Marilyn. "'Peter Pan' sans big names." *The Shreveport Times*, Dec. 28, 1986.

Beer, Janet. *Kate Chopin, Edith Wharton and Charlotte Perkins Gilman: Studies in Short Fiction*. Palgrave, 1997.

Beer, Janet. "Introduction." *The Cambridge Companion to Kate Chopin*. Cambridge University Press, 2008.

Benstock, Shari. *No Gifts From Chance: A Biography of Edith Wharton*. Charles Scribner's Sons, 1994.

Berkove, Lawrence I. "Fatal Self-Assertion in Kate Chopin's 'The Story of an Hour.'" *American Literary Realism*, 32.2, Winter 2000.

Bernard, Kenneth. "Imagery and Symbolism in *Ethan Frome*." *College English,* 23.3, Dec. 1961.

Berriault, Gina. "Zenobia." *The Threepenny Review*, No. 64, Winter 1996.

Björkman, Edwin. *Voices of To-Morrow: Critical Studies in the New Spirit of Literature*. Mitchell Kennerley, 1913.

Blackall, Jean Frantz. "Edith Wharton's Art of Ellipsis." *The Journal of Narrative Technique*, No. 17, Spring 1987.

Bloom, Allan. *The Closing of the American Mind*. Simon & Schuster, 1987.

Bloom, Harold. "Introduction." *Bloom's Modern Critical Views: Edith Wharton*. Chelsea House Publishers, 1986.

Bloom, Harold. "Introduction." *Bloom's Modern Critical Views: Kate Chopin*. 1987. Infobase Publishing, 2007.

Bloom, Harold. *Novelists and Novels*. Chelsea House Publishers, 2005.

Blumberg, Edith, ed. "Morningside Reviewed." *The Barnard Bulletin*, Feb. 26, 1926.

Bobbin, Jay. "'Ethan Frome': Challenge for PBS." *The Palm Beach Post*, Nov. 13, 1994.

Bogel, Fredric V. *New Formalist Criticism: Theory and Practice*. Palgrave Macmillan, 2013.

Boswell, Parley Ann. *Edith Wharton on Film*. Southern Illinois University Press, 2007.

Bradford, Jack. "Hollywood." *The Pittsburgh Post-Gazette*, Apr. 2, 1968.

Brennan, Joseph X. "*Ethan Frome*: Structure and Metaphor." *Modern Fiction Studies*, 7.4, Winter 1961-1962.

Brooks, Cleanth. "Keats's Sylvan Historian: History Without Footnotes." *The Well Wrought Urn*. Harvest Books, 1947.

Burke, Kenneth. "Symbolic Action in a Poem by Keats." *A Grammar of Motives*. University of California Press, 1962.

Butler, Marilyn. *Romantics, Rebels and Reactionaries*: *English Literature and its Background, 1760-1830*. Oxford University Press, 1985.

Cahir, Linda Costanzo. "Wharton and the Age of Film." *A Historical Guide to Edith Wharton*. Carol J. Singley, ed. Oxford University Press, 2003.

Chait, Jonathan. "Not a Very P.C. Thing to Say: How the Language Police are Perverting Liberalism." *New York Magazine*, Jan. 26, 2015.

Chatfield, Caroline. "Friendly Counsel." *The Atlanta Constitution*, Nov. 30, 1934.

Chapman, John. "Looking At Hollywood." *The Chicago Tribune*, July 6, 1941.

Chopin, Kate. "The Dream of an Hour." *Vogue*, Dec. 6, 1894.

Chopin, Kate. *The Awakening*. 1899. Avon Books, 1972.

Connolly, Mike. "TV Topics." *The Philadelphia Inquirer*, Sept. 29, 1963.

Considine, Shaun. *Bette and Joan: The Divine Feud*. Graymalkin Media, 2017.

Cooke, Elizabeth. *Zeena: A Novel*. St. Martin's Press, 1996.

Cool, Una H.H, ed. "Ethan Frome." *The San Francisco Call*, Jan. 14, 1912.

Crosby, John. "'Ethan Frome' a Season's Highlight." *The Detroit Free Press*, Feb. 23, 1960.

Custred, Glynn. *A History of Anthropology as Holistic Science*. Lexington Books, 2016.

Daly, Maggie. "Director Wyler quits retirement for Bette." *The Chicago Tribune*, June 27, 1977.

David, George L. "Bette Davis Gets New Contract." *The Rochester Democrat and Chronicle*, June 29, 1943.

Davis, Owen. *My First Fifty Years in the Theatre*. Walter H. Baker Co., 1950.

Davis, Owen and Donald Davis. *Ethan Frome: A Dramatization*. Charles Scribner's Sons, 1936.

Davis, Suanna H. "Limiting Topics Brings Knowledge to Life." *Teaching College English*, Dec. 13, 2014. < http://www.teachingcollegeenglish.com/2014/12/13/hof-limiting-topics-brings-knowledge-to-life/ >

Dawson, Melanie. "Biography." *Edith Wharton in Context*. Laura Rattray, ed. Cambridge University Press, 2012.

DeVoto, Bernard. "Introduction." *Ethan Frome*. Edith Wharton. 1911. Charles Scribner's Sons, 1938.

Dock, Julie Bates. *"The Yellow Wall-paper" and the History of Its Publication and Reception*. Pennsylvania State University Press, 1998.

Douglas, Ann. *The Feminization of American Culture*. 1977. Noonday Press, 1998.

Dixon, Hugh. "Hollywood Movie Memos." *The Pittsburgh Post-Gazette*, Aug. 3, 1948.

DuBois, Andrew. "Close Reading: An Introduction." *Close Reading: The Reader*. Frank Lentricchia and Andrew DuBois, eds. Duke University Press, 2003.

Dwight, Eleanor. *Edith Wharton: An Extraordinary Life*. Harry N. Abrams, 1999.

Ebert, Roger. "'Ethan Frome' Has Sinned: But It's The Audience That Pays." *The New York Daily News*, Mar. 12, 1993.

Editor. "Bleak and Bitter." *The Boston Globe*, Oct. 14, 1911.

Editor. "The Home Front Reports To The Fighting Fronts." *The Burlington Free Press*, Mar. 27, 1945.

Editor. "Library Notes." *The Edwardsville Intelligencer*, June 14, 1950.

Editor. "TV Key Preview." *The Tampa Times*, Feb. 18, 1960.

Edmundson, Mark. "On the Uses of a Liberal Education: As Lite Entertainment for Bored College Students." *Harper's Magazine*, Sept. 1997.

Edmundson, Mark. *Why Read?* Bloomsbury, 2004.

Emerson, Ralph Waldo. "The American Scholar." 1837. *The Essential Writings of Ralph Waldo Emerson*. Modern Library, 2000.

Epstein, Joseph. "What Killed American Lit.: Today's Collegians Don't Want to Study It—Who Can Blame Them?" *The Wall Street Journal*, Aug. 27, 2011.

Epstein, Joseph. "Who Killed the Liberal Arts? And Why We Should Care." *The Weekly Standard*, Sept. 17, 2012.

Epstein, Joseph. *A Literary Education and Other Essays*. Axios Press, 2014.

Evans, Sara M. *Born for Liberty: A History of Women in America*. The Free Press, 1989.

Faulkner, William. "A Rose for Emily." 1930. *Collected Stories*. Vintage Books, 1977.

Feinberg, Wilfred. Davis v. DuPont De Nemours & Company, 240 F. Supp. 612. S.D.N.Y. 1965. < https://law.justia.com/cases/federal/district-courts/FSupp/ 240/ 612/2145392/ >

Ferris, Earle. "Right Out Of The Air." *Bernardsville News*, Jan. 18, 1940.

Fidler, Jimmie. "In Hollywood." *The St. Louis Star-Times*, June 19, 1945.

Fidler, Jimmie. "In Hollywood." *The Montgomery Advertiser*, Aug. 20, 1949.

Flanner, Janet. *Paris Was Yesterday, 1925-1939*. 1940. Mariner Books, 1988.

Flaubert, Gustav. *Madame Bovary*. 1856. Wordsworth Editions, 1998.

Fournier, Suzanne J. *Edith Wharton's* Ethan Frome*: A Reference Guide*. Praeger, 2006.

French, Marilyn. "Introduction." *The House of Mirth*. Edith Wharton. 1905. Berkley Publishing, 1981.

Frye, Northrop. "Archetypes of Literature." 1951. *The Educated Imagination and Other Writings on Critical Theory, 1933-1963*. Germaine Warkentin, ed. University of Toronto Press, 2006.

Frye, Northrop. "Science and the Public Critic." 1957. *Anatomy of Criticism: Four Essays*. Princeton University Press, 1971.

Fryer, Judith. *Felicitous Space: The Imaginative Structures of Edith Wharton and Willa Cather*. University of North Carolina Press, 1986.

Gajowski, Evelyn. "Series Editor's Preface." *Shakespeare and New Historicist Theory*. Neema Parvini. Bloomsbury Publishing, 2017.

Gill, Joanna. "'The absorbed observation of her own symptoms': *Ethan Frome* and Anne Sexton's 'The Break.'" *Edith Wharton Review*, 17.2, Fall 2001.

Gilman, Charlotte Perkins (Stetson). "In Duty Bound." 1884. *In This Our World, and Other Poems*. J.H. Barry and J.H. Marble, 1895.

Gilman, Charlotte Perkins (Stetson). "The Yellow Wall-Paper." 1892. Small, Maynard & Company, 1899.

Gilman, Charlotte Perkins. "Why I Wrote The Yellow Wallpaper?" *The Forerunner*, October 1913.

Gilman, Charlotte Perkins. *The Living of Charlotte Perkins Gilman*. 1935. University of Wisconsin Press, 1991.

Graham, Sheilah. "Hollywood Today." *The Kingsport News*, Mar. 25, 1946.

Graham, Sheilah. "Hollywood Today." *The Louisville Courier-Journal*, Apr. 7, 1946.

Graham, Sheilah. "In Hollywood Today." *The Indianapolis Star*, Sept. 13, 1946.

Graham, Sheilah. "Hollywood Today." *The Honolulu Star-Bulletin*, June 13, 1947.

Graham, Sheilah. "Hollywood Today." *The Honolulu Star-Bulletin*, Nov. 11, 1947.

Graham, Sheilah. "Hollywood Today." *The Honolulu Star-Bulletin*, Jan. 29, 1948.

Graham, Sheilah. "In Hollywood." *The Tampa Times*, Mar. 11, 1948.

Graham, Sheilah. "In Hollywood." *The Tampa Times*, Nov. 10, 1948.

Graham, Sheilah. "Hollywood Today." *The Honolulu Star-Bulletin*, May 14, 1949.

Graham, Sheilah. "In Hollywood." *The Tampa Times*, Sept. 15, 1951.

Graham, Sheilah. "In Hollywood." *The Tampa Times*, Feb. 23, 1953.

Grasty, Charles H, ed. "New England Story By Edith Wharton." *The Baltimore Sun*, Nov. 26, 1911.

Grimm, Herbert L., ed. "Broken On The Wheel Of Life." *The Gettysburg Times*, June 24, 1924.

Gussow, Mel. "Theater: 'Ethan Frome' is Revived." *The New York Times*, Apr. 25, 1982.

Gwynn, Edith. "Hollywood In Review." *The Philadelphia Inquirer*, July 18, 1949.

Held, David. *Introduction to Critical Theory: Horkheimer to Habermas*. University of California Press, 1980.

Herman, Arthur. *The Cave and the Light: Plato versus Aristotle, and the Struggle for the Soul of Western Civilization*. Random House, 2013.

Herndl, Diane Price. *Invalid Women: Figuring Feminine Illness in American Fiction and Culture, 1840-1940*. University of North Carolina Press, 1993.

Hester, William, ed. "Some Strong Novels." *The Brooklyn Daily Eagle*, Oct. 7, 1911.

Hopper, Hedda. "Looking At Hollywood." *The Chicago Tribune*, Mar. 17, 1943.

Hopper, Hedda. "Looking At Hollywood." *The Chicago Tribune*, June 11, 1943.

Hopper, Hedda. "Looking At Hollywood." *The Los Angeles Times*, July 7, 1943.

Hopper, Hedda. "Looking At Hollywood." *The Los Angeles Times*, Jan. 6, 1944.

Hopper, Hedda. "Looking At Hollywood." *The Los Angeles Times*, Sept. 22, 1944.

Hopper, Hedda. "Warners' Big Three Set to Play in 'Ethan Frome.'" *The Detroit Free Press*, July 18, 1945.

Hopper, Hedda. "Looking At Hollywood." *The Chicago Tribune*, Sept. 7, 1945.

Hopper, Hedda. "Looking At Hollywood." *The Chicago Tribune*, Oct. 3, 1945.

Hopper, Hedda. "Looking At Hollywood." *The Los Angeles Times*, Dec. 10, 1947.

Hopper, Hedda. "Modern 'Joan' Will Spotlight Goddard." *The Los Angeles Times*, Aug. 4, 1948.

Horney, Karen. "The Problem of Feminine Masochism." 1934. *Feminine Psychology.* W.W. Norton, 1993.

Horowitz, Helen Lefkowitz. *Wild Unrest: Charlotte Perkins Gilman and the Making of "The Yellow Wallpaper."* Oxford University Press, 2010.

Hotchkiss, L.D., ed. "Movieland Events." *The Los Angeles Times*, Mar. 2, 1955.

Hovey, R.B. "*Ethan Frome*: A Controversy about Modernizing It." *American Literary Realism*, 19.1, Fall 1986.

Hutchinson, Stuart. "Unpackaging Edith Wharton: *Ethan Frome* and *Summer.*" *The Cambridge Quarterly*, 27.3, 1998.

Hymowitz, Carol and Michaele Weissman. *A History of Women in America.* Bantam Books, 1978.

Johnson, Erskine. "Bette Davis Is Turned Down For Role In 'Ethan Frome.'" *The Jackson Sun*, Sept. 27, 1951.

Jones, Chris. "Cold winter of 'Ethan Frome' a bit bloodless." *The Chicago Tribune*, Mar. 7, 2011.

Kallevang, Britta. "Ethan Frome (1993)." *American Film Institute*, 2017. < https://catalog.afi.com/Catalog/moviedetails/59513 >

Kazin, Alfred. "Edith Wharton and Theodore Dreiser." *On Native Grounds: An Interpretation of Modern American Prose Literature.* 1942. Houghton Mifflin Harcourt, 2013.

Kellogg, Grace. *The Two Lives of Edith Wharton.* Appleton-Century, 1965.

Kennedy, John F. *Let the Word Go Forth: The Speeches, Statements and Writings of John F. Kennedy, 1947 to 1963.* Theodore Stevenson, ed. Laurel, 1988.

Killinger, Amy. "The Making of 'Ethan Frome.'" *The Burlington Free Press*, Feb. 9, 1992.

Kissel, Howard. "Wharton Made Worth-While." *The New York Daily News*, Jan. 21, 1994.

Koloski, Bernard, ed. "Kate Chopin: The Story of an Hour." *The Kate Chopin International Society.* 2005. <https://www.katechopin.org/the-story-of-an-hour/>

Koloski, Bernard. "Introduction." *Awakenings: The Story of the Kate Chopin Revival.* Louisiana State University Press, 2012.

Kowalewski, Michael. *Deadly Musings: Violence and Verbal Form in American Fiction*. Princeton University Press, 1993.

Krasny, Michael. "Chekhov, Love, and 'The Lady with the Dog.'" *The Great Courses: Masterpieces of Short Fiction*. DVD. The Teaching Company, 2008.

Lapham, Frank "Leave It To Lydia." *All-Story Weekly*, 94.2, Feb. 22, 1919.

Lauer, Kristin O. and Cynthia Griffin Wolff, editors. *Ethan Frome. A Norton Critical Edition*. Edith Wharton. 1911. W.W. Norton & Co., 1995.

Lee, Hermione. *Edith Wharton*. Vintage Books, 2007.

Lewis, R.W.B. *Edith Wharton: A Biography*. Harper & Row, 1975.

Lodge, David. *Language of Fiction*. 1966. Routledge, 2012.

Longinus. *Longinus on the Sublime*. Cambridge University Press, 1899.

Lowery, Cynthia. "Hayden, Harris Make Ethan Frome Exciting." *Wellsville NY Daily Reporter*, Feb. 20, 1960.

MacCallan, W.D. "The French Draft of Ethan Frome." *Yale University Library Gazette* Vol. 27.1, 1952.

MacDonald, Dwight. *On Movies*. Prentice-Hall, 1969.

Malone, Mary T. *Women and Christianity, Volume III: From the Reformation to the 21st Century*. Orbis Books, 2003.

Manners, Dorothy. "'Air Cadet' Lead Latest Part of Gail Russell." *The Rochester Democrat and Chronicle*, Sept. 4, 1950.

Mannweiler, David. "'Frome' as slow as molasses in winter." *The Indianapolis News*, Apr. 30, 1993.

Mantle, Burns. "Gordon, Harris Go Ahead With Movie Support." *New York Daily News*, June 16, 1935.

Mantle, Burns. "'Ethan Frome' Tragically Human." *New York Daily News*, Jan. 22, 1936.

Marshall, Megan. *Margaret Fuller: A New American Life*. Mariner Books, 2013.

Martin, Linton. "The Call Boy's Chat." *The Philadelphia Inquirer*, Jan. 12, 1936.

Masters, Edgar Lee. *Spoon River Anthology: 100th Anniversary Edition*. Signet Classics, 2007.

McIntyre, O.O. "As O.O. McIntyre Sees It." *The Shreveport Times*, Oct. 19, 1934.

Meherin, Elenore. *Chickie*. "Chapter XLIII: Reconciliation." *The San Bernardino County Sun*, Feb. 26, 1924.

Mencken, H.L. "Women Novelists Suffer Because Truth-Telling Creates A Scandal." *The Baltimore Evening Sun*, Jan. 24, 1925.

Mill, John Stuart. "On the Subjection of Women." 1870. *The Basic Writings of John Stuart Mill*. The Modern Library, 2002.

Miller, Arthur. *The Crucible*. 1953. Penguin Books, 1982.

Mitchell, Amanda. "With so much to choose from, reading can be fun." *The Marshfield News-Herald*, Feb. 10, 2008.

Moers, Ellen. *Literary Women: The Great Writers.* 1977. Oxford University Press, 1985.

Moore, Sue V. Editor. *St. Louis Life.* Jan. 5, 1895.

Mulroy, David. *The War Against Grammar.* Boynton/Cook Publishers, 2003.

Nelson, Richard. "Flying Without Columbus." *The London Guardian*, Mar. 30, 1991.

Nelson, Richard. Screenplay. *Ethan Frome.* DVD. Miramax, 1993.

Nevius, Blake. *Edith Wharton: A Study of Her Fiction.* 1953. University of California Press, 1976.

Nichols, Tom. *The Death of Expertise: The Campaign Against Established Knowledge and Why it Matters.* Oxford University Press, 2017.

Nicholson, William. Screenplay. "Life Story." *Horizon.* BBC Television, 1987.

Nilsen, Helge Normann. "Naturalism in Edith Wharton's *Ethan Frome.*" 1995. *Readings on Ethan Frome.* Christopher Smith, ed. Greenhaven Press, 2000.

Ochs, Adolph S, ed. "Three Lives in Supreme Torture." *The New York Times*, Oct. 8, 1911.

Ogle, Connie. "'Arsonist' torches pretensions." *The Lansing State Journal*, Sept. 16, 2007.

Olmstead, Andrea. "The Rome Prize from Leo Sowerby to David Diamond." *Music and Musical Composition at the American Academy at Rome.* Martin Brody, ed. Boydell and Brewer, 2014.

Papke, Mary E. "Kate Chopin's Social Fiction." *Bloom's Modern Critical Views: Kate Chopin.* Infobase Publishing, 2007.

Parrington, V.L. *Main Currents in American Thought: The Beginnings of Critical Realism in America, 1860-1920.* Harcourt Brace & Co., 1927.

Parsons, Louella O. "In Hollywood." *Middletown Times Herald*, Oct. 21, 1941.

Parsons, Louella O. "Hollywood Is Quick to Register Title For 'Kelly of the U.S.A.'" *The Atlanta Constitution*, Dec. 24, 1941.

Parsons, Louella O. "Wanger Plans Film on Marine Battalion." *The Philadelphia Inquirer*, Mar. 17, 1943.

Parsons, Louella O. "Davis to Appear For Warners in Ethan Frome." *The Rochester Democrat and Chronicle*, June 22, 1943.

Parsons, Louella O. "Bette Davis Visits In Atlanta Before Joining Humphrey Bogart For Ethan Frome." *The Fresno Bee*, Sept. 27, 1944.

Parsons, Louella O. "Illegal Entry of Undesirable Aliens Into U.S. Will Be Theme of New Picture." *The Fresno Bee*, Feb. 6, 1948.

Parsons, Louella O. "Hollywood Today." *The Arizona Republic*, Dec. 23, 1949.

Peattie, Ella W. "Among the New Books." *The Chicago Tribune*, Oct. 28, 1911.

Pike, Albert. "To the Mockingbird." *Gen. Albert Pike's Poems.* F.W. Allsopp, 1900.

Pollock, Arthur. "'Ethan Frome' Joins the Broadway Play List." *The Brooklyn Daily Eagle*, Jan. 22, 1936.

Price, Michael H. "Blizzard of boredom buries 'Ethan Frome.'" *The Cincinnati Inquirer*, Mar. 20, 1993.

Pristin, Terry. "Old Novels, New Screenplays." *The Los Angeles Times*, Apr. 26, 1992.

Quirk, Lawrence J. *Fasten Your Seat Belts: The Passionate Life of Bette Davis*. Signet, 1990.

Radway, Janice A. *Reading the Romance: Women, Patriarchy, and Popular Literature*. University of North Carolina Press, 1984.

Rattray, Laura. "Edith Wharton: Contextual Revisions." *Edith Wharton in Context*. Cambridge University Press, 2012.

Roberts, Robert. *The Classic Slum: Salford Life in the First Quarter of the Century*. Penguin Books, 1978.

Rose, Alan Henry. "'Such Depths of Sad Initiation': Edith Wharton and New England." *The New England Quarterly*, 50.3, Sept. 1977.

Roth, Michael S. *Beyond the University*. Yale University Press, 2015.

Ruland, Richard and Malcolm Bradbury. *From Puritanism to Postmodernism: A History of American Literature*. Penguin Books, 1991.

Russell, Candice. "Romantic Tragedy." *South Florida Sun-Sentinel*, June 29, 1993.

Ryan, Sam J., ed. "Final Program of Expression Students." *The Appleton Crescent*, May 22, 1913.

Ryerson, James. "The Philosophy Giant You've Never Heard Of." *The New York Times Book Review*, Sept. 30, 2018.

Schallert, Edwin. "While the Films Reel By." *The Los Angeles Times*, Jan. 4, 1942.

Schallert, Edwin. "Olivia Signs Termer; Bette May Act 'Queen.'" *The Los Angeles Times*, Nov. 5, 1946.

Schallert, Edwin. "Longden Life Story Planned; Gary Merrill Stars With Bette Davis." *The Los Angeles Times*, Mar. 25, 1950.

Scharnhorst, Gary. "The Two Faces of Mattie Silver." *Ethan Frome* and *Summer*. Edith Wharton. Houghton Mifflin, 2004.

Scorsese, Martin. *A Personal Journey with Martin Scorsese through American Movies*. DVD. British Film Institute, 1995.

Scull, Andrew. *Hysteria: The Disturbing Story*. Oxford University Press, 2009.

Sedgewick, Ruth Woodbury. "Ethan Frome." *Stage*, 13.5, Feb. 1936.

Sexton, Anne. *Love Poems*. 1969. Houghton Mifflin Harcourt, 1999.

Shakespeare, William. *Romeo and Juliet*. 1591. Yale University Press, 2008.

Shakespeare, William. *Julius Caesar*. 1599. Yale University Press, 2006.

Shapiro, Karl. *In Defense of Ignorance*. Vintage, 1952.

Shaw, Len G. "Harris Postpones 'Ethan Frome.'" *The Detroit Free Press*, Jan. 13, 1935.

Sherman, Thomas B. "Youthful Violinist Performs Admirably." *St. Louis Post-Dispatch*, Feb. 13, 1943.

Shuman, R. Baird. "The Continued Popularity of *Ethan Frome*." 1971. *Readings on Ethan Frome*. Christopher Smith, ed. Greenhaven Press, 2000.

Smith, Imogen Sara. *Buster Keaton: The Persistence of Comedy*. Gambit Publishing, 2008.

Smith-Rosenberg, Carroll. *Disorderly Conduct: Visions of Gender in Victorian America*. Oxford University Press, 1985.

Smith-Rosenberg, Carroll and Charles E. Rosenberg. "The Female Animal: Medical and Biological Views of Women and Her Role in Nineteenth-Century America." *Women and Health in America*. Judith Walzer Leavitt, ed. University of Wisconsin Press, 1999.

Soanes, Wood. "Curtain Calls." *The Oakland Tribune*, Dec. 12, 1934.

Sontag, Susan. "Against Interpretation." 1964. *Against Interpretation and Other Essays*. Picacor, 2001.

Speers, W. "Another Ice-T concert is frozen out by the police." *The Philadelphia Inquirer*, Dec. 17, 1992.

Springer, Marlene. *Ethan Frome: A Nightmare of Need*. Twayne's Masterwork Studies No. 121. Twayne Publishers, 1993.

Stackpole, Albert H., ed. "Massey Stars Wednesday." *The Harrisburg Telegraph*, June 15, 1940.

Stanfill, Francesca. "The Secret of Ethan's Wife." *The Los Angeles Times*, Dec. 22, 1996.

Stein, Erin Kirsten. "Pedantic Poetics." *Arizona Daily Wildcat*, Nov. 6, 1997.

Steinbeck, John. "The Chrysanthemums." 1938. *The Long Valley*. Penguin, 1995.

Stern, Harold. "Television Show Was 'Big Break.'" *The Munster Indiana Times*, May 10, 1960.

Swindell, Larry. "Movie took long route to become honorable failure." *The Manhattan Mercury*, Sept. 3, 1993.

Taine, Hippolyte. *History of English Literature*. The Colonial Press, 1900.

Thomas, Bob. "Bette Davis Is Prepared For Free Lancing." *The Tucson Daily Citizen*, Mar. 2, 1950.

Toth, Emily. *Kate Chopin*. University of Texas, 1990.

Toth, Emily. *Unveiling Kate Chopin*. University of Mississippi Press, 1999.

Trilling, Lionel. *The Liberal Imagination*. 1950. Harcourt, Brace & Jovanovich, 1978.

Trilling, Lionel. *A Gathering of Fugitives*. 1956. Harcourt, Brace & Jovanovich, 1978.

Trilling, Lionel. *Beyond Culture: Essays on Literature and Learning*. 1965. Harcourt, Brace & Jovanovich, 1978.

Tucker, George. "Manhattan." *The Fitchburg Sentinel*, Mar. 1, 1940.

Van Doren, Carl. *Contemporary American Novelists, 1900-1920*. 1922. Macmillan, 1931.

Van Horne, Harriet. "'Ethan Frome' Holds True To Book in Fine Show." *The El Paso Herald-Post*, Feb. 19, 1960.

Wadsworth, Charlie. "On TV, The Acting Is What Counts." *The Orlando Sentinel*, Feb. 19, 1960.

Wagner-Martin, Linda. "Wharton and Gender." *Edith Wharton in Context*. Laura Rattray, ed. Cambridge University Press, 2012.

Waid, Candace. *Edith Wharton's Letters from the Underworld: Fictions of Women and Writing*. University of North Carolina Press, 1991.

Walker, Danton. "Danton Walker." *The Philadelphia Inquirer*, Sept. 19, 1951.

Wald, Elijah. *How The Beatles Destroyed Rock 'n' Roll: An Alternative History of American Popular Music*. Oxford University Press, 2009.

Walton, Geoffrey. *Edith Wharton: A Critical Interpretation*. Farleigh Dickinson University Press, 1970.

Ward, Candice. *Great Short Stories by American Women*. Dover Publications, 1996.

Warga, Wayne. "Whatever Happened to Ruth Davis?" *The Los Angeles Times*, Feb. 27, 1977.

Warren, Joyce W. *Women, Money and the Law*. University of Iowa Press, 2005.

Weber, Bruce. "Big Movies on Little Budgets." *The New York Times*, May 17, 1992.

Weisser, Olivia. *Ill Composed: Sickness, Gender, and Belief in Early Modern England*. Yale University Press, 2016.

Weitz, Rose. "A History of Women's Bodies." *The Politics of Women's Bodies: Sexuality, Appearance and Behavior*. Rose Weitz and Samantha Kwan, eds. Oxford University Press, 2014.

Wellek, René. *A History of Modern Criticism: 1750-1950, The Later Nineteenth Century*. Yale University Press, 1965.

Wharton, Edith. "The Choice." 1908. *Xingu and Other Stories*. Charles Scribner's Sons, 1917.

Wharton, Edith. *Ethan Frome*. 1911. Charles Scribner's Sons, 1922.

Wharton, Edith. *The Reef*. D. Appleton & Co., 1912.

Wharton, Edith. *The Writing of Fiction*. 1925. Touchstone, 1997.

Wharton, Edith. "The Writing of *Ethan Frome*." 1932. *Ethan Frome: A Norton Critical Edition*. Lauer & Wolff, eds. W.W. Norton & Co., 1995.

Wharton, Edith. *A Backward Glance*. 1934. Charles Scribner's Sons, 1964.

Wharton, Edith. "Foreword." *Ethan Frome: A Dramatization*. Owen and Donald Davis. Charles Scribner's Sons, 1936.

Wharton, Edith. *My Dear Governess: The Letters of Edith Wharton to Anna Bahlmann*. Irene Goldman-Price, ed. Yale University Press, 2012.

White, Barbara A. "The New England Setting." 1995. *Readings on Ethan Frome*. Christopher Smith, ed. Greenhaven Press, 2000.

Wilson, Edmund. "Edith Wharton." 1923. *Edmund Wilson: Literary Essays and Reviews of the 1920s & 30s*. The Library of America, 2007.

Wilson, Edmund. "Stephen Crane." 1924. *Edmund Wilson: Literary Essays and Reviews of the 1920s & 30s*. The Library of America, 2007.

Wilson, Edmund. "The All-Star Literary Vaudeville." 1926. *Edmund Wilson: Literary Essays and Reviews of the 1920s & 30s*. The Library of America, 2007.

Wilson, Earl. "Myopic Critic Sees All But Plays Through Rose-Haze." *The Miami News*, July 25, 1945.

Wilson, Earl. "Off Broadway." *The Delaware County Daily Times*, Nov. 14, 1973.

Wolff, Cynthia Griffin. *A Feast of Words: The Triumph of Edith Wharton*. 1977. Addison-Wesley, 1995.

Woolf, Virginia. *A Room of One's Own*. 1929. Harvest Books, 1989.

Wordsworth, William. "Preface." *Lyrical Poems, with Pastoral and Other Poems*. Longman and Rees, 1802.

Ziff, Larzer. *The American 1890s: The Life and Times of a Lost Generation*. Viking, 1966.

Index

Butler, Marilyn, 21
Cahir, Linda Costanzo, 159, 208, 354-355, 361
Cather, Willa, 35, 127
Charleville, Victoria, 47
Chekov, Anton, 86
Chickie, 363
Children, The, 333
"Choice, The," 179-180
Chopin, Kate, 12-13, 21, 33, 35-36, 40, 43, 46-50, 52, 65-67, 69, 82, 95, 108, 118-119, 121, 127, 145, 149, 151, 166, 178, 193, 224-225, 274, 379
    background, 46-48, 52; feminism, 48; New Orleans, 48, 52; writing, 36, 48-49, 65-66, 71, 82
Chopin, Oscar, 47-48, 82
"Chrysanthemums, The," 171, 237-238
Civil War, American, 43, 47, 59, 63, 105, 125-126
close reading, xiii, 18, 30, 66, 114, 273, 293, 358
Coleridge, Samuel Taylor, 125
context of *Ethan Frome*, 44-45
    biographical, 109, 111, 116, 121-123, 162, 196, 226, 230, 241, 278, 296-297; historical, 109, 124-126, 267; literary, 137, 141, 179-180
contextual analysis, 9-12, 14-18, 20-22, 26, 30
Cooke, Elizabeth, 368-376
Crane, Stephen, 126
critical theory, 25
criticism of *Ethan Frome*, 31, 38-41, 43-45, 125-127, 130-131, 289-304
Crucible, The, 12, 328
Daisy Miller, 132
Darwin, Charles, 141
Davenport, Marsha, 301-302
Davis, Bette, 327, 334-344
Davis, Donald, 295-296, 308, 311-312, 315, 326-329, 335
Davis, Owen, 295-296, 308, 311-315, 326-327, 335
Davis, Rebecca Harding, 34
deconstructionism, 5, 7-9, 12, 17, 26, 29

Denis Eady (character), 142-143, 151, 154, 158, 167-174, 176, 178, 200-204, 214, 222, 267, 273
Depression, The Great, 291, 310, 312, 334
Deutsch, Helen, 329, 335
DeVoto, Bernard, 299
Dickens, Charles, 8, 11, 40, 43, 126
Dock, Julie Bates, 71, 100-101
Dostoevsky, Fyodor, 126
Douglas, Ann, 17
"Dover Beach," 227-228
Dreiser, Theodore, 127, 130
DuBois, Andrew, 11, 22, 30
Dunbar-Nelson, Alice, 35
Dwight, Eleanor, 162
dynamic character, 60-64
Edel, Leon, 326
Edmundson, Mark, 2-3, 5-7, 14-15, 27
Eliot, T.S., 11
Elm, The, 309
Emerson, Ralph Waldo, xi, xvi
Epstein, Joseph, 6, 8-11, 29-30
"Ethan Brand," 137
Ethan Frome (character), xvii, 38, 42-43, 50, 66, 103-104, 110-116, 118-119, 123, 132-134, 135-288, 292-298
    background, 120, 138, 143, 148, 151, 159, 193-194, 246; conflict, 150, 152-153, 167, 170, 200-201, 204, 209, 231-233, 251, 259, 275-276; delusion, 118, 156, 159, 164-165, 186, 191-192, 201-202, 208, 212, 251, 268, 274-275; dialogue with Mattie, 169, 173-178, 202, 260, 262, 264, 267-270; fear, 165, 168, 175-176, 181, 186, 188, 193, 215, 232, 268; gender reversal, 38, 42, 113-116, 119, 123, 131, 161, 164, 166, 168, 189, 196, 198, 208, 218, 221, 230-231, 235, 237, 244-245, 247-248, 250, 255-256, 274, 286, 292-294, 298; graveyard, 178, 200, 202, 245, 275, 282, 287; imprisonment, 112, 136, 144, 178, 186, 194, 216, 250, 254-255, 278, 301; jealousy, 158, 176, 200-201, 204, 266; light/

277-278; character names, 137, 154-155, 175; clouds, 151-154, 156, 166, 169, 176, 219, 251, 275-276; death, 146, 167, 177, 179, 181-182, 190, 214, 224, 264, 275; doors/windows, 149, 151-152, 179, 184-186, 219, 224, 228, 257, 277; gender reversal, 38, 42-43, 134, 141, 144, 164, 166, 218, 237, 247-248, 286, 292-295; granite outcroppings, 128-129, 146, 157, 163, 286; light/dark, 149, 150-154, 156, 164, 169, 173-174, 176-177, 179-182, 186, 200, 211-212, 218-219, 224, 227-228, 235, 250-251, 261-262, 264, 269, 275, 277; mouse, 216-217, 277-278; pickle dish, 204-206, 209, 286; sexual, 159-160, 207-209, 240-245; sky, 150, 184-185, 275, 277; snow, 145-146, 150-151, 186, 221, 245, 261, 263, 278, 301; sun, 184-186, 188, 251; weather, 141, 144-145, 148, 188, 221, 278, 287

Taine, Hippolyte, 11-12

teaching of literature, xiii-xvi, 1-17, 26-27, 29

higher education, 1-17, 26-27, 29; secondary school, 1, 7, 13, 15

To Kill a Mockingbird, 157, 348

"To the Mockingbird," 54

Toth, Emily, 35, 47-48, 50, 52, 64-66, 119

Trilling, Lionel, 5-6, 38-45, 64, 113-114, 130-132, 141, 290, 300, 303, 360

Tristan, Flora, 160

Tyler, Elisina Royall, 328-329, 335, 377

Twain, Mark, 126, 150

Uncle Tom's Cabin, 59, 118, 230

Van Doren, Carl, 110-111

Wagner-Martin, Linda, 111, 121-123

Waid, Candace, 149, 277, 286

Walton, Geoffrey, 157, 274, 300-301

Ward, Candice, 34-35

Wharton, Edith, xi, xvi-xvii, 18, 21, 27, 30-33, 36-45, 82, 94, 102, 103-111, 116, 118, 121-123, 124-126, 141, 159, 162, 179-180, 196, 216, 226, 230, 241, 278-279, 280, 285, 295-301, 308-311, 333, 377, 379

affair, 107, 109, 162, 279, 296-298; autobiography, 131, 299, 303; background, 94, 104-110; death, 299, 308, 309; Europe, 105, 107, 109-110, 196, 279, 302, 310-311; feminism, 103-104, 122-123; gender reversal, 116, 121-123; marriage, 106-107, 113, 121-122, 196, 226, 230, 241, 278-279; New England, 107, 109-111, 124, 128-129, 131, 141, 143, 195, 278, 290, 299-302; suicide, 279; writing, 31-32, 36-39, 82, 105-111, 116, 121-123, 124-129, 133-134, 136, 141, 159, 179-180, 230, 280, 285, 300-302, 379

Wharton, Edward Robbins "Teddy," 106-107, 109, 162, 180, 196, 226, 230, 241, 278-279, 297

White, Barbara A., 141

Whitman, Walt, 126

Wild Unrest, 16, 68, 78

Wilder, Thornton, 287, 328

Wilkins, Mary E., 35, 299

Wilson, Edmund, 31

Winthrop, Egerton, 141

Wolff, Cynthia Griffin, 32, 94, 116, 133-134, 137, 149, 163-164, 187, 207, 209, 230, 236-238, 243, 285, 298-299, 377-378

women, 18-22, 38-45, 50-51, 53-54, 59-63, 72-73, 75-77, 81-82, 97-98, 103-104, 113-123, 140-141, 150, 160-161, 180, 185, 194, 197-199, 213-214, 221, 229-230, 237-238, 247-248, 254-256, 266-267, 271, 274, 278, 288, 292-294, 298-301

health, 18, 39, 40, 68-69, 87, 116-117, 189, 292; legal status, 21, 44, 47, 50-51, 53-54, 58, 60, 88, 109; marriage 35, 40, 44, 47-48, 50-51, 58-62, 65, 68-71, 84, 88, 95, 100, 109, 115, 160-161, 180, 197-198, 237, 244, 247-248, 266, 294, 300; money and finance, 48, 50-51, 53,

About the Author

Eric B. Olsen is an independent film analyst and literary critic. His previous works of non-fiction include *The Death of Education*, an exposé of the public school system in America, *The Films of Jon Garcia: 2009-2013*, an analysis of the work of the acclaimed Portland independent filmmaker, and a collection of essays entitled *The Intellectual American*. He lives in the Pacific Northwest with his wife.

Please visit the author's web site at https://sites.google.com/site/ericbolsen author/home or contact by email at neslowepublishing@gmail.com.

Printed and bound by PG in the USA

USA2019PGIL